THE LIE
AT THE HEART OF
WATERLOO

THE LIE

AT THE HEART OF

WATERLOO

THE BATTLE'S HIDDEN
LAST HALF HOUR

NIGEL SALE

To the memory of Robert Osborne

Front cover: **Charge of the 52nd under Sir John Colborne at 8pm** by William Barnes Wollen 1857–1936 (Courtesy of the Royal Green Jackets (The Rifles) Museum, Winchester)

★The artist has erred in illustrating the men wearing the 'Belgic' shako, with a flange at the front, instead of the old 'stovepipe' which is sported by the officer.

Back cover: **A Private of the 52nd**
'There,' said the Duke, 'it all depends on that article whether we do the business, or not. Give me enough of it, and I am sure.'

First published 2014
by Spellmount, an imprint of The History Press
The Mill, Brimscombe Port
Stroud, Gloucestershire, GL5 2QG
www.thehistorypress.co.uk

© Nigel Sale, 2014
Maps by Nigel Sale

The right of Nigel Sale to be identified as the Author
of this work has been asserted in accordance with the
Copyright, Designs and Patents Act 1988.

British Library Cataloguing in Publication Data.
A catalogue record for this book is available from the British Library.

ISBN 978 0 7509 5962 9

Typeset in 11/13.5pt Bembo by The History Press
Printed in Great Britain

CONTENTS

FOREWORD

It is no longer fashionable to write of 'decisive' battle, as did Sir Edward Creasy in 1851. Creasy's Fifteen Decisive Battles of the World, ranging from Marathon to Waterloo, were engagements that had changed the course of history for the better. Thus, for Creasy, such admirable traits as Greek wisdom, Roman virtue, European Protestantism, and English liberty had all been preserved for posterity by battle. Yet, there is no denying that, from the moment the guns fell silent, its contemporaries regarded Waterloo as a pivotal moment in history. Where once that implied the battle's military and political significance, it was increasingly seen as equally important in terms of its social and cultural legacies. Waterloo loomed large in art, literature, and popular memory. Not surprisingly, it has generated a vast literature, and has raised enduring historical controversies, not least how the Duke of Wellington chose to represent his victory.

The long accepted version, deriving from Wellington's own Waterloo Despatch, has been that, at the climax of the battle, the British Guards routed Napoleon's Imperial Guard to ensure victory. Wellington himself had chosen the decisive moment, his stirring 'Up Guards and at 'em' becoming one of the most celebrated phrases in British military history. But there were other versions, which detracted from his reputation, that Wellington found it convenient to suppress. As the veteran of the Peninsular War and renowned military historian, William Napier, once wrote, there was a 'secret politics' of Waterloo. The contribution of the Prussians to the victory was one such uncomfortable factor to be discounted. But so, too, was the role of the 52nd Foot in delivering a flanking attack that destroyed the left wing of the Imperial Guard's advance. As Nigel Sale shows, the 52nd shattered the major and final French assault, and harried the remainder from the field.

It may be thought that there is little new to say about Waterloo on the approach of its bicentennial year. By focussing on the critical last stage of the battle, and the role of the 52nd Foot, however, Nigel Sale presents a persuasive case that offers a major re-interpretation of the existing historiography. The confusion of accounts as to the formation taken up by the Imperial Guard, the direction of its advance, and its precise composition as its elements encountered the British 1st Guards Brigade and the 52nd, is all expertly dissected. Based on an exhaustive study of the contemporary and near-contemporary evidence, the ground, and the military probabilities, Nigel Sale radically recasts the sequence of events in the late afternoon and evening of 18 June 1815. It is also a story of how the officers of the 52nd who knew the truth, such as John Colborne, William Leeke, and George Gawler, saw their contribution to victory, and that of their men, ignored by Wellington and forgotten by history. In this, too, Nigel Sale adds materially to the story of Wellington's many historical deceptions. The Prussian contribution to Waterloo is now widely recognised. In the light of Nigel Sale's outstanding historical detective work, the 52nd deserves no less.

Professor Ian F. W. Beckett,
Professor of Military History,
University of Kent.

LIST OF ILLUSTRATIONS

ACKNOWLEDGEMENTS

Although the embers of determining exactly what happened at the end of the battle had smouldered in my mind for decades, they were fanned into life in the early twenty hundreds by the enthusiasm of retired Colonel David Stanley, when we toured some of the battlefields in Belgium and Normandy in which our regiment had been involved. The resulting fire has kept me warm for many years and provided many eureka moments.

I am indebted to two helpers with my research. On the one hand, John Franklin of 1815 Ltd has been generous with his provision, both online and in book form, not only of newly published material, particularly from Hanoverian and Netherlands sources, but also of British accounts, to add to the mass that has been in the public domain for over one and a half centuries. On the other hand, retired Colonel Robert Osborne, a long-standing army friend, was a tower of strength both in seeking material from otherwise inaccessible academic resources and in acting as a very well informed sounding board for ideas. His death in 2009 was an immeasurable loss.

I am indebted to Leonard Bentley for the intriguing information about the 1st Guards' nickname mentioned in the epilogue, gleaned in the process of his transcribing handwritten Metropolitan Police Orders for historical purposes. My thanks go, too, to Christine Pullen of the Royal Green Jackets Museum for her help with images and to Cressida Downing, book analyst, for the controversial title.

I am very grateful to two readers of successive drafts – retired Lieutenant Colonel Ewan Sale, Royal Marines, and Mrs Judy Goodland, not a retired colonel but ex-headmistress of a well-known girl's public school and therefore of the same sterling quality – both nobly read and commented upon my early manuscripts. The final reader was history Professor Ian Beckett to whom I shall be eternally grateful for valuable advice and support.

It would be amiss of me not to pay tribute to the patience exhibited by Shaun Barrington, of The History Press, in guiding me through the painful process of publication with exemplary patience.

PREFACE

I entered the world some thirty-nine days before Hitler invaded Western Europe so it is no surprise that my first interest in history was the Second World War. However, by the time I decided to take up soldiering my horizon had expanded to include Wellington's Peninsular War in Spain. This was natural because I hoped to be accepted for service in the Oxfordshire and Buckinghamshire Light Infantry, the parent regiment of my father's Territorial Army unit, the 1st Buckinghamshire Battalion, which he had commanded during the war, especially during the Normandy landings.

During that war the officers of the 'Ox and Bucks' unofficially referred to their two battalions as the 43rd and the 52nd, these having been separate regiments before the amalgamations of the Cardwell reforms in the late nineteenth century. So proud of their antecedents were the men of the Ox and Bucks that, when the next reshuffle occurred, they ensured the numbering was perpetuated in their new title of the 1st Green Jackets, 43rd and 52nd.

Why was such loyalty merited? The answer lies in the Napoleonic period: the 43rd and the 52nd were the first two British regiments to be converted to light infantry and each had then become the core of one of the two brigades that made up Wellington's elite Light Division, which – supported by men of the 95th (the Rifle Brigade), Portuguese light infantry and the Chestnut Troop of the Royal Horse Artillery – fought with such distinction throughout the Peninsular War.

When I joined the 43rd and 52nd I was not surprised to find the deeds and ethos of the regiment's forebears were still celebrated and followed, its reputation carefully nurtured. We were all aware of the emphatic statement by General Shaw-Kennedy, who was present at Waterloo as a brigade major and wrote in 1865:

> No man can point out to me any instance in ancient or modern history of a single battalion so influencing the result of any great action as the result of the Battle of Waterloo was influenced by the attack of the 52nd Regiment on the Imperial Guard.

In the regiment it was common knowledge that the 52nd had struck the decisive blow at Waterloo, so I was puzzled to find there was neither mention of this in the histories nor sign of any public recognition of the sort accorded to the Grenadier Guards, whose very title stems from their inferred achievement in the battle. As the Battle of Waterloo held such an important place in European history why had the 52nd received no recognition? Was the 52nd's claim a figment of the imagination? Were all the oil and watercolour paintings of the 52nd's action at Waterloo spurious attempts to gain undeserved glory? Certainly, it was regimental style not to make a song and dance about its achievements but, to me, total reticence in this case seemed misplaced.

At the time, life was too full to allow me to pursue the subject. Ten years of multi-faceted army life followed. Deployment in the United Kingdom was followed by active service in the jungle of Borneo, protecting the newly formed Malaysian Federation from the predatory President Sukarno of Indonesia.

Then there was more active service, first with the United Nations force in Cyprus, followed by two years in Berlin surrounded by less-than-friendly Soviet forces, and, finally, a stint as a staff officer on the 1st (and only) British Corps Headquarters in Germany. Of the many lessons I learned over the years there are two with special relevance to this book. One is that the problems of co-ordinating troop movement across country have not changed since Napoleonic times; the other, a fact also unchanged since war itself began, is that the famous law, which states that if something can go wrong it will go wrong, is still on the statute book.

When the moment finally came to retire I was able to concentrate at last on the big question – what did the 52nd actually do at Waterloo; was it important and – if so – why is it not fully recognised? The search for the truth has taken over eight years. It has been a time of patient detective work punctuated by astonishing discoveries and exciting insights. There is even a 'smoking gun' (or should that be a dripping pen?) which has been in print for well over a century.

Although much new material has been published during the past decade and new material continues to appear, the most puzzling aspect is that much of the evidence needed to establish the truth – in the form of letters, reports and memoranda written by men who were at the battle – has been in the public domain since 1891. There can be no doubt that many subsequent authors have been aware of this corpus because they have quarried it for quotations to support their own, invariably incorrect version of the action. The realisation that no one has deduced the correct version creates the suspicion that there is some underhand aspect to the whole affair, which both demands discovery and heightens the need to treat all evidence with a jaundiced eye.

Waterloo is the first battle in recorded history about which a large number of private accounts were written and published. Historians of Waterloo have been uniquely blessed by the gathering of hundreds of individual British participants' accounts of the battle by one man, Captain William Siborne, although it is to be regretted that he waited for nigh on a quarter of a century after the battle before he sought the information. Regrettable too is that he omitted to seek reports from many of the other national contingents within the Allied army such as the Dutch, the Belgian and the Hanoverian. Fortunately, much evidence was recorded by the allied troops and is now available. Although Siborne consulted the Prussians in detail, neither he nor his son published their correspondence.

Siborne had been officially commissioned in 1830 by General Sir Rowland Hill, by then commander-in-chief of the British Army and had commanded Wellington's 2nd Corps at Waterloo, to construct a model of Waterloo for a 'United Service Museum'. The full story of the model is told in Peter Hofschröer's *Wellington's Smallest Victory*. Given that a model can illustrate only one moment Siborne selected to show the battle's turning point, when the French Imperial Garde attacked the Allied line in high hopes of claiming the victory, but were repulsed in total confusion. This moment had already been dubbed 'The Crisis' but the details of what actually happened were singularly unclear. So he determined to write to as many Waterloo officers as were traceable, asking:

> What was the particular formation of the [unit] at the moment (about 7 p.m.) when the French Imperial Guards, advancing to attack the right of the British Forces, reached the crest of our position?

Interestingly, when, some years later, his interpretation of the responses to his letter was revealed in his *History of the Waterloo Campaign*, the then current version of the battle's last moments bore little relationship to the evidence he had gathered:

> Anxious to ensure the rigorous accuracy of my work, [the model] I ventured to apply for information to nearly all the surviving eye-witnesses of the incidents which my model was intended to represent. In every quarter, and amongst officers of all ranks, from the general to the subaltern, my applications were responded to in a most generous and liberal spirit, and the result did indeed surprise me, so greatly at variance was this historical evidence with the general notions that had prevailed on the subject.

There are two volumes of responses to Siborne's letter from participants in the battle. Both are immeasurably important to an understanding of the events of the battle. The first, *Waterloo Letters*, a selection of about half the responses, was published in 1891 by his son, Major General Herbert Taylor Siborne. Needless to say the son's choice of letters for publication, far from being unbiased, was dictated by a desire to support his father's detailed interpretation of the course of events, and to avoid undermining it. There is evidence, for example, that he omitted parts that were critical of, or contradicted, his father's text, and he probably published at least one memorandum which the originator had expressly asked his father to destroy.

Publication of the second volume containing the remainder of the responses – *Letters from the Battle of Waterloo* – had to wait until 2005, edited most admirably by Gareth Glover. They throw light on several of the unexplained incidents, such as the death of Major Howard, 10th Hussars, leading a charge against a Garde square.

This is the appropriate moment to explain that the use of Garde with English adjectives such as Old (Vieille), Middle (Moyenne) and Young (Jeune) is to ensure clarity in a discourse that contains many mentions of the British Guards.

I hope the wide use of quotations from firsthand evidence will enhance the period feel of the text rather than be an obstacle to its free flow. I have endeavoured throughout to quote the sources verbatim, to avoid any suspicion that I might be twisting or misinterpreting them.

Another book that has been invaluable is Mark Adkin's *Waterloo Companion*, without which no one with an interest in the battle can afford to be. Almost any question of fact, be it French battalion strengths, the profile of a section through the battlefield or a discussion on infantry versus cavalry tactics, can be answered by application to this fascinating tome.

I make no apologies for adding to the massive total of books on the subjects of Napoleon, Wellington and Waterloo – as far as I am aware, there has been no book dedicated purely and solely to elucidating the end of the battle although the truth about the Crisis of Waterloo has been sought by many historians of the whole battle. My conclusions are startling and may be unpalatable to some. Nevertheless, I must confess to a certain satisfaction at having resolved (at least to my *own* satisfaction) a conundrum that has puzzled men and women since the immediate aftermath of the battle.

For a fuller appreciation of some of the finer points of the military techniques of Napoleonic times, I recommend that some readers might find a perusal of the appendix useful before starting the first chapter.

1

THE REASON WHY

Waterloo, fought on Sunday 18 June 1815, is – arguably – the world's most famous battle. The story of how this titanic struggle ended is well known; how the British 1st Foot Guards, directed by Wellington himself, repulsed Napoleon's Garde Impériale, and how Wellington ordered his entire army to make a general advance which drove the emperor's army off the field in a state of absolute confusion. Some will know that the Prussians were involved, even to the extent of being credited with the ultimate victory; a few other Allied units are allowed walk-on parts. What, then, is the justification for yet another book about Waterloo, let alone one that examines only the climax of the battle, the moment that has been known ever since as the 'Crisis'?

Regrettably, this story is untrue in all respects bar one; it is referred to henceforth as 'the myth'. Consider – did the Garde attack alone? No. Did the Guards repel the whole Garde force? No. Was it the last Garde force? No. Was it the bulk of the Garde force? No. Did Wellington's general advance clear the French from the field? No. Were the troops whom the Guards repelled called grenadiers? Yes, although even that is disputed – some say the Frenchmen were châsseurs.

After any battle the victors write the history, and the Battle of Waterloo is a case in point, yet the final minutes of the battle are still unclear. The battle's 200th anniversary is an appropriate moment at which to establish the truth. But doing so has inevitably raised the questions as to how the myth gained currency and why. Both questions have additional intrigue in the light of a statement by Wellington's contemporary, the author of the *History of the War in the Peninsula and in the South of France*, Major General Sir William Napier, who introduced an air of mystery when he wrote in a letter:

> Depend upon it, Waterloo has a long story of secret politics attached to it, which will not be made known in our days, if ever.

The aim of this book is to establish the truth about the Crisis of Waterloo, the moment when potential defeat was turned into victory. Most readers and

many – perhaps most – historians will be unaware that the current versions
are at complete variance from what the evidence reveals. So, despite Napoleon
having said 'The only author who deserves to be read is he who never
endeavours to influence and direct the opinion of the reader', this author will
endeavour to do just that. But, rather than writing yet another version and
expecting everyone to accept it as true, in the face of the entrenched opinions
of two centuries, the evidence will be presented in the words of the men who
were there.

Some modern historians have disputed the term 'Crisis' being applied to
the event that this book examines, considering other major events during the
daylong fighting to have been more critical. Indisputably each might have
been critical but if one event in a battle deserves the title of the Crisis it must
be the moment when the enemy is still attacking, when the Allied army is
exhausted and defeat is imminent, yet suddenly, inexplicably, the coin of fate
flips, defeat is averted and the enemy is completely routed. The real Crisis –
known as such by those who fought in the battle – came when the long, hard
hours of defence by Wellington's army turned suddenly into glorious victory.
Napoleon's elite troops of his Garde Impériale had been sent to win the
battle, as they had in previous campaigns, but instead they were sent packing
in disarray.

This was a pivotal moment in history, from which stemmed forty years of
peace in Europe. Indeed, so important a moment was it that it is reasonable
to assume that every detail of what actually happened has been thoroughly
researched and that every version, be it in book, magazine or television documentary, will be alike, at least in its essential details. But they are not. It is
difficult – perhaps impossible – to find two versions of the Crisis that tally
just in important detail, let alone the minor too. Since the middle of the
nineteenth century there has been a growing mass of eyewitness evidence
in the public domain, from which the facts of the Crisis could have been
deduced, yet, strangely, no one has successfully established the truth. In fair-
ness, some have tried but have either not dug deep enough or, more likely,
despite the best of intentions, have been subconsciously in thrall to the myth.
One such was the American historian, Jac Weller, who studiously walked and
overflew the battlefield, photographed its salient places and read widely; but
he still admitted:

> We know more of the uniforms worn by the contending armies than we do
> about their offensive and defensive formations. For instance, no one can be
> sure how the French Imperial Guard was formed at the crisis of the battle,
> nor how and by what units it was defeated … this is the most confused por-
> tion of a battle that abounds in confusion.[1]

Such expressions of doubt about the facts of their version are rare among authors: most histories of the battle speak authoritatively about the 'facts' of the Crisis without quoting the evidence to justify conclusions. The very first version was Wellington's own, taken from a letter, dated 19 June 1815, to Earl Bathurst, Secretary of State for War and the Colonies, a letter better known as the *Waterloo Despatch*:

> These [cavalry] attacks were repeated till about seven in the evening, when the enemy made a desperate effort with the cavalry and infantry, supported by the fire of artillery, to force our left centre, near the farm of La Haye Sainte, which, after a severe contest, was defeated; and having observed that the troops retired from this attack in great confusion, ... I determined to attack the enemy, and immediately advanced the whole line of infantry, supported by the cavalry and artillery. The attack succeeded in every point; the enemy was forced from his position on the heights, and fled in the utmost confusion, leaving behind him, as far as I could judge, one hundred and fifty pieces of cannon.[2]

There is so little detail in this statement that – despite additional information provided by other witnesses – historians have been forced to invent their own, leading to widespread confusion. To illustrate this confusion it is illuminating to take a general view of a sample of over forty historians' accounts, selected from histories published during the two centuries since the battle, and including French and Prussian sources as well as British. Many of these historians are still alive, so – following the military adage 'no names: no pack drill' – they have not been listed.

There are only two 'facts' on which there is consensus. First, all agree that the attackers were a force comprised of five battalions of the Middle Garde supported by a reserve of three battalions of the Old Garde. Most accounts say the Garde advanced in column; some – very few – claim the battalions were in square. There is much talk of the first and second column, which, given that eight were involved, is confusing. How this arose will be explained later. Two German brigades in the Anglo-Allied line are said by some to have been forced out of the line by the first Garde battalion – some say two. Others say another French infantry corps, not the Garde, dealt with the German brigades. There is little said about the next two battalions in the Allied line which were struck by one, or perhaps two, Garde battalions; it is uncertain how many were involved. Even less is said of the precipitate withdrawal from the line by these British troops, creating a huge gap. Next to be struck by one (some say two) Garde battalions (whether they were grenadiers or châsseurs is disputed) was the British Guards brigade, of two battalions, although there is

The Duke led on a brigade consisting of the 52d & 95th Regt 33. Vol.1.

The Duke led on a Brigade consisting of the 52nd and 95th Regiments.
This is an entirely fictitious incident, but the action it purports to illustrate is so clearly
suicidal that it probably reflects both awareness that something important and dramatic
involving the 52nd and 95th had occurred, and absolute confusion as to what. Copenhagen,
not unreasonably, looks a little dubious about attacking cavalry with infantry in line.

no agreement on whether one or both battalions were involved in the action.
This action is described variously as a prolonged fire fight, or as just two
volleys of musketry, followed by a charge, whether by one Guards battalion or
both is unclear.

That the commands to the Guards were given by Wellington himself is
the second point of consensus, although his actual words have been much
debated. The Guards charged about 100 yards downhill before confusion set
in and the men hurried back to the safety of the ridge. The charge is always
included although the rush for the ridge is hardly ever mentioned. The intervention by a Dutch division in the repulse of this early part of the Garde's
attack is generally ignored, but, when it is included, opinions vary as to its
effect. At this moment a British light infantry battalion is introduced into the
narrative in a few accounts. One has this battalion firing, from their position
in the Allied line, at the flank of the approaching Garde 'column' but others
speak of the light infantry being brought out of line, wheeling and charging
the flank of one large – and supposedly the last – Garde battalion. Some versions have the British Guards firing at the head of the French column while
the light infantry assault the flank. One version even has the Guards charging the head of the French column while the light infantry charge the flank,
which sounds like a recipe for disaster.

Almost invariably (when they are mentioned at all) the three Old Garde battalions in reserve are said to have chosen retreat rather than engagement, a curiously defeatist response from such veterans. Then nearly all accounts mention the general advance, which Wellington claimed had seen off the French Army, but only six authors support his claim. Several accounts include Wellington's own words, recorded in some of the eyewitness statements, but the events to which they are applied vary from historian to historian. One account has the light infantry appear with Wellington during the advance, without any explanation as to why. No one has fully addressed why the French Army fell into confusion as the result of the repulse of just one battalion of infantry, albeit of the Garde, nor why the three Old Garde battalions in close reserve did not support the attack.

This simplified summary of versions hides the apparent infinity of permutations that exists. Logic suggests there must be a reason why it has proved impossible, even after the passage of 200 years, to reach a consensus about the Crisis. Could the reason be that the original version is intentionally incomplete or even false? Since the original version is Wellington's, the inescapable possibility is that he was responsible for the confusion. If that hypothesis is pursued there are three questions that arise: did he know what actually happened, and if so, why did he omit the missing events; and was this forgetfulness or intentional misinformation?

2

THE CAMPAIGN
SO FAR

Since the subject of this book – the Crisis – lasted not much more than thirty minutes and because there are so many excellent accounts – excepting the Crisis – of the entire battle currently in print, it would be pointless to try to emulate them here. But, for those new to the battle or in need of a reminder, this book will limit itself to a summary of the campaign's opening and of the battle itself up to the Crisis. However, special mention will be made of the actions by those units of all sides that featured in the Crisis. 'All sides' is not an error. It is important to remember that Napoleon, albeit unintentionally, fought two battles simultaneously on 18 June 1815 – one against Wellington's Anglo-Allied army and another with Blücher's Prussian army.

Napoleon's attempt to bring all of Europe under France's hegemony had begun in 1799. Britain's first involvement was the Walcheren Expedition which failed because of dithering by the 'Grand Old Duke of York' and the dire effects of malaria. In Portugal in 1808, Wellington beat the French at Vimeira but was superseded by two senior generals, who ignominiously made peace by the Convention of Cintra, which included returning the French Army, with its spoils, back to France in British ships.

Over the years some six coalitions of varying countries – Prussia, Austria, Spain, Russia, the German states and Poland – had been formed, often with Great Britain as instigator and paymaster. As often, each coalition had been broken by one or more of the major states being forced by defeat, or persuaded by apparent self-interest, to side with France. In 1809 the British had again entered the continental land battle by sending a small, volunteer army to Portugal, initially under the command of General Sir John Moore. Vastly superior French forces, briefly under Napoleon himself, ejected Moore's army at Corunna, but another army was sent to Portugal under Sir Arthur Wellesley, best known at the time for his successes against the Marathas in India. Then followed what is famously known as the Peninsular War. It was here, in Spain, that the Light Division earned its legendary status in the annals of the British army.

By October 1813 Wellington's army had fought its way into France. On 12 April 1814 Wellington entered Toulouse and was dining with the prefect thereof when news arrived of Napoleon's abdication. Invaded from north and south, France had lost the political will to continue the struggle. Napoleon's support had collapsed and he found himself, with a miniature army, exiled to the island of Elba, between mainland Italy and his original homeland, Corsica.

Representatives of the continental powers – including Wellington for Great Britain – now sat down at the Congress of Vienna, celebrating their success and redistributing minor states, such as Saxony, to new masters. To their surprise, in March 1815, after he had been in captivity for less than nine months, Napoleon took ship to the south of France, won the hearts of the troops sent to apprehend him – including that of Maréchal Ney, who had promised King Louis that he would bring Napoleon back in a cage – and resumed his emperorship.

The opposing powers promptly signed a joint treaty binding them not to make any separate peace with Napoleon, the weakness that had broken so many coalitions in the past. The monarchies of Great Britain, Russia, Austria, Prussia, with Switzerland and Upper Italy, now re-armed in a hurry, intending to invade France and to put paid once and for all to this troublesome pseudo-republican. Napoleon meanwhile wasted no time conjuring troops and equipment out of long-suffering France, not wanting to go to war until he was ready but knowing he had to strike first to survive, let alone win. Mark Adkin, in *The Waterloo Companion*, reminds us that Napoleon was also faced with internal revolts, which absorbed some 77,000 troops in nine separate armies, leaving him with 123,000 men for his Armée du Nord.[1]

But the gathering of sufficient men was perhaps the least of his worries because conscription enabled him to tap into the youth of France. Turning conscripts into useful soldiers, however, was a different matter and none were sufficiently trained in time to be engaged in the campaign. Replacing the supply of horses, so uselessly depleted by starvation – some 186,000 dead – in his Moscow campaign of 1812, was even harder.[2] A mammoth manufacturing effort struggled to provide essentials such as muskets and shoes. Uniforms were also in short supply, even for the one part of his force that was not skimped, his Garde Impériale.

In the Russian campaign the Garde had been as strong as an army in its own right, but had been the least used of all Napoleon's forces. Originally formed in 1804 as an elite bodyguard of some 5,000 infantry, 2,000 cavalry and twenty-four guns, it had ballooned into an army of 102,000 by 1814. Its purpose was to enable Napoleon to resist any of his marshals, in the event of their developing delusions of grandeur. To ensure the Garde's loyalty, all ranks were better paid, more generously supplied and better housed than the rest of

Emperor Napoleon, 1769–1821, in front of the Grenadiers of his Garde.
He became first consul of the French Republic by coup d'état in 1799 and crowned himself Emperor of France in 1804. Attempted to enforce hegemony over most of continental Europe but overreached himself in the Peninsular War and the invasion of Russia in 1812. Escaped from captivity on Elba and resumed rule until final military defeat at Waterloo and being outmanoeuvred politically in Paris in 1815.

his forces, who had to show due deference by clearing the road and presenting arms when the Garde passed.[3] So much for l'égalité.

All this privilege led to animosity within the French Army. Their nickname, 'the immortals', may have referred to the few casualties the Garde suffered through not being sent into action very often, but also hints at the recognition of its reputation, which achieved success without its having to go into action. Napoleon had wanted to field a Garde of 35,000 for this new campaign but had to make do with 12,700. To achieve even this, he had to make a levy on Ligne battalions because too few of his pre-abdication Garde had returned to the eagles.[4] The original criteria for selection were that, for the Old Garde – the 1er (Premier) and 2e (Deuxième) Regiments of grenadiers and châsseurs – soldiers should have twelve years' service.[5] For the Middle Garde – the 3rd and 4th regiments of grenadiers and châsseurs – eight years were required, and for the Young Garde, the regiments of tirailleurs and voltigeurs, four years.[6] For the Waterloo campaign the criteria were very much less stringent in all units of the Garde, but especially for the Young Garde.

Meanwhile, the rest of the continental nations were racing to re-establish armies of their own. As usual at the end of hostilities, much disbandment had occurred. Britain had discharged 47,000 men, including eleven vet-

Generalfeldmarschall Prince Gebhard Leberecht von Blücher, 1742–1819. A hussar officer of somewhat wild temperament who began military service for Sweden. Having transferred to the Prussian army he offered a rude resignation to Frederick the Great, but was later reinstated. He was promoted Field Marshal when the war of liberation from the French began in 1813.

eran first battalions, twenty-four second battalions and 7,000 artillerymen. The cavalry was severely cut as well. In Britain's case a war against the United States (which had aggressively invaded Canada) had claimed the attention of many of the experienced battalions of the Peninsular War. The war had ended at Christmas 1814 but the difficulty of shipping troops back to Britain meant that many battalions were not available for the emergency now presented. The 43rd Light Infantry, for example, arrived at Ostend on the day Waterloo was fought. By contrast, the 43rd's erstwhile comrades from the Light Division, the 52nd Light Infantry, had been delayed by a contrary wind from sailing to America and had been diverted to Belgium instead. Wellington was appointed commander-in-chief of the Anglo-Allied army and assumed his post in early April, taking over from the young Prince of Orange. He found a multi-national army, more than half of which did not speak English.[7] Being fluent in French himself he could communicate with the Belgian element but the contingents from Hanover, Nassau and Brunswick — all Germans — and the Dutch would have presented difficulties. The King's German legion, although German too, was part of the British Army and had integrated completely with the British during the war in Spain.

The Prussians were allies too, but under the separate command of 72-year-old Feldmarschall Gebhard Leberecht von Blücher. Wellington was no stranger to having to combine allies into a cohesive force, having employed Portuguese light infantry in the Light Division, as well as acting as commander-in-chief of the Spanish armies for a brief and intensely frustrating period during the Peninsular War. Wellington's forces in Belgium totalled some 112,000 men, while Blücher commanded about 130,000.

However, simple numbers do not tell the full story: quality is of greater importance in any battle. The French Army was likely to be completely loyal to its emperor. Wellington expected no French desertions apart from a few senior officers. By contrast, he was concerned about the inexperience of many of his troops, and even more dubious about the loyalty of some, especially those of the Dutch-Belgian contingents, since many of them had been under Napoleon's command less than a year before. His answer to both problems was to mix the Anglo/experienced with the Allied/dubious, as far as national sensitivities allowed. Mark Adkin tells us Wellington had detached some 17,500 to defend an alternative route that Napoleon might use to reach Brussels or to cut the British lines of communication to the coast. He had also lost 4,600 casualties in the clashes before Waterloo. Others were detached on garrison and other duties so the Allied army numbered some 73,200 at Waterloo. Blücher could field only 49,000 at Waterloo, having lost – through battle and desertion – some 30,000, and having left about 25,000 at Wavre. His remaining 26,300 were still en route to the battle. So, on 18 June 1815, the Allies fielded 122,200 against Napoleon's 77,500.

Of the emperor's original 123,000, an estimated 15,500 had become battle casualties, and no less than 30,000 were to be detached, supposedly pursuing the 'defeated' Prussians.[8] On paper, then, the allies outnumbered the French to an overwhelming degree when the final clash came at Waterloo. But numbers often lie. Many of Wellington's allied troops were little better than recruits and even appreciable numbers of the British contingent were inexperienced. Peter Hofschröer in his *1815 The Waterloo Campaign* describes the Prussian troops being mostly 'raw levies'.

Before the campaign opened, Napoleon's dilemma was whether he should continue to build up his forces and try to defend France's borders against each of the surrounding nations' forces either in turn or in combination, or to strike first. He had the advantage of having short lines of communication and of being able to dictate strategy. He chose to attack. The first armies in the field against him were the Allies and the Prussians and so these inevitably became the first targets. The two armies – the Prussian on the left and the Allied on the right – were facing the French border, of necessity spread widely throughout the Belgian countryside, for food supply and because the

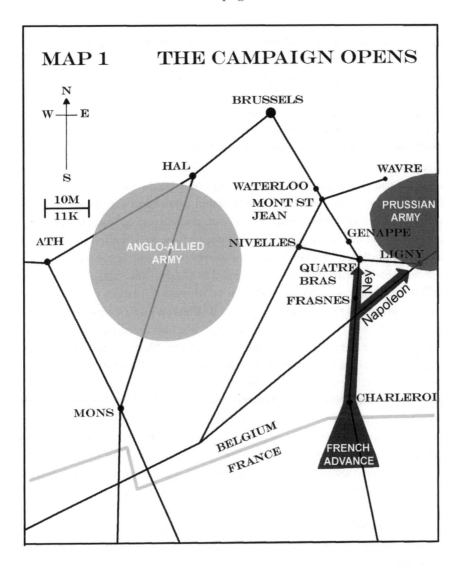

MAP 1 — THE CAMPAIGN OPENS

commanders did not know for sure which route Napoleon would take, or where his attack would fall.

Napoleon's ultimate aim would probably be to take Brussels. He had a choice of routes: via Mons, Ath and Hal or via Charleroi, Quatre-Bras and Waterloo. Wellington believed the first route – via Hal – was the one he would have used, had he been in Napoleon's shoes, the latter being noted in his younger days for his skill at manoeuvre. So Wellington detached a division to block this route, and left it in position even when it was reasonably clear Napoleon had chosen the other route. The Waterloo route was, arguably, the most likely point of attack because it was the boundary between the two armies, always a weak point. Success here would offer the opportunity of despatching one numerically inferior army before turning on the other. Once defeated – Napoleon believed – the Prussians would retire eastwards, towards Prussia, and the British to the west, towards Ostend or Antwerp, for the customary evacuation. The allied part of Wellington's army would either disperse homewards or rejoin the French Army.

On 15 June the French Army crossed the border into Belgium south-west of Charleroi and made contact with the Prussian I Corps under Lieutenant General Hans von Zieten. This corps' effective fighting withdrawal allowed time for the rest of the Prussian army to concentrate around the village of Ligny. Wellington was informed but hesitated, awaiting confirmation that this was indeed Napoleon's main thrust and not just a diversion. That evening, supposedly to avoid alarming the Brussels population, he attended the Duchess of Richmond's ball in a coach maker's warehouse. There he received news of a second French thrust, under Ney, aimed at Quatre-Bras, and at last he gave orders for his forces to concentrate around Nivelles. Distances for many units were so great and time so short that, had Wellington's initial movement order been followed, Ney's thrust probably could not have been held. Fortunately the quartermaster general (chief of staff) of the Netherlands contingent, Major General de Constant-Rebècque, ignored Wellington's instructions and redirected the Nassauers of Major General Prince Saxe-Weimar's brigade of the 2nd Netherland's Infantry Division to hold the crossroads until reinforcements arrived. During the Peninsular War, Wellington had often been extremely unforgiving of any deviation from his strict instructions, as will be described later. It is hard to imagine he would have been similarly put out by de Constant-Rebècque's independent action, which saved the day. The two men were certainly still on speaking terms at Waterloo.

On Friday 16 June two battles took place: at Ligny and at Quatre-Bras, where Maréchal Ney made no move to capture the strategically important crossroads until 1430hrs, leaving Wellington time to ride the 5km to meet Blücher, and to agree to come to the Prussians' support, if possible, since it was the two commanders' plan to fight Napoleon together on the same battlefield. Wellington's subsequent failure to do so confirmed in the mind of Lieutenant General Gneisenau, Blücher's chief of staff, that Wellington was not to be trusted. This was unreasonable, for Ney had a vastly superior force of 28,000 men to the Allies' initial 8,000 defenders of the crossroads. Holding the crossroads was essential if communication with the Prussian army was to be kept open. But this strategic commitment forced Wellington into holding ground he would otherwise have considered the worst possible for the sort of defensive battle at which he was so skilled. Initially the battle was fought by Dutch troops, who had fought for Napoleon less than a year before but were now commanded by the Prince of Orange. It was to be late afternoon before sufficient troops – he never had enough cavalry – reached the battlefield for Wellington to take the offensive.

He was on the verge of ordering withdrawal when the first reinforcements arrived. These were Lieutenant General Sir Thomas Picton's 5th British Infantry Division, led by the riflemen of the 1st Battalion of the 95th, who were immediately tasked with holding the left (east) flank of the Allied line, just south of the east–west road. As further battalions arrived, a second line was formed just north of the crossroads. An attack by French columns was successfully repulsed by the 79th and 32nd Regiments in line, in echelon. Then the Duke of Brunswick's contingent came in, some 6,244 strong and uniformed in black, but the men were mostly new recruits. One battalion was sent east to support the 1/95th, now under severe pressure, and the remainder were deployed west of the north–south road. The five squadrons of Brunswick cavalry, led by their duke, charged – but failed to break – some French squares. The Duke of Brunswick was killed.

The Prince of Orange was only in his early twenties and had seen service with the British Army in the Peninsula, accompanied by de Constant-Rebècque. Now, for political reasons, the prince was in command of the Allied I Corps which comprised two Netherlands divisions stiffened by the inclusion of Cooke's 1st British (Guards) Division and von Alten's 3rd British Division. He led the Dutch, Belgian and Brunswick cavalry forward in double line but, faced by inferior numbers of French light cavalry, they nevertheless refused to charge, turned and streamed back, pursued by the French, who nearly caught Wellington. He escaped by ordering the men of one side of the 92nd's square to lay down their muskets (so as not to deter his horse, 'Copenhagen') and jumping into the protective box. This and the squares of the 42nd and 44th Regiments saw off this attack and a subsequent one by the French heavy cavalry, the cuirassiers. But, after the latter had withdrawn, the French gunners were once again able to play havoc with these squares, ideal artillery targets. The Allied skirmishers were unwilling to go forward to harry the gunners in response, because of the imminent threat of cavalry attack, to which skirmishers were most vulnerable. The French cavalry attacked yet again, but to no avail, although the Allies' ammunition was running short by this time. The French all-arms co-operation was excellent at this stage of the campaign.

The Allied low point had now been passed as reinforcements in strength began to arrive. Picton, ordered by Wellington to handle the deployment of the newly arrived four battalions of Sir Colin Halkett's brigade, placed the Highlanders of the 69th in square on the west flank of his division and the remaining three – the 30th, the 73rd and the 33rd – in squares in echelon to support the Brunswickers holding the Bossut Wood in the south-west quadrant of the crossroads.

The Prince of Orange now began to exert his baleful influence on the battle.[9] Aggrieved – one suspects – at this interference in what he perceived as his area of authority, he first ordered the 69th back into line and then went to the other three squares and did the same. The result was disastrous. Jacques Logie describes how Ney ordered Kellermann – the French cavalry commander – to charge to capture the crossroads of Les Quatre-Bras, and how the first regiment encountered was the 69th, composed of Scotsmen, who discharged their muskets at a range of twenty paces, but the cuirassiers, far from being stopped, fell on them full tilt, destroyed them completely and bowled over all who were in their way.[10] The 69th had been caught by surprise and completely destroyed – at least for this day. One of its colours was taken, the first and only one lost during all of Wellington's campaigns.[11] The other battalions had a few moments warning of the cuirassiers' charge: nevertheless – being in line, not square – the 73rd and 33rd both broke and rushed into Bossut Wood, the 33rd losing about a third of its strength and the 73rd almost as many.[12]

The 30th managed to form square and survived, although suffering some casualties. This battalion finally finished in the wood too. Wellington managed to restore, to some degree, the morale of the young men of the three less damaged battalions, but the 69th was beyond immediate repair. Never before had Wellington had an entire brigade broken by cavalry.

Fortunately, Ney had now shot his bolt and had no more reserves. At the same time, Major General Cooke's 1st British Infantry (Guards) Division arrived, exhausted from its long and rapid march to the sound of the guns. Unfortunately, it was fed piecemeal by the Prince of Orange into Bossut Wood to clear it of Frenchmen before Wellington could start his advance. Maitland's Brigade, consisting of the second and third battalions of the 1st Foot Guards, lost about 500 casualties from an initial strength of 2,050. Nevertheless, the Allied line was stabilised well south of Quatre-Bras and the battle petered out.

The battle for Quatre-Bras was no simple precursor to the main event of the campaign but a major battle, in which Wellington displayed his skill in defence when the terrain was not of his choosing and the advantages of initiative and numbers were decidedly in favour of a French victory.[13] One more commander – a Frenchman – needs to be introduced. Comte d'Erlon, who commanded Napoleon's 1st Army Corps of some 20,000 men, was allocated by Napoleon to Ney's thrust at Quatre-Bras. Some writers suggest that Napoleon saw Ney's role being simply that of a pin, as in chess, to hold the Allied army away from providing support to the Prussians. This view is borne out by Napoleon's order, direct to d'Erlon, to march to his aid at Ligny, where he found himself outnumbered and in difficulty. Napoleon failed to inform Ney, who discovered d'Erlon's absence and, no doubt, reacted as any red-haired man would, before demanding his return. So d'Erlon dutifully turned

Field Marshal Arthur Wellesley, 1st Duke of Wellington, 1769–1852.
Commissioned in 1787, by 1796 he had purchased command of the 33rd Regiment and learned, in the Walcheren Expedition, how not to carry out operations. In 1803, serving as his brother's army commander in India, he defeated the Maratha Confederacy at Assaye. He proposed the British Government should provide armed support for the Spanish revolt against French occupation, and led the first and subsequent invasion forces. The victor of some twenty-four battles and sieges he lost only one, the siege of Burgos.
Only three and a half months older than Napoleon he was immeasurably fitter, being able to ride continuously for over sixteen hours at Waterloo.

his corps about and marched back towards Quatre-Bras but he did not arrive in time to take any part in the battle. This must give rise to one of the most important 'what-ifs' in history. His veteran troops, added to either Ney or Napoleon, could, plausibly, have contributed to a French victory and break-through at either point – Quatre-Bras or Ligny – allowing whichever was the victorious 'wing' to outflank and defeat the other allied army.

The Battle of Ligny began at about 1430hrs with the Garde's artillery opening fire on the village of Saint Armand-la-Haye. Thereafter a ding-dong struggle for the two villages ensued, ending at around 2030hrs with the infantry of the Old Garde finally ejecting the Prussians from Ligny. Napoleon was convinced he had inflicted a crushing defeat on Marshal Blücher. 'Alte Vorwärts' as he was known had indeed been 'forwards', and was certainly old by the standards of the time but, nevertheless, he had been leading a desperate cavalry counter-attack in his own inimitable fashion, when his horse was brought down. Blücher was stunned and trapped beneath it. With his commander temporarily out of the battle, his chief of staff, Gneisenau, assumed command and ordered withdrawal. Gneisenau knew that the logical direction in which to retire was towards Prussia – eastwards: and Napoleon knew that too. Gneisenau also knew that Blücher had promised to work in tandem with Wellington's army, currently lying due west; but Wellington had failed to meet his promise to support the Prussians at Ligny. What is more, Gneisenau had a long-standing antipathy to – and distrust of – Wellington. So he decided to hedge his bets and withdrew northwards, to a small village called Wavre, whence the Prussians could – given time – move west to support Wellington or east if the Allied army did not stand. The four Prussian corps were deployed at each of the four cardinal points of the compass around Wavre: Thielemann to the north; von Pirch in the south; von Bülow, east; von Zieten, west.

The morning of 17 June dawned to find Wellington already back at Quatre-Bras, but there were few signs of activity by his enemy. Wellington was aware that the French, dependent as they were on marauding for their supplies, were unlikely to be ready to move before 1000hrs. So, ignoring the desultory skirmishing shots, and conscious of the privations all his troops had suffered the day before, he ordered a meal to be cooked and eaten. He then withdrew all his infantry and foot artillery northwards, leaving only cavalry and horse artillery. These fought a brilliant withdrawal when Napoleon eventually instigated a belated attack. Wellington had escaped.

Napoleon also spent a leisurely morning, letting his veterans feed and water themselves. He also failed to reconnoitre forwards to be sure the Prussians were moving eastwards as expected, but around 1100hrs he sent the newly-promoted Marshal Grouchy with 30,000 men, in an ad-hoc corps, to pursue the Prussians and prevent their rejoining battle while he dealt with the Allied army. Grouchy faithfully headed north-east and did not connect with the Prussian force. Napoleon then led his now depleted army north-westwards to Quatre-Bras, only to find that all he could do was pursue Wellington's highly mobile rearguard. As he did so, a massive and persistent storm broke over all the armies. The thunderous downpour continued throughout the withdrawal (the British Army never retreats) to the previously chosen defensive position on the ridge just south of the hamlet of Mont-Saint-Jean, some 2km south of a small village with the strange name of Waterloo, apparently named after a marshy meadow since at least the year 1145, according to Jacques Logie, in the English edition of his *Waterloo, The 1815 Campaign*.[14] The rain continued all through the night, only to cease around dawn of Sunday 18 June. Most troops on both sides had no food, shelter or firewood. Only those posted near the few buildings in the area were able to burn furniture or doors, creating at La Haie Sainte, in the middle of the battlefield-to-be, a problem for its defenders at the height of the clash to come. Amidst all the misery the Peninsular veterans found consolation – most of Wellington's great victories in Spain had been preceded by just such intemperate weather.

HARD POUNDING THIS, GENTLEMEN

The night had been grim. Torrential rain had fallen incessantly since early the evening before. Very few men in all three armies had found shelter. On arrival on the continent the British had been issued with blanket tents but a pre-campaign test run had shown them to be deeply deficient, as one might imagine a system of buttons and loops supported on muskets would have been. The 'tents' had been left behind – after all, it was midsummer. Fortunately the night was hot. The best that most men could do was to find some straw on which to lie, even if that involved taking the newly thatched roof off a barn in which a brigade commander was quartered.[1] William Leeke lay down on his straw in the middle of a ploughed field. He had his boat cloak as cover but it was minus its cape and hood, which Leeke had lent to his commanding officer, Sir John Colborne. At about 2200hrs he was ordered to move his company. Having settled again, his efforts at getting some rest were thwarted by half a dozen loose horses galloping back and forth. He and his comrades could only avoid being trampled by jumping up and scaring them off. The morning dawned and was blessedly fine. The men's first duty was to check that their firearms were serviceable after the rain. Next they would have had breakfast had there been any to be had – the commissariat had failed. Leeke had one biscuit and a half mouthful of soup.

The final, titanic battle of the Napoleonic wars was to be fought on one of its smallest battlefields (see Map 2, Colour section). Where distances had been measured in kilometres at Austerlitz, Jena and Borodino, here they were in metres – or in decent imperial yards. The French and Allied armies, drawn up on ridges about 1,200 yards apart, would face each other across a shallow valley no more than 5,000 yards long. The countryside between the two ridges was gently rolling farmland, intersected by a few hedges marking fields of nearly full-grown crops, especially rye. Then, rye was much longer in the stalk than it is now, creating a visual barrier and an obstacle to movement – standing or trampled – especially for the 'poor bloody infantry'. There were no major streams. The few roads and the network of tracks were only paved in parts. Some stretches of the roads were sunken. The main road between Charleroi to the south and Brussels to the north ran through the centre of the battlefield providing an axis for both armies. Brussels was Napoleon's target.

From his slightly higher ridge at La Belle Alliance, on the axis road, Napoleon could survey Wellington's defensive position on the next ridge. Since he was dismissive, if not completely ignorant, of Wellington's skill in defence and in particular his technique of hiding his troops and their movements behind a ridge, the implications of the topography may have eluded him. To his extreme right-rear was the village of Plancenoit on the road to the east. To his right front the terrain looked to be far more suitable to defence than attack, being especially awkward for cavalry and artillery, complicated, as it was, by several small hamlets, woods, hedge lines, watercourses and lanes, some seriously sunken. By contrast, the ground directly in front of him on both sides of the axis road was open. The enclosed farmstead of La Haie Sainte, on the left of the road, obviously provided a redoubt to the enemy's advantage as did the buildings, garden, kitchen garden, orchard and wood of Château au Goumont to his half left.[2] If La Haie Sainte, to his immediate front a mere 200m from Wellington's ridge top, could be captured it would be like a dagger in the chest of the enemy, especially as an artillery post. To the left – west – of La Haie Sainte, Wellington's ridge was more pronounced, with a projecting tongue of land, but the ground was open as far left as the redoubt of au Goumont.[3]

Beyond au Goumont, the ground became quite steep and unsuitable for an outflanking attack. But the flanks were unimportant since the centre looked very inviting and the axis road led straight to Brussels. In his view, Wellington had made the mistake of fighting with his back to an almost impenetrable forest, which would provide the anvil for the French Army's hammer.

So Napoleon's initial plan was to draw the Allied reserves away from his centre to Wellington's right and to hold them there while a massive attack in the centre would break through and open the road to Brussels. As a secondary benefit the assault against Wellington's right might offer an opportunity of rolling up his line from that flank. To this end he would make a feint against au Goumont, to force Wellington to reinforce it, and then put down an intimidating bombardment on Wellington's centre from a Grande Batterie of his beloved artillery before launching a massed infantry attack, supported by cavalry, just to the east of the axis road.

By contrast, Wellington's appreciation of the situation was affected by the knowledge that Napoleon would dictate the course of events. From his stance by the elm tree at the crossroads just south of Mont-Saint-Jean, it was clear to him that au Goumont and La Haie Sainte would serve as strong points, as too would the buildings of Frichermont, Smohain, La Haye and Papelotte to

The Morning of Waterloo. Wellington, on Copenhagen, takes tea with the 1st/95th on the way to battle. Of mixed English Thoroughbred and Arabian blood, Copenhagen was born in 1808 and raced twelve times, winning twice. Wellington bought him from a fellow officer in Spain. Having carried Wellington continuously throughout the sixteen-hour battle, when his rider dismounted, understandably tried to kick him. He received a full military funeral at Stratfield Saye in 1836.

his left. Like many of his Peninsula positions, this one also had the vital transverse track behind the ridge which would allow rapid and secret movement of troops to the critical point. He was not concerned by having the Forêst de Soignes behind his position, astride the road to Brussels, as he knew it to be reasonably passable to his army and its vehicles, and would provide good cover for his 'Spanish' troops to fight a rearguard action in the event of withdrawal being necessary.

Given Napoleon's reputation as a master of manoeuvre, Wellington's chief concern was that he might outflank him, either by attacking his – Wellington's – right flank or by sweeping well to the west and cutting the British line of communication with Ostend. To meet the latter possibility, Lieutenant General Sir Charles Colville had already been detached with a mixed force of some 17,000 men to defend the route through Hal, 8 miles (12km) to the west. To protect his immediate right flank Wellington initially posted the 52nd Light Infantry 'en potence', borrowing a French phrase meaning T-shaped ('gallows' in French) implying a deployment at right angles to the line. Some 2,000 yards further back he positioned the 3rd Netherlands Infantry Division in the hamlet of Braine l'Alleud, not only to defend that flank but also – possibly – because he was uncertain of the division's loyalty. The Dutch troops were dressed in French blue since the units had served under Napoleon until a few months before; their general, David-Hendrik Chassé, had been created baron by the emperor. He in particular was to prove where his loyalty lay, later in the battle. Behind his right centre Wellington placed, in reserve, the Brunswick contingent. In front of that was Clinton's 2nd British Infantry Division, in defensive depth and an effective reserve. Clinton's division contained Adam's 3rd British Infantry Brigade (the Light Brigade), the 1st King's German Legion (KGL) Brigade and Colonel Hugh Halkett's 3rd Hanoverian Brigade.[4]

The front line of the right centre comprised – reading westwards from the crossroads at the centre – Count Charles Alten's 3rd British Division consisting of Colonel Ompteda's 2nd KGL Brigade, a Brunswick brigade, and Sir Colin Halkett's 5th British Brigade. The latter had been reduced to two composite battalions – 30th/73rd and 33rd/69th – by the heavy casualties incurred at Quatre-Bras. Finally, on the flank, unadulterated by the inclusion of other nationalities, stood George Cooke's 1st British Guards Division of two brigades, Peregrine Maitland's 1st British Guards brigade and Sir John Byng's 2nd British Guards brigade. Both brigades had two battalions; Maitland's the 2nd and 3rd battalions of the 1st Foot Guards, and Byng's the 2nd battalion of the Coldstream Guards and the 2/3rd Fusilier Guards aka the Scots Guards. The latter brigade, with some Nassauers, eventually garrisoned au Goumont. A separate contingent of Nassauers under August von Kruse was held as part of Wellington's reserve.

The left wing was less strongly manned with only two divisions – Sir Thomas Picton's 5th British Infantry and Perponcher's 2nd Netherlands. Half of the latter division – Prince Bernard of Saxe-Weimar's German Nassauers – were deployed forward of the line, manning the strong points. Picton was noted for his fighting ability so his men were purposely posted to hold the gap in the ridge through which the vital road to Brussels lay.

Cavalry was customarily posted on an army's flanks but Wellington, recognising that the topography of neither flank was suitable for cavalry, held the two brigades of his heavy cavalry – the Household Brigade and the Union Brigade – behind his centre, together with all bar two brigades of light cavalry. The latter, Vivian's and Vandeleur's were despatched to the flank of the Allied left wing. However the ground in front of them was so steeply contoured, the tracks sunken and the fields bounded by thick hedges as to make cavalry assault almost out of the question.

Wellington's whole front was about 4,200 yards in length. His skirmish line – in theory at least – was placed between the northern most points of the four 'redoubts' while his main line followed the ridge and the road that ran behind it. From the air it would have seemed an untidy and apparently formless array. Napoleon's, by contrast, was neat and almost symmetrical. His left wing found

Reille's II Corps in an arc south of au Goumont, backed by Kellermann's cavalry corps and the Garde's heavy cavalry. D'Erlon's I Corps was drawn up in a tight formation on Napoleon's right wing, backed by Milhaud's IV Cavalry Corps and the light cavalry of the Garde. Further east still, Napoleon posted Jacquinot's 1st Cavalry Division, with uncanny prescience. His reserve, tightly packed astride the axis road, was the 11,000 men of Lobau's VI Corps and, behind that 20,000 more, the three elements of the Garde, the Young Garde in front of the Middle Garde in front of the Old Garde. Finally he added his Grande Batterie of artillery on a subsidiary ridge directly in front of d'Erlon's Corps. The Gunner-Emperor massed some eighty cannon – a paltry total compared to his earlier battles but impressive nevertheless – including his 'beautiful daughters,' the 12-pounders. The gun line, its limbers, and four lines of ammunition caissons (four wheeled wagons) occupied the entire area in front of the infantry corps and must have presented a very disruptive barrier to the latter's advance, as and when it might be ordered.

Like Wellington, Napoleon had also detached a major portion of his army. After a leisurely start that morning, Marshal Grouchy had taken his 30,000 men with orders to pursue the retreating Prussians. Believing them to have been soundly beaten at Ligny, two days before, Napoleon gave Grouchy specific instructions as to which direction he should take. That Gneisenau had not gone in the expected direction meant that Grouchy's 30,000 were a crucially wasted asset.

After the retreat from Ligny, the Prussians had bivouacked around the village of Wavre while Gneisenau and his revived commander, Blücher, argued as to whether the Prussians should support Wellington or escape to safety. Blücher won the argument and Gneisenau issued the orders. The Prussian advance was to be two pronged: one corps to attack the French right by taking the village of Plancenoit and threatening his rear, the other to effect a junction with the Allied left wing. For Plancenoit, Gneisenau chose Bülow's IV Corps; this had not been involved in fighting at Ligny. But IV Corps had the furthest to go and had to negotiate its way through the narrow village of Wavre and the bivouac area of another corps.

Bülow set off at 0400hrs. His corps was halted for two hours due to a fire in Wavre. Gneisenau could have advanced another corps to speed the promised provision of assistance to Wellington, but, surprisingly, he declined to do so. His reasoning behind this decision is understandable but might – and nearly did – have dire consequences. According to the American historian Jac Weller, the Prussian chief of staff was mistrustful of Wellington before the campaign began and

... warned Müffling to be much on his guard with the Duke of Wellington, for that by ... his transactions with the deceitful Nabobs, this distinguished general had so accustomed himself to duplicity, that he had become such a master in the art as even to outwit the nabobs themselves.[5]

Gneisenau's concern had been increased by Wellington's failure to provide support for the Prussian army at Ligny. Whilst he now knew why Wellington had been unable to come to his aid two days before, Gneisenau was determined to avoid irretrievable involvement at Waterloo until he was absolutely certain that Wellington was going to fight, rather than withdraw, which would have left the Prussians at Napoleon's mercy. Hence he pulled his punches and both corps were seriously delayed. At about 1300hrs Bülow's IV Corps was spotted by the French, and Napoleon despatched Lobau's Corps, his first reserve, to block the Prussians beyond Plancenoit. Bülow suffered further delays from narrow bridges, mud and ravines before pushing Lobau back and assaulting Plancenoit for the first time at about 1800hrs.

Zieten's I Corps had been selected to support Wellington directly but did not start until 1400hrs, to avoid tangling with Bülow's corps, whose route had to be crossed. Zieten's advance guard reached Ohain, just east of Wellington's line at about 1800hrs. And there, *pro tem*, we will leave the Prussians and return to Waterloo.

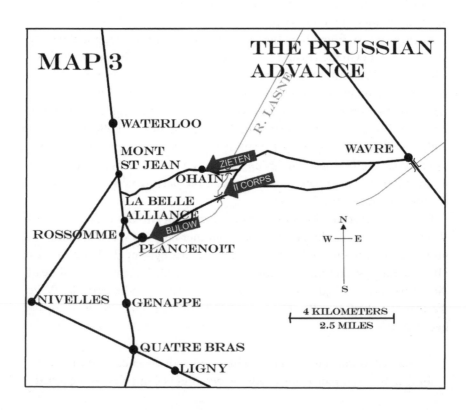

Napoleon had intended to make the first move in the battle at 0900hrs, but the difficulties created by the overnight weather slowed down the arrival of his troops: the Garde did not even leave its bivouac area until 1000hrs. As he welcomed his army's arrival and placed them, in all their sodden glory, on the forward slope of his ridge, to those few on the Allied side able to watch it must have seemed he was orchestrating a review. However, if it was intended to intimidate his enemies it failed, for very few of Wellington's men could see the array, hidden as they were behind their ridge to the north. Of course, Napoleon was blind to Wellington's strength and dispositions from the same cause.

This reverse-slope deployment had a third advantage. When the Grande Batterie finally opened fire, aiming to pulverise the Allied centre, it too failed. The direct fire of the guns had no targets on the forward face of Wellington's ridge, except a brigade of Dutch troops, who were hurriedly withdrawn. Cannonballs did not even ricochet usefully, due to the soft ground. The howitzers, of which there were about a third the number of guns, fared better with lobbed case shot, so long as it burst in the air: ground bursts were also absorbed by the soft soil. Again, the ridge prevented observation by the French gunners of the results of their shooting. However, perhaps the most serious failing of the Grande Batterie, and certainly its most surprising, is that no attempt was made to destroy the fortifications of La Haie Sainte.

The first cannon shot came at 1130hrs, not from the Grande Batterie but at au Goumont, signalling the start of the attempt to draw in Wellington's reserves. The château and its grounds were surrounded by a hedge but, internally, can be envisaged in thirds. The northern third contained the buildings and formal garden, themselves in a partially brick-walled compound, and the apple orchard. The southern two thirds contained the wood and cultivable land.

The original garrison consisted of all four light companies of the four Guards regiments but the 1/2nd Nassau Battalion was sent as reinforcement early on the eighteenth. The wood was initially manned by a selection of German light infantry companies. Subsequently the entire Coldstream and Scots Guards Battalions were sent into au Goumont but the two light companies of the First Guards, commanded by Captain and Lieutenant Colonel Lord Saltoun, were later withdrawn and rejoined their battalion in line behind the ridge.[6] The defenders had been forced back into the buildings and the orchard before 1400hrs. By about 1500hrs the French already had committed twenty-four battalions to Wellington's three.[7] What had been intended as a feint had become an all-out attempt to capture, having the opposite effect to that intended by Napoleon: his reserves – not Wellington's – had been depleted. Despite the efforts of Reille's corps, the buildings of au Goumont remained throughout the battle in Allied hands to act as an inhibiting factor to any advance Napoleon made on the western half of the battlefield.

The retention of au Goumont was much aided by the six howitzers of Bull's troop, which were able to lob spherical case shot – shrapnel – into the wood over the heads of the defenders.

The Grande Batterie expended some 3,600 rounds in thirty minutes to very little effect, unknown, of course, to Napoleon.[8] Now, no doubt full of optimism, he ordered what was intended to be his masterstroke, the massed attack by d'Erlon's corps on the east side of the Brussels road. It was to include an assault on La Haie Sainte and cavalry support on its left flank. The infantry's frustration at having to thread its way through the hundreds of wagons, horses and men of the Grande Batterie must have been audible. The military sin of having to form up for an attack in sight and within range of the enemy's artillery suggests over-optimism or a fading military genius. But form up they did, in massed close columns, before they set off up the slope, slowed by the tall, wet rye to confront Wellington's thinly held line. Only four batteries and a thin red line of infantry manned the hedges of the ridge-top road, but they were backed – fortunately – by the English, Irish and Scots dragoon regiments of the Union Cavalry Brigade. The other heavy cavalry, the four regiments of the Household Brigade, were positioned to the west of the axis road (see Map 4 Colour section).

D'Erlon's columns reached the summit of the ridge and were stopped by the infantry of Picton's 5th British Infantry Division and Bijlandt's 1st Netherlands Brigade. Picton was shot through the forehead, leading his division's bayonet charge. Now the British cavalry came to the rescue. The Union Brigade, in line, was brought forward, the infantry parted to let the horses

Lieutenant General Sir Thomas Picton, 1758–1815.
Commissioned in 1771, his early career was as part soldier, part government official in Trinidad, where he earned a reputation for brutality and a quick temper. Nevertheless his ability as a commander was recognised by Wellington, who appointed him to command a division in Spain. Despite not receiving the peerage given to other divisional commanders in 1814, in 1815 he accepted command of the 5th Division for the Waterloo campaign. His uniform had not arrived before Napoleon moved so Picton was in civilian dress when shot in the forehead while successfully counter-attacking d'Erlon's mass assault.

through, they struggled through the hedges and across the road, and eventually came to grips with the enemy. So tightly packed were the French that the British cavalry, initially, could only chip away at the columns' edges until panic finally broke them and the men streamed away. Only now could the cavalry move at more than a trot in pursuit. In wild, slashing excitement they galloped (as fast as the mud would allow) down into the valley and up the opposite slope to the Grande Batterie. Meanwhile the Household Brigade had also moved forward to beat off the cavalry on the French infantry's left flank. These latter too were heavy cavalry, cuirassiers, in steel breast- and back-plates. After a mammoth struggle, the French, outnumbered, broke and the survivors fled southwards. The Household Brigade, as excited but inexperienced as the Union Brigade, now joined the latter in the race for the French gun line.

Lord Uxbridge, to whom Wellington had given complete control of the Allied cavalry, had spotted the opportunity, given the orders and led the Household Brigade. The heavy cavalry had successfully seen off Napoleon's first attempt at winning through to Brussels. However, as so often with British cavalry, all control had been lost in the quest for glory. Having 'taken' the Grande Batterie but without the means to tow away the cannons or to spike their vent holes, the horsemen milled around aimlessly. French General Jacquinot had carefully brought forward his 2,400-strong mixed cavalry force, initially to protect d'Erlon's eastern flank, and was now presented with a perfect target, and took it. The British cavalry was much more than decimated: losses amounted to nearly 50 per cent and neither brigade took any further major part in the battle.

Some historians claim that d'Erlon's massed infantry assault was the crisis of the battle. Certainly it was Napoleon's main set-piece move to win the victory he craved, but it was defeated, in the same way nearly all French attacks in column had been defeated by the British line for the past decade. The Allied army was still intact and fresh: there was no serious sign of weakness that might suggest it was likely to collapse, although the cavalry arm was seriously depleted. The moment properly known as the 'Crisis' was to come later. There was now a pause of about one and a half hours before the next phase of the battle.

Attacks on au Goumont and La Haie Sainte had continued throughout the day and, just before 1600hrs, Maréchal Ney observed from La Haie Sainte that the Allied line directly to the north appeared to be crumbling. At this point the ridge was less pronounced than elsewhere and what was going on there was accordingly more visible. Although he was mistaken, Ney assumed that an immediate and massive blow would achieve a breakthrough at last. Whether he consulted his emperor or Napoleon gave the order is still debated but Ney ordered a massed cavalry charge against the Allied line between La Haie Sainte and au Goumont, a distance of no more than 1,000 yards. He also had artillery brought forward, able to fire over the heads of the cavalry as they crossed the valley. However this was only partly effective since firing had to cease when the cavalry actually attacked. This was an attempt at all arms co-operation but was flawed: no infantry was involved and the over-large mass of cavalry so filled the cramped space that it not only precluded the use of infantry but also prevented the employment of horse artillery in close support (see Map 5, colour section).

Faced by the threat of cavalry the Allied infantry formed into battalion squares in a loose chequerboard pattern. Despite its magnificent and awe-inspiring appearance, the cavalry's charges had practically no effect on the squares. Faced with a slope of sodden rye, the French horsemen could ride at no more than a trot and the horses unhelpfully refused to impale them-selves on the bayonets. Wave after wave simply parted and flowed round the squares, whose men actually welcomed their presence – what they hated was the artillery barrage that knocked them over when the horsemen were absent. Astonishingly not one Frenchman thought to spike the Allied guns, even to hammer a pistol ramrod into the vent of a gun as a makeshift spike, which might have turned the cavalry attacks into a battle-winning sacrifice.[9] Instead the Allied gunners were able to shelter in the squares, as instructed by Wellington, and then run back to their cannons and open fire on the horse-men's backs. Some of the British squares were so well drilled they were able to deploy from square to a four-rank line in order to fire on the cavalry as they retired, and to return to square again before the horsemen could retaliate. No battalion square was broken.

Wellington and his staff were far from inactive during these attacks, moving about the battlefield encouraging and repositioning as necessary. He and his aides frequently had to take refuge in a square, as did other senior officers as well as the gunners, whose cannon remained untouched although surrounded many times by enemy horsemen. Immediately after the first cavalry charge Wellington detected the Brunswick squares in their positions in the line to the immediate north-east of au Goumont were unsteady. In order to stiffen their morale and to provide a breakwater against the repeated waves of horseflesh up the slope, Wellington moved Adam's Light Brigade, whose units were all 'Spanish' veterans and hitherto held in central reserve to deal with real emer-gencies, to the forward slope of the ridge northeast of au Goumont.[10] The 71st (Glasgow) Light Infantry was furthest out, on the Allied right, with two companies of the 3/95th. The 52nd (Oxfordshire) Light Infantry – the strong-est British battalion in the Allied army at about 1,000 men since the 2nd and 3rd battalions of the First Foot Guards had suffered severe casualties in

Bossut Wood at Quatre-Bras – formed two wing-squares in the centre, while six companies of the 2/95th squared up on the left.

Ensign William Leeke, newly commissioned into the 52nd and from whom we shall hear more later on, described how the veteran officers of his battalion reckoned the bombardment to which they were now subjected was far worse than any they had experienced in the Peninsular War. To make matters worse, the British shrapnel rounds fired overhead were bursting short and inflicting serious damage on the 52nd. Word was sent back to the gunners to desist. After several surges of cavalry had failed to break the Allied line, Ney belatedly realised his error in not involving his infantry, and ordered forward Bachelu's division and a brigade of Foy's, both involved in the persistent assault on au Goumont. The French columns, upwards of 6,500 strong but tired by their hours of struggle to capture the 'strongpoint', marched initially into an artillery cannonade from the ridge and then into Adam's brigade alongside au Goumont, whose musketry broke them; Bachelu's columns fled first taking Foy's with them. General Foy described this encounter as follows:

I kept my left flank at the hedge [of au Goumont].[11]

In front of me I had a battalion deployed as skirmishers. When we were about to meet the English, we received a very lively fire of canister [probably shrapnel fired over the heads of the light infantry and riflemen] and musketry. It was a hail of death. The enemy squares [Adam's brigade] had the front rank kneeling and presenting a hedge of bayonets. The columns of Bachelu's division fled first and their flight precipitated the flight of my columns. At this moment I was wounded. ... Everyone was fleeing.[12]

From the Allied side General Adam also recorded this episode, after the first cavalry assault:

... the Enemy's Cavalry retired. Shortly after this the 3rd Brigade was ordered to advance, which it did in the order in which it was formed, to the Nivelles road, on the edge of which it remained for some time exposed to the fire of Artillery, by which a considerable number of men were disabled. After crossing the Nivelles road the Duke of Wellington personally directed that the Brigade should form line *four* deep 'and drive those fellows away,' meaning some French Infantry. There was not space to form the 52nd in line with 71st and 95th, and the 52nd consequently was a sort of reserve to the Brigade.

The Enemy's Infantry were very soon disposed of, ... and the Brigade continued to advance to about ... [left blank for no known reason, but the Light Brigade was roughly in line from the south-east corner of au Goumont angled back towards the Allied line but not in contact with it, acting as a sort of groyne to take the surge out of the cavalry assaults] where the Cavalry of the Enemy, being prepared to attack, the Brigade was formed in columns and then squares. The interval between the 71st and the 95th was larger than desirable, and when the Cavalry were just reaching the 71st Sir John Colborne brought down the 52nd to fill up the space, and [threw] in a most effective fire on the Cavalry, which were in the act of attacking the 71st Regiment.[13]

Adam goes on to tell how the right of his brigade seemed too close to the enclosure of au Goumont and likely to be enfiladed from it, and that, at the suggestion of Colborne, the Light Brigade was brought back to the ridge, when a deserting French officer galloped up to announce Napoleon's preparation for his final assault. It is important to note that this action beside au Goumont was emphatically not part of the final action against the Imperial Garde, as some historians would have it. Foy's description of the British being beside au Goumont precisely matches Adam's telling of the action when his Light Brigade was posted on the forward slope, well forward of the Allied line, during the massed cavalry attacks. It is also worth noting, in passing, that Colborne seemed to be taking all the important decisions on behalf of his brigade commander. This is not altogether surprising as Colborne had often commanded at brigade level in the Peninsula. Eventually the French cavalry charges petered out.

Meanwhile, at about 1800hrs, two brigades of Bülow's IV Corps took the village of Plancenoit. Napoleon, recognising the dire consequences of losing control of the roads and tracks to his rear, sent all eight battalions of the Young Garde to retake it. This was achieved, but at the cost of depleting his reserve. After further attempts by the Prussians to regain possession, the French ill-advisedly advanced beyond the bounds of Plancenoit and were cut to pieces by combined Prussian infantry and cavalry, again losing control of the village, especially of the churchyard, the strongest defensive point. Desperate to avoid encirclement, Napoleon ordered two battalions of his valuable Old Garde, to retake the village. The 1/2e Grenadiers à Pied and the 1/2e Châsseurs à Pied were despatched with specific orders – it is said – to use only the bayonet. This may sound like bravado but actually was a wise military precaution. Maintenance of momentum is crucial to success in hand to hand fighting – halting to fire and reload would have lost it. The Garde duly achieved what was asked of it, Plancenoit was once more in French hands and would be retained until after the rout that ended the battle.

Meanwhile, the French at last scored a success, although not all of their own making – they captured La Haie Sainte. The garrison had run out of ammunition and was forced to withdraw. Initially the farm had been held by 400 men of the 2nd Light Battalion KGL. They had later been joined by two companies of 1st KGL and one company of 5th KGL. Finally the Light Company of 2/1st Nassau had been sent in. The garrison had been in difficulty from the start. Through a failure of leadership during the night before, the men had been allowed to burn a barn door and several farm vehicles for warmth, leaving a gaping hole in the surrounding wall beside the road and little with which to barricade it. The same incompetence had allowed all the pioneer equipment, which would have allowed the creation of loopholes and platforms from which to fire over the walls, to be sent to au Goumont. The final and most telling error was the failure to provide the men with a proper supply of ammunition, since it must have been clear they would be besieged and replenishment would probably be difficult, if not impossible. Most of the men were armed with rifles, whose ammunition was specific to the weapon. Resupply was requested five times but none came, although reinforcements arrived successfully. Nevertheless the garrison put up a magnificent fight. Those few that remained alive retired to the ridge at about 1815hrs, leaving some riflemen of 1/95th forward of the line, in the sandpit just north of La Haie Sainte but on the opposite – the east – side of the axis road. The French renewed their attacks on the Allied centre with new enthusiasm.

Colonel Ompteda, commanding the brigade which included the 5th KGL, was ordered by his divisional commander, von Alten, to recapture La Haie Sainte. Colonel Ompteda demurred, because the French cavalry were very much in evidence. But the Prince of Orange insisted the divisional commander's orders be carried out: the men of 5th KGL duly advanced to their deaths. They lost 93 per cent of their strength. It is fair to ask why 5th KGL did not advance in square for protection against cavalry, as they were very experienced troops and the technique had certainly been used by British light infantry regiments in the Peninsula.

Ney, sensing the opportunity to break through the Allied centre that the capture of La Haie Sainte offered, sent an officer to Napoleon with a request for more infantry, only to receive a crusty refusal, since the Young Garde had only just been sent to Plancenoit, no doubt much against Napoleon's wishes but with his better judgement. Ney, himself, may have ridden back to beg his emperor for support, but none was given and the opportunity had passed. Nevertheless Ney continued to maintain pressure on the Allied centre, bringing fresh infantry across from the eastern flank. Either Ney or Napoleon sent horse artillery forward of La Haie Sainte on the east – the French right – of the axis road, within 150m of the 1/95th Rifles, who had retired from the sandpit, which had proved untenable. The artillery's effect is described by Captain Shaw, quartermaster general of 3rd Infantry Division which was holding the Allied line to the immediate west of the axis road:

The possession of La Haye Sainte by the French was a very dangerous incident. It uncovered the very centre of the Anglo-Allied army and established the enemy within 60 [more accurately 200] yards of that centre. The French lost no time in taking advantage of this, by pushing forward infantry supported by guns, which enabled them to maintain a most destructive fire upon Alten's [3 Infantry Division] left and Kempt's right, and to drive off Kempt's light troops that occupied the knoll in his front. By this fire they wasted [depleted] most

the ranks of the left of Alten's and the right of Kempt's divisions; so much so that Ompteda's brigade having been previously nearly destroyed, and Kielmansegge's much weakened, that were now not sufficiently strong to occupy the front which was originally assigned to them.[14]

The battery's fire, which so reduced the other units of Ompteda's brigade, and those of Kielmansegge's brigade too, that they all had to be withdrawn from the Allied line, would soon suppress the troops of Brunswick and Nassau that were moved forward to replace them.

It was clear that Napoleon must now make one final and decisive move: should it be attack or retreat? He chose attack and selected – as he always did when chestnuts needed pulling out of the fire – his Garde Impériale, or, at least, what was left of it. The Crisis had arrived: the Garde was to strike a hammer blow to Wellington's centre on the west of the axis road. But the attack was not to be a lone thrust by his elite. Napoleon ordered d'Erlon on the right and Reille on the left to support the Garde with one final assault. He demanded a general attack, to crush the Allied army before racing for Brussels whilst turning on the Prussians. With hindsight this may seem wishful thinking, but Napoleon clearly thought he had the upper hand, that the day was won. But he was wrong: General Armand de Caulaincourt, Napoleon's Minister of Foreign Affairs, recorded his emperor's words on 21 June 1815, three days after the battle:

Well Caulaincourt, here's a pretty to-do! A battle lost! How will the country bear this reverse? All the material is lost. It is a frightful disaster. The day was won. The army had performed prodigies; the enemy was beaten at every point; only the English centre still held. Just as all was over the army was seized with panic. It is inexplicable.[15]

The explanation follows.

4

Formez le Carré!

'Form square!' came the order from Général de Division Comte Antoine Drouot, acting general officer commanding the Garde Impériale at Waterloo. Octave Levasseur, who was aide-de-camp to Maréchal Ney, described, in his *Souvenirs Militaires*, the moment when the remaining Garde battalions were prepared for the final assault on the Allied line: 'Up came Drouot and called out: "Formez le Carré!"'[1]

Thus it would seem fairly certain that square was the formation in which each battalion was to be during its approach to the enemy line, although the assumption must have been that they would deploy into line just prior to the clash, as dictated by standard practice. Yet here we have the first of many controversies relating to the 'Crisis' that continue to be argued over to this day. Many sources, French as well as Allied, say the Garde was in column, and, because there are many more who claim column than square, column has become the received wisdom. The situation is complicated by the two very different meanings given to the word column, one specifying a battalion in rectangular formation and the other being shorthand for column of battalions, one behind the other, as detailed in the appendix.

The contentious question of whether the Garde was formed in square or in column is of much more than pure academic interest – it bears directly on the way the Garde's attack developed. It is important to resolve the controversy because the deployment of the battalions, i.e. the way they were positioned, each in relation to the next, is almost entirely dependent on knowing whether they were in square or in column. On their deployment hangs the question as to which Garde battalion struck which Allied unit, and only this will reveal to whom the accolade of having 'defeated the Garde' should be awarded.

Since Ney was to command the Garde's assault, it is fair to assume that his aide-de-camp would be a good witness with no obvious axe to grind. His memory of the moment might have been sharpened by the rarity of such an order when a formal assault was anticipated. But he was not alone in recording square as being the formation of choice. He is supported by

Maréchal Michel Ney,
1769–1815.
Son of a cooper, he rose
through the ranks of the
Revolutionary and Napoleonic
armies earning the sobriquet
of 'bravest of the brave' and the
titles of Prince de la Moskowa
and Duc d'Elchingen. After
Napoleon's abdication he swore
allegiance to King Louis XVIII
but reverted to Napoleon.
Seriously disadvantaged by
being invited to take command
of the French left wing after the
Waterloo campaign had already
begun, Ney made a series of
misjudgements which helped
lose Napoleon's final battle. He
was shot for treason..

the nineteenth-century French historian, Henri Houssaye, who wrote:
'He [Napoleon] ordered Drouot to bring forward, in the formation of squares
previously adopted, nine battalions of the Guard … '[2]

This seems conclusive enough but Houssaye was not an eyewitness.
Maréchal Jean-Martin Petit, however, was. He was in command of the first
and second battalions of 1er Grenadiers, which were the senior battalions
of the Garde. Both battalions had been retained by Napoleon as a reserve
of last resort south of La Belle Alliance. Petit was ideally placed to see or to
discover what happened both before and after the Garde's final attack. Yet, far
from being universally believed, Petit has even been accused of inventing the
'fiction' of an attack in square to provide an excuse for the defeat.

Regrettably his account is not without its ambiguities but they can generally be resolved by cross-referencing with other versions. Petit will provide
confirmation of many important facts as the story progresses. As a senior,
highly experienced officer of the Garde, who saw the attacking force form up,
advance and retire precipitately, it is difficult to justify questioning his word
on such a basic question of their initial deployment, especially if confirmation
comes from other sources.

He starts by describing the night's downpour, how the Garde became disorganised and men were still rejoining the ranks during the morning of 18 June.
He describes how, at 1400hrs the entire Young Garde was sent to Plancenoit, and
1/2e Grenadiers and 1/2e Châsseurs of the Old Garde were later sent in support.

By about 1900hrs the remaining twelve Garde battalions were positioned as follows: 1/1er Châsseur at La Caillou, a farm well to the rear of the French Army, guarding the emperor's treasure; the 1st and 2nd battalions of 1er Grenadiers at La Belle Alliance; and the rest of the attacking force in squares by battalions on the left (west) of the road (see Map 6, colour section). He then says:

> They were formed and placed thus: the 1st battalion of the 3rd Regiment [1/3e Grenadiers] with its right resting on the main road. The 2nd battalion was immediately detached at less than full artillery range to the left to watch and check a movement which the enemy was making at that point.

It is not clear what movement this was but the account suggests 2/3e Grenadiers was several hundred yards to the west of La Belle Alliance, possibly astride a track. The account continued:

> The Emperor placed himself with this battalion.

This is ambiguous but he must be referring to 1/3e Grenadiers, not 2/3e Grenadiers because all accounts, including Petit's, agree Napoleon led the leading battalion of the assault force. Petit continued:

> A little in the rear and echeloned to the left of the 1st battalion of the 3rd regiment of Grenadiers, were formed successively the 4th regiment of Grenadiers and three battalions of Chasseurs: they were, as has been said, in squares, but all drawn up close to one another.[3]

The three battalions of châsseurs were 1/3e, 2/3e and 4e. Unhelpfully, Petit does not mention the three battalions of the Old Garde, in reserve, but the remaining Garde battalions, by a process of elimination, were 2/2e Grenadiers, 2/2e Châsseurs and 2/1er Châsseurs. That aside, Petit, having already stated the Garde was in square, supports this by his statement 'A little in the rear and echeloned to the left …' Whilst it is *possible* that battalions in column could have been deployed 'in echelon to the left', it is *certain* that battalions in square would have been in echelon, especially if they were close to each other, since the essence of being in square was that volleys could be fired from any face of the square, with ease of fire control, especially in the Garde where each battalion's four companies provided one company per side under the command of its company commander. It follows that squares would be in echelon to avoid volleying straight at a neighbouring square, should they be either beside them in line, or in front or behind, as in column of battalions.

Some witnesses on the Allied side did recognise the Garde had attacked in square. One of these was Sir John Colborne, commanding officer of the 52nd Regiment. G.C. Moore Smith records in his *The Life of John Colborne* that Colborne wrote: 'The Great Column was formed in ... squares of battalions.'[4]

The evidence for the Garde being formed in square seems to be solid, yet, from that day to this, belief has persisted that the battalions were in column. Why? There are four factors that could lead to this misapprehension.

First we have force of habit. From their experience in Spain and Portugal, the British had concluded that the French always attacked in column and had even made something of a joke about it. Hence we have Wellington saying 'They came on in the same old way and we saw them off in the same old way' – or words to that effect. The French continued with this tactic, despite its being so ineffective against the British two-deep line, because the compactness of column gave a sense of confidence to conscripts. The drill manual specified that the column should halt and deploy into line just out of enemy musket range. Given their veteran status it is reasonable to assume the men of the Garde would have been perfectly capable of advancing to the attack in square. But the Garde had not been met in the Peninsula (except on the retreat to Corunna many years before) so the British would have been unaware of this skill. Therefore the French were expected to be in column.

Secondly we have visibility. There was by no means as much smoke obscuring the view as is sometimes supposed. For example, several officers – Sir John Colborne amongst them – tell of watching the Garde form up, at a range of nearly 1,000 yards. Many Allied guns had run out of ammunition and there was a lull in the fighting while the general attack was prepared, and so less smoke. However, as the Garde came closer, the view would have been much less clear and it is important to remember that the great majority of Allied officers and men were behind the ridge and unable to see the Garde until the last moment, and then only briefly. Under these circumstances it was far from easy to determine the distinction between column and square, especially since few on the Allied side would have expected anything but column.

Thirdly we have the appearance of the Garde battalions. Frankly, despite the endless possibilities offered by working out numbers of men in the front rank and hence the frontage and depth of the phalanxes of men approaching up the hill, both in close column and in square, there would have been little difference: both would have appeared to be solid blocks of men. The most obvious difference, to an observer, between square and column would have been that, in square in defence, officers – and in particular mounted field officers – would have been inside the formation, whilst in column they would have been outside. However, this rule would not apply when advancing in square: on this occasion, presumably because the threat of cavalry was more a possibility than a probability and in order to exert their powers of leadership, the officers were outside the square, thus supporting the erroneous impression of the Garde being in column. Napoleon – or Ney, who is said to have been a noted proponent of the square in attack – ordered the Garde to advance in square because he did not know just how depleted the Allied cavalry was and he wanted to avoid a repeat of the debacle that had occurred earlier in the battle when d'Erlon's massive corps attack had been shredded by the heavy cavalry of the Household and Union brigades.

Fourthly, there is a perceived difficulty of moving in square. The ability of the Garde to advance in square as opposed to column is doubted by some historians, on the grounds that it was not used by the British. This is to ignore the facts of history. The Battle of Fuentes d'Oñoro, in 1811, provides a good example of movement in square under attack. The French were trying to relieve their garrison of Almeida and their cavalry had driven in the British right flank, apparently capturing Major Ramsay's battery of Horse Artillery. But he and his men, at full gallop, suddenly burst out of the encircling French, whereupon the 14th Dragoons rode to his support. However they were scared off by the arrival of the French main body of 7,000 cavalry with artillery and took shelter behind the Light Division, which was in reserve. The Light Division immediately formed square in echelon and remained in that formation while it moved for over 3 miles while Wellington repositioned his line, proving that at least the 43rd, 52nd and 95th Regiments were perfectly capable of this manoeuvre, even if it was perhaps not standard practice in other regiments.

Moving in square actually had one advantage over column that has gone unnoticed – command and control in the event of attack by cavalry would have been much simpler in square than in column. In column the front and rear of a four-company strong Garde battalion would have comprised one company under command of its own company commander but each side would have comprised the flank men of four companies, including those of the front and rear companies. Any hurried attempt to face cavalry attacking a flank by turning the sides outwards – say three files of each company – might have ended in chaos since the order to turn outwards would have had to come either from the battalion commanding officer or from each company commander. Once turned outwards there would be confusion over fire control since there would be no one officer designated as in command of each side. In square, however, the single command 'Outwards turn' would have produced an instant defence against cavalry since whole companies would have acted in unison, either on the battalion commander's order or those of their own company commanders.

In Summary

The loose use of the term 'column' has led to much misunderstanding. In Napoleonic warfare the term column was used specifically either to describe a battalion in the formation called column, where companies were positioned one behind the other like layers in a cake, or incorrectly to describe a number of battalions, one behind the other, when the correct term would be column of battalions. Many accounts, both Allied and French, speak of the Garde advancing in column, on the grounds that the French in the Peninsula always advanced in column; that they looked like columns; that movement in square was too difficult to be contemplated by the British Army, and, by inference, by the French. Against these opinions we have two senior Garde commanders specifying square, and, in addition, Ney having a known liking for attacking in that formation; an experienced British officer stating the Garde was in square; officers being outside the square when moving, giving a false illusion of column; movement in square by the British being well attested in the Peninsula; square would have been a sensible choice in the light of the repulse of d'Erlon's corps earlier; square provided a more efficient fire control to the flank than did column; deployment from square into line for the final assault would have been as easy for experienced troops as it would have been from column.

With so many factors in favour of square it is difficult to avoid the conclusion that most British officers were mistaken in thinking the Garde battalions began their advance in column. Assuming, as a hypothesis, that the Garde battalions started in square, it follows that the likelihood of the battalions' relationship to each other was echelon, as described by several sources and in the appendix. In the next chapter we find the echelon formation is confirmed by the major influence it had on how the action developed.

EN AVANT LA GARDE!

The Garde was not to advance alone. Napoleon's plan was to renew the fighting along the entire Allied line while the Garde delivered the coup de grâce in the Allied right centre. To this end, d'Erlon's corps engaged Kempt's brigade in a musketry duel to the east of the Brussels road. Brevet Major Leach of 1/95th describes, in a letter to Siborne, how the capture of the farmhouse of La Haie Sainte had allowed the French to fill it with 'sharpshooters' and also to establish a strong and numerous line of infantry extending along the front of Kempt's brigade. He adds:

> This [the loss of La Haie Sainte] was highly disastrous to the troops of Picton and Lambert [to the east of the axis road], for the French instantly filled the house with swarms of sharpshooters [the French did not have rifles], whose deadly fire precluded the possibility of our holding the knoll and the ground immediately about it, and they established also a strong and numerous line of Infantry, extending along the front of Kempt's Brigade.[1]

He continues to emphasise that, from the time La Haie Sainte fell until the general advance, the fight in his part of the position was of uninterrupted musketry only, at about 100 yards distance, despite vain efforts by the French officers to induce their men to advance. Meanwhile the French right wing progressively became engaged with Bülow's Prussian corps and changed front to face east, attempting to delay its advance. On the French left wing Reille's corps did not manage to go into action at au Goumont before the Garde was finally repulsed. Hence the ground where the only chance of success lay was to the west of the crossroads, between au Goumont and La Haie Sainte.

Five battalions of the Middle Garde, supported by three battalions of the Old Garde, dutifully deployed to the west of the axis road in square in echelon. The Middle Garde comprised the first line with 1/3e Grenadiers leading on the right, then 4e Grenadiers, then the three châsseur battalions, 1er,

2/3e and 4e. Behind 4e Châsseurs, with a visible gap, were positioned 2/2e Grenadiers, 2/2e Châsseurs and 2/1er Châsseurs. These last three were of the Old Garde. Their deployment and location have been matters of some uncertainty but it is reasonable to assume they too were in square and in echelon in rear (possibly directly behind, i.e. 'refused'. See the appendix) of 4e Châsseurs. The remaining Middle Garde battalion – 2/3e Grenadiers – was placed (as Petit has already told us) as long stop, about a cannon shot's distance from Napoleon's headquarters at La Belle Alliance towards au Goumont, probably athwart the track that ran across the battlefield.

As they stepped off, the men saw, with approval, that their emperor was leading them into battle, but their enthusiasm was probably dulled somewhat when they neared La Haie Sainte and Napoleon stepped aside, handing command to Maréchal Ney (see Map 7, colour section). But that was the least of Ney's worries. Immediately, the apparently simple plan of advancing parallel with the axis road to attack the wavering German troops to the west of the crossroads – like so many military plans both before and since – went awry. Ney found the ground, over which the following squares of the Middle Garde were expected to advance, was blocked by a battery ('compagnie') of horse artillery, firing from the west side of La Haie Sainte. Even more of an obstacle than the cannon was their invisible arc of fire. What had gone wrong? Why were the gunners here? From Lieutenant Pontécoulant, one of the officers of the Garde Horse Artillery, we learn that he understood that Napoleon himself

> … detached two batteries of the Guard [Garde] horse artillery, which he ordered to advance as far forward as they could go. It was 5.30pm. They deployed to the left [west] of the farm of la Haye-Sainte, which the enemy no longer disputed with us, on the slopes of the Mont-Saint-Jean plateau that had been occupied for some time by our own cavalry, and soon swept the whole English line with balls and case shot. The author of these lines found himself amongst the officers who commanded one of these batteries, and can assure you that, in the most celebrated battles of the Empire, there was not another example of fire so lively and accurate. The Guard artillery was composed of élite men in an élite corps. All our gunners appeared to be galvanised by the danger of the crisis that we could see coming but could not prevent; each of our shots struck home, and we were so close to the enemy, that we could distinctly hear the cries of the English [The troops under bombardment were German: Brunswickers and Nassauers.] officers, closing up the thinning ranks of their weakened battalions with strong curses and the flats of their swords, to fill the gaps that we were making. Unfortunately, not having any infan-

try or cavalry, we were not able to advance or bring about a decisive result, and our role for the next two hours was confined to a murderous exchange of balls and shells with the enemy, whose fire was also very lively, but which seemed to be to maintain a purely passive attitude, as one could see they made no move to take the offensive which, however, would have been favourable to them as at this moment our available infantry and cavalry were all exhausted.[2]

A Garde Horse Artillery battery was armed with six 6-pounders – four guns and two howitzers – and could bring devastating fire, especially by canister, on the Allied centre at a range of 150m. Major Leach also tells us that the guns (on the east of the axis road) were supported by infantry and that the combined effect drove light troops off a knoll, but by no means out of action. The light troops referred to were the six companies of the 1st/95th. Major Leach of the Rifles emphasises that the riflemen were far from subdued:

> …knelt down, and exposed only their heads and shoulders to our fire, and in this manner the contest was carried on between them and us until the General Advance of the whole of the Duke of Wellington's Army against the French position immediately after the total defeat of the Imperial Guards.[3]

The French infantry made difficult targets, even for rifles, but the French artillerymen had to stand to reload, making perfect targets for the riflemen of 1/95th who duly made their position untenable, as Lieutenant Pontécoulant confirms:

> … [the enemy skirmishers] … spread out in all the folds in the ground from behind which cover, and equipped with muskets of long range [we can presume he was referring to rifles], killed our gunners at their pieces almost with impunity, because of the ineffectiveness, at this period, of the arms of our own infantry gave them a marked inferiority in this kind of skirmishing.[4]

There were no Allied riflemen on the immediate west of the crossroads above La Haie Sainte so it seems safe to deduce that Pontécoulant was incorrect in saying both batteries of horse artillery went to the west of La Haie Sainte. One must have gone to the east and it was this one that was driven off by the 1/95th Rifles, leaving the battery to the west to cause Ney to change the direction of the Garde's attack. It may well be that some or all of the 'eastern' guns moved round to join the 'western' battery, seeking protection from the fire of the 1/95th by sheltering behind the buildings, walls and hedges of the farmstead.

Henri Houssaye, the nineteenth-century French historian, confirms the artillery's presence, albeit indirectly, but, more importantly, as a historian he is possibly unique in identifying Ney's change of direction:

> It appears that Ney gave an ill-advised order and a wrong direction to the Guard. Instead of forming one single column strong enough to pierce through the enemy's line, the Marshal left the battalions divided. Instead of marching straight up to the plateau from the lowlands of La Haye Sainte by the Brussels road, over which the column had barely 400 yards to traverse and where the embankments sheltered it from the slanting fire of the artillery, he took an oblique course by the unprotected slopes which the cuirassiers had climbed in their first charge. The five battalions of the Middle Guard, formed into as many squares, advanced in echelons, the right [square] leading.[5]

In other words, for a reason that neither Houssaye nor (apparently) any other historian has correctly deduced, Ney altered direction by about 30° from north, following the road, to near north-west and led 1/3e Grenadiers diagonally up the slope. We learn from Colonel Crabbé, senior ADC to Maréchal Ney, that Napoleon's declared intention was the obvious one, to break through the Allied centre north of La Haie Sainte. Crabbé was despatched to put Ney straight:

> Marshal Soult, Duc de Dalmatie, the Chief of Staff summoned me. He told me that the emperor had confided his ultimate reserve to Maréchal Ney; all that remained of the Guard, to make a decisive attack on the English lines. He demanded an experienced officer of the headquarters to carry supplementary orders.
>
> I reached the rise near the farm of La Belle Alliance where the emperor was located … Slumped in his chair, he appeared to me both exhausted and angry. One of the ADCs informed him of my arrival. Without even turning to me, he said out of the blue. 'Ney has acted stupidly again. He has cost us the day! He has destroyed my cavalry and is ready to destroy my Guard. He manoeuvres like a good-for-nothing. He attacks the plateau obliquely instead of assaulting at the centre. Go at best speed and order him to modify his march and to pierce the centre of the English position in a compact mass …'[6]

If Crabbé's words are correct – and there seems no reason to suspect they are not – Napoleon's wish that Ney attack 'in a compact mass' suggests the latter's choice of formation was not Napoleon's, who would have attacked in column of battalions. This point is worth bearing in mind when the manoeu-vres of the châsseur battalions are discussed. That Napoleon acquiesced in Ney's choice of formation is entirely concordant with his delegation of tactics to subordinates throughout the battle.

The result of Crabbé's mission will be revealed in due course; first, the reason for Ney's deviation must be clarified. There are two possible causes for this sudden change of direction. One alternative – suggested by several historians – is that there were already other, non-Garde troops in action on the western side of the Brussels road, obstructing the Garde's line of advance. Many modern accounts claim that troops of General Donzelot's division of d'Erlon's corps were attacking the Allied line immediately west of the cross-roads, but there are many reasons to doubt this. It is unlikely such an attack would have gone in without Napoleon's or Ney's knowledge and it is unlikely to have been sanctioned since the axis road was an ideal inter-unit boundary. More importantly, Napoleon's aim was to break through the Allied centre to gain the road to Brussels so it would have been senseless to deploy less than the best available troops for the purpose. An attack by Donzelot's men would have been visible from La Belle Alliance so it could have been halted before the Garde advanced, had Napoleon so wished. And, if these reasons are insufficient to prove the point, to judge by Napoleon's leading the 1/3e Grenadiers along the road as far as La Haie Sainte, the plan was for the Garde to follow the road – the presence of other troops would have obstructed this.

Those accounts, that do not claim Donzelot's involvement, have the Brunswick and Nassau brigades, who were holding this section of the Allied line, 'brushed aside' by 1/3e Grenadiers of the Garde, but this is highly ques-tionable, both on the grounds that it ignores Ney's dramatic deviation and also because a reliable witness, Ensign Edward Macready of the 30th/73rd, expressly tells us there were no battalions of the Garde to the left of Colin Halkett's brigade:

A heavy Column of Brunswickers came up on our left (30th and 73rd Regiments) in the evening of June 18th. A remark on them in my Journal states that 'they fell back at first bodily, but were rallied and afterwards stood their ground.' ... But I do not think they were engaged with the Guard. I saw no troops of the Guard to the French right of that Column which advanced on us (30th and 73rd) ...[7]

Admittedly Macready does not expressly rule out troops, other than those of the Garde, being involved, but, had they been, surely he would have mentioned them? As discussed earlier, it really seems most unlikely that infantry other than the Garde were in action on the west of the axis road, and that the leading

Garde battalion was the one that struck the 30th/73rd. So the next questions to resolve are: what is the origin of the myth of the Nassauers and Brunswickers being 'brushed aside' by – variously – the Garde or troops of Donzelot's division, and what actually drove back the Allied troops in this sector? Fortunately the reports from the commanders of these Nassau and Brunswick troops are available to us.

First we hear from General von Kruse's brigade of Nassauers. The Nassauers were some 2,500 strong, in green uniforms with white covered shakos. Smart and highly visible they may have been, but the men were little more than inexperienced recruits although they had many veteran officers. The German town of Nassau provided some 10 per cent of Wellington's infantry at Waterloo. One strong brigade's worth were in Dutch pay and served as the 2nd brigade of the 2nd Netherlands Infantry Division. A weaker brigade known as the Nassau Contingent, comprised of two battalions of the 1st Nassau Regiment and a Landwher Battalion, served as part of Wellington's reserve under the command of von Kruse. It was the latter brigade with which we are concerned here. That they were manning such a crucially important position in the line is surprising. Wellington must have been very short of dependable, experienced men.

Von Kruse's account is dated 21 June 1815, i.e. before hindsight had set in. The account is somewhat confused and requires careful interpretation:

> The enemy artillery inflicted heavy losses on the various infantry battalions, in particular the I. Battalion of the I. Nassau Regiment, and our artillery having for the most part exhausted its ammunition or been destroyed, the enemy cavalry appeared in immense masses and attacked our infantry …
> At this moment the I. Battalion wavered under the terrible fire the French artillery poured into them with their canister. The Cuirassiers, who were quite near, charged … However, this encounter had weakened the French cavalry very much and it withdrew … [8]

He has conflated the massed cavalry attacks with the subsequent artillery assault. He is certainly describing an artillery assault, which is not the morning's opening barrage by the Grande Batterie since his brigade had been well in rear of the position then, and he has already described in his report the initial heavy barrage. Since one of the criticisms made of Ney is that he failed to co-ordinate artillery and infantry with the cavalry attacks, the gunfire could not have been from horse artillery during the cavalry charges. The conclusion is that he is describing the effect of the artillery brought forward to La Haie Sainte when the farmstead was eventually captured after the cavalry charges had ceased. His next statement is equally confusing:

... and it was replaced by the elite of the infantry, Napoleon's Garde Impériale, which advanced to capture the plateau, from which our infantry withdrew only 100 paces.

Once again this does not ring true. Kruse is trying to give the impression that the Nassauers actually engaged 1/3e Grenadiers in a fire fight and then a bayonet charge. But, had this actually occurred and the Nassauers been repulsed, would the Nassauers have retired as little as 'only 100 paces'? Had they been so engaged and won, then surely a spirited description of the action could be expected – none is forthcoming. To judge by other accounts, it would have been an achievement even to stand firm in the face of such an assault, such steadfastness was not to be expected of raw recruits. To attempt a bayonet charge with them against some of Napoleon's elite would have been sheer madness, although Orange's previous record of rashness might tempt one to believe it possible. Major General de Constant-Rebècque, chief of staff to Orange's I Corps, wrote of them in the battle, showing how fragile their morale was:

> However, I was regularly obliged to go some distance to the left from the Prince to rally the three squares of the Nassau contingent (Kruse's brigade), which were composed of young soldiers who were under fire for the first time, and often retired. I brought them back several times. At one point one of these battalions was put into complete disorder when a shell exploded amidst their ranks. I rode ahead of them and fortunately managed to bring them back.[9]

Von Kruse continued his previous statement:

> A violent fire fight broke out, and, showing as much courage as foresight, the Crown Prince, who had been in command on the plateau throughout the entire battle, attempted to resolve with a bayonet charge. For this honour, he called upon the Nassau troops. Thus, I [von Kruse] ordered the II. Battalion to move forward and I advanced with them in column; the remainder of the I. Battalion joined with them. The attack took place with the utmost courage. I saw one side of a square of the French Garde turn back when, perhaps due to the fall of the Crown Prince who was wounded, a wave of panic descended upon the young soldiers and at the moment of their greatest victory, the battalion fell into confusion and fell back. The remaining battalions in the first line soon followed, so that the plateau was only held by small bodies of brave men, to which I added the Landwher Battalion and the remainder of the II. Battalion, but in such a way that the enemy fire could have little effect on them.

That is a clear decription of troops sheltering behind a ridge from artillery fire, for which there is corroborative evidence, from a very junior Nassau officer. Fähnrich (Ensign) Heinrich von Gagern, of the 2/1st Nassau Regiment, tells of his experience:

> ... until shortly after seven o'clock. Now our battalion was ordered to attack a battalion of French Guards with fixed bayonets. At that time the crisis had already started, because the Prussians, who had long been expected, had still not arrived. Some of the Allied battalions were quite dispersed, and the French attacked with renewed courage. Our battalion, however, with the Landwehr Battalion on our left, and slightly behind, advanced while covered by the cavalry [Vivian's 6th Cavalry Brigade, breathing down their necks to dissuade them from decamping]. One of the main mistakes was that our artillery had completely run out of ammunition, and no cannon was able to support us. We charged twice and were repulsed twice. The brave Hereditary Prince of Orange rode alongside our square the first time ... Shortly after, I saw our gallant Prince riding back past our square with his wound.
>
> After we had [been] repulsed [in] the first attack I sat down on a drum and happily went to sleep despite the musket fire which was raging. However, I was woken by the start of the second attack.[10]

Leaving aside comments on the ability of young men to fall asleep anywhere at any time, Gagern's remark about doing so between advances indicates his battalion was temporarily hidden from the enemy fire that plagued it when forward on the summit of the ridge (see Map 6, Colour section). This adds weight to the supposition that it was cannon fire from below the ridge that was the cause of their discomfiture, not musketry from close range: infantry would not have been firing at an invisible target. His mistaken reference to musketry can reasonably be attributed to his hearing light canister balls passing overhead while the sound of the cannon shot would have been muffled by the intervening ground. He further confirms the Nassauers had no artillery support; that they made two advances; the prince was wounded in the first, and that he supposed a battalion of the Garde was their target. The lack of any description of an engagement with the Garde suggests that no such combat took place.

There is no doubt that the Nassauers were led forward by Orange for it was during this event that the prince received a minor shoulder wound, which is commemorated by the Lion Mound. But was the advance against the Garde or against some other target? That von Kruse 'saw one side of a square of the French Garde turn back' may well be true but that is not a convincing description of his brigade actually attacking a Garde unit. It sounds more as if he witnessed at a distance the first retreat of 1/3e Grenadiers, of which we shall hear in due course. He tells us his brigade broke in the face of an unattainable target and could only be rallied when screened from its fire by the form of the ground, some distance in rear of the front line. In other words, the dreadful pummelling from which his men were suffering each time they advanced was from canister, fired by the company of French cannon at La Haie Sainte. Lacking effective artillery with which to silence it, the Nassauers bravely, but uselessly, tried twice to assault the French battery. While the first of these attacks was in progress – apparently the one led by the Prince of Orange – the 1/3e Grenadiers had come up across their front and been repulsed by another unit to the Nassauers' right. The Brunswickers were on the Nassauers immediate right, but it was not they who had turned the Garde: the Brunswickers were also suffering from the fire of the French artillery at La Haie Sainte. Three battalions were repeatedly ordered forward to maintain the line, but were as often driven back behind the ridge.

The Brunswick contingent was about 5,500 strong and now commanded by Colonel Olfermann, since the Duke of Brunswick's death at Quatre-Bras. The entire contingent was also part of Wellington's Reserve Corps. In a report dated 9 o'clock in the morning of 19 June 1815, Oberst (Colonel) Johann Elias Olfermann wrote at length to the Secret Council of Braunschweig (Brunswick):

At this time [during the cavalry attacks] the Duke of Wellington sheltered in the squares of our corps … Soon afterwards the Duke of Wellington ordered me to advance with three battalions in square and to cross the height. This movement was executed with the utmost calm, although everybody supposed that a violent infantry and canister fire would await us on the other side of the height. This supposition was only too true. Hardly had we crossed the said height when whole ranks within the battalions were shot down in a very short period of time. The enemy soon realised the effectiveness of his fire and now he supported the cavalry [the cavalry attacks had already ceased] with the horse artillery. It was impossible for us to remain in the position any longer and so I ordered a retreat to the former position. Shortly thereafter we were attacked again with the utmost violence, but the enemy were unsuccessful as the 2nd and 3rd Light Battalions and the 3rd Line Battalion in particular stood like rocks. The Duke of Wellington remained close to us and he again sent orders to advance. This was attempted, but the enemy advanced with increased strength, especially the artillery, and the losses our infantry battalions incurred were severe. The three aforementioned battalions repeatedly occupied the other side of the slope, but each time we had to retire to the old position, where we remained despite the continuous enemy attacks and the fact that the Allied artillery was almost destroyed. During one of these attacks my right hand, including the fingers, was shot to pieces, so I was forced to retire ... Towards 7 o'clock the most complete victory was obtained.[11]

Unlike von Kruse and Gagern, Olfermann did not explicitly claim involvement with the Garde but by his phrase, '... the enemy advanced with increased strength, especially the artillery' he hints at more than artillery fire being involved. This suggestion that more troops, other than artillery, were opposed to them suggests that to be suppressed by gunfire alone was somehow dishonourable. In fact his account of repeated advances to the forward slope followed by retirement out of the direct line of artillery fire clearly shows the Brunswickers experienced the same devastating fire as the Nassauers on their left. In none of the descriptions is there evidence of a clash with infantry – let alone with the Garde – to convince us that they had more than an artillery barrage with which to contend. If further proof of its existence and efficacy is needed, it comes from Major Heinrich Müller of the Bremen Light Infantry Battalion, which was part of Count Kielmansegge's 1st Hanoverian Brigade. This brigade is often incorrectly said to have been in this part of the Allied line, on the Nassauers' left, at this moment in the battle. In fact it had been there earlier but, severely reduced by the gunfire, had now retired to Mont-Saint-Jean.

Müller relates how his brigade also suffered terribly from the artillery fire from La Haie Sainte. Even before the battle reached its crescendo, with the Garde's attack, the 1st Hanoverian Brigade had lost more than half its men to artillery fire and had, in fact, been withdrawn to Mont-Saint-Jean to reform. The butcher's bill was so large the Bremen Battalion had to be amalgamated with another but still could only muster a four company unit. The brigade did not return to the line until after the Crisis was over. It did not join the general advance and bivouacked on the battlefield.[12]

The answer to this bombardment would have been counter-battery fire. This had been expressly forbidden by Wellington before the battle started, as a waste of ammunition, but it is unlikely he would have objected to suppression of the French battery – or batteries – at La Haie Sainte, had the Allied cannon been able to respond. They were not. And to confirm the lack of Allied artillery support in this part of the line we have a quotation from Sir John Colborne, whose Peninsular-experienced eyes and ears recorded the situation, as he viewed the battlefield from horseback on the top of the ridge some 700 yards to the west, at this precise time:

The guns under Colonel Gould [Gold] on the cross-road [i.e. along the ridge] were all silent, there was scarcely any firing except in rear [i.e. the allied side] of La Haye Sainte and on that part of our centre.[13]

It is clear from these accounts that the problem the German infantry could not overcome, lacking Allied artillery support, was the canister fire from the six or more cannon of the French artillery at La Haie Sainte, possibly augmented in the later stages of this phase by the two cannon of Garde horse artillery that came forward in support of the Garde on the right flank of 1/3e Grenadiers. Like von Kruse, Olfermann, it seems, was unwilling to acknowledge openly that his brigade had been defeated solely by artillery. In neither case need any shame have been felt: infantry *en masse* were – and are – very vulnerable to sustained multi-bulleted fire, be it from canister-firing cannon or quick-firing machine gun. However, the point is made: neither the Nassau nor the Brunswick Contingents were directly engaged with a battalion of the Garde, but were effectively neutralised and forced out of the line by cannon fire, both from La Haie Sainte and the Garde horse artillery section.

So here is the reason for Ney's change of direction: not only were there at least six cannon as an obstacle but more dangerous and less visible, was the battery's arc of fire (see Map 7, Colour section). Thanks to Pontécoulant's testimony, we know Napoleon was clearly aware of the guns' presence yet, it seems Ney was not:

He [Napoleon] moved them [the Garde battalions] to the bottom of the valley, in front of La Haye-Sainte, next to two batteries of horse artillery of the Guard, that, placed on the slopes of the plateau, had not ceased their fire, and which again showered the English squares with balls, so that he could preside over the grand attack that he planned on the centre of the enemy army… This was the last time I saw Napoleon. He came and placed himself a few paces to the rear of [these] two batteries, of which I was a part … Napoleon's face was sombre and very pale …[14]

We should note that Pontécoulant's report of continuous and highly effective artillery fire from La Haie Sainte completely negates any suggestion that attack by French line infantry suppressed the Nassau and Brunswick contingents. Moreover, Ney seems to have been caught by surprise by the obstacle in his way, or did he decide he had a better plan than Napoleon's? To halt the Garde's movement would have risked losing the essential momentum of the advance and could have resulted in chaos at a critical moment. He could have sent an order to the artillery to cease fire but he probably could see how effective the barrage was being and, remembering how the cavalry charges had failed for lack of support from the other arms, he may have concluded the gunfire was worth maintaining and that striking the first blow by the Garde slightly further west would not necessarily be a disadvantage. This was a highly pressured moment at the end of a far from restful day – he may just have shrugged his shoulders, spoken a single word and changed direction to his left – with unforeseen consequences.

The first consequence was that Ney missed an opportunity to win the battle, or at least to defeat the Allied army. He could have ordered the battery to cease fire or, better still, to move forward in direct support of the Garde. Had he been able to co-ordinate the artillery fire with the arrival of the Garde in a succession of blows against the Nassauers and Brunswickers there seems a distinct likelihood he would have broken through the line. The unfortunate young Germans were in no fit state to repel a determined assault by French veterans. As Captain Mercer, commanding his horse artillery battery to the Brunswicker's right during the cavalry attacks, had earlier observed of the Brunswickers in square in the front line:

> … they were in such a state I momentarily expected to see them disband.
> … standing like so many logs, [they] were apparently completely stupefied
> and bewildered. I should add they were all perfect children. None of the
> privates, perhaps, were above 18 years of age.[15]

Had Ney broken through it might be argued that the Garde would have had to face two brigades of light cavalry, those of Vivian and Vandeleur. But this would not have been a serious problem since his battalions were already in square. The extra horse artillery fire that could have been deployed in support would have been invaluable. It is pointless to surmise further but there is no doubt Ney, by deviating, missed an outstanding opportunity.

The second consequence of Ney's decision to deviate from his planned line of advance was that his carefully deployed formation of squares in echelon was thrown into confusion, with a knock-on effect throughout his entire force. Evidence for this will be detailed in a later chapter.

We have established that the Germans under Kielmansegge had retired to Mont-Saint-Jean and the troops of Nassau and Brunswick were forced back from the Allied line by the artillery fire from La Haie Sainte and, latterly from the two gun section of Garde horse artillery, but no Garde infantry battalion had yet come into action. The leading Garde battalion was now heading at a point in the Allied line a full 500m west of the point to which they should have struck, had Ney maintained Napoleon's intention of following the axis road. Now 1/3e Grenadiers were approaching Sir Colin Halkett's 5th British Infantry Brigade.

SLAP CAME THEIR GRAPE

The four battalions of Sir Colin Halkett's 5th British Infantry Brigade had suffered severe casualties at the battle for Les Quatre-Bras crossroads two days before. The 69th had lost its regimental colour. Numbers and morale were both very low, so low in fact that the four-battalion brigade had been amalgamated into two battalions, the 33rd with the 69th (neither of which had fought in the Peninsula) and the 30th with the 73rd. Their run of bad luck was now to continue. Both 'battalions' were about to be involved in action against the first two Garde battalions to strike the Allied line, together with their supporting horse artillery sections, which were to prove more dangerous than the infantry.

Appropriately our first witness is Sir Colin Halkett himself. He starts by describing the cavalry phase and then the subsequent loss of La Haie Sainte to the French:

> I beg to inform you that … the 30th and 73rd Regiments, were formed in [one] square, and that they were by the French Cavalry charged several times without effect. They also made a movement to the farmhouse [La Haye Sainte] when taken by the Enemy, but without effect and with considerable loss.
>
> These are the *two only* subjects worth mentioning, excepting having sent out the Light Company of [I think] the 69th Regiment to skirmish with the Enemy, and having the Enemy on their flanks in La Haye Sainte, they were nearly annihilated. This was done on the positive order of the Prince of Orange, and seeing their unprotected state I recalled them.[1]

The Prince of Orange had already tried – and failed – to retake La Haie Sainte with a Nassauer battalion, so the purpose of sacrificing the 69th's Light Company was not necessarily to retake La Haie Sainte. Another account suggests its aim was an attempt to exclude the enemy from the high ground of the tongue, that projected forward of the Allied position. The wisdom of achieving this would shortly be made clear. But if, when the Light Company of the 69th was ordered forward, the French horse artillery company had already reached the north-west corner of the farmstead (as described in the previous chapter), the 69th's light company would have been subjected to close range canister fire. Although canister was not usually employed against skirmishers because they were small targets, the suppression of the Nassauer and Brunswick brigades by this same artillery company suggests there was no shortage of canister rounds.

When the leading Garde battalion approached Halkett, his brigade was formed with both composite battalions in the front line, the 33rd/69th on the right and the 30th/73rd on the left, with no reserve. Ensign Edward Macready of the 30th Regiment is one of our most trustworthy and honest witnesses. Although only 17 years old at the time, he finished the battle in command of the 30th's Light Company. His men had also been out on the forward slope but were forced back by the canister fire. Their trial by fire was far from over. He vividly tells what happened next:

> French artillery trotted up our hill, which I knew by the caps to belong to the Imperial Guard, and I had scarcely mentioned this to a brother officer, when two guns unlimbering at a cruelly short distance, down went the portfires and slap came their grape into the square. They immediately reloaded, and kept up a most destructive fire. It was noble to see our fellows fill up the gaps after each discharge. I had ordered up three of my light bobs, and they had hardly taken their places when two falling sadly wounded, one of them (named Anderson) looked up in my face, uttering a sort of reproachful groan, when I involuntarily said, 'By God! I couldn't help it.'[2]

These two guns were the section in support of 1/3rd Grenadiers. Henri Houssaye was convinced of both the formation and the presence of the guns:

> The five battalions of the Middle Guard, formed into as many squares, advanced in echelons, the right leading. Between each echelon the mounted gunners of the Guard drew two cannons of 8, the total forming a complete battery – company – under the orders of Colonel Duchand.[3]

Mark Adkin, in his *Waterloo Companion*, tells us that Duchand commanded the Old Garde Horse Artillery and says there were only six cannon per Garde horse artillery company.[4] David Chandler, when a lecturer in War Studies at RMA Sandhurst, suggested there were two companies, not one.[5] If Houssaye and Chandler are correct there would have been two guns with each of the eight Garde battalions, which seems most likely. Napoleon's evidence has already largely confirmed this.

Captain Robert Howard, also of the 30th, tells us that action was taken to lessen, as far as possible, the devastating effect of this close range gunfire:

> It [the 30th, forming one square with the 73rd] was lying down to avoid as much as possible the artillery of the enemy which at that time was very destructive, under cover of which in our flank, or perhaps a little to our left in the direction of La Haye Sainte a very heavy column of French infantry advanced steadily with supported arms to almost if not quite within the range of musketry when it halted, having witnessed as we afterwards supposed, the result of their attacks upon our right.[6] This was the only body of the enemy I remember seeing at the time.[7]

Howard makes several more informative remarks (see Map 8, Colour section). Ignoring his reference to a column, which was probably a square, he tells us that 1/3e Grenadiers approached from the direction of La Haie Sainte, as is to be expected in the light of Ney's deviation, and halted not directly in front of the 30th/73rd but off to their left flank. To halt just beyond effective musket range would have been standard practice, in order to deploy into line before attacking, but one of the advantages of Wellington's technique of having troops behind a ridge, possibly supine, was that the enemy did not know how close they were to their opponents and, as a result, halted to deploy much too close and found themselves under close-range fire. It is worth noting, too, that 1/3e Grenadiers would not have known whom they would meet but found themselves confronted by a gap on their right front, with the Brunswickers cowering 100 yards back, and – to the 1/3e Grenadiers' left – a formed body of British infantry. It may be Ney paused to decide what to do, bearing in mind the artillery section on the right of this leading battalion could continue subduing the Germans but would be unable to fire on the British battalion when the French Grenadiers moved forward and screened them, and also that he could not immediately stop the gunfire from La Haie Sainte.

Howard's comment '... having witnessed as we supposed, the result of their attacks upon our right' refers to the opinion held by several officers, including Macready, that the rapid retirement of the 1/3e Grenadiers, that was about to occur, was caused by their being outflanked by the British counter-attack that subsequently came across their front from the right. Timings make this unlikely even though events would happen very rapidly now, but his recalling this counter-attack strongly suggests that such a movement took place during this fast-moving phase, as will be recounted in a later chapter. Most important is Howard's statement that this was the only body of the enemy he saw at this time. In other words he saw no sign of a following battalion: 1/3e Grenadiers were on their own. Macready gave a more colourful account of their arrival:

Our Colours were ordered to the rear [the 69th had lost one at Quatre-Bras
and the 33rd nearly so] ... Our square was ordered to open out its rear face,
and wheel up right and left into line four deep ... when a column [actually
a square] of the Imperial Guard ... came over the ridge in splendid order.
As they rose step by step before us, with their red epaulettes and cross belts
put on over their blue greatcoats, and topped by their high, hairy caps, and
keeping time, and their officers looking to their alignment ... I certainly
thought we were in for very slashing work.[8]

In his letter to William Siborne, the model-maker and historian of the battle,
Macready first describes the Brunswickers' fate and then the Garde's arrival
and its almost inexplicable, immediate departure:

A heavy Column of Brunswickers came up on our left (30th and 73rd
Regiments) in the evening of June 18th. A remark on them in my Journal
states that 'they fell back at first bodily, but were rallied and afterwards stood
their ground.' ... But I do not think they were engaged with the Guard.
I saw no troops of the Guard to the French right of that Column which
advanced on us (30th and 73rd), and which, though it came over the hill in
beautiful order, was an inconceivable [*sic*] short time before us, turning and
flying to a man at the single volley we fired, and the hurrah that followed
it. Having expected great things from them, we were astonished at their
conduct, and we young soldiers almost fancied there was some 'ruse' in it.
The men I spoke to as they lay wounded were all of the 'Moyenne Garde.'[9]

That Macready had the opportunity to talk to the French wounded was due
to 30th/73rd not moving forward when the general advance was ordered –
the men of his battalion were too exhausted and depleted in numbers. It's
a pity he did not enquire of them as to why these supposed veterans of the
Middle Garde decamped, apparently without firing a shot. But we can surmise. It may seem banal but feasible to suggest that one of a number of factors
might have been the men's physical state. They had been seated for hours,
waiting for a possible call to action, in the strong sunshine of a continental
summer, after a night of heavy rain guaranteeing high humidity, followed by a
stiffish climb up a slope, in their greatcoats! Heat exhaustion might have been
the result. Indeed, Richard Holmes noted that, the day before, a rifleman of
1/95th had gone mad and died from the excessive heat.[10]

Allied gunfire against the Garde is usually described as being heavy and
effective but, in fact, this seems not to have been the case. We should not forget
that the gunners had been in action, humping ammunition, heaving guns
forward after each discharge, often under fire or cavalry attack, for six hours.

Macready had something to say on the subject, and we should not forget that the Nassauer and Brunswick commanders both spoke of a lack of artillery support. Macready was bitter about it, clearly believing this was a moment of extreme danger to the Allied cause:

> To my way of thinking, no body of the French Army could have passed over our front so little molested as the Imperial Garde. When they passed, where were the well-served batteries that had thundered on ...? The soldiers of Lloyd, Cleeves [battery commanders] ... In both cases all silent.[11]

It has been claimed that some Allied batteries ceased firing because of barrels overheating (leading to premature firing) rather than from lack of ammunition. Other accounts have some batteries going to the rear for ammunition resupply and not returning. Sinclair's battery might have provided Halkett's brigade with much needed artillery support had it not been ordered to move westwards near to au Goumont. According to Lieutenant Wilson of Sinclair's, the battery was in the process of moving when 1/3e Grenadiers attacked, missed the assault of 4e Grenadiers and was not engaged when the final Garde attack came in – a wasted asset.[12] Lieutenant Colonel Ross's troop presents another puzzle. He tells how he was ordered to move when his current position north of La Haie Sainte became untenable after the farmstead was captured. Is this further evidence of the French battery's fire? H.T. Siborne's map of the final positions of the British troops and batteries show Ross's posted in front of the Brunswickers.[13] However, this is questionable as there is no trace in the record of his presence there; his troop's fire could have provided an antidote to the bombardment from La Haie Sainte that so suppressed the men of Olfermann and von Kruse. Unfortunately Ross himself admits that he 'cannot speak positively as to the precise spot'. Perhaps he was ashamed to do so. He does not tell of engaging the Garde at any time. The first repulse of 1/3e Grenadiers can not be attributed to Allied gunfire.

Another reason for a collapse of the French grenadiers' morale might be a loss of leadership. We know that Maréchal Ney was leading the attack and was, presumably ahead of the leading battalion, 1/3e Grenadiers. At some point during the advance up the slope his horse had been shot and fell, but now Ney was back on his feet. The commanding officer of the Old Garde Grenadier division (and therefore presumably accompanying Ney), was Général de Division Comte Louis Friant. Although he had served Bourbon King Louis, Friant was admired by Napoleon, who had summoned him to take this most prestigious of divisional appointments. He was wounded during the advance, retired to where Napoleon was and reported an imminent victory. From Napoleon himself we read that:

General Friant, who had been wounded, and was passing by at this moment, said that everything was going well that the enemy appeared to be forming up his rear-guard to support his retreat, but that he would be completely broken, as soon as the rest of the guard deployed.[14]

It is pure surmise that Friant based his judgement on the sight of the Nassauers and Brunswickers cowering behind what little shelter the ridge here afforded and the visible effect the section of guns with 1/3e Grenadiers was having on 30th/73rd as the Grenadiers crested the slope; but there is no obvious alternative.

We do know that the loss of a leader can have catastrophic effects, as Général de Division Maximilien Foy learned at the Battle of Orthez, in southern France in February 1814, when the 52nd had made an unexpected approach through a marsh; as William Napier tells us:

Foy [was] dangerously wounded; and his troops [a division], discouraged by his fall and by this sudden burst from a quarter where no enemy was expected, for the march of the fifty-second [52nd Light Infantry] had been hardly perceived save by the skirmishers, got into confusion; the disorder then spreading to Reille's wing ...[15]

General Petit, in the next quotation, confirmed that loss of leadership was a crucial factor in the first repulse of the 1/3e Grenadiers, '... an excited move-ment ...' is a nice euphemism for precipitous retreat. It should be noted that Petit then states the battalion recovered and advanced again to the assault. This confirms that the second attack on the 30th/73rd was by the same Garde battalion, the 1/3e Grenadiers, and strongly suggests there was no second bat-talion behind it:

At this moment, General Friant, commander-in-chief of the movement, was grievously wounded, and General Michel [Michel was second in com-mand of the Châsseur Division.] was killed. The death of the latter caused an excited movement amongst his troops. But very soon, in response to General Poret, commander of the 3rd regiment of Grenadiers, the 1st battal-ion of that regiment regained its vigour, then resumed its advance, marching at the pas de charge with loud cries. ... The other battalions of Grenadiers and of Chasseurs, [sic] equally resumed their progress.[16]

But, while the grenadiers had temporarily retired, their horse artillery sec-tion had stayed in position and continued to pump a hail of canister into the unfortunate 30th/73rd. And at this point we must leave them to their torment and briefly switch our attention (see Map 9, colour section) to Halkett's other battalion, the composite 33rd/69th. Halkett describes how:

> The remaining part of the Brigade (33rd and 69th Regiments) were [*sic*] in double column formed on the centre in support, but on the Enemy advancing upon the Guards, I moved them forward towards the position of the French Guards, and in their front, which had the good effect of arresting their progress; this movement created a heavy loss both of officers and men. [17]

Those are the words of Sir Colin Halkett himself, by which he reveals that he swung out and to the right the 33rd/69th, the right hand of his two composite battalions, in order to fire into the front and flank of the next Garde battalion square, which, it should be noted, was 'advancing on the Guards', not on the 33rd/69th. That statement alone should be sufficient to dismiss any theory of the 33rd/69th being attacked by 4e Grenadiers (the next in sequence after the 1/3e Grenadiers) – the fact that the men of the 33rd/69th were swung out shows clearly there was no infantry directly opposing them.

Major General Sir Colin Halkett, 1774–1856. Elder brother of Hugh Halkett, from 1811 he served in the Peninsular War with the KGL; promoted to Major General twelve days before Waterloo at which he was wounded four times including through both cheeks. Governor of the Royal Hospital Chelsea from 1849 until his death.

The next battalion in the Allied line was the 3rd Battalion of the 1st Regiment of Foot Guards. The 2nd Battalion, 1st Foot Guards stood on their right, the two together comprising the 1st British (Guards) Brigade, commanded by Major General Peregrine Maitland. The Garde battalion was 4e Grenadiers, which was a very new unit and had been unable, in the few weeks available, to recruit a second battalion. About 520 men strong, they were dressed and equipped in a mixture of uniforms and arms, reflecting the variety of units from which they had been recruited.[18]

Nevertheless sufficient men had the tall bearskin, the most visible insignia of the Old and Middle Garde, by which to identify them. Telling grenadier from châsseur at any distance was harder and best achieved if they were wearing their plumes – red for grenadier, red and black for châsseur. With 4e Grenadiers came another section of two cannon of Garde Horse Artillery, which took post on the summit of the tongue, a commanding vantage point, marginally higher than the Allied ridge.

In the next chapter we will explore in detail the reception of 4e Grenadiers by the British Guards. But this action by the 33rd/69th deserves to be noted since it suggests that accounts of the famous repulse of 4e Grenadiers by the Guards have failed to give proper credit for the assistance provided by Halkett and half of his brigade. This action is also described by a young participating officer of the 33rd, Frederick Hope Pattison, who years later wrote of his experiences at Waterloo in a series of letters to his grandchildren, letters which were subsequently brought together into a book in 1870, and republished in 1997. He was rather given to hyperbole. He starts:

> Each Regiment having been formed four deep, right wing in front, took its relative position, when our brave and gallant General, Sir Colin (with what feelings of love and admiration did I behold him!) placed himself in front of the centre of his Brigade, and taking one of the colours (I think of the 73rd) supported it on his right stirrup and gave the word of command for the Brigade to advance.[19]

Pattison was mistaken in thinking the whole brigade was involved. Halkett himself specified only the 33rd/69th – the 30th/73rd was otherwise engaged with 1/3e Grenadiers. Pattison continued:

> The contest soon became fierce and exterminating, men dropping in quick succession all around. My right-hand man, a brave fellow, was at this instant shot right through the head. He leaned on me in falling: the ball had entered his left temple, and I can never forget the expression of his countenance in the momentary transition from life to death …

Although the contest could not have lasted more than ten or fifteen minutes, the losses on both sides must have been prodigious. Our brave General was shot right through both cheeks and removed from the field. ... On the removal of Sir Colin, the command devolved on Colonel Elphinstone ...

It is fairly certain that the opposing fire came, not from the 4e Grenadiers, but from that battalion's artillery section on the top of the tongue. Indeed his eye for detail – 'the ball had entered his left temple', – may give weight to this conclusion, suggesting both Pattison's right-hand man and the brigade commander were shot from the side. His estimate of time is almost certainly over-generous – time seems to stand still in periods of great stress or excitement. Then he makes an intriguing statement, which indicates that morale in the Allied line was beginning to weaken:

... and well do I recollect that matters became so serious as to create much apprehension as to the final issue of the contest ...

The likely reason for this will be described shortly but it is time to rejoin the men of the 30th/73rd, who, having seen off 1/3e Grenadiers, are being assailed by a hailstorm of canister from the grenadiers' supporting cannon section. Edward Macready again:

Late in the day the French had brought up two Guns on the crest of our position, which fired grape into our Square (30th and 73rd) with very deadly effect. Some one in authority must have thought that the bank of a hedge which ran a very short distance in our rear would afford us some cover, and in an evil moment we received the command to face about and march down to it.

Our little Square retained its formation, and we had all but reached the hedge, when a body of men (British) rushed in amongst us, turned us altogether into a mere mob, and created a scene of frightful confusion. Fortunately the Enemy took no advantage of it.

The falling back in Halkett's Brigade, and of the Brunswick Column occurred very near together, and I can readily conceive this to have been the period to which the French 'témoin oculaire' ['eyewitness', source unspecified] alludes when he speaks of Battalions being seen 'en débandade' [rout or disorder] on our height.[20]

Macready later expanded his description of this potentially catastrophic event. In his journal he wrote:

There was a hedge to our rear, to which it was deemed expedient to move us, I suppose, for shelter from the guns. We faced about by word of command, and stepped off in perfect order. As we descended the declivity the fire thickened tremendously, and the cries from the men struck down, as well as from the numerous wounded on all sides of us who thought themselves abandoned, was terrible … Prendergast of ours was shattered to pieces by a shell; McNab killed by grape-shot, and James and Bullen both lost their legs by round shot during this retreat. … as I recovered my feet from a tumble, a friend knocked up against me, seized me by the stock [stiff leather collar], and almost choked me, screaming, (half-maddened by his five wounds and the sad scene going on), 'Is it deep, Mac, is it deep?' At this instant we found ourselves commingled with the 33rd and 69th Regiments; all order was lost, and the column (now a mere mob) passed the hedge at an accelerated pace. The exertions of the officers, added to the glorious struggling of lots of the men to halt and face about, were rendered to no avail by the irresistible pressure … they [the officers] were themselves jammed up against them and hurried on with the current, literally for many yards not touching the ground … I cannot conceive what the enemy were about during our confusion. Fifty cuirassiers would have annihilated our brigade …[21]

At this moment, with the Nassauers and Brunswickers suppressed behind the ridge by gunfire from La Haie Sainte and Halkett's two composite battalions mixed together 'en débandade', there was a massive gap in the Allied line of some 700 yards. Astonishingly it seems no mention of it appears in the record (see Map 9, colour section). No wonder Wellington described the battle as 'a near run thing'. Here was a missed opportunity the French must regret to this day. Macready was right to be worried as there may have been cuirassiers about. Several accounts allude to cavalry attacks but, since none were effective, their movements have not been included in this analysis. In fact, the reports of cavalry attacks may have been imaginary, an excuse to cover up the supposed shame of retiring in confusion.

Fortunately, as Macready tells us, the 30th/73rd recovered themselves, and the 30th Light Company – now a mere fourteen strong – was sent forward to cover the reformation. This was effected without difficulty (see Map 10, Colour section). They had returned to the line just in time to receive the second assault by 1/3e Grenadiers. The latter, no doubt thoroughly ashamed of their precipitate withdrawal from their first encounter with the 30th/73rd, and, probably abused verbally and physically by their officers, had been persuaded to try again.

General Petit's evidence aside, can we be sure these attackers were the same ones that had earlier turned and run after one volley, and not a fresh battalion, namely the next in line, 4e Grenadiers? Evidence to prove a negative is always hard to find but nevertheless there is enough to put the conclusion beyond reasonable doubt. There is no eyewitness evidence of a second, subsequent battalion being involved. The likelihood of their being in square and therefore in echelon renders a follow-up battalion, directly behind the first, unlikely. The sudden, unexpected change in direction by Ney, and the subsequent confusion in the echelon formation that it caused, almost certainly precludes the possibility of a second, fresh battalion appearing behind the first. The very considerable space – 250m – between 1/3e Grenadiers and 4e Grenadiers, when they eventually struck the Allied line, shows very clearly how much wider than intended was the spacing, resulting from the 4e Grenadiers' square altering course more than 1/3e Grenadiers.

It might be argued that the change of direction might well have brought the leading battalion directly in front of the second. But that second battalion was 4e Grenadiers, and there were no more grenadier battalions in the assault force. It is almost certain that the next battalion to hit the Allied line was a grenadier battalion (justification for this conclusion is provided in the next chapter) – it cannot have been in two places at once. It is also worth pointing out that, had there been a follow-up by a fresh battalion immediately behind the first, Macready's 'fifty cuirassiers' would not have been needed; the fresh battalion would probably have broken through. Again, had there been a second battalion behind the first, it is reasonable to suppose the lead battalion would not have broken so easily nor run so far. This point is illustrated in reality with the repulse of 4e Grenadiers; but that has yet to come.

Macready's account has now revealed that the 'body of men (British) [who] rushed in amongst us, [and] turned us altogether into a mere mob', were the combined 33rd and 69th. There is no evidence to suggest this retreat of the 33rd/69th had been brought about by the actions of 4e Grenadiers, whose attentions were directed at the infantry that had just popped up in front of them, namely 3/1st Guards. Credit for the 33rd/69th's sudden rush to the rear must go to the section of horse artillery that had come forward with 4e Grenadiers. Once again artillery had proved to be the most effective arm in attack. It is even possible that the guns that came up with 4e Grenadiers, and were positioned on the summit of the tongue, which was higher than the ridge top, were thus able to fire down into the re-entrant in the reverse slope of the ridge down which the 30th/73rd retired, and which Macready describes as 'the declivity'.

Wellington, passing the spot at about 1830hrs, a minute or two before Halkett's brigade retired *en débandade*, and seeing the confusion, said to his staff in general, 'See what's wrong there.' Major Dawson Kelly, of the 73rd, but currently acting as an assistant quartermaster general on the duke's staff, rode over and questioned Sir Colin. At that moment Halkett was shot through the mouth and was obliged to leave the field. The next senior officer was Colonel Elphinstone of the 33rd. Exhibiting signs of his later indecisiveness and lack of judgement, he – a full colonel – asked Major Kelly, 'What is to be done? What would you do?' to which Kelly replied:

> At this period the attacking column was again retiring, and having observed that the different Battalions of the Brigade had got intermixed from the frequent formation of squares, [Kelly may not have been aware of the amalgamation of battalions] I advised Colonel Elphinstone to order both officers and men to resume their respective stations, to form as extended a front as possible, directing them to cover themselves as best they could by lying down, to renew, or check their flints, and to fresh prime, so as to meet the next attack with the best means left us.[22]

Kelly's phrase 'the attacking column was again retiring' must refer to the French column against which Halkett had deployed the 33rd/69th, namely 4th Grenadiers who had been met and repulsed by 3/1st Guards, as described in the next chapter because his description of the second attack by 1/3e Grenadiers is yet to come. It is clear this exchange took place before the 33rd/69th collapsed under the hail of shot from the horse artillery section with 4e Grenadiers, and rushed down the slight re-entrant to their left rear, only to collide with the 30th/73rd, who, according to Macready, had been ordered to retire to the putative shelter of a hedge in the same re-entrant.

The suspicion must be that Elphinstone gave the order that gave rise to the whole brigade's near-catastrophic reversal. Given that Elphinstone's chief claim to fame is having effortlessly lost a complete British Army in Afghanistan during the First Afghan War of 1839–1842, was this debacle at Waterloo an early manifestation of what might be termed 'the Elphinstone touch'? Macready has told how he and fourteen men, the remains of the Light Company, were sent forward to cover the reformation of the 30th/73rd, but there seems to be no evidence for the 33rd/69th having returned to the line before the battle ended. In fact there is evidence that suggests the contrary.

Before the rush to the rear, Kelly left the 33rd/69th and joined the 30th/73rd at the request of two serjeants of the 73rd – to which he belonged – that he should take command of their battalion since all its experienced officers were dead or wounded. It is unlikely he gave the command to retire to the hedge – since both battalions retreated simultaneously to the 'shelter' of the same hedge, it has the hint of acting brigade commander, Elphinstone, about it. Kelly continues his account with the second assault by 1/3e Grenadiers, naturally omitting all reference to the more-than-momentary hiccough:

Lieutenant Colonel William Elphinstone, 1782–1842.
He entered the British Army in 1804 and saw service throughout the Peninsular War. In 1841, by now a major general, he was put in command of the British Garrison in Kabul, having last seen active service at Waterloo. He died of dysentery in Afghanistan while his army of about 16,500 men and camp followers was massacred almost to a man – and woman – attempting to retreat from Kabul in the First Afghan War, 1842. His grave is unmarked.

Thus situated we remained a short time inactive, when the *last attacking Column* [his italics] made its appearance through the fog and smoke, which throughout the day lay thick on the ground. Their advance was as usual with the French, very noisy and evidently reluctant, the Officers being in advance some yards cheering their men on. … until they reached nearly on a level with us, when a well-directed volley put them into confusion from which they did not appear to recover, but after a short interval of musketry on both sides, they turned about to a man and fled.[23]

'… the last attacking Column …' refers to the renewed assault by 1/3e Grenadiers, brought back reluctantly by energetic officers, but repulsed with almost as little effort as the first assault. Kelly reiterated his story in a subsequent letter:

I can therefore only say that when the last attacking Column emerged from the smoke in *our front* … whether they were of the Imperial Guard, or of D'Erlon's Corps we had no opportunity of judging. I should rather think the latter, for after some firing between us the Enemy retreated without any *very apparent cause.*[24]

Before we discuss the real cause of this Garde battalion's second and final retreat, Kelly provides here a clue about the origin of the persistent belief that troops of d'Erlon's corps, variously claimed to be from Donzelot's or Quiot's divisions, 'brushed aside' the Nassauers, the Brunswickers and even the 30th/73rd too. Is this somewhat ingenuous statement by Kelly the cause of this misunderstanding? It is ingenuous because he had the same means of discovering who the enemy were as Macready had, namely going forward and asking them, when he would have learned they were of 'La Moyenne Garde'. Being English, an insufficient grasp of the French language may have hindered him, but the tall, hairy headdress that some of the enemy were wearing should have given him a clue. The brigade commander, Colin Halkett, was equally bemused:

> They halted and fired – I think badly. We returned the volley – ported – and, giving a 'hurrah!' came to the charge. Our surprise was inexpressible when through the clearing smoke we saw the backs of the Imperials flying in a mass. We stared at each other as if mistrusting our eyesight. Some guns from the rear of our right poured in grape among them, and the slaughter was dreadful. Nowhere did I see carcasses so heaped upon each other. I never could account for their flight …[25]

This quotation is slightly puzzling because the first part sounds very much like Macready's description of the first repulse, yet it could apply equally well to the second. That Halkett witnessed the second repulse is possible despite his just having retired with a musket ball through one or both cheeks of his face. He would hardly have had time to go to the rear, since events were following one upon another with mind-numbing rapidity. Halkett was definitely describing the second repulse of 1/3e Grenadiers. His mention of 'some guns' is the clue to the effortless repulse of the French at this point; they were those of Captain Krahmer's battery of the 3rd Netherlands Infantry Division. Who had brought them so opportunely to this critical spot? (See Map 10, colour section)

The answer is one of Napoleon's erstwhile generals. Lieutenant General Baron David Hendrik Chassé had fought for Napoleon in the Peninsula, where he had earned the grudging respect of the British and the sobriquet 'General Baïonnette'. After the emperor's abdication he had switched allegiance to the King of the Netherlands, to whom he remained loyal, despite Napoleon's expected mass desertions to his cause by those who had fought for him before his abdication. Chassé's division was originally posted in reserve on the Allied right flank, around the village of Braine l'Alleud. Around 1500hrs he was ordered to move his division into close reserve in the right centre where they came under fire. Chassé himself takes up the account:

Towards evening, I noticed that the fire of [Allied] artillery upon the height in front of us was slackening considerably, although not stopping completely; I immediately went there to enquire the reason and I was told that they were running out of ammunition. Seeing at the same time that the French Garde Impériale was moving to attack this artillery, and so I did not hesitate one moment; I ordered our artillery upon the same height and its commander, Major Van der Smissen, commenced a heavy fire.[26]

Van der Smissen was the divisional artillery commander; the battery commander was actually Captain Krahmer. Van der Smissen does not deserve the credit he is given in this and many other accounts, since he could not immediately be found, as we learn from Captain Frederick van Omphal, erstwhile French Army officer and now aide-de-camp to Chassé:

As a result [of 'provisional measures' being needed] van Omphal was ordered to advance the divisional artillery, which he only found after searching for a long time, because Major van der Smissen, who commanded this arm, on his own initiative had decided to place them further away from the position he had been allocated.[27]

Fortunately Krahmer brought his six cannons into action on the right of what remained of Halkett's brigade and was able to engage the French guns both on the summit of the tongue and those originally with the 1/3e Grenadiers. It was probably this fire that was largely responsible for finally repulsing the latter, not the volley from the 30th/73rd, which could not have been more than half-hearted after their unsettling experience. What is more, by suppressing the Garde artillery section on the tongue, Krahmer neutralised the artillery support that was supposed to assist the 4e Grenadiers in its tussle with 3/1st Guards. However, a glance at the map of the 4e Grenadiers' attack will show that the French gunners probably could not fire at 3/1st Guards at the critical moment of contact because their line of fire was masked by their own Garde battalion's presence. They had, however, already inflicted much damage on Mercer's troop from their vantage point on the tongue, some 400 yards to the east, as Mercer describes:

… when under cover of the smoke a Battery came (we could not conjecture whence) and established itself a little in advance of our left flank, from which it could not have been distant more than four hundred yards, and thus almost enfilading our line, besides being on higher ground; the fire it poured in upon us was the most destructive we had experienced, and could not have failed to annihilate us, had we not been saved by a Battery of Belgic Horse Artillery which came up soon after on our left, and thus taking them almost in flank, soon drove them from their position.[28]

To be doubly sure that the 1/3e Grenadiers were seen off, infantry was also sent forward. Chassé claimed to have initiated this deployment, as he went on to describe in his report to the Prince of Orange:

> I then ordered Major General d'Aubremé to remain in two columns, one behind the other, en echelon, and I advanced together with the 1st Brigade, under the command of Colonel Detmers, in closed column against the enemy, and I had the pleasure to witness the Garde Impériale retire from the confrontation with our brigade. I followed the fleeing enemy until the darkness of the night prevented us from doing so any longer.[29]

However, Chassé was being intentionally circumspect in saying he saw the Garde retire from the confrontation with his brigade: his sense of honesty prevented his claiming they had physically met and had repulsed the Garde. He is less accurate when he gives the impression that he initiated both the move by Krahmer's battery and of Detmers' brigade. In fact the call for infantry probably came from Wellington, if Chassé's very precise and observant chief of staff, Lieutenant Colonel Carl van Delen, is to be believed. On 11 November 1815, van Delen reported to Constant-Rebècque, after describing how Chassé discovered the need for artillery and had sent orders to van der Smissen:

> Meanwhile, an English Aide-de-camp came to Colonel Detmers and rode off quickly again, having ordered him to place himself with three battalions in the first line, whereupon the colonel marched with the 35th Jäger Battalion, the 2nd Line Battalion and the 4th Militia Battalion in columns by divisions ... Meanwhile his Excellency [Chassé] had returned with the division and after having made a short but very zealous and appropriate speech, he moved the three remaining battalions of the 1st Brigade forward, ... and now assembled all the battalions of the 1st Brigade and advanced in closed column at the head of the 1st Brigade towards the enemy ... when suddenly the French Garde Impériale, upon which our attack was aimed, left its position and disappeared from our front.[30]

Assuming it was Wellington who had sent the aide-de-camp, it would seem that he too had foreseen the urgent need for reinforcement of the line. Chassé's contribution was to double the number of battalions to six, which might be seen as over-insurance against one battalion, even of the Garde. His chief of staff, van Delen, went ahead to reconnoitre a space in the line for this considerable body of men and guns. By his description he manages to confirm not only where Detmers' brigade came through the line but also to confuse us as to when. It is likely van Delen first went forward to recce; then returned to Detmers' brigade and Chassé; then he led them forward. It seems the men of Detmers' brigade arrived just as the 33rd/69th broke and quitted the line, and were temporarily held up by them, only being able to proceed when the gap in the line had been created by the 33rd/69th's rush to the rear. Captain Gerard Rochell, with the Flanker (Light) Company, 19th Militia Battalion, in the group sent forward by Chassé, describes the moment:

> We advanced at attack pace and soon caught up the three leading battalions. At the same time an English division began to waver, as well as a Brunswick brigade; this caused some confusion in our column and the men were pushed against each other. It was impossible to get away with so many troops on one spot, so that our situation became precarious … But the order within the column was soon restored and with renewed courage we advanced further.[31]

Rochell does not describe any direct engagement with the Garde. However, his was one of the rearward battalions so it might be argued that the unexpected halting of the column of battalions marked the moment of the clash. But his later evidence of inebriation in his battalion, bolstered by Macready's observation below, raises serious doubts that direct contact was actually made. However, after the battle, Chassé was concerned that his 1st Brigade's supposed clash with 1/3e Grenadiers had not been given its due recognition. However, Chassé's suggestion that his division had seen off a Garde battalion is contradicted by evidence from Macready, who describes the Dutch/Belgians arrival after 1/3e Grenadiers had finally retreated. In its noisy exuberance, their style was very much in the mode of the French, not unexpectedly since they had been their allies not so many months before:

> A heavy column of Dutch infantry (the first we had seen) passed, drumming and shouting like mad, with their shakos on the top of their bayonets, near enough to our right for us to see and laugh at them, and after this the noise went rapidly away from us. Soon after we piled arms, chatted, and lay down to rest.[32]

Chassé's account – 'I had the pleasure to witness the Garde Impériale retire from the confrontation with our brigade' – implies, but does not specifically claim, that Detmers' column came into direct contact with the French. In the same report Chassé had written:

I would not have added thereto the report of our movements and of what the Division accomplished, being persuaded that General Lord Hill (under whose command I found myself by your Royal Highness' order) had done so; but the Duke of Wellington's report makes me see very distinctly how much I have been deceived in my just expectation. I therefore took the liberty of addressing myself to Lord Hill on that account, and I have the honour to send herewith a copy of my letter.

To Hill, who had commanded the 2nd Allied Army Corps at the battle, Chassé had complained that Wellington's despatch gave no mention, let alone credit, to the actions of the men of his division, despite Hill having congratulated Chassé, two days after the battle, on the performance of his artillery, but not, it should be noted, of his infantry. This last may be significant. Lord Hill duly replied.[33] He claimed that he had indeed mentioned in his report to Wellington the excellent service provided by the 3rd Netherlands Division but that, unfortunately, the duke's report had been despatched before Hill's reached him.[34]

Returning to Macready's description of the exuberant Dutch advance, given his obvious honesty, it is difficult to believe he invented something as bizarre as this cheerful Dutch courage. It is equally difficult to believe the Dutch/Belgians, with their shakos over the muzzles of their muskets, actually scared the Garde. Even allowing for Chassé's Dutch/Belgian officers having been in the French Army a year before (although most of his men had only about ten weeks service) this style of attack seems somewhat unprofessional. It has been suggested that the good people of Braine l'Alleud had been over-generous with alcoholic refreshment during the hours spent around the village during the early phases of the battle. Despite denials, this was the case. Gerard Rochell reveals that almost all of his battalion, the 19th Militia of the 1st Brigade, but excluding his company, were tipsy:

We had every reason to be content with our men and I was even more satisfied, because we were the only company in the battalion that had not received alcohol, which was because our marketer, the wife of our serjeant wagon master who was with the frying pans, had gone missing on the 16th and remained with her husband. I had some advantage over the other companies, who still had their marketers and received alcohol. Some flankers now protested, but I told them it would be much better to fight sober and nothing could be more shameful than to have drunk too much as it spoils one's courage.

During this advance our battalion became separated; everywhere one could see small groups of men together; I was lucky to keep my loyal company together and they followed me the whole time.[35]

There is a strong possibility that Detmers managed to halt his brigade as a body before they came level with La Haie Sainte. It seems they were seen by Ensign William Leeke, the youngest officer in the 52nd Light Infantry, who had the time to look about him because he was forward of the Allied line and was carrying the regimental colour, and so had no other responsibilities. The question of how the 52nd happened to be well out in front of the Allied line will have to wait, but this is what he had to say:

> Directly after the guns were driven in on our right by Gawler, we distinctly saw on our left, 300 or 400 yards up the British position, and on the Hougoumont side of La Haye Sainte, four battalions in column, apparently French, standing with ordered arms. According to all accounts they were too far down the British position to be Dutch Belgians; they certainly were not English. It was thought they were French, [because Dutch-Belgians were dressed in blue French uniforms] and part of Donzelot's division, who did not know how to get away, and therefore remained quietly where they were until the 52nd had passed.[36]

Men of Donzelot's division, it is true, had been responsible for capturing La Haie Sainte but the case for their not being involved in the Garde's attack has been argued earlier, so this attribution sounds wrong. Equally it seems unlikely the farm's garrison would have been drawn up in this position and, besides, a description of the hurried and uncontrolled departure of the garrison when it found itself outflanked will appear later. The troops Leeke saw were almost certainly Detmers' brigade, which Chassé records as being in column. They were in the blue uniforms of their previous service under Napoleon. They had halted and ordered arms, so their pursuit was on hold for the time being.

In Summary

1/3e Grenadiers were received with such a volley from the composite 30th/73rd that Ney was dishorsed, Friant wounded and (according to Petit) Michel killed. Morale collapsed and the grenadiers retired. Macready complained of the lack of Allied artillery support and of the dreadful effectiveness of the Garde Horse Artillery section that continued its onslaught even after the French infantry had retired, albeit temporarily.

Many accounts record a second attack on the 30th/73rd, and assume this was an assault by another battalion marching with the 1/3e Grenadiers, but this is incorrect. Given the echelon formation, which follows from the battalions being in square, it is very unlikely there would have been a second battalion behind the first at this stage. Moreover, there is no credible primary evidence of an accompanying battalion, no mention of two units being sighted simultaneously. More conclusively, Petit recounts that the 1/3e Grenadiers were rallied – 'renewed their vigour' – by their commanding officer and advanced again.

Before 1/3e Grenadiers struck a second time, the 30th/73rd and their comrades the 33rd/69th had been ordered to retire (probably by Elphinstone), did so and intermingled in confusion. Just in time, the men of the 30th/73rd managed to extricate themselves and return to the line where they were able to help Krahmer's Dutch battery of horse artillery to repel 1/3e Grenadiers for a second time. Detmers' Netherlands Brigade – as a few historians mention – did follow the retiring men but halted shortly after leaving the line and neither fired on, nor came into contact with, the French. This may have been fortunate since many of the soldiers were inebriated.

Some accounts claim that the 33rd/69th was struck by another Garde battalion. There is no evidence to support this and the truth, deduced from the evidence, is very different. The brigade commander, Sir Colin Halkett, seeing the second Garde battalion – 4e Grenadiers – approach the 3/1st Foot Guards on his brigade's right, swung the 33rd/69th out of the line and fired on the flank of 4e Grenadiers while 3/1st Guards fired at its front. The Foot Guards were doubly fortunate in that the Garde's horse artillery section, in support on the 4e Grenadiers' right, chose to fire not at the Guards but at the 33rd/69th instead.

Up guards and at 'em

> Your last point is whether the Duke made use of the words 'Up, Guards, and at them.' I did not hear him, nor do I know of any person, or ever heard of any person that did. It is a matter of no sort of importance, has become current with the world as the cheering speech of a great man to his troops, and is certainly not worth a controversy about. If you have got it I should let it stand.[1]

These immortal but singularly unsoldierly words – etched into the nation's memory on a par with Nelson's 'Kiss me, Hardy' – were supposedly invented by that master myth maker, Sir Walter Scott, but he may have cribbed them from a letter dated 22 June 1815, by an anonymous Guards officer, whose words were 'Up Guards and at them again.'[2] That they were ever spoken is dismissed in the quotation above, which is taken from a letter to William Siborne – modeller and historian of Waterloo – written by the then Major General Lord Saltoun. Saltoun had been the senior unwounded – and hence commanding – officer of the 3rd battalion the 1st Foot Guards when the Garde launched their final attack in the evening of the battle, so he is best placed to know what Wellington said.

Whilst the phrase's wording is in serious doubt, its ability to stick in the mind, and to convince generation after generation that Wellington and the Guards beat Napoleon with those five words, is unquestionable, supported by the certain knowledge that the duke did indeed give commands to the 3/1st Guards. But to discuss this question further now would be to advance too fast. We must retire, not just to the time in the previous chapter when Colonel van Delen, while guiding Detmers' brigade in their pursuit of 1/3e Grenadiers, heard the Guards volleying, but to the few moments earlier still when the next Garde battalion appeared, marching with difficulty over the dead and dying men and horses of the cavalry attacks, climbing the slope towards the 3rd Battalion of the 1st Foot Guards.

While the men of the second Garde battalion are slogging up the slippery slope to the drum beat of a pas de charge and shouts of 'Vive l'Empereur!' this

"Up Guards and at them." 63. Vol. 1.
Published by J. Booth, Dec' 30, 1816.

'Up Guards and at them'.
Wellington's apocryphal command to the 3rd Battalion of the Foot Guards. The book in
which this illustration appears, must have been one of its earliest manifestations.

is a good time to deal with a major controversy that has wracked historians
for decades – namely, were the troops, who met the British Guards, grenadiers
or châsseurs?

The officer commanding the 1st (Guards) Infantry Brigade – Peregrine
Maitland – was convinced that they were grenadiers. In his letter of November
1834 he told William Siborne that '…while the Grenadiers of the French Guard
were advancing up the slope'.[3] Could Maitland have genuinely recognised them
as grenadiers? It is true that some in the British Army were largely unfamil-
iar with Garde uniforms, having met the Garde only briefly in the Peninsula
during the Corunna campaign but Maitland had served therein. Moreover, it
seems likely that the Garde's distinctive uniforms could have been known to
senior officers – many had visited Paris during Napoleon's time-out on Elba,
and there were copious illustrations available in Britain, making their tall bearskin caps a well known distinction by which to identify the Garde.

The safest way of distinguishing grenadiers from châsseurs was by the
colour of their plumes. But that might not have been easy at Waterloo, not
only because of obscuration by the clouds of smoke but also because the
plumes differed only slightly – red for grenadier, red over black for châsseur.
And, to make matters more difficult still, the châsseur's black was next to

Major General Sir
Peregrine Maitland,
1777–1854.
A pious, strongly moral
but somewhat sickly
man. Ensign in the
Foot Guards in 1792,
he was promoted to
major general fifteen
days before Waterloo.
Lieutenant Governor
of Upper Canada for
ten years, then of Nova
Scotia and finally of
Cape Colony.

the bearskin and so merged with it while the red part projected above it. That in turn raises the question as to whether or not bearskins were worn at Waterloo. It has been said they were carried in the men's knapsacks, ready for their triumphal entry to Brussels. The obvious riposte to that is – just how smart would a crushed bearskin look? Surely the men would have worn them into battle: their purpose was to increase both the impressive size of the soldier and of his ego, as the symbol of his elite status. Besides, if you are going to die, would you not want to be in your best kit? Much is made of the evidence of Captain Rees Gronow, veteran of the Peninsular War and serving in 1/1st Guards in 1815. His battalion was not detailed for the campaign, so he had promptly taken leave of absence and joined the 3rd Battalion on the Continent. Often quoted in subsequent accounts, his description seems definitive enough:

> … their red epaulettes and crossbelts put on over their blue greatcoats [giving] them a gigantic appearance, which was increased by their hairy caps and long red feathers, which waved with the nod of their heads as they kept time to a drum in the centre of their column.[4]

Red epaulettes and long red plumes sound definitive enough, but the question – were they grenadiers or châsseurs – cannot be resolved for certain by appearance alone.

There is another way. The conclusion that the officers of the Guards were mistaken, and that their attackers were not grenadiers but châsseurs, probably stemmed from the mistaken belief that both French grenadier battalions had been expended in assaulting either the Brunswickers and Nassauers, or Halkett's brigade, or both. But if the reader has been convinced by the evidence, so far adduced, of the Garde's attack, and by the conclusions based on that evidence, then the answer is clear, thanks to the rigidity of protocol of most armies of the time, and especially of the militaristic French Imperial Army. By a process of elimination the battalions that actually took part in the attack have been identified, as has been discussed earlier.

Protocol gave precedence to grenadiers before châsseurs. Precedence dictated positioning in the line of each regiment, and of each battalion of the same regiment – the senior being stationed on the right. So the two grenadier battalions of the Moyenne Garde would have been positioned on the right of the châsseur battalions, with the 3e Grenadiers battalion taking precedence over the 4e Grenadiers. Additionally we should remember there is no evidence to indicate the existence of another battalion with 1/3e Grenadiers, either beside it or behind it. It was the first Garde battalion in action and its second assault should not be mistaken as a separate battalion. Therefore the second Garde unit to strike the Allied line, the battalion that came face to face with the 3/1st Guards, would have been the 4e Grenadiers.

Mark Adkin, in *The Waterloo Companion*, tells us that 4e Grenadiers had not been able to recruit a second battalion before the campaign began. Furthermore, the men had been together for a mere six weeks, so the bonding process that provides the glue that gives a unit its esprit de corps, had not yet set. Nor had this process been helped by the disparity in uniforms – many lacked Garde uniform, brass-mounted musket and headgear. Moreover they had been heavily engaged against the Prussians at Ligny, two days before, and were now reduced to about 520 men.[5]

It might be asked why it is of more than esoteric interest to know that the Guards faced the second grenadier battalion of the Garde force. Not only is it important to have this fact correct, to clarify the grenadier/châsseur argument, but it tells us there were still three Middle Garde battalions in the offing together with the reserve of three Old Garde battalions, a total of six battalions still to be defeated. The relevance of this becomes clear in the next chapter.

The 4e Grenadiers had now reached the summit of the tongue and still had more than 200m of ground to cover in full view of the Allied artillery. In contrast with the Allied line further east, the artillery here was active.

Captain Pringle, of Captain Bolton's battery of foot artillery, on the right of the 1st Guards Brigade, describes the moment in graphic detail:

> The battery fired case shot from the moment they appeared on the crest of the hill (about 200 yards), and during the advance along the plateau, from which they suffered severely, the Column waving, at each successive discharge, like standing corn blown by the wind.[6]

Some accounts speak of these guns being double-shotted with ball and canister: Pringle makes no mention of firing ball. On the other hand, it seems odd to be firing case shot – shrapnel – when canister would seem to have been the ammunition of choice. Apart from the possibility that the battery may have fired most of its canister rounds at the cavalry charges, shrapnel with a very short fuse could – indeed seems – to have been as effective if not more so. Air-bursting shrapnel would, in fact, have been the most suitable ammunition at this moment because of the need to lob shot over the heads of the Guards' skirmishers, who were forward of the line under the command of Ensign Thomas Swinburne (see Map 9, colour section):

> On their gaining the crown of the hill (if I may so call it), there was a call for skirmishers to check the French advance. I went forward with a few men pretty close to the French, who continued advancing to the spot where our battalion was lying. I got back to the company I had command of, shortly before we were ordered to rise and fire a volley and charge. This the French received and I think they were not more than 15 yards from us; they were so close that some of our men fired from the charging position (I mean without bringing the musket to the shoulder).[7]

We should briefly pause to note there is no mention here of French skirmishers, and that Swinburne's return to the battalion occurred just before the French main body arrived, the two points together strongly confirming there were no skirmishers with the Garde.

The presence or otherwise of French skirmishers is another of the finer points of history that has created much debate over the centuries. Logical reasoning suggests there were none. First, the Garde battalions were in square for protection against cavalry attack of the sort that had demolished d'Erlon's attack. Skirmishers, alone or in pairs, were not much afraid of musketry or gun fire, to which they offered no mass target, but were very vulnerable to cavalry. As the Garde battalions were in square, prepared to face cavalry, it would have been illogical to deploy skirmishers. Secondly, there were only four large companies to a Garde battalion. Hence a four-sided square would have required detachments from each company to be formed to act as skirmishers. Henri Houssaye was adamant there were no French skirmishers with the Garde. It is difficult to disagree with him. At moments when witnesses complain of the fire from tirailleurs, light canister from artillery was probably the culprit.

The most important point made here by Pringle and Swinburne is that the 4e Grenadiers appeared on the crest of the hill – i.e. the knoll on the top of the tongue – 200 yards in front of the Allied line. The Garde battalion had to traverse this open ground, in full view not only of the Allied artillery but also of the mounted field officers of the Guards, thanks to the latter's equine high-seats. So the Grenadiers' arrival should not have been the surprise that some accounts make it. Most accounts record the encounter between the Guards and the Garde battalion at between forty and sixty paces. The exact distance is unimportant: that they were quite close is unarguable. Apart from the skirmishers, the men were lying behind a low bank on the reverse slope of the ridge so their view forward would have been a few feet, until they stood up, to the surprise of the French.

Swinburne's observation that some guardsmen fired from the hip is interesting. Had the French actually been only 15 yards from them this might have been a reasonable action, delivering a quick response when accuracy was not a problem, but, if the range was greater – which seems more likely – firing from the hip would have been very inaccurate, and sounds more like the knee-jerk reaction of inexperienced troops. Captain Weyland Powell, also of 1st Foot Guards, embellishes the story:

> … Suddenly the firing ceased and as the smoke cleared away a most superb sight opened on us. A close Column of Grenadiers (about seventies in front) of La Moyenne Garde, about 6,000 strong, led, as we have since heard, by Maréchal Ney, were seen ascending the rise at the pas de charge shouting 'Vive l'Empéreur'. They continued to advance till within fifty or sixty paces of our front, when the Brigade was ordered to stand up.[8]

This brief extract raises several questions, so once again, the action must be paused. Powell was wrong about Ney, who was some 250 yards away with the previous, leading battalion. His comment that 'the firing ceased' suggests that not only the Grande Batterie had ceased firing to avoid hitting their own infantry but also that the artillery section, that was giving close support to 4e Grenadiers, had stopped firing at the Guards, although the two guns of this section probably continued to fire on the 33rd/69th until Krahmer's battery drove them off.

Furthermore Powell is assuming that his battalion was opposed to the entire Garde; his estimate of numbers can only be understood as 'an imposing body'

Captain and Lieutenant Colonel Alexander Fraser, the 17th Lord Saltoun, 1785–1853.
He served with the 1st Foot Guards at Corunna, on Walcheren and in Spain and France in 1814. At Waterloo he commanded first a force of Light Companies in the orchard of au Goumont, before they were withdrawn and he assumed command of 3/1st Guards on the ridge. He was promoted to major general in 1837 and commanded the British force at the end of the first Anglo-Chinese war, 1842–43.

– 6,000 would have comprised at least ten battalions. However it raises the question of comparative numbers and its corollary, firepower. He assumed, incorrectly, that the enemy was formed in column, and that assumption was reinforced by the mathematics of the square formation. In column, standing in three ranks, each full company would have had about thirty-five in the front rank, and he guessed their frontage was the French standard for ligne battalions of two companies providing a total frontage of what Powell called 'seventies'. In fact he seriously overestimated the strength of the 4e Grenadiers, which, as noted earlier, was less than 520 strong. These 520 men, in an even-sided square would have presented 130 men on each side, which gives, in the French regulation three ranks, a frontage of forty-three, allowing eighty-six to fire, or possibly 130 if the third rank dared to fire too, despite the risk to their comrades in the two ranks in front of them. This, apparently, they did.

Lieutenant Charles Ellis, of the 1st Foot Guards, reports '… they began firing from the rear of their column and killing themselves …'[9] By comparison, 3/1st Guards was about 750 strong in four ranks (i.e. double line – four ranks – as a precaution against cavalry, on the orders of the duke,) and assuming a loss of 250 at Quatre-Bras, giving a frontage of about 180. If only the two front ranks fired, a volley would deliver 360 musket balls to the Garde's maximum 130 – nearly three times the firepower. And we should not forget that the 33rd/69th was also firing into the Garde's right flank.

We return to the battle, with the 4e Grenadiers having advanced for some 200m under fire, not only from the guns of Bolton's battery but also – in the later stages – from the muskets of the 33rd/69th. Lord Saltoun, last mentioned commanding two Light Companies in au Goumont, due to casualties was now in command of his battalion, 3/1st Foot Guards, just behind the summit of the ridge. He had watched a formed body of French troops advance across the small plateau in front of him. His brigade commander, Maitland, was close by and he was aware that the commander-in-chief was just behind his battalion too. It must have been a somewhat daunting situation for a young man: who was to give the orders, and what orders, and when? The French had almost reached the summit before the answer came: Wellington himself.

Wellington, behind the Guards and with a longer view from Copenhagen's back than from ground level, called, in his high-pitched, far-carrying voice, 'Now, Maitland, now's your time!' and then before Maitland could respond (or perhaps because he failed to) 'Stand up, Guards. Make ready, present, fire!'

The first volley stopped the French in their tracks, caught completely by surprise. Various accounts describe how they attempted to deploy from square into line whilst returning fire. The impression given is that up to ten volleys were exchanged and there is no doubt the young and inexperienced men of the Guards were fully tested – serjeants are reported leaning hard on their spontoons against the guardsmen's backs to keep them in line. Finally the French began to crumble, turned and ran. Lord Saltoun, commanding the 3/1st Guards, shouted 'Now's the time, my boys' (according to Powell, but Saltoun himself does not claim it – perhaps it echoes Wellington's command 'Now Maitland, now's your time') and they charged.

Maitland spoke with the voice of experience, having seen considerable service in the Peninsula, as evidenced in this quotation from his response to Siborne's letter:

About seven o'clock … p.m., the Duke of Wellington, aware of the Enemy's preparations for a new attack, desired me to form the 1st Brigade of Guards in line four files deep, his Grace expecting that the French cavalry would take part in the affair.

The formation of the Brigade was scarcely completed before the advance of the Enemy became apparent. The force employed by the Enemy in this service consisted of two strong Columns of Infantry; a third Corps, consisting of both Cavalry and Infantry, being in reserve.

The attacking columns were alike composed of the Infantry of the Imperial Guard, the Grenadiers forming one Column, the Chasseurs [sic] of that Corps the other.

As the attacking force moved forward it separated, the Chasseurs inclined to their left. The Grenadiers ascended the acclivity towards our position in a more direct course, leaving La Haie Sainte on their right and moving towards that part of the eminence occupied by the 1st Brigade of Guards. Numerous pieces of ordnance were distributed on the flanks of this Column.

He confirms the change of direction of the Garde attack but fails to notice that the leading grenadier battalion– 1/3e Grenadiers – had already struck Halkett's brigade 250 yards or so to his left. It may be he did not – or could not – see it. He also confirms the presence of sections of artillery accompanying the Garde. He specifically mentions that 'As the attacking force moved forward it separated, the châsseurs inclined to their left.' The likely causes of the grenadiers and châsseurs separating are examined in the next chapter. He continues:

The Brigade suffered by the Enemy's Artillery, but it withheld its fire for the nearer approach of the Column. The latter, after advancing steadily up the slope, halted about twenty paces from the front rank of the Brigade.

The diminished range of the Enemy's Artillery was now felt most severely in our ranks; the men fell in great numbers before the discharges of grape shot, and the fire of the musketry distributed among the Guns.

This can only refer to the supporting fire of the 4e Grenadiers' gun section as mentioned in the previous chapter. It seems unlikely these guns would have been able to continue firing at 3/1st Guards when they and 4e Grenadiers were face to face, but his statement undoubtedly reflects the terrible casualties caused by these two guns, before they were driven off by Krahmer's battery. Musketry is unlikely since there were no skirmishers, and infantry mixed with guns seems equally unlikely. Perhaps the guns were firing both heavy and light canister, the latter giving the impression of volleys of musketry. Next he confirms:

The smoke of the Artillery happily did not envelop the hostile Column, or serve to conceal it from our aim.

So the smoke was not as dense as some historians claim. As the opposing units were very close to each other, plume colouration would have been clearly visible. He continues:

The fire of the Brigade opened with terrible effect …

The Enemy's Column, crippled and broken, retreated with the utmost rapidity, leaving only a heap of dead and dying men to mark the ground which it had occupied.

The Brigade pressed on the retreating Column, and was in some measure separated from the general line of our position.[10]

Here Maitland's report is strangely opaque. He does not claim to have given the orders, but perhaps is trying to hide the embarrassing fact of Wellington's having temporarily taken command of one of his battalions. The last sentence is a surprisingly understated way of describing the charge, an event that, according to Wellington, put the French Army terminally into confusion. Another question mark hovers over his use of 'the Brigade' by which he implies that both battalions of 1st Guards acted together, because there is no corroborative evidence – at least neither in H.T. Siborne's *Waterloo Letters* nor in Gareth Glover's *Letters from the Battle of Waterloo* – of the 2/1st Guards having been involved in any way.

There is, however, a statement that specifically excludes 2/1st Guards from taking part in the action. It is contained in an interesting version of the charge from a senior warrant officer who took part in it. Such men are known for their honesty and outspokenness. His account, however, was recorded by an ex-officer of the 52nd Regiment – William Leeke – and is therefore hearsay. Leeke's own account of the 52nd's action will feature strongly in the next chapter and so he must declare an interest. In later life Leeke took Holy Orders and there is nothing to suggest he intentionally altered or fabricated any part of his evidence. On the other hand he certainly misinterpreted some of what he saw and made incorrect statements about some events he didn't see. Such mistakes will shortly be revealed. But he reports what he saw and heard with great clarity of memory, having kept notes, which ultimately became his *History of Lord Seaton's Regiment, (The 52nd Light Infantry) at the Battle of Waterloo* together with a *Supplement* thereto.

A sceptic might ask why somebody would take notes over a period of fifty years before publishing a 'history'. There are two aspects to the question. First, why did he feel so strongly on the subject and, second, why did he take so long to go public? To the first question the answer is straightforward: he was highly disgruntled that his regiment had received no public acknowledgement – let alone reward – for carrying out an action, which, from any period of history, he thought should have resounded down the ages. The answer to the second question is more complex. His stated reason was that, as the youngest and most junior officer in the 52nd, having joined only six weeks before the battle, he could not accept that it was his place to write an 'official history'.

There were indeed many senior officers better qualified to do so: we shall hear from them in due course.

This digression on William Leeke is intended to acknowledge – and, to a large extent, to dispel – the view of some historians that Leeke is unreliable. It seems likely that the difficulty they have with Leeke is that he diametrically contradicts the basic assumptions of the (almost) universally accepted versions of the Crisis. However, upon long and carefully researched acquaintance, in comparison with the histrionic extravagances of many other eyewitnesses, he stands out as a paragon of accuracy. That he made some mistakes by no means proves all is wrong. Indeed, an absence of disagreements with others might well suggest collusion in a fabrication. The serjeant major's account, as recorded by William Leeke, ran as follows:

> Several years ago I received from an officer, who told me that he was serjeant-major of the 3rd battalion of the 1st Guards at Waterloo, and noted it down the day after, the following information with regard to what his battalion really did at the crisis of Waterloo. I copy a portion of it from my history of the battle – they were attacked by a 'column' of twelve or fourteen hundred men, and that these troops opened fire upon them at a distance of fifty or sixty paces; that the Duke coming along from their left, observed how this 3rd battalion of the 1st Guards was suffering from the heavy fire of the mass of troops in their front, and desired the commanding officer to form line on the front face of the square, and 'drive those fellows off', which they did in very gallant style, and followed them for some eighty or a hundred yards down the slope; then there was an alarm of cavalry, and the 3rd battalion of the Guards, some of them thinking they were to form square, got into confusion and retired hastily over the crest of the position and beyond it on the reverse slope. This officer also told me most positively that this was the only movement the 3rd battalion of the 1st Guards made against the enemy's infantry at Waterloo, *and that their 2nd battalion was not with them. It will be seen therefore, that the two battalions of which Maitland's brigade consisted, could not at any time have advanced together, as Siborne and other writers have asserted. ... The 3rd battalion, being in square* [no – four deep line but against cavalry] *at the time, must have been at a considerable distance from the 2nd battalion on its right; when in a four-deep line there would still be a great interval between the battalions.* [Original author's italics.][11]

As usual, the serjeant major's estimate of the number of enemy troops is about twice reality, but much nearer the mark than many others. It must be recognised that estimating such numbers in the few available minutes (if not seconds) whilst in a state of considerable excitement (if not worse) must have been extremely difficult. Greater dependence can be placed on judgements of length i.e. frontage or – as will be apparent in the next chapter – of distance front to rear. He refers to a 'column' where 'column of battalions' would have been correct usage by someone responsible – as he was – for a battalion's drill, had there been more than one. So thereby he supports the contention there was no follow-up battalion, and that 2/1st Guards did not charge but were some considerable distance away to the right. 3/1st Guards had performed the standard British charge of 80–100 yards. But, before they could retire in good order, something went seriously wrong. Confusion about an order led to loss of control and cohesion. The battalion rushed back behind the ridge in disorder.

The serjeant major was confident in claiming an alarm of cavalry was the cause of the Guards confusion but others have concluded the scare was prompted by the appearance of the so-called second column. The three châsseurs battalions of the Middle Garde had come round the outer end of the tongue and had coalesced into a column of battalions. They may already have been joined by two or three of the Old Garde battalions in reserve (see Maps 7–10).

Any infantry in line – let alone young and inexperienced recruits – at the extremity of a charge might well have panicked at the dreaded cry of 'cavalry!' So, how experienced were the men of 3/1st Guards? Ensign Robert Batty of that battalion tells us:

> … too much cannot be said in praise of the division of Guards, the very largest part of whom were young soldiers and volunteers from the militia, who had never been exposed to the fire of an enemy, or witnessed its effect.[12]

Maitland continues his description of the action:

> The Enemy's second attacking Column advanced towards that part of the position which had been vacated by the second Brigade of Guards, when it moved to Hougoumont.[13]

The use of the word 'second' suggests the previous unit, repulsed by 3/1st Guards, was the first Garde column and this, over the years, has given rise to much misunderstanding. In particular, when established as part of the myth, it ruled out any possibility of there having been a previous attack by a Garde unit, or in other words, that the attack by 1/3e Grenadiers on the 30th/73rd had never happened. His description of the apparent target of the 'second column' being the ground 'vacated by the second Brigade of Guards' is incorrect, on his own admission. He himself says, two lines later, that the ground that had been occupied by the 2nd Brigade of Guards was now occupied by Adam's brigade, but in fact he was still wrong. Had the oncoming column of French battalions been aimed directly at Adam's brigade, the latter could not have been swung out against their flank. However, it does tell us that the head of the column of battalions was seen ascending the distinct re-entrant on the west of the tongue, but its target was 2/1st Guards, further east, judged by men of Adam's brigade from their different viewpoint (see Map 10). Then he claims:

> The Brigade began to change front towards its right.
> The Light Brigade under Sir F. Adam occupied the ground vacated by the 2nd Brigade of Guards, and opened its fire on the Enemy's Column. The latter retreated with the utmost haste pursued by Sir F. Adam's Brigade.[13]

We should note that he does *not* claim that his brigade fired on the '2nd column'. Is it not reasonable to expect him to have recorded this, had it done so? His use of the word 'occupied' is also misleading, suggesting movement in response to the French advance whereas the Light Brigade had been in that position since the end of the cavalry attacks. Moreover, he gives the impression the Light Brigade opened fire from its position in the line, which is contrary to the evidence adduced in the next chapter but has nevertheless been quoted as fact by at least one historian. However Maitland is absolutely correct when describing the Light Brigade's action.

Saltoun also responded to Siborne's enquiry and it is printed in *Waterloo Letters*, but its content bears little relationship to Maitland's.[14] Indeed, the supposed battle-winning affray with the French grenadiers is hardly detectable. The preamble, marked by the mention of 'the last cavalry attack,' reads:

> In this position we received the last Cavalry attack I saw that day, who, refusing us, passed between us and the *inward rear angle* of the orchard, receiving our fire; did not charge between us and the 52nd, where the Rifles were, but rode along the front of the 52nd with a view of turning their right flank, and were completely destroyed by the fire of that Regiment [writer's italics].

That event is not mentioned by any one else and seems to be pure invention. Strangely, Saltoun then omits any mention of his battalion's successful repulse of 4e Grenadiers but fabricates another non-event before returning to the true story:

After this we, the 3rd Battalion, retired to our original position in square, as I conclude the 52nd did also, as the next I saw of them was their attack with the rest of General Adam's Brigade on the 2nd Column of the Imperial Guards.

His next three paragraphs are given over to trying to cover up his battalion's unfortunate and slightly humiliating (but perfectly understandable) rush back to the ridge. He completes his letter:

The left shoulders were then brought forward, and we advanced against the second Column of the Imperial Guards, but which body was defeated by General Adam's Brigade before we reached it, although we got near enough to fire if we had been ordered so to do; and as far as I can recollect at this distance of time we did fire into that Column.

Saltoun hesitantly claiming some possible participation by his battalion in this action is unconvincing. First, his phrase 'if we had been ordered so to do' is questionable. Why, if he was in command of the battalion, would someone else have given the command? Maitland did not claim to have done so, and it has never been attributed to Wellington. If both first and second battalions of 1st Guards had advanced towards the 'second' column Maitland might have been expected to give the order but – as we shall learn in a moment – there is no evidence from 2/1st Guards that they did anything at all, so the duty of command should have devolved on Saltoun.

Since he was writing eighteen years after the battle, his memory might possibly have failed him over lesser matters but this was supposed to be the crux of the battle, the moment when the 1st Guards supposedly defeated the majority – if not the entire – Garde attack. This was the unforgettable moment to savour for a lifetime – unless it was untrue. Written in 1838, his hesitant claim of possibly having fired on the final Garde assault preceded the appearance of Siborne's model of the Crisis, first displayed in 1839, and before Siborne published his history in 1844. Both model and book would eventually give some credit to the 52nd for helping to defeat the Garde but both would also show the Guards firing into the enemy column, in direct contradiction to the statements by the two senior Guards officers.

Unfortunately, the myth that the 1st Guards defeated the Imperial Guard was already firmly established when Saltoun penned his account, yet here he was faced with denying the myth, one which had already gained great honours for himself and his regiment. To have denied that his battalion fired could have caused an almighty ruckus; and no doubt he was an honourable man and took no pleasure in telling an outright lie. So he took the only course open to him – he settled on a very British compromise, a fudge: 'and as far as I can recollect at this distance of time we did fire into that Column'.

It is difficult to accept Saltoun's hesitant claim as a genuine suggestion, let alone definitive proof of the 1st Guards firing into the final Garde column. Maitland made no such claim. Had they fired on the next column, knowing how much the maintenance of the myth depended upon their having done so, surely both officers would have claimed as such, vociferously. Had they genuinely repulsed a battalion or a column of battalions and thereby routed an army there would have been long and detailed descriptions of the action. Instead, there is silence.

By contrast, here is evidence to support the contention the Guards did not fire. From Colonel Colborne we hear:

> Sir John Byng mentioned to me, at Paris, that he observed our movement in front of his Brigade, [the 1st Guards Brigade, although he was commanding the Guards Division at this stage] and that at this time his Brigade had no more ammunition left. Lord Hill mentioned to me also that he was near the Brigade of Guards when he observed the 52nd moving across the plain, that some men of the British Guards were retiring, that he ordered them to advance, waving his hat to them.[15]

Leeke recalls his colonel telling him that during the same conversation Byng said to Colborne 'How do you fellows like our getting the credit of doing what you did at Waterloo? I could not advance when you did, because all our ammunition was gone.'[16] Sceptics might think that hearsay evidence from two officers of the 52nd on this count is suspect, but we have an independent witness to the lack of ammunition, to support their testimony. Henry Rooke of the 3rd Foot Guards told Siborne via a friend in 1835:

> I am sorry to say that I was not with the First Brigade at the moment he [Siborne: the Crisis] particularly refers to, and left them about two minutes previous to that. The Division was in want of ammunition. Two or three officers had been sent to order it up but could not find it and Sir John Byng wished me to go as I knew where it was placed. Before I got back the attack had been made and the Brigade had since advanced.[17]

At the start of the battle, Major General Byng commanded the 2nd Brigade of Guards (which was defending au Goumont) but had by now assumed command of the Guards Division from Lieutenant General George Cooke, who had lost his left arm. When command devolved on him, Byng immediately rode over to the 1st Guards Brigade, where the action was. The day after the battle he reported to the Duke of York:

> I had also to witness the gallantry with which the last attack made by Grenadiers of the Imperial Guard ordered on by Bonaparte himself; the destructive fire they [the British Guards] poured in, and the subsequent Charge, which together completely routed the Enemy, a second attempt met with a similar reception and the loss they caused to the French of the finest Troops I ever saw, was immense. I beg you, Sir, understand, that my presence or advice to General Maitland never was required, I merely stayed with him as an humble Individual, when assistance of everyone was required. His own judgement and Gallantry directed everything that was necessary. I cannot say too much in his praise, or in that of the several Commanders his Battalion had …[18]

Since this missive was for the eyes of the Duke of York, was Byng primarily carrying out the apparent first duty of every commander of every period, eulogising his subordinate commanders in the hope that the glory of their successes would add lustre to his own? Or was this letter to cover up their failures? Is there a certain air of defensiveness detectable in his praise for Maitland's judgement and command? Could this reflect concern about Maitland's apparently being struck dumb at the critical moment, leaving Wellington to give the necessary orders to his brigade?

Byng's description of the action, if taken at face value, can be construed to be confirmation that both battalions of 1st Guards Brigade had been responsible for repulsing two successive attacks by the Garde but that is questionable. In fact, he tells us only one battalion was involved by his phrase '… of the several Commanders his Battalion had …' thereby subliminally confirming he was thinking of Maitland's control (or lack of it) of only one battalion. His saying 'a second attempt met with a similar reception …' may have been intentionally ambiguous – it certainly does not confirm the repulse was attributable to the Guards. Had it been so, we should expect him to have said so with emphasis. Since he did not, we can conclude the repulse was achieved by another unit, and that Byng's phrasing was obfuscation, intentional or otherwise.

As to the failure to have sufficient ammunition, Leeke tartly observes that the experienced and thoughtful Colborne, anticipating a full day's pounding, had the men of the 52nd supplied with two days' issues of cartridge (120 rounds), and that La Haie Sainte might not have fallen if a similar double ration had been issued to the KGL garrison under Major Baring.

Of course, had the Guards fired they would probably have hit the men of the 52nd, who, as both Maitland and Saltoun have already told us, were in the line of fire. Had 3/1st Guards also charged, the two battalions would have collided in an unseemly heap, always assuming the Guards had somehow avoided the six companies of 2/95th, who were also in their way, as becomes clear in the next chapter. Leeke points out that George Gawler, in his book, *The Crisis of Waterloo*, of 1833, observed that if 3/1st Guards had had a hand in the defeat of the '2nd column' of the Garde they would have 'crossed' the 52nd, by which we must assume he meant 'collided with'. Gawler did not suggest they fired on the Garde since, had they done so, they would then have been firing on the 52nd, and he clearly assumed the Guards would not commit such a basic error.[19] Yet it is this very error that Saltoun, Siborne and subsequent historians have perpetuated ever since.

Leeke also asks, if 3/1st Guards had actually fired into the head of the Garde column of battalions, why did Maitland not then move in support of Adam's brigade?[20] 2/1st Guards were posted on the right of their fellow men of the 3rd Battalion and might have been well placed to assist. Indeed many accounts speak of the 1st Brigade – comprised of the two battalions of the 1st Foot Guards – having defeated the Garde. Yet, puzzlingly, there seems to be no evidence in published primary sources that 2/1st Guards took any part whatsoever in the action. For example, in all of the published correspondence amassed by William Siborne there are only two letters from officers of and about 2/1st Guards, and they were rejected for publication by Siborne's son, only surfacing in 2005 in *Letters from the Battle of Waterloo*, thanks to Gareth Glover.

The only officer of 2/1st Guards to reply to Siborne's letter was Lieutenant Charles Lascelles. His letter, dated 19 March 1835, in which the italics are the questions posed by Siborne, reads in full:

Sir,

I had the honour to receive your letter last night, enclosing a plan of the Battle of Waterloo, requesting me to answer the following questions.

What was the particular formation of the 1st Foot Guards at the moment, (about 7 o'clock pm) when the French Imperial Guards advancing to attack the right of the British forces reached the crest of our position?

We were formed in line four deep.

What was the formation of the enemy's forces immediately in front of the Regiment?

The Imperial Guard came up in close column, and began to open out into line, but did not complete the manoeuvre.

I do not recollect anything about the crops as it is so long since the Battle of Waterloo. I have marked your map as well as I can remember at this length of time where the battalion was formed at this time of the attack of the Imperial Guards, as also their position (the Imperial Guards) at the bottom of the hill at the moment of that attack.

The Light Infantry Companies of the 2nd and 3rd Battalions' were detached under the command of Lord Saltoun at Hougoumont. If I remember right the 95th Rifles (part of General Adam's brigade) were on the right of the 2nd Battalion, between it and Hougoumont. I beg leave to state I was in the 2nd Battalion 1st Foot Guards during the campaign of 1815.

I have the honour to be, Sir, your obedient servant, [21]

C F R LASCELLES

Remarkably he gives no hint of 2/1st Guards doing anything. Once he has described the Grenadiers' attempt to deploy in front of the Regiment (by which he would have meant both battalions of 1st Guards) he immediately changes the subject to crops. Is it realistic to believe he could have resisted the opportunity of blowing his battalion's trumpet, had there been anything about which to blow it, concerning its share in the repulse of the Garde?

The almost complete lack of letters from the 2/1st Guards is even mentioned by another officer of the 1st Guards, Lieutenant Charles Ellis, writer of the second letter from 2/1st Guards. He specifically bemoans the failure of the 2/1st Guards officers to communicate:

> It is very strange, and I regret it much, that no officers who were present at the time should have answered your letter; for I feel, myself, that love of my old corps, in which I served nearly twenty years, that I cannot bear to think that their services on that day should not be duly recorded. [22]

There is, however, one letter of 2/1st Guards' origin, from Captain Nixon to his father – not to Siborne – written a day after the battle:

> At 8 o'clock the enemy moved forward his Old Guard who was received by the 1st Brigade of Guards, and a Dutch brigade with Saltoun at their head, with such fire that they took to their heels. Their whole army fled in the greatest disorder, and ours followed in sweeping lines, as fast as the lines could move. [23]

He concludes by stating the 2/1st Guards mustered only 340 men after the battle, so they had indeed manfully stood their ground in the face of heavy punishment, mostly from the French artillery. It is telling that he names Saltoun as the leader of the Guards Brigade suggesting only 3/1st Guards were involved. His letter is riddled with inaccuracies, compounded by poor punctuation, especially the lack of a comma after Dutch brigade), but what he says is immaterial – only the fact that he makes no play with his own battalion's performance is relevant. The inevitable conclusion must be that 2/1st Guards did not fire at 4e Grenadiers.

Did they, as is usually assumed, take part in the charge? Many accounts speak of how 'the Guards Brigade charged'. Of course, use of 'the Guards Brigade' can be shorthand for a portion of the brigade such as in 'the Green Jackets won the shooting trophy at Bisley', which does not imply the entire three battalions were shooting, only a small team from one battalion.

William Siborne promulgated the myth of the 2/1st Guards' involvement by describing how, having charged, they were successfully lined up by Maitland parallel with the flank of the oncoming Garde column of battalions, but that 3/1st Guards misunderstood the command and, imagining it to have been to form square, 'fell into confusion', and rushed back to the ridge. Once there the men immediately formed up next to 2/1st Guards, who – if Siborne was correct – by some miracle had already returned there before them. It has proved impossible to find any evidence that might have supported Siborne in this apparent fabrication. Siborne's imagination was running ahead of the facts. His desire to propagate the myth, and hence to ingratiate himself with Wellington, is evident.[24] Siborne's relationship with Wellington is considered in a later chapter.

The clear logic of arithmetic suggests 2/1st Guards did not join in the charge. The frontage of the Garde's square was about forty-three men; that of 3/1st Guards in four ranks about 180 men, so there would have been an overwhelming overlap on both sides. There would also have been a long gap between 3/1st Guards and the 2nd battalion on its right, due to both being doubled up, i.e. with one half being formed behind the other in four ranks, not the usual two. There would have been nothing at which another battalion could charge, unless there had been a follow-up battalion, another square of the Garde. There was almost certainly not.

The prime reason for assuming there was no such follow-up is the lack of evidence that there was! If the use of the term 'column' implied one column behind another, a follow-up battalion must have manifested itself in the historical record. However, had there been a column behind 4e Grenadiers, these troops might not have been hit by the Guards' volley (their being down the forward slope and the Guards on the other side of the crest) but, instead, could and should have held fast and perhaps deployed into line, able to meet the Guards' charge when it came. Alternatively the rearward column's presence would have prevented – or at least inhibited – the retreat of the leading battalion. At the very least, if the leading battalion retired and collided with the rear battalion there must have been a major check to the Guards' charge.

An important facet of the debate about the quantity of battalions involved at each phase of the Garde's assault is that Siborne had to make sense of two directly conflicting 'facts': on one hand the 'first and second columns' had become set in mythical stone and, on the other hand, the evidence from the responses to his enquiry showed clearly that there had been a genuine first column – 1/3rd Grenadiers – that struck the 30th/73rd. The 4e Grenadiers became known, incorrectly, as the 'first column', through the term's use in the 1st Guards Brigade's account, which became the accepted myth. This caused a problem for William Siborne when writing his *History of the Waterloo Campaign*, because he now knew there had been a 'first attack' already. To circumvent this difficulty he invented an unlikely manoeuvre:

> During the advance of the first attacking column, one of the battalions had moved out from the mass to its right [by which he presumably means it moved out to its own right] … which brought it in front of … the 30th and 73rd British regiments …[25]

He is at least acknowledging the attack by 1/3e Grenadiers but, by including this battalion in 'the first attacking column' he neatly avoids having to refer to 1/3e Grenadiers as the 'first column', which would have been true but at odds with the myth. He is also incorrectly inferring that there were two (or more) battalions together, further muddying the waters of history.

In Summary

The theory that 3/1st Guards were opposed by châsseurs, not grenadiers, is effectively dispelled by logic. First, Napoleon had led his men down to La Haie Sainte proving the Garde's attack was meant to drive along and beside the Brussels road aimed at the part of the Allied line, to the west of the road, where Ney had earlier seen the defenders retire, leaving a potential weak point. Secondly, the hierarchy of military precedence placed the two grenadier battalions first, and the second of the sequence of battalions struck 3/1st Guards.

Maitland, commanding the Guards Brigade, confirmed that the Middle Garde formation of battalions in square in echelon split into two: the two grenadier battalions in one part, and the three châsseur in the other, as independent evidence tells us. The two grenadier battalions then diverged and the second one – 4e Grenadiers (not châsseurs) – struck 3/1st Guards, whose skirmishers had briefly opposed them. The latter did not report French skirmishers and the fact that the Grenadiers were in square suggests skirmishers would not have been deployed. Reports of musket fire can be attributed to canister fire from the Garde's accompanying guns.

The 33rd/69th of Colin Halkett's brigade was swung out to fire on the Frenchmen's flank but was, in its turn, severely treated by one of the two guns with 4e Grenadiers. 3/1st Guards were also under close-range artillery fire until shielded by the advance of 4e Grenadiers, when the French gunners switched target. After a lengthy fire-fight 4e Grenadiers were seen to waver and run from the Guards' charge. As was standard practice, the Guards' charge was halted about 100 yards out. Inexperience and a misunderstood order combined to send the Guards rushing back to the 'safety' of the ridge.

2/1st Guards appear to have taken no part either in this part of the action, nor in the next phase. Reference to the 'first' and 'second' attacks should be ignored as they were in fact the second and third. Maitland's failure to give orders seems to have raised questions.

There was no evidence of another infantry unit supporting 4e Grenadiers. Nor had there been two battalions involved in 1/3e Grenadiers' attack, merely two assaults by the same unit, so the theory that only 4e Châsseurs remained to be seen off is a fallacy.

Neither Guards battalion fired at the column of battalions. Saltoun's hesitant claim that they may have done so is the squirming of a man compelled to tell a lie – and hating doing so. He was honest enough to confess that Adam's brigade 'flanked and pursued' the column of battalions and this was confirmed by Maitland, Saltoun's superior. The 3/1st Guards were out of ammunition, as their divisional commander, Byng, admitted, and this was confirmed by the officer sent to fetch more. The myth that the Guards fired on the head of the column while it was attacked in the flank is unsupported. To suggest that they charged the head of the final column ignores the fact that both the 2/95th and the 52nd would have collided with them, as will shortly be made clear.

Most notably, here we have clear admissions from both senior officers in command of 3/1st Guards that the final attack by the Garde was 'flanked' and pursued' by the 52nd Light Infantry, not by 1st Guards, admissions that have been in the public domain but ignored for over 122 years. But questions remain – how many battalions were there in the column of battalions, and how were they repulsed?

8

MAKE THAT COLUMN
FEEL OUR FIRE

In his letter to William Siborne, which was quoted at length in the previous chapter, General Maitland made an observation that subsequent historians seem to have ignored:

> The attacking columns were alike composed of the Infantry of the Imperial Guard, the Grenadiers forming one Column, the Chasseurs [*sic*] of that Corps the other.
>
> As the attacking force moved forward it separated, the Chasseurs inclined to their left. The Grenadiers ascended the acclivity towards the 1st Brigade.[1]

Since there were two grenadier and three châsseur battalions in the main body of the attack, his statement proves Maitland is using the term column loosely to signify a column of battalions. Next, let us be absolutely clear, while he was right in recognising that the two grenadier battalions had separated from the three châsseur battalions, he was wrong to conclude that both grenadier battalions approached his brigade since we know (perhaps he had not registered) the leading Garde battalion – 1/3e Grenadiers – assaulted Halkett's brigade. Thus only one grenadier battalion remained to attack his brigade: further proof – if more were needed – that 3/1st Guards had only one battalion with which to contend.

Out of the five battalions that made up the Middle Garde element of the attacking force, three – 1 and 2/3e Châsseurs and 4e Châsseurs – still remained. These together with three Old Garde battalions in reserve – 2/2e Grenadiers, 2/2e Châsseurs and 2/1er Châsseurs – made six battalions still in the offing. These six battalions totalled three-quarters of the total attacking force. In fact the eyewitness evidence, together with the theory of 'Inherent Military Probability', suggests convincingly that these six battalions came forward in a genuine column of battalions and represented a very real threat to the Allied line. Can we determine how this might have happened, why and with what results?

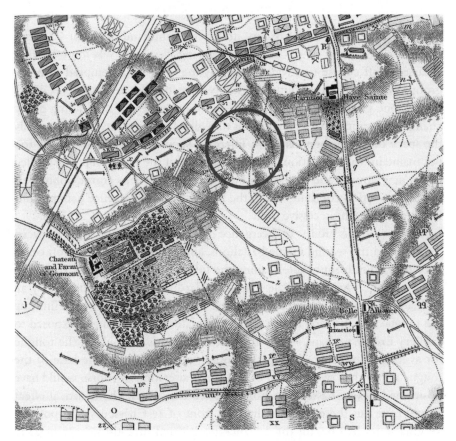

The Tongue.
This land feature notably contributed to the Garde's change of formation. The map, from which this is extracted, was engraved in October 1816 and so predates the destruction of the feature (ringed) that I have called the tongue. The hachuring indicates a rising slope, so the white area is the plateau referred to by several eyewitnesses. The tongue is illustrated in colour plate No 3.

Like any good infantry officer, let us look first at the ground. Reference has already been made to the tongue of land which projected forward from the ridge, roughly in the middle of the right centre of the Allied line, culminating in a knoll slightly higher than the ridge itself. It is clearly shown (in colour plate 3) in a watercolour painting by Charles Turner from drawings made by Captain George Jones and published on 20 May 1816, before the whole tongue was shovelled away to create the Lion Mound.

The explanation stems from Ney's sudden decision to veer leftwards as he led the 1/3e Grenadiers past La Haie Sainte. The effect of that divergence was to 'push' 4e Grenadiers sharply to its left, away from the leading battalion, so that it struck the Allied line nearly 250m further west, as is clear from Map 7. Following the rules of battlefield etiquette, the next battalion was the senior châsseur battalion, 1/3e Châsseurs, under the command of Major Cardinal. The knock-on effect of 4e Grenadiers' veering westwards was to push 1/3rd Châsseurs off course (see Map 7). As anyone who has attempted to move groups of people across country in line will recognise, any change of direction by one group has a knock-on effect on the others. If the leading group changes direction it takes time for this to register with the next group. Initially the space between them narrows. Then the second group alters course too but maintains the correction beyond the moment the first group has steadied on its new course, and so the gap between them widens considerably. This reaction to action continues down the line, with the divergence being amplified between each successive unit.

At Waterloo this process of divergence created a gap of some 250m between the first and the second Garde battalions, and sent the third battalion on to a separate, roundabout route, leading the following five battalions. It is quite apparent when looking at the map that Cardinal, forced to the left by 4e Grenadiers' change of direction, decided that – to avoid the steep climb up the tongue and the long march across the 'plateau' of the tongue exposed to artillery fire or, perhaps, simply to shelter from this fire behind the tongue for as long as possible – the better route would be round the base of the tongue rather than over the top of it. A sharp alteration of course would have positioned 1/3e Châsseurs in front of 2/3e Châsseurs. The identical effect would have put these two battalions in front of 4e Châsseurs. It is possible 4e Châsseurs had begun the advance positioned directly in rear of 2/3e Châsseurs, being 'refused' in contemporary parlance, to provide flank protection against cavalry (a threat that, judging by the battalions being in square, was evidently being taken seriously). Yet another possibility is that the commander of the 4e Châsseurs was unwilling to shift further to his left because of the threat of enfilade fire from au Goumont, parts of which were still occupied by Allied troops.

There are two further possible reasons why the battalion commanders may have decided to change from the prescribed formation of line in echelon into column of battalions. The first is that they may have considered the echeloned line formation to be potentially ineffective (in spite of Ney's known enthusiasm for it), whereas a column of battalions had the back-up and penetrating power that was obviously required. Unknown to them the châsseurs had already been proved right, by the failures of the two grenadier battalions. The second reason – pure surmise but based on modern experience – is that there was probably a sense of rivalry between grenadiers and châsseurs, just as there used to be and may still be, between the British Grenadier and Coldstream Guards for example. Such competitive spirit would naturally have led the châsseurs to tackle a similar problem with a different solution.

Whatever the reasons, the châsseurs of the Middle Garde had now formed a column of battalions (see Map 8).

What were the Old Garde battalions doing in the meantime? Most historians dismiss the Old Garde reserve, suggesting that the three battalions merely watched what happened to the Middle Garde and then retired out of harm's way. This must be nonsense. The aim of a reserve in attack is to back up the troops ahead of it, not to stand back and watch the attack fail. Is this really the likely action of veterans whose only desire was to serve and die for their emperor? Certainly General Petit did not think so. His firsthand account, with the phrase 'pas de charge', supports the likelihood of the Old Garde's involvement, although of only two battalions:[2]

> Meanwhile, the two 2nd battalions of Grenadiers and Châsseurs of the 2nd regiments had been brought up at the pas de charge, commanded by Generals Christiani and Pelet.[3]

Petit believed that 2/1er Châsseurs, under Cambronne, had remained with Napoleon near La Belle Alliance. However, he seems to have been mistaken – that Old Garde battalion was shortly to be pursued by Colonel Hugh Halkett from near au Goumont. It may be that Cambronne's battalion was initially reserved by Napoleon but moved forward on its commander's own initiative and had just caught up to become the sixth of the column of battalions. Alternatively, Cambronne may not have quite reached the column of battalions but it seems certain, as will become apparent later, that he and his men were somewhere in the valley bottom when the column of battalions was broken.

In order to allay any suspicion that the evidence that follows was a fabrication by officers of the 52nd it is worth noting now that two of the four prime witnesses – Lieutenant George Gawler and Ensign William Leeke – fell out in public over their differing interpretations of the event. It is well known that, if a story has been invented and witnesses have agreed to tell a set version, all accounts will probably be identical. There is no such collusion evident here, despite Colborne and Leeke agreeing on most points. This agreement is explicable on two grounds. They were both placed in the centre of the 52nd's line (although Colborne would have been mounted and mobile) so shared a similar viewpoint but, nevertheless, each man adduced evidence not shared by the other. We must not forget, too, that Leeke, at the time of the battle, was a very young and inexperienced officer who would quite naturally have seen Colborne as a role-model, if not the object of hero worship: Leeke had lent Colborne his cloak for the battle. The one would naturally follow the other's lead. We are fortunate that the other two witnesses were posted at extreme ends of the 52nd's line, Gawler on the right and Cross on the left.

Colonel Sir John Colborne, 1778–1863.
In 1794 he was commissioned into 20th of Foot and gained all subsequent promotions without recourse to purchase. Exchanged into the 52nd in 1811, he commanded the assault on a commanding fort at the siege of Cuidad Rodrigo, when he was wounded twice. He led the 2nd Brigade during the battles of the Pyrenees, with distinction. Retired as Field Marshal Lord Seaton. Latterly lieutenant governor of Upper Canada.

Our first witness to the blow that broke the Garde is Colborne, who had served in the Peninsular War with both Sir John Moore and the Duke of Wellington. Under the latter he had often commanded a brigade and so was well known to Wellington and largely trusted by him, although Colborne is said to have had a reputation for rashness. In an army accustomed to doing only what was ordered by its commander, to avoid incurring his displeasure by making an error through taking independent action, it was probably easy for initiative to be considered rash. Colborne's description of the body of troops he watched, climbing towards the ridge top to his left was that 'The Great Column was formed in … squares of battalions.'[4] So there we have further support for believing the unusual choice of square for the attack formation – experience gained in Spain would have enabled him to make the distinction. His use of 'Great' and 'battalions' in the plural, must surely indicate this was a column of several battalions and certainly not a single battalion, the 4e Châsseurs, as is suggested in many modern versions of the Crisis.

George Gawler, commanding the 52nd's right-hand company reported precisely the route taken by this body of the Garde (although at this stage of the post-battle correspondence – 1834 – he seems still not to have been aware of the previous attacks by two grenadier battalions) but he does confirm that the Garde had come round the tongue, not over it. By 'Moyenne leading' he as good as says there were Old Garde battalions behind the Middle Garde:

Brevet Lieutenant Colonel Sir Charles Rowan, 1782–1852. Born in Ireland, of Scottish descent. Commissioned into the 52nd as ensign in 1797, he so impressed General Sir John Moore that he bought Rowan his captaincy. Thereafter all his promotions were on merit. By 1809 he was brigade major to the Light Division and assistant adjutant general in 1811. He was colborne's second in command at Waterloo. He eventually commanded the 52nd in Ireland until, on retirement, he was given the task of setting up the Metropolitan Police, which he commanded for twenty-one years.

> ... the Enemy pushed on very heavy masses composed *entirely* of the Guard, the *Moyenne* leading rather on the Western side of the projecting tongue of ground.[5]

Colborne recognised that this column of battalions represented a major threat to the Allied line and, having discussed with Lieutenant Colonel Charles Rowan, one of his wing commanders, 'the necessity of menacing the flank of the French Columns', he decided the 52nd should advance.[6] His regiment, as ordered previously by Wellington, was in a four-deep formation, an order best complied with – in Colborne's opinion – by positioning the left half of each company (a subdivision) in rear of the right half. This would have kept each company as a compact unit with its company commander on its right front with sufficient space between the two lines (each of two ranks) for wheeling to left or right by half-companies, if the need arose. This displayed the wisdom of an experienced campaigner:

> The 52nd thus, at seven o'clock, were formed into two lines not four deep, but each left sub-division in rear of its right, the whole forming two complete lines, the rear line keeping the wheeling distance of a subdivision from the front line.[7]

Colborne then said to the adjutant, Captain Winterbottom, 'We must bring the regiment up on their flank,' to which Winterbottom replied, 'We cannot do it; we cannot wheel the regiment.' To which Sir John replied, 'Wheel the left company, and the others will conform to it.'[8] Left wheeling the whole regiment with a frontage of over 200 yards would have had the right-hand men sprinting to keep up, whereas a left form would have been practicable, with the left-hand company as marker. This movement was as per Sir John Moore's instructions, and is illustrated in the appendix. Sir John Moore had suggested retaining the command 'Left wheel' while actually executing the left form. Winterbottom seems to have forgotten this: and he the Adjutant, too! (See Map 11, Colour section.)

It is important to stress that his forward movement out of the line was carried out entirely on Colborne's own initiative, with no direction from any senior commander. Referring to himself in the third person Colborne wrote:

> He received no directions from anyone for the wheeling of the regiment and the attack on the flank of the French column …[9]

This decision must have required courage and confidence on Colborne's part, founded on his years of fighting in the Peninsula, because Wellington was notorious for insisting that major decisions of this sort should be left to him alone. Colborne risked not only Wellington's ire but almost the whole continent's opprobrium by opening a large gap in the front line, a dangerous manoeuvre had there been an enemy force able to take advantage of the opportunity offered.

Colborne continued: 'The French column being, as usual, flanked by skirmishers …' this is the first mention by Colborne of skirmishers and it seems unlikely there were any, since the French were in square against the threat of cavalry. Equally, there is no definite evidence of skirmishers contacting the hidden British line before the squares themselves did. Was Colborne mistaking – as did Leeke, as we hear in a moment – the remnant of the 4th Grenadiers for skirmishers? They were certainly in view because Colborne offered the 'skirmishers' as a target to the riflemen on the right of the Light Brigade:

> Sir John Colborne desired to throw out some answer to them, and requested the officer commanding two companies of the Rifle Corps (attached to the brigade) to deploy for this purpose.

These two companies must have been those of the 3/95th. According to some accounts, these two companies were formed on the right of the 71st, and therefore some considerable distance from the 52nd but Colborne's action suggests the riflemen were between the 52nd and the 71st. The 2/95th was on the 52nd's immediate left but to have depleted the latter in the face of the oncoming attack would have been unthinkable:

> He refused, and then Sir John Colborne ordered out the right [his error – left] companies of the 52nd, checking, for the moment, the advance of the regiment.[10]

Now we hear from Captain William Rowan who had joined the 52nd in 1803 and was afterwards a Field Marshal, had served at Corunna and in the Peninsula, earning the General Service Medal and eight bars. Rowan explains that the 52nd's strength was actually about 1,000, not its stated strength of 1,148, as absentees would include sick, batmen and detached. He may also not have taken account of casualties incurred during the actions beside au Goumont with both cavalry and infantry and also from artillery fire, both French and Allied, the latter being limited hitherto to shrapnel, fired over the men's heads – more 'friendly' fire was to come in a few seconds. Rowan refers here to the 52nd as 'the Regiment' as it had received all the able bodied men from the second battalion, which had already returned to England. Because the Guards Brigade had lost some 500 men at Quatre-Bras the 52nd was now the strongest British battalion at Waterloo.

As the 52nd moved forward again, William Rowan, tells us that Charles Rowan, his elder brother, was 'knocked off his horse about the same time we wheeled to the left, by the fire from the flank men of the French column and previously to our returning the fire', by which he may mean the Garde's volley, although there is a more likely alternative culprit, who will be revealed shortly.[11] John Cross takes up the story as Colborne ordered out his No 9 Company, now the left-hand company, No 10 Company (Lieutenant Anderson and around 100 men) having already gone forward to skirmish, suffering many casualties including two out of its three officers:

> Captain Cross commanded [what was now] the left company [No 9] of the 52nd Regiment … And at the period now generally termed the crisis of this battle, Captain Cross by *order of Sir John Colborne*, wheeled his company about the eighth of a circle, [The Garde's line of advance was not at right angles to the Allied line, but approaching diagonally up the re-entrant] to the left in order to effect a change of position [in other words, to act as left marker for the 52nd's change of position], so as to throw the front of the 52nd line on the left flank of the French attacking column …[12]

As soon as the skirmishers fired on the French, the latter halted and 'formed a line facing the 52nd'.[13] This suggests the companies forming the sides of the Garde squares were able to turn outwards instantly, a movement that would have been much slower and more disorganised had the battalions not been in square. While the 52nd was carrying out the left-form to bring it parallel to the Garde's flank, Major General Frederick Adam, the Light Brigade's commander, came up and asked, 'What are you about?' to which Colborne tells us he replied, 'Don't you see that advancing column?'[14] In case that sounded too much like a disrespectful response to a superfluous question, in his reply to Siborne's letter (which he may have suspected would eventually be published, hence referring to himself in the third person) Colborne says he replied, 'to make that column feel our fire', toning down somewhat his obvious sense of irritation.[15] Adam made himself useful by riding away to order the 71st to follow and support the 52nd. At some stage he was wounded in the knee but continued to ride behind his brigade.

Meanwhile the 52nd, in two lines (each line of two ranks) of half-companies, the rear line at ten paces distance from the front, gave the standard British three cheers on advancing. With several years of campaigning behind him, Colborne knew that rapid action was the key to success. Not waiting for his entire regiment to come parallel to the Garde, Colborne gave the historic order. John Cross again:

> … and as soon as either *two or three* of the companies on the left of this line had fired, Sir John Colborne ordered the line to charge, which broke the French column …[16]

This gives the lie to versions of the Crisis that talk of a lengthy musketry duel between the 52nd and the Garde. Moreover, Colborne was adamant no other unit (he was referring to the Guards) fired before the 52nd and he made no mention of French artillery. All the French guns were on the Garde's battalions' right flanks so, mercifully, they could not be deployed against Adam's brigade, and were swept away in the rout.[17] However Colborne reports little action by the Allied artillery either:

> The guns under Colonel Gould [Gold] on the cross-road [i.e. along the ridge] were all silent, there was scarcely any firing except in rear [i.e. the allied side] of La Haye Sainte and on that part of our centre.[18]

The firing 'in rear of La Haie Sainte' was probably the French cannonade that was suppressing the Brunswickers and Nassauers. Ramsay's battery had been firing at the Garde since it set off but those cannon too were now silent.

Ensign William Leeke, 1797–1879. He was the youngest ensign at Waterloo, where he carried the 52nd's regimental colour. He proudly wears his Waterloo Medal. Author of *The History of Lord Seaton's Regiment* in which he wrote 'the truth, with regard to what we knew the 52nd had achieved at Waterloo, ought to see the light.' He was rrdained priest in 1830 and in 1840 appointed perpetual curate of St Michael's Church, Holbrook in Derbyshire.

Gawler confirms the lack of artillery support, probably from lack of ammunition or, possibly, from being suppressed by the Garde's supporting artillery firing until its target was masked by the leading Garde battalion.[19] Colborne also mentions Byng's brigade (meaning Maitland's brigade under Byng as divisional commander) was stationary and not firing – as we learnt in the previous chapter, they had run out of ammunition.[20]

But some of the artillery was still firing. Lieutenant Maule, RA, was with Rogers' battery's five cannon in their third position during the battle, at the angle formed by the 2/1st Guards and the 2/95th. He perfectly remembers 'the French Guard coming up in front, and nearly to our Guards, and their being taken in flank by Adam's Brigade and my guns', which had been reduced to three at that stage.[21] In fact his men were dangerously overactive. Corporal Aldridge of the 2/95th recounted that one artilleryman, lying under his gun, jumped up and loosed off two or three guns, just as the six companies of the 2/95th passed through them.[22] Aldridge does not mention any casualties to 2/95th arising from this salvo but the 52nd may not have been so lucky, as we shall shortly hear.

Ensign William Leeke takes up the story. Leeke had been with the 52nd for only five weeks and was glad to have been nominated to carry the regimental colour since he had no experience of commanding troops in battle. He was fortunate – the ensign who had been carrying the King's colour was already dead, bowled over by a round shot, along with his colour serjeant, while retiring from the 52nd's post in the valley forward of the line during the cavalry attacks. Leeke himself had already narrowly escaped a similar fate. Earlier in the battle, after standing in square forward of the line for about an hour, a shaft of sunlight had drawn his attention to a brass cannon, which a French gunner was assiduously loading. It was pointing directly at his square and when it was discharged he saw the ball flying directly at him:

> I thought, shall I move? No! I gathered myself up, and stood firm, with the colour in my right hand, but I think two seconds elapsed from the time that I saw this shot leave the gun until it struck the front face of the square. It did not strike the four men in rear of whom I was standing, but the four poor fellows on their right. It was fired at some elevation, and struck the front man about the knees, and coming to the ground under the feet of the rear man of the four, whom it most severely wounded, it rose and, passing within an inch or two of the colour pole, went over the rear face of the square without doing further injury. The two men in the first and second rank fell outward, I fear they did not survive long; the two others fell within the square. The rear man made a considerable outcry on being wounded, but on one of the officers saying kindly to him, 'O man, don't make a noise,' he instantly recollected himself and was quiet.

Leeke adds that a similar shot striking the 71st's square killed or wounded seventeen men. But now he was leaving the shelter of the ridge to advance the regimental colour as the focal point of the whole regiment. He was positioned in the centre of the front rank of the four-rank formation and in close proximity to his colonel, who was as usual riding in front of the centre of his regiment while his two lieutenant colonels led their respective wings:

> As we passed over the crest of our position, we plainly saw, about 300 or 400 yards from us, in the direction of La Belle Alliance, midway between the inclosures [*sic*] of Hougoumont and La Haye Sainte, … two long columns of the Imperial Guard of France, of about *equal* [original author's italics] length, advancing … in the direction of Maitland's Brigade of Guards … There was a small interval of apparently not more than twenty paces between the first and second column; from the left centre of our line we did not at any time see through this interval.[23]

It is fascinating to find Leeke recording 'Two long columns … of about equal length', which sounds like the three battalions of the Middle Garde, closely closed up, followed, with only a small gap, by the three battalions of the Old Garde, just as other evidence suggests. He seriously overestimated the French strength at 10,000, but that was understandable for a young man of little military experience.[24] However, aware of this possible criticism, he justifies his estimate on the grounds of his having seen all 6,833 men of Sir Henry Clinton's division on parade. He was still a long way out but his guess indicates there were a sizeable number of battalions involved. His description of two long columns (of battalions), one behind the other with a small interval between them is his way of reconciling what he saw with the subsequent myth of 'first and second columns'. In fact, it is probably confirmation that the three Middle Garde battalions had been joined by the two – possibly three – Old Garde battalions, the reserve.

Sceptics may argue that, because these witnesses are members of the 52nd, their evidence is inevitably partisan and hence suspect. That they are mostly of the Light Brigade is unavoidable since it was they alone who carried out the movement on the forward slope of the ridge and were therefore largely unseen by the Allied army on the reverse side of the ridge, and whose view was further obstructed by smoke. However there are some independent records of the action, which dispel doubts on this score. The clearest comes from Lieutenant Sandilands, now commanding Major Ramsay's Troop of Royal Horse Artillery, shown on Siborne's *Plan showing General Positions of Troops and Batteries of Artillery*, posted in front of the 71st, i.e. to the 52nd's right.[25] He claims his battery fired on the Garde columns from forming-up to arrival on the position but then ceased fire as:

> … the Duke of Wellington, who had brought up three Infantry Regiments from the right, deployed them on the flank of the French Columns, and shut them out from our view.[26]

Sandilands erred – not unreasonably – in concluding that Wellington had brought them, but here is a statement from a disinterested witness that confirms the duke was with the Light Brigade, and that the Light Brigade (there is absolutely no evidence to suggest it might have been any other) had struck the French columns (note the plural) in the flank. As his battery was positioned on the forward slope of the ridge between the 52nd and the 71st, Sandilands could hardly have been mistaken about the Light Brigade's movement itself.

Leeke continued by describing how the Garde's shouts of 'Vive l'Empereur' were answered by the three tremendous British cheers for the King. When the left of the regiment was in a line with the leading company of the Garde it began to mark time and the men automatically touched in to their left. The Garde battalions were now not quite 200 yards from the 52nd. Then came the order 'Right shoulders forward' to begin the left form. There was a slight dip (the re-entrant?) between the 52nd and the Garde. In this dangerous and exposed advance, Colborne was on the right of his regiment keeping an eye on a large mass of the enemy's cavalry.[27] That he was sensitive about cavalry was understandable since the 52nd, under his command at Albuera on 11 May 1811, was (uniquely for the British) broken by French cavalry whilst manoeuvring in line, caught in a sudden storm of rain and sleet which blinded them and soaked their musket charges.

Fortunately, at Waterloo, no cavalry attack developed and Leeke was able to concentrate on events around him, reporting that:

> From the left centre of the 52nd line we saw a numerous body of skirmishers of the Imperial Guard running towards, and then forming about 100 yards in front of, their leading column …
>
> I recollect seeing a French officer strike, with the flat of his sword, a skirmisher, who was running farther to the rear than the point at which the others were forming; at that time I could see 300 yards up the slope of the British position to our left, and not a British Regiment or a British soldier was in sight.[28]

All his life Leeke was convinced these Frenchmen were skirmishers, because he failed to register the existence of the first two grenadier battalions. Instead, being himself in the grip of the myth, he believed the 52nd had dealt with both the 'first' and 'second' columns, which – in his opinion – were separated by the 20-yard gap, of which he wrote earlier. But in this assumption, the observant young man was wrong – these were no skirmishers but the remnant of 4e Grenadiers, repulsed and much reduced in numbers, having taken the easiest and fastest route – the re-entrant – away from the charge by the 3/1st Guards (see Map 10 in colour section). Their officers, keen to resume the attack, were attempting to reform their battalion.

We can be sure they were not skirmishers – had they been they would not have been attempting to reform, let alone directly ahead of an advancing formed body. Skirmishers were trained to retire round the flanks of an oncoming column or line and to reform in the rear. If necessary they would lie down to allow the column to pass without hindrance. The survivors of a recently repulsed body were unlikely to behave in this manner. The large majority of the men would not have been of the light company so such evasive action would not have occurred to them. The officers would have been concentrating on stopping the flight and reforming. It is possible to make an informed guess at the likely numbers of these survivors of 4e Grenadiers. Captain Powell (whom we met in the previous chapter) claimed the Guards' volleys brought down 300 men.[29] Like all guesses about numbers in battle, that is almost certainly an over-estimate – 200 is probably nearer the mark.

The 4e Grenadiers began the battle about 520 strong, so the survivors numbered around 320.[30]

Leeke's mention of 'a numerous body of skirmishers', running back, seems not to have been picked up by any historian, possibly because it does not fit the myth. Yet it has great significance because it helps to confirm that 4e Grenadiers were on their own – had there been more than one battalion of the Garde pitted against the British Guards two alternative scenes should have presented themselves to Leeke, either there would have been many more 'skirmishers' reforming if the supporting battalion had also broken, or the more-or-less formed body of a supporting follow-up battalion would have been visible. Leeke would surely have reported the presence of a formed body but did not as there was none. However, there must have been some remnant of 4e Grenadiers after its repulse: they could not have disappeared into thin air. It is strange no historian seems to have recognised that Leeke's observation is the answer. He was in the right place at the right time, but reached the wrong conclusion. That in a roundabout way supports the credibility of his evidence.

The advancing column of battalions can now reasonably be considered to contain the three châsseur battalions of the Middle Garde and General Petit confirms at least two of the Old Garde battalions were involved in the attack and the subsequent rout by the 52nd. Completing the section of his report that was recorded at the start of this chapter, he continued with unusual Gallic understatement:

> Meanwhile, the two 2nd battalions of Grenadiers and Châsseurs of the 2nd regiments had been brought up at the pas de charge, commanded by Generals Christiani and Pelet. They were determined to regain the offensive, but the enemy continued their progress; there was disorder; it was necessary to retire.[31]

There remains the question of whether 2/1er Châsseurs had caught up with its fellow Old Garde battalions to join the fray. Lieutenant Gawler throws light on this by observing:

> That the flank of the Enemy was much longer than the front of the 52nd Regiment seems to be established by the fact (which I have verified from the Regimental Books) that the loss of men was as great in the right Companies as in the left.[32]

George Gawler tells us the 52nd's right flank was overlapped by the Garde. Because Captain Diggle had been wounded, Gawler was now in command of the right flank company, so he was best placed to know, but, by stating

Lieutenant George Gawler,
1795–1869.
He joined 52nd as an ensign in
1810, in January 1812 he went with
the 52nd to Spain and took part in
the capture of Badajos, wounded
and saved by one of his soldiers
who lost his own life in so doing.
He fought at Waterloo, assuming
command of the right-hand
company on Captain Diggles'
death as the regiment left the
line, then took his company on
detachment to see off a section of
French cannon during the 52nd's
advance. Lieutenant colonel by
1834. In 1838 he was appointed
governor of South Australia, where
droughts nearly destroyed the
colony but it was saved by Gawler,
who nevertheless was criticised
and replaced, but later exonerated.

that the *Regimental Record* showed this, by noting casualties were as bad at his end of the 52nd's line as they were elsewhere, he seems to be conscious of the possible accusations of self-interest that might arise from his simply declaring an overlap. A computation of column lengths would appear to support his point.

He is emphasising that the French column of battalions was at least as long as the 52nd's frontage, ensuring there were muskets facing the 52nd's extreme right wing. At 1,000 strong in four ranks with a parade ground distance of 27 inches per man (standard 21 inches for line regiments, plus an extra 6 inches for Light Infantry) the 52nd would have stretched for a minimum of 188 yards on a parade ground. To maintain such precise and close spacing would have been impossible at the charge, given the speed at which they were moving (at the double), the state of the ground and the obstacles underfoot. Let us assume the 52nd had a frontage of about 200 yards. What length would the Garde's column of battalions have been?

The first question must be, how strong were those six battalions? And to that there is no definitive answer. When an army is routed it is unrealistic to expect that precise strengths will have been recorded. The estimated strengths, based on Mark Adkins' figures – for there are none more convincing – are 530 for each battalion of 3e Châsseurs, 840 for 4e Châsseurs, 545 for the second battalion of 2e Grenadiers, 580 for 2/2e Châsseurs and 650 for 2/1er Châsseurs.[33] If we assume that the squares were equal sided (rather than oblong, each Garde battalion being comprised of four companies, rather than the six of Ligne battalions), then 530-strong battalions would have had sides totalling about 130 men. In three ranks they would have had frontages of forty-four men. Allowing 27 inches (like the British) per man, a forty-four-men sided square would have a side of 33 yards; 545-men 34 yards; 580-men 36 yards; 650-men 40 yards, and 840-men would form a square of 53 yards a side. Allowing 5 yards between battalions and 20 yards (as identified by Leeke) between the Middle and Old Garde contingents, the length of the column of battalions would have been 270 yards if 2/1er Châsseurs had joined, and 225 yards if it had not.

The comparable length of the 52nd of a maximum of 200 yards suggests the Garde column definitely included the two Old Garde battalions, 2/2e Grenadiers and 2/2e Châsseurs, and that 2/1er Châsseurs had probably joined them. However, the fact that the 52nd went into the charge before the right-hand companies had come fully into line suggests the Garde had a very considerable overlap, which explains why the three Old Garde battalions were able to retire in some sort of order. The crucial point to note is that (probably) six Garde battalions, comprising some 3,675 men to the 52nd's 1,000, were together at the moment the 52nd struck. Since it was standard practice to consider a balance of forces of three times the attacking force to one of the enemy to be essential to having a good chance of success, the balance here was massively inverted, emphasising both the risk Colborne had taken and the dramatic success of the 52nd's manoeuvre.

The calculation of the Light Brigade's total frontage, based on unit strengths published in 1816, each unit being in four-rank line and allowing 27 inches per man, is a total of 490 yards as follows:

52nd	1,000 men	frontage 200 yards
71st	800 men	frontage 150 yards
2/95th	580 men	frontage 105 yards
3/95th	190 men	frontage 35 yards[34]

But enough of arithmetic, it is time to return to the battle. Ensign Leeke describes how 'The Garde column of battalions did not halt and return the fire until it was fired on by No 5 Company.'[35] Leeke erred in specifying No 5 Company; the young and inexperienced ensign believed the 52nd's left wing (companies Nos 6–10) was in rear of the right wing (Nos 1–5), whereas Colborne said that the 52nd was in four ranks with each half-company (sub-division) behind it's other half. It was No 10 Company that was sent to skirmish.

Sending out the skirmishing company before changing direction may have been standard Light Infantry practice but was inspired in this instance. Colborne's problem was the precise timing required to bring the 52nd's left flank level with the moving target that was the head of the advancing column of battalions, given, too, that the latter was moving diagonally in relation to the 52nd's line of advance, while the 52nd had to be taken forward at least 100 yards, then formed to the left and then advanced to charging distance from the enemy. The solution was to halt the Garde column, to provide a stationary target. This the skirmishers achieved before they rejoined the 52nd:

> As the 52nd closed, No 5 Coy [company] fell back but two of the three officers were severely wounded and many men killed.

No 9 Company, under Captain Cross, was wheeled to the left to act as the 52nd's left marker.

To the volley and charge it is clear the Garde responded in kind with an effective, even if rushed and ragged, volley, possibly two. Leeke continues:

> The 52nd opened fire without halting. Though maintaining a compact line the 52nd occupied nearly double the normal depth of a four rank line.

In other words, the front rank halted and fired and subsequent ranks passed through and fired in turn while those who had fired 'partly halted' to reload, in accordance with Sir John Moore's instructions. This is another nail in the coffin for accounts which speak of a prolonged fire fight. The 52nd's musketry is likely to have been more effective than that of a line battalion since men of the latter were ordered simply to 'level' their muskets whereas light infantry were taught – and commanded – to 'aim', and, what is more, they had rear sights on their light infantry pattern muskets, a luxury not deemed necessary for line infantrymen. Volleying by rank on the move and reloading on the move too, is evidence of the 52nd's high state of training. And it is fascinating to discover how little musketry was needed before the Garde broke, as Leeke describes:

> As we closed towards the French Guard, they did not wait for our charge, but the leading column [of battalions, i.e. the three the Middle Garde battalions before the 20-yard gap] at first somewhat receded from us, and then broke and fled; a portion of the rear column also broke and ran; but three or four battalions of the Old Guard, forming part [all?] of this second column,

retired hastily, in some degree of order, towards the rising ground in front of La Belle Alliance, with a few pieces of the artillery of the Guard, which must have been on their right flank when they advanced, as we did not see them, and those which were left by the gunners on the ground, until the French Guard had given way; indeed, had those guns been on the left flank of the columns of the Imperial Guard, when we were bringing our right shoulders forward, they might have plied our line with grape, and have caused us the most serious loss; or, possibly, had they been there, Sir John Colborne would not have ventured on the movement at all.[36]

The 52nd was indeed fortunate not to have to contend with the Garde's guns. Some may have been dispersed by the rout but some of those with the Old Garde battalions retained their cohesion and appear in the record, if only briefly, a few minutes later, in the next chapter. But the 52nd had to face Allied gunfire, as well as musketry from the Garde.

William Rowan says his brother Charles 'was knocked off his horse about the time we wheeled to the left, by the fire from the flank men of the French column and previously to our returning the fire'.[37] William Rowan's horse, was killed and Charles wounded by canister shot. According to Leeke, Colborne also lost his horse at this moment, just before the charge.[38] Later, both Colborne and William Rowan, finding some French horses still attached to abandoned French guns (presumably those sections supporting the Garde) mounted them and asked their men to cut the traces. But they were unable to oblige since no one had a knife and the issue musket bayonet had no edge. The two officers had to dismount hurriedly.

Fortunately they soon found many loose, saddled horses.[39] For field officers (major and above) to be mounted was essential, not laziness. A horse enabled them to roam and transmit orders speedily, as well as providing the extra height to see over their own troops and undulating ground, looking especially for approaching cavalry. Colonel Colborne encouraged all his officers to be mounted because – as William Leeke reminds us – mounted officers were more useful in very many ways; they were less tired after a long march and more ready for other duties; they were able to bring up stragglers in a long march; they could be used as extra staff officers if required. But at Waterloo all officers' mounts, except those of field officers, had been sent to the rear.

Several writers say Colborne's horse was shot by a 52nd man. Whilst admitting that mistakes can occur with even the best trained men, this calumny, nevertheless, seems most unlikely to be true. We heard from Cross and Leeke that only the left-hand companies of the 52nd actually fired and Colborne was well away from them, somewhere to the right of the 52nd, scouting for enemy cavalry. It is much more likely that the animals and Charles Rowan –

and possibly many of Colborne's men, especially in the two companies that were acting as skirmishers and markers – were hit by canister shot from the over-keen gunner of Rogers' troop of 9-pounders, who, as recounted earlier, loosed off his guns without checking his aim, just as the 2/95th advanced through them. Indeed, Roger's troop may have accounted for a major proportion of the 52nd's 130 plus casualties, as well as several horses.

Before we leave the critical moment when possible victory for Napoleon (at least on this side of the battlefield) was turned into defeat, we must re-examine the claim in some versions of the Crisis that the British Guards were firing at the head of the 'second' column while the 52nd – sometimes implausibly said to be the entire Light Brigade – was attacking its flank. This contentious claim was considered in some depth in the previous chapter but there are further points that confirm it is untenable.

First we hear from Captain John Cross, who was commanding the 52nd's left-hand company, and, hence, would have been best placed of all the 52nd officers to observe the Guards' actions, or the lack of them.[40] He reiterates that the start of the 52nd's advance was the deployment of a strong company under Lieutenants Anderson and Campbell (George, not Patrick Campbell, from whom we hear later) to skirmish. He states the Guards were stationary and not firing and that the 52nd was about 200 yards in front, which we might interpret as meaning the Regiment had advanced that distance before beginning its wheel to the left. Cross's company was the battalion's left-hand marker, upon which the remainder would have formed.

There are disparities between the various accounts about the distance the 52nd moved forward, disparities which might cause doubt about their veracity. They should not. The cause of these differences is essentially the considerable length of the 52nd's front. Cross, on the left flank, had less far to advance before wheeling than did Leeke in the centre before starting the left-form, and Gawler on the right flank had farthest of all to travel. Cross was aimed at the head of the oncoming column of battalions and thus left space for the 2/95th to wheel and disperse the reforming 4e Grenadiers, who must have been at least 100 yards down the slope.

Next we have a statement by Lieutenant Thomas Smith, who was the adjutant of the 2/95th, on the immediate right of the Guards Brigade. Just as Corporal Aldridge could not see 2/1st Guards, neither could Lieutenant Smith, so he did not register the repulse of 4e Grenadiers. Instead, judging by his description of the Guards' 'near being driven out of their own position', he probably saw them recovering from the rush back to the ridge after their successful charge. The Guards do not sound as if they were sufficiently recovered at this crucial moment to be able to fire at an approaching column. This is what Smith said:

I have no hesitation in stating that I firmly believe the 1st Brigade of Guards were in rear of the cross roads [NB Not the modern meaning] which runs along the ridge of the position and unites the two high roads upon this head I am positive for a short time previous to the crisis the battalion I belonged to being stationary in square I rode to the left for the purpose of looking at the Brigade of Guards in action and they were certainly in the rear of the road and neither as I think they ever crossed it, and as far from their having driven back the attacking column, they were very near being driven out of their own position and which would most decidedly have been the case had it not been for Sir F. Adam's brigade and a brigade of cavalry [presumably he is referring to Vivian's Brigade of Light Cavalry, which came through the line an appreciable time after the Light Brigade's departure. Smith would not have witnessed this. See chapter 10] which charged on the moment of the former brigade [Adam's] moving to its left …[41]

Smith's punctuation – or rather the lack of it – is all his own. Finally, apropos the question as to whether or not the Guards were involved in routing the final Garde attack, it is worth quoting Colborne, writing in the third person:

On our approach the French halted and retired in confusion, receiving a severe fire from the two … [indecipherable, but clearly referring to the 52nd and the 2/95th] regiments which, bringing up their left shoulders, [now heading diagonally across the battlefield] pursued them so that the 52nd passed over the ground on which the enemy's column had advanced. It is evident that had the guards charged the head of the column, they must have been intermingled with the left of the 52nd, [not to mention the 2/95th!] whereas, in fact, as to Byng's Brigade [referring to Byng's commanding the division which included the 1st Guards Brigade] they were stationary, doing nothing, like a regiment on parade, and this was accounted for shortly after by Sir John Byng, who told Colborne that they had no ammunition left, adding, 'I was very glad to see you coming in our front.'[42]

The lack of ammunition was real: we have already heard how Henry Rooke had been sent to find more but had not returned by the time the Crisis occurred. We must now complete Captain Smith's statement to highlight the involvement of his battalion in the coup de grâce:

… and when the 2nd 95th Regiment gave their fire I do not think the final column could have been more than twenty paces from them and which fire well given in made most dreadful slaughter.[43]

Having the shortest distance to travel before making contact with the disordered remnants of 4e Grenadiers, these six companies of the 2/95th met little or no resistance at this stage of their advance and held their fire until only twenty yards separated them from their adversaries, who, desperately trying to reform ahead of the approaching column of battalions, were probably unaware of the blow about to hit them.

Captain Budgen of the 2/95th assumed the duke had ordered the Light Brigade's advance:

> ... Immediately before or during the right shoulder movement of the Brigade, the Duke of Wellington rode along our line. I conclude he himself directed the movement. It was the only moment I saw him during the day. He spoke to the men, they cheered him in return.[44]

Most officers, certainly all who were not actually involved in the 52nd's action, would naturally have reached the same conclusion, that Wellington had directed the movement, since no one else could have dared to take such an extraordinary risk. Indeed, it is probable that he set the 2/95th in motion since there is no record of General Adam having so ordered and Adam was at this moment on his way to bring forward the 71st. On the other hand the duke's involvement may be questioned not only because of Budgen's saying he may have appeared 'during' the left wheel – in other words the movement had already started – but also because, at what must have been a time of great urgency, he had the time to speak to the men. But the most telling reason for giving Wellington the credit is that it is unlikely even a Rifles' commanding officer would have dared move out of the line without a senior officer's sanction, especially if the latter was in the vicinity. But there is no doubt that the 2/95th was hurriedly wheeled out of the line and, being on the inside of the circle, came up along side, or perhaps slightly in rear of, the 52nd (see Map 11, colour section). That the riflemen were able to cross in front of the Guards Brigade, without – apparently – suffering casualties from the latter is a further pointer to the Guards' not firing at the head of the Garde column of battalions.

So, two units of Adam's Light Brigade were on their way – what of the third unit, the 71st with two companies of the 3/95th? General Adam himself, after speaking briefly to Colborne, had ridden off to order forward the 71st Light Infantry, and to request support from General Clinton to cover his brigade's right flank.

The 71st, under the command of Colonel Thomas Reynell, had advanced on the orders of General Adam. Having been posted in the line on the right of the 52nd, the 71st, also in four ranks, had a considerable distance to wheel before they could form line with the 52nd but, as they too were light infantry, this was not a serious problem. However, their advance took their right flank close to the corner of the au Goumont enclosure, from the cover of which some French were able to kill or wound several of the Scots, as they passed.[45]

With the 71st came the two companies of 3/95th, one of them commanded by Brevet Major William Eeles, posted to the right rear of the 71st. Thus the start of the brigade's counter-attack was probably not visible to him. He himself says smoke prevented his seeing what happened initially but he advanced with the 71st and, when the smoke cleared, he found they were 'moving between both armies, and driving some French before us in the greatest disorder'. His company was sent out to skirmish while the other remained between the 52nd and the 71st.[46] Last – but by no means least – a battalion of the 3rd Hanoverian Brigade joined the advance, apparently at the request of General Adam to General Clinton, the 2nd (British) Division's commander, for support, expressly to cover the Light Brigade's flank, which was now dangerously exposed to cavalry attack. The 3rd Hanoverian Brigade's commander, Colonel Hugh Halkett, led out the Osnabrück Landwehr Battalion and sent his Brigade Major, Captain von Saffe, to bring forward two of the other three battalions of his brigade. Unfortunately von Saffe was killed en route and the order was never delivered. The Osnabrückers' fortunes will be traced in a later chapter.

When examined in detail, the 52nd's claim to have trounced the major and final part of the Garde's assault at Waterloo is entirely credible, yet, not unexpectedly, there are very few independent accounts of the 52nd's action. This may be because the bulk of evidence about the battle was gathered at least a decade after the event and after the myth of the Guards having gained the victory had taken firm hold of the nation's psyche. Many witnesses must have had conflicting thoughts about speaking out or keeping quiet. Of the former there are three interesting examples. The first comes from an officer also of the Light Brigade, Captain S. Reed, who was in command of the right flank company of the 71st. He explicitly recounts that:

As you [Siborne] particularly mention the hour of seven, I have marked [on a general plan] our advance, bringing our right shoulders forward, leaving Hougoumont to our right. In this movement the Regiment was formed four deep, supporting the 52nd in a charge on the Imperial Guard, who, I think, were either in square or column.[47]

The second account – admittedly hearsay – is convincing nonetheless, since it comes from an officer of the 1st Foot Guards no less. In 1835 Captain William Moore wrote:

> I regret extremely that it is not in my power to give you any information,
> worthy of communication, respecting the position of the 2nd Division at
> the moment you have selected, [the Crisis] as I was at that time in the wood
> (or orchard) of Hougoumont. You will of course have learnt from various
> publications that the 52nd Regiment, commanded by Sir John Colborne,
> brought up its right shoulders and fired into the flank of the Columns [note
> plural] of the Imperial Guard, which was advancing to the attack of our
> centre. It is certain that the movement took place, although I did not see it
> myself from the cause I have above mentioned.[48]

So, although not an eyewitness, Moore was convinced of the 52nd's action
and of the strength of the column of battalions. Since he was an officer of the
1st Foot Guards, his failure to support his regiment's claim to fame (which is
examined later) and his alternative support of the 52nd might not have made
him popular with his fellow officers – perhaps this accounts for his later transfer to the 60th Rifles, of which he would latterly be colonel-in-chief.

Moore's letter to Siborne is coincidentally – but intriguingly – juxtaposed,
in Gareth Glover's *Letters from the Battle of Waterloo*, with another from an
officer also of the 1st Foot Guards. Both were staff officers on the headquarters of 3rd Infantry Brigade – the Light Brigade. Yet their accounts of the
breaking of the Garde could not be more different. Captain Lord Charles
Fitzroy has 'the Guards' – he does not specify whether this was the 3/1st
Guards or the entire Guards Brigade – brought forward 'on the left of Adam's
brigade with a wide interval', the latter having been ordered to advance.
He then colourfully claims:

> The whole advancing brought the Guards in immediate contact with the
> Imperial Guards; an honour which others (Adam's brigade) claimed, but
> had no more right [to] than a ship in sight when another ship engages and
> captures an enemy.[49]

Fitzroy was both mistaken and right. He was correct in believing 3/1st Guards
had repulsed the Garde – but only one battalion thereof – without the help of
the 52nd, but was, apparently, unaware that the 52nd had then despatched the
last five or six battalions unaided by the Guards.

It is expecting too much of French historians to give a full and true
account of the Garde's discomfiture but one – Edgar Quinet – although not
an eyewitness was sufficiently confident of his facts to record, in 1862, the
name of the regiment he concluded was responsible for the Garde's demise.
Admittedly he does not specify how many battalions or what proportion of
the Garde was crushed but his words surely signify it was the main part:

The 52nd Charging the Imperial Guard at Waterloo.
One of very few depictions of the event, and perhaps less evocative than the cover image, but useful.

Le 52e régiment Anglais [52nd English regiment] en profite venire auda-cieusement se déployer sur le flanc gauche. Quand le régiment Anglais l'eut débordée [outflanked it] tout entière, il ouvrit son feu á brûle-pourpoint [point blank range] … qui l'écrasait [crushed it].[50]

But that was only an historian's opinion; the soldier on the spot knew what had happened but felt he had to be more circumspect. General Petit put the French situation in the best light possible, but the rout had clearly started:

They [the Old Garde battalions] were determined to regain the offensive, but the enemy continued their progress; there was disorder; it was necessary to retire … The whole army was in the most horrible disorder, infantry, cavalry, artillery all hurrying in all directions.[51]

So the 52nd, supported by its comrades in the Light Brigade, had routed the bulk of the Garde's assault force, Napoleon's last opportunity to achieve victory, however forlorn it might seem to have been in the harsh light of hindsight. The 52nd's unprecedented and unexpected riposte to Napoleon's expected coup de grâce could only have been achieved by officers and men with the self-confidence and experience gained in years of war.

The three Middle Garde battalions were completely shattered by the 52nd's assault and disappear from the history of the battle from this moment. Their dispersal and the sight of the three battalions of the Old Garde in full retreat threw into confusion – but did not break – the left wing of the emperor's army, which had to be urged into a panicked rout by the Light Brigade's next move, a drive across the battlefield to the axis road before turning south to thrust at Napoleon near La Belle Alliance. Arguably even more important to the achievement of victory than the breaking of the Garde, the pursuit had begun.

In Summary

Care must be taken, when interpreting the term 'column', to differentiate between a battalion in column and a column of battalions. The column of Garde battalions had formed through the effect of Ney's change of direction causing a knock-sideways effect, combined with the influence of the tongue or spur that projected from the Allied ridge. That this important battlescape feature was eliminated to construct the Lion Mound is regrettable to say the least.

There is compelling evidence that the Old Garde battalions in reserve closed up from behind to join the column of châsseur battalions. The 2/1er Châsseurs, under Cambronne, may not have quite reached the column when the whole was blown apart by the 52nd's flank attack. That question is explored further in the next chapter. There is little doubt that the column of battalions was at least five battalions strong, around 3,000 men, representing nearly three-quarters of the total Garde force: a potent threat.

Although the bulk of evidence about the breaking of the Garde inevitably comes from officers of the 52nd who took part, there are other accounts confirming the event from officers with no obvious interest in falsifying the record.

The 52nd was brought forward out of the line and manoeuvred by Sir John Colborne, entirely on his own initiative. At the moment of contact between the 52nd and the Garde column of battalions there was no prolonged fire fight. One company of light infantrymen had been sent out to halt the column by engaging it: a stationary target was needed so the next left-hand company could be wheeled opposite the head of the column as a left marker for the 52nd. The remaining 800 men of the 52nd went into a left-form, anchored on the left-hand company, which had halted level with the head of the now-stationary column. Knowing that speed and surprise were his most potent weapons, Colborne – even before all the companies had reached a position parallel to the French – had the first two companies fire a volley – probably on the move (as described in the appendix) – before the regiment went straight into the charge. Talk of a ten-minute exchange of fire is fantasy. The three Middle Garde battalions were shattered but the Old Garde battalions retired in some sort of order. Sent forward by Wellington, the six companies of the 2/95th, on the 52nd's left, easily dispersed the remnant of 4e Grenadiers.

If any doubts about the total number of Garde battalions involved still linger, the arithmetic of frontages must dispel them. This was certainly not the single battalion – 4e Châsseurs – that so many accounts mistakenly count as the sole victims of the 52nd.

It is worth reiterating that the Guards neither fired nor charged at the head of this column of battalions, on the evidence of their brigade and battalion commanding officers. The 52nd was fortunate that the Garde's sections of horse artillery were posted on the right of their respective battalions and hence screened by the latter from firing on the regiment. The 52nd did, however, take casualties, not only from the Garde's volley but also from blind fire by British artillery.

So the Garde was broken and finally repulsed. The shock of seeing this sudden reversal of fortune must have seriously unsettled the French morale, but it is unlikely the rout occurred directly as a result of it. With the return of the Old Garde battalions to the French line it might have been possible to effect a fighting withdrawal. What happened next caused and maintained the rout.

9

DON'T LET THEM RALLY

The pursuit had begun, and one element of its success would be the speed of the Light Brigade's advance. Some accounts – including that of the 52nd's commanding officer – speak of the Light Brigade moving at the double (running). But in reality this cannot have been the parade ground double but more of a lope, and by no means in step. Nevertheless, it must have been an amazing sight. Their rapidity is all the more remarkable in light of the unspeakable 'going' they had to contend with, as Captain Albertus Cordemann faced when the 3rd Line Battalion of the KGL took part in the general advance:

> … we found such obstacles to our advance that at first we lagged behind, in part because the terrain was so soft and deep that people could only get through with some difficulty, and some lost their shoes in the process; in part also because the field before us was so covered with killed and wounded enemy soldiers and cuirassiers, horses and weapons of all sorts that we could not keep our ranks closed, but continually had to split up to avoid humans and horse, the latter of which often kicked about with their hoofs.[1]

Of course the men of the Garde would have found movement at speed equally trying, but they had panic to speed them on their way (see Map 12, colour section). Not unexpectedly there is no record of the direction taken by the three completely shattered Middle Garde battalions. Imagination suggests each man would have made a beeline for the perceived safety of the French position, retreating in an arc between south-east and due south, trying to escape the attentions of the pursuing light infantry. The three Old Garde battalions, shaken but not yet broken, retired diagonally across the battlefield towards the French command centre near La Belle Alliance. It seems that 2/2e Grenadiers, 2/2e Châsseurs and 2/1er Châsseurs all reached their objective.

The 52nd, flanked on its left by the six companies of the 2/95th, had been moving nearly parallel with the Allied line when it struck the Garde but now Colborne ordered left shoulders forward to change direction slightly to the right: the rest of the Light Brigade followed suit. It is intriguing to wonder what was in his mind. Did he have a clear plan or was he simply chasing the fleeing enemy and was loath to make a major change of direction for fear of losing impetus and allowing the broken battalions to reform. Why did he not turn more towards the French position and pursue the unbroken squares? It is reasonable to believe that he made a conscious choice, based on his very considerable experience in the Peninsular War. His new line of advance would not only sweep the broken Garde battalions off the field but would also outflank La Haie Sainte where the most serious threat to the Allied line lay. Intentional or not, it had the required effect, according to Major Leach of the 1/95th:

> A very short time (a few minutes only I think) before Picton's Division joined in the General Advance against the French position, the French suddenly evacuated the farmhouse of La Haye Sainte and the ground near it, and retreated in haste; and this, I conclude, was in consequence of the total repulse of the Imperial Guards, and the forward movement of a part of the Duke of Wellington's right wing.[2]

Most effectively of all, Colborne's choice of direction would bring his regiment and the Light Brigade to the axis road where a 90° change of direction would enable a thrust to be made at the nerve centre of the French Army – Napoleon. But the Light Brigade's progress was not to be without incident. Corporal Aldridge of 2/95th introduces a potentially catastrophic mistake by British cavalry. Previously he has noted in his statement, transmitted via George Gawler, the British 'friendly' artillery fire – now he introduces a 'friendly charge' by British cavalry:

> [Aldridge] Saw the 52nd move forward to the right of the 2nd 95th and charge these columns. About the same moment Wellington rode up and enquired who was in command. There was some hesitation as Colonel Norcott and Major Wilkins had just been wounded. Eventually Captain Logan gave the command 'Forward.'
>
> One artilleryman, lying under his gun, jumped up and loosed off two or three guns. Left of 2/95th passed through the guns. Joined immediately with the 52nd pursuing the enemy. Almost immediately saw small body of English Light Dragoons pass forward to his left, saw them driven back by French cavalry towards the front of the 52nd. Soon after a part of 2/95th extended to skirmish.[3]

Colborne himself describes how:

At this moment two or three squadrons of the 23rd Dragoons appeared ... approaching rapidly towards the [52nd's] line. The two Companies on the left halted and fired into them, supposing them to be the Enemy ... which interrupted our march. The Duke of Wellington came to the rear of the left of our line near the two Companies which had fired. I said to his Grace, 'It is our own Cavalry that has caused this firing.' His Grace replied, 'Never mind, go on, go on.'[4]

John Cross adds, 'the three adjoining companies wheeled back to form square'.[5] William Leeke injects a little more colour. He tells us how the cavalry was seen approaching just after the 52nd had passed the dead and wounded of the Garde.[6] When they were twenty yards off, the line opened about 6 or 8ft. Leeke thought this was bad form – they should be received on bayonets – and he tried to draw his sword but the sword-knot caught on the button of his scabbard. Giving up on his sword, he then took the colour staff in both hands to use it as a lance but the horseman was shot by a man of the 52nd and fell in front of Leeke, who then recognised him by his stripes as a British serjeant. More fell behind the 52nd's line than in front but then the mistake was recognised and firing ceased immediately. The uniform of the light dragoons was of a similar blue colour to those of the French grenadier à cheval.

Leeke rather tartly observes the need to avoid dressing like the enemy if 'friendly fire' is to be avoided. Given that the 23rd looked like Frenchmen and had charged directly at the 52nd it is hardly fair – as some historians do – to claim that the 52nd made the mistake. The controlled manner in which the light infantrymen changed from charge-in-line at the double into defensive square and back again into line also gives the lie to those who state the 52nd was 'in great disorder'. It is fair to say this interruption was unwelcome.

At this point it is necessary to sound a warning about some of the evidence attributed to Colborne by Colborne's son, James. In a memorandum, composed from his father's letters, conversations and other sources, he has the contretemps with the 23rd Light Dragoons occur before or while the 52nd struck the Garde's column of battalions.[7] He states 'the battalion at the time was under a heavy fire from the Imperial Guards'. This could not be true since the cavalry would have had to penetrate the Garde column to reach the 52nd.

How did the 23rd Light Dragoons report this event? Lieutenant John Banner says the mission of the 23rd Light Dragoons had been to dissuade some French cavalry from trying to silence Allied guns. His squadron drove the French cavalry back to a French square (could this have been 1/3e Grenadiers before their second advance, or men of Donzelot's who had taken La Haie Sainte?) behind which – he claims – the cavalry took shelter. The 23rd Light Dragoons took casualties from this square on retiring and '... and in consequence of their experiencing a similar annoyance on approaching the British line [the 52nd], they were induced to move to its flanks ...', eventually attaching themselves to the 18th Hussars in Vivian's brigade, despite a less-than-welcoming response from the Hussars' commanding officer, Lieutenant Colonel Henry Murray.[8] The 18th Hussars were part of Vivian's brigade so this establishes that this light cavalry brigade was still static within the Allied line while Adam's Light Brigade was already well on its way to La Haie Sainte, a fact that will have importance when the cavalry's contribution to the rout is considered.

Another officer of the 23rd Light Dragoons, Major P.A. Latour, made some slight amends by recording the 52nd's triumph:

> ... where we remained until the evening [when the enemy] on our right, led on by the Imperial Guards, advanced again to force the position occupied by the British, and in which they were successfully repulsed; and it struck me, as well as I could judge from the immense smoke and confusion at that moment, that a part of the Imperial Guards were [*sic*] overthrown and driven back by the 52nd Light Infantry.[9]

Charging one's own infantry might be considered poor form at the best of times – doing so at the very moment the infantry is trying to defeat Napoleon's final assault was unhelpful, to say the least. However, this was not an isolated instance of bad luck by the 23rd Light Dragoons. They had been part of the Peninsular army at the Battle of Talavera, during which Wellington decided to use his cavalry against some French infantry columns, who had fought the previous night and that morning, and were past their best. The 23rd Light Dragoons and the 1st Hussars KGL charged and the French formed square. The 23rd, at speed, fell foul of a hidden, dry watercourse and many came to grief. Some went on with the hussars to attack but the 23rd lost almost half its officers and men.

Despite writing approvingly of the charge in his despatch, Wellington nevertheless concluded – perhaps a little unfairly – that the 23rd Light Dragoons were of no further use and sent them back to England.[10] Apparently they were rehabilitated by 1815 and were present in Belgium. During the retirement from Quatre-Bras, the Dragoons blotted their reputation yet again by refusing Lord Uxbridge's request to attack some French lancers, when Uxbridge wished to rest the 7th Hussars. In disgust, Uxbridge ordered the 23rd Light Dragoons to stand aside and instead sent in the 1st Life Guards to repel the lancers.[11]

To be fair, this error at Waterloo is excusable. The sudden appearance of the 52nd and the rest of the Light Brigade way out in front of the Allied line had already caught the Garde by surprise: the dragoons would have found it equally unexpected. But this unfortunate riding at one's own infantry might have had serious consequences. Although the Garde had been broken, and disorder amongst the French frontline troops was beginning, there was no absolute certainty at this moment that the French Army would not be able to keep or recover its balance. Fortunately, however, the well-trained and experienced men of the 52nd were able to cope with this emergency without falling into confusion, forming square and then reforming line as if they were on a parade ground. Fascination with this unfortunate incident may have caused the reader to miss a statement whose importance will become apparent when we consider how and why the myth originally took hold:

> The Duke of Wellington came to the rear of the left of our line near the two Companies which had fired.[12]

The statement's significance lies in its establishing that Wellington had ridden out and joined the 52nd immediately after the breaking of the Garde and was present during the episode with the 23rd Light Dragoons. He could not have failed to witness the elimination of the final Garde assault. If Colborne's word is insufficient to prove the point then there is another witness. Another officer of the 52nd reported the duke's appearance from the left of his regiment, as would be expected as the 52nd was now moving at right angles to the Allied line. Captain Patrick Campbell tells how:

> … Having been on leave of absence, I was unable to join my regiment until about four o'clock on the memorable 18th June. I found it drawn up in line with the Rifles on its left, I think about an hour after I joined we were very sharply engaged with an immense column of the enemy who appeared to me to be retreating and in confusion, about this time the Duke came up to the left of the regiment, and was very much exposed to a sharp fire of musketry.[13]

This rather strange example of partial memory (written in 1834) has been used to claim that the Garde was already in retreat before the 52nd attacked but the evidence already adduced is surely sufficient to show Campbell was mistaken. Perhaps he did not think to mention the 52nd's movement out of line because he is admiringly describing the moment the duke joined them under fire. This lapse of memory might also be explained by the fact that Campbell retired on half pay in 1818 at his own request on account of his wounds, including the loss of an eye, having served throughout the Peninsular War, even commanding the 52nd at the battles of Nivelle and Nive, and being wounded twice. Campbell's mood may not have been improved by his having missed promotion to brevet lieutenant colonel by being absent from the 52nd when the battle started. The most important element of his evidence is his statement that Wellington joined the 52nd at the moment of sharp musketry, which – whether it was French or British canister – shows the 52nd had already left the line. In other words, not only did he confirm Wellington joined the Light Brigade after the 52nd broke the Garde, but it also shows that it cannot be claimed – as some accounts do – that the duke had both ordered and led the 52nd's movement out of line in the first place.

The men may have been cool under the stress of apparent cavalry attack but they and their officers were clearly exultant about their success. Colborne relates that he called for the officers commanding Nos 1 and 2 companies to come into

> … good line, [Being on the outside of the left form, they were having diffi-
> culty catching up.] and whilst I was restraining the disorderly impetuosity of
> these companies under great excitement, several officers in front, Colonel
> Churchill and Colonel Chalmers, were cheering and waving their hats and
> caps in front.[14]

Churchill and Chalmers had both been appointed brevet lieutenant colonel and had assumed command of the left and right wings of the 52nd, which was a thousand strong at the start of the battle and merited being subdivided. This was certainly not the usual English sangfroid! But perhaps such unseemly behaviour can be excused because they had just achieved something extra-ordinary. Colborne continued:

> At this time the 71st formed on our right flank and I ordered the bugles to
> sound the advance …[15]

However this announcement of the 71st's arrival may have been premature: there is evidence to suggest the 71st rejoined the other two battalions in the Light Brigade some minutes later.

The next event in the 52nd's progress, recorded by Leeke, which he says followed immediately after the Dragoons' debacle, was a shower of can-ister shot on the 52nd's right flank from guns in the direction of La Belle Alliance.[16] He believed (as logic suggests) these guns had been with the Old Garde battalions. Gawler, now commanding the right-hand company, asked if he should 'drive them in' and was ordered to do so. When the gunners saw the red coats advancing towards them they retired. Captain Cross recounted how the 52nd had pushed on:

> … as far as a small coppice to the right of La Haie Sainte where the 52nd
> and Rifle Corps made a momentary halt and opened fire upon the fugitives

[Middle Garde or garrison of La Haie Sainte?] (this halt did not exceed one minute and a half.) The 52nd then pursued on along the high ground to the right of the Genappe road leaving a large body of the enemy behind them in this hollow road, which seemed to make it doubtful [questionable] whether the 52nd had pushed on too far from the general line without support. The word, Halt, was given and at that instant the enemy rushed out of the hollow road to form on the ground which the 52nd then occupied, but the attempt was very feeble.[17]

Unsurprisingly, none of Cross's letters was deemed worthy of publication by H.T. Siborne, presumably because they contradicted his father's version. We are indebted to Gareth Glover for bringing them into the light of day. Cross enlarged his account in a later, undated memorandum (see Map 13, colour section):

… where those regiments stopped about three or four minutes firing on the fugitives … but keeping on the bank to the right hand side of the hollow road, by which means the 52nd got ahead of a great body of the French and again made a momentary halt, and at this instant the fugitives rushed out of the hollow road apparently with the intention of forming on the very ground the 52nd occupied, and at this instant, Captain Cross called out they were going to surrender and not to fire upon them, but this proved quite a mistake for the foremost of the enemy commenced firing as they got up the bank, but were unable to make the slightest stand there.[18]

It has to be said that the 52nd was very fortunate that the French in La Haie Sainte did not make a better showing, for they might have delivered a stab in the back to the Light Brigade. The demoralising effect achieved by surprise is evident in the enemy's 'feeble' response but it seems the six companies of the 2/95th were less lucky for they had to deal directly with the French occupants of the farmstead. Leach of the 1/95th has already observed the evacuation but was not aware that his comrades in the second battalion had suffered in the process, as Corporal Aldridge tells us:

The French were very thick to the left of a house [La Haie Sainte – did he mean right?] 2/95th lost most men here. Went on to attack the rear guard.[19]

Aldridge did not clarify what he meant by 'rear guard'. Was it the men who debouched behind the 52nd or was he referring to the three squares, which were the Light Brigade's next adversaries? The latter seem most likely. As usual, George Gawler has something to add, not only with his eye for detail but also because his detachment – referred to here as 'the section' – was currently acting independently of the 52nd, having dealt with the guns that had fired on the 52nd's right flank:

> I was clear of the Imperial Guards smoke, and saw three squares of the Old Guard within four hundred yards farther on. They were standing in a line of contiguous squares with very short intervals, a small body of cuirassiers on their right, while the guns took post on their left ... They were standing in perfect order and steadiness ... The section advanced to within 200 metres of the squares and halted until joined by the main body of the 52nd.[20]

What is not clear is why Gawler had to be detached to see off opposition that should have fallen to the 71st, on the brigade's right flank, or even to the men of 3/95th on the 52nd's immediate right, unless the 71st had still not caught up. It is possible the 71st – despite Colborne's earlier statement – had not come alongside the 52nd during the episode with the 23rd Light Dragoons but only now caught up. The 71st's absence until now would explain Gawler's detachment to drive away the artillery (see Map 13, Colour section).

Gawler had cut a corner, so to speak, but his 'section' neatly rejoined the main body when, just south of La Haie Sainte, Colborne halted the 52nd to reform after its dash over half a mile of corpse-encumbered ground, and to change direction to the south. Leeke records Colborne halting the 52nd to dress the line. The regimental colour carried by Leeke, and his 'covering-serjeants' had been sent forward as markers when the duke, with Lord Uxbridge and Sir Colin Campbell, rode up to Colborne in rear of the 52nd.[21] Leeke, as he looked back from in front of the centre heard Wellington say 'Well done, Colborne! Well done! Go on, don't give them time to rally.'[22] At this critical moment Leeke was only ten paces or so in front of Colborne, Wellington, Uxbridge and Sir Colin Campbell, when he heard Uxbridge say 'For God's sake duke, don't expose yourself so, you know what a valuable life yours is,' to which the duke replied, 'I'll be satisfied, when I see those fellows go.'[23] Lord Uxbridge's own version of this exchange had Wellington say, more colourfully but with much the same intent: 'Oh, damn it. In for a penny, in for a pound.'[24]

Gawler's account continues:

> Up to this moment neither the guns, the squares of the Imperial Guard, nor the 52nd had fired a shot. I then saw one of the guns slewed round to the direction of my company and fired, but their grape [canister shot] went over our heads. We opened our fire and advanced; the squares replied to it, and then faced about, retired...the cuirassiers declined the contest and turned. The French proper right square brought up its right shoulders and crossed the chaussée [the axis road to Genappe], and we crossed it after them.[25]

Lieutenant General Henry Paget, Earl of Uxbridge, 1768–1854. He commanded the cavalry during Sir John Moore's campaign in the Peninsula in 1809. Created 1st Marquess of Anglesey after Waterloo. Sired eighteen children by two wives, the second having been poached from Wellington's brother, Henry. Lord Lieutenant of Ireland twice. Retired as field marshal.

Uxbridge's concern for Wellington's safety was well founded for he himself was struck on the knee by one of the canister balls fired by that cannon (see Map 13). Leeke did not witness Uxbridge's wounding, nor did any officer of the 52nd as all were concentrating on the enemy to their front. Neither did he hear the famous exchange but was told of it by Sir Colin Campbell. Uxbridge: 'I've lost me leg, egad.' and Wellington's offhand reply: 'Egad, so you have!'[26] The duke's apparent lack of concern has been attributed to the fact that Uxbridge, some years before, had eloped with Wellington's sister-in-law, the wife of Henry Wellesley, Wellington's younger brother. True or not, such long-held resentment seems very unlikely, especially in the light of Wellington's own propensity for philandering with other men's wives. He even joked about the elopement, saying at the start of the campaign:

> … Lord Uxbridge has the reputation of running away with everybody he can. I'll take good care he don't run away with me.[27]

Wellington's apparent lack of sympathy can much more plausibly be attributed to a lack of interest, concentrating, as he was, on the French Army (which was also running away), in case there were any signs of resistance. At this particular moment, situated perilously, hundreds of yards in front of his army, the duke was much more concerned with maintaining the momentum of the 52nd's advance – of the French retreat – than he was with Uxbridge's state of health. Wellington's apparently heartless response was much the same as Colborne's at the Battle of Orthez when told that Lord March, then serving with the 52nd, had been wounded: 'Well I can't help it. Have him carried off.' In battle there are moments when sympathy is not top of the agenda for commanders.

Lord Uxbridge had his leg amputated to save his life from the otherwise inevitable gangrene, and it was buried in the village of Waterloo, subsequently becoming something of a tourist attraction. We can be certain the event happened but historians' perception has always been that Uxbridge and the duke were positioned within the Allied line at the time, just prior to the general advance. They are mistaken – thirty-seven years after the event Lord Uxbridge himself recorded that he was wounded:

> ... in the low ground beyond La Haye Sainte, and perhaps a quarter of an hour before dusk, at the moment when I was quitting the Duke to join Vivian's Brigade of Hussars which I had sent for ...[28]

The phrase 'beyond La Haye Sainte ... ' clearly implies 'as seen from the Allied line' and, therefore, can only mean south of the farm, precisely where Leeke's account places both the event and the Light Brigade, moving forward to chase off the Old Garde squares. This anecdote confirms Wellington had accompanied the 52nd and the other battalions of the Light Brigade across the battlefield and so was undeniably aware of their meteoric action. Further corroboration of Wellington's presence with the Light Brigade at this time will follow in a few pages time.

Incidentally, by its independent confirmation of Leeke's story, Uxbridge's leg gives added credence to the latter's other evidence. It also raises the question as to why Lord Uxbridge waited thirty-seven years before revealing this important information. That debate must wait for a later chapter. Wellington did, however, record his cavalry commander's misfortune in the *Waterloo Despatch*, but, ungenerously, gave nary a whiff of approval of his performance during the battle. However he did give a useful additional clue about its timing:

> The Earl of Uxbridge, after having successfully got through this arduous day, received a wound, by almost the last shot fired, which will, I am afraid, deprive his Majesty for some time of his services.[29]

Unaware of the little drama of Uxbridge's leg being played out behind him, the 52nd's colonel describes how his regiment

> ... then passed on to the attack of a body of apparently between 2,000 and 3,000 of the Guards, who had preserved their order [a remark that suggests he had observed their movement across the battlefield after the breaking of

the Garde column of battalions] and occupied a hill rather to the left of the direct line of advance towards La Belle Alliance. I think there were three battalions of them. They opened a heavy fire on us as we advanced in line till we came within 50 or 60 yards, when moving off in good order, our men being rather blown with their long run, by the time we got to the crest of the hill they had disappeared on the other side and we saw no more of them. In going over this ground the Duke was immediately in rear of the 52nd, and when, in consequence of seeing that parties of Cuirassiers, who were retiring before us were continually trying to form, apparently with the intention of charging us, several of the officers were rather checking the pace of the men for fear of the ranks becoming disordered, he two or three times called out, 'Go on, go on,' and so it was that these Cuirassiers were fairly driven off without ever being able to make any head.[30]

So Colborne confirmed that Wellington was still with the 52nd, and that elements of the French cavalry were prevented from making an attack by being kept on the move. The duke clearly appreciated that the momentum of the advance had to be maintained. But the regimental field officers were equally correct in exercising caution in the face of potential cavalry attack and in maintaining tightly controlled cohesion, for it was the impression of invincibility that this projected, which frightened off the cavalry. Let us not forget that the men of the brigade had been moving at speed across hazardous terrain for a distance of some 1,500 yards and must have been tiring. Captain John Cross, as early as 1821, recorded in the 52nd's *Orderly-room Record*:

> The squares of the Imperial Guard were standing formed on the summit of the hill to check the pursuit; but, although single-handed, [not strictly true, assuming 2/95th had caught up after the wheel south of La Haie Sainte] the Regiment could not be intimidated, and it continued approaching the squares in the double quick march, preserving an excellent line, and when arriving within sixty or eighty yards of the enemy, both squares fired a volley, broke, and dissolved in the general mass of fugitives.[31]

The value of this account lies in its relatively early date, six years after the battle, in contrast with the later correspondence with William Siborne and in public documents, which did not take place until at least ten years later. It is interesting to note that so little interest had been shown in the subject that Cross was unaware that the other battalions of the Light Brigade had been alongside the 52nd.

Colborne's guess at the total strength of the three squares was on the high side but 1,700 would not be an unreasonable estimate, assuming the three squares were as follows: the 2/3e Grenadiers, which had been held back between au Goumont and La Belle Alliance and in which – according to General Petit – Napoleon had now taken refuge, together with the first two of the three Old Garde battalions that had retired in formation from the disaster on the ridge, namely 2/2e Grenadiers and 2/2e Châsseurs.[32]

So now the Light Brigade was heading south (see Map 14, Colour section) and Gawler, precise as ever, confirms it was formed from left to right; the 2/95th, the 52nd, two companies of the 3/95th, and the 71st, and that the 52nd continued four deep to the close of the day.[33] It was at this stage, when the 52nd was facing up to the three Garde squares, that the 71st fully became part of the advance. Colonel Reynell's account is a rather cursory description of the action. Having told us his battalion suffered casualties as they came past the corner of au Goumont he continues:

When apprehension of further annoyance from the Enemy's cavalry had ceased, we took advantage of the ground to display our full front by obliquing, in opposite directions, the two wings, and directed our march upon two Columns of French Infantry, which from the first had appeared at the bottom of the hill. These Columns did not wait our approach but made off, and from the circumstance of our finding an immense quantity of arms lying against the walls of the houses in the village of Caillou [Rossomme?], I should incline to believe that they had broken without order and dispersed.[34]

Reynell usefully confirms the lack of any threat from French cavalry. With rather more detail, the observant Captain Reed of the 71st tells us:

In this movement the Regiment was formed four deep, supporting the 52nd in a charge on the Imperial Guard, who, I think, were either in square or column ... We here charged three Squares of the Guard, whom we broke and pursued, crossing the road leading to Genappe, when we brought left shoulders forward, the right of the 71st resting on La Belle Alliance ... The French Squares having separated, the 52nd pursued what had been their right square; the other two fell to our lot.[35]

The Old Garde squares now dispersed. One hundred yards to the south of the enclosure of 'Primotion' (as named on some maps – actually Trimetiou), which was just south of La Belle Alliance and on the other side of the road, the 52nd came to a sunken road – Leeke calls it hollow – 'up which a column of artillery and infantry was hastily retreating.'[36] One artillery officer attempted to surrender; his commander did not and was immediately bayoneted by a

The 52nd Captures a French Battery.
The artist, based on William Leeke's account, has produced an impressive picture but, to judge by the spire of Plancenoit church in the background, he has the French battery heading in the wrong direction.

man of the 52nd. One group of about 100 infantry on the left of the 52nd climbed out of the road in an offensive manner but hurriedly retired again when the left company of the 52nd 'brought up its right shoulders'. The artillery set their horses at the steep bank and finished up in a state of chaos. There was no firing. That the French were in a formed body suggests they were not under immediate pressure from the Prussians, but were definitely retiring from the battle.

It seems extraordinary, but surrender was assumed. The 52nd abandoned its 'prisoners' in order to maintain the momentum of the pursuit. Leeke passed through the French troops and was the first up on the top of the opposite bank, so that the battalion could be reformed on the regimental colour. It was getting somewhat 'duskish'. Leeke describes what happened next:

At a distance of about 200 yards we observed four French staff-officers. McNair who was on the right of No. 4 [his own company, No 9, being in the rear] gave the word, 'No. 4, make ready,' when I, who was next to him on his right, begged him to 'let those poor fellows off.' He replied, 'I dare not, I know not who they may be.' He then completed the word of command, and No 4 fired a volley; No 3, on the right did the same ... The horse of one of the French officers fell, and we soon lost sight of them. I have thought it was probably Maréchal Ney, who thus had his horse shot under him. It tallies with his own account; he speaks of lingering on the field, and all of his horses being shot. When McNair said, 'He did not know who they might be,' he was thinking of Napoleon, and thought it was not right to let him get away, if he could prevent it.[37]

This tantalising possibility cannot be proved but it is certain that the emperor did shelter briefly in one of the two squares of the 1er Grenadiers, which – General Petit tells us – retired in good order, firing on non-Garde fugitives trying to break into his squares but also stopping frequently to gather fugitives from other Garde battalions.

About a quarter of a mile before Rossomme the 52nd came across a quantity of knapsacks which Leeke assumed had belonged to the Garde battalion they had been pursuing. The 52nd finally came to rest at Rossomme farm and, piling arms, they bivouacked. Leeke was given a slice of bread, liberated from a French haversack. This was the first food he had eaten in twenty-four hours, except for one biscuit. He heard later that the duke had ordered the halt, and Colborne confirmed that the duke had indeed come up to the left of his regiment from the direction of La Belle Alliance and left a message to that effect.

The 2/95th bivouacked near the 52nd but the 71st bivouacked at La Caillou, south of Rossomme, and, according to Captain Reed, 'We were here passed by a body of Prussian Light Cavalry, their music playing *God Save the King*.'[38] The two companies of the 3/95th bivouacked with the 71st but at Rossomme, according to Major Eeles of the 3/95th.[39] Leeke faithfully recorded the time the 52nd halted as a quarter after nine o'clock, and that the first Prussian column arrived three-quarters of an hour after that. They broke into slow time, playing the national anthem, and a mounted officer embraced the regimental colour, exclaiming 'Brave Anglais'.[40] The observant reader will have noted that General Adam has not been mentioned since his being wounded when the 52nd charged the Garde column of battalions and going back to the line to order forward the 71st. Throughout the dash across the battlefield and the pursuit south, Wellington is recorded, by both Colborne and Leeke, as addressing Colborne as if he were commanding the brigade, and Colborne gives the necessary commands such as to sound (as one does with a bugle) the advance. It is difficult to detect Adam's presence with his brigade even from his letter to Siborne since he wrote in the third person.[41] Leeke expressly states that Adam did not accompany the Light Brigade but this is no proof. In fact, Adam's brigade major, Hunter Blair, comes to our – and Adam's – rescue, when he describes how:

After the repulse of the Squares of the Old Guard (I do not exactly recollect the spot) [but it is clear from Blair's letter that it was before the Light
Brigade passed La Belle Alliance] Sir Frederick Adam desired me to ride on
the prolongation of our right in order to observe if any part of the Enemy
seemed to threaten our right flank – then apparently quite unprotected.
Having gone some distance, I met the Duke of Wellington moving at a
quick pace, followed by one individual to whom I spoke. His answer was,
'Monsieur, je ne parles pas un seul mot d'Anglais.' I told him in French the
order I had received. He replied, 'Le Duc lui-même a été voir; il n'y a rien à
craindre.' I rejoined the Brigade.[42]

It was, no doubt, reassuring to all concerned that there was nothing to fear.
However, whilst confirming Adam was with his brigade despite his wound,
this paragraph establishes, without doubt, a much more important fact, namely
that Wellington had indeed ridden about the battlefield in front of his army,
leaving the rest of his troops still in line behind him.

The non-English-speaking officer's name was Comte de Sales, a Sardinian.
De Sales confirmed his meeting with Blair when he responded in French to
William Siborne's letter, which clearly was seeking not information to aid the
construction of the model of the Crisis but for confirmation that de Sales was
the foreign officer whom Blair had met. De Sales replied on 19 December
1842 in the affirmative:

On this memorable day, upon which I was, in effect, at all times in the Duke
of Wellington's retinue, I can confirm in addition that, during the period to
which you refer in your letter, I found myself as the only one of his retinue,
accompanying him for half an hour.

I subsequently had to inform an officer who was asking me for information, that I could not speak English, but I do not remember at all what it was
he wanted to know nor his name or to whom he was sending this message.

I can only reply to confirm the fact that you appear to want to establish
that the Duke of Wellington was to be found towards the most advanced
positions of his army at the moment he gave the order to attack, and yes, all
the corps [battalions of the Light Brigade] were just in front.

The movement to attack was made so quickly and with such fervour, the
Duke being at all times towards the front, that, upon arriving at the position
which had just been abandoned by the French troops …[43]

That he was the only officer with Wellington might be accounted for by the
unexpected suddenness of the latter's decision to ride out to join Colborne
and the 52nd. The penultimate paragraph could be misconstrued as referring

to the general advance, were it not firmly tied to the Light Brigade's dash both by its link to Major Blair and also by the wording of the last paragraph. What is particularly important is that his confirmation of his meeting Major Blair establishes as fact that Wellington was now moving freely and rapidly around the battlefield, having left the Light Brigade when he was certain the three squares were no threat.

It is clear from this that the French, especially formed bodies of their cavalry, had either lost any aggressive urge or had completely departed. The other question is – what was Wellington doing, roaming freely and unescorted, hundreds of yards in front of his army? We learn from Blair's letter that he was checking that the ground east of au Goumont was free of formed enemy cavalry, but what did he do next? The answer must wait until a later chapter.

Apart from General Adam, there is one more player in this drama who has not reappeared since it began: Colonel Hugh Halkett and his Osnabrück Landwher Battalion. Having set off to cover the Light Brigade's right flank Halkett manoeuvred separately from it – possibly ahead of it – and was involved with the British light cavalry that now came forward, whereas the Light Brigade was not. So it is more logical to describe Halkett's adventures in the next chapter. In the meantime it might be helpful to highlight some crucial facts arising from our narrative.

In Summary

Despite being charged by the 23rd Light Dragoons the Light Brigade's meteoric passage, at the double, diagonally across the muddy, body-strewn battlefield and then directly at the enemy commander, can surely be claimed as unique in Napoleonic battles. How fortunate Europe is that the 52nd was sufficiently experienced to handle the collision with the 'friendly' cavalry: how different history might have been if the 52nd's advance had ended here.

The 52nd's effect on the French left wing was to cause a complete loss of discipline and cohesion. First the pursuit prevented the Middle Garde from reforming and then outflanked the French garrison of La Haie Sainte. On reaching the axis road the Light Brigade changed direction and confronted the three Old Garde battalions that had also moved across to rejoin Napoleon at La Belle Alliance. The varied descriptions may have confused more than clarified what actually occurred with the three squares. The 52nd dealt with the left-hand square, which passed to the east of La Belle Alliance. The 2/95th, on the 52nd's left was not engaged. The 71st with 3/95th's two companies saw off the two right-hand squares, which went to the west of La Belle Alliance. It was here and now – neither back in the Allied line nor during the general

advance – that Lord Uxbridge, as he himself admitted, was severely wounded
in the knee, neatly proving that Wellington was still with the 52nd, having
ridden out to join them just before the 23rd Light Dragoons had so unhelpfully ridden into them.

Wellington left the Light Brigade at that stage to reconnoitre to the west
with only one staff officer; his precise movements will be examined shortly.

After reaching the axis road, turning and pausing to straighten the line,
encouraged by Wellington the 52nd and its comrades of the Light Brigade
set off up the hill to disperse the three Old Garde squares and to drive at
Napoleon and his headquarter staff. Meanwhile, satisfied that the Light
Brigade could be left to its own devices and that the French rout was well
under way, Wellington, accompanied by a single Sardinian officer (and possibly
Colonel Campbell), rode to the west to check whether the panic had caught
hold around au Goumont, thereby proving the French had flown.

Incredibly, sufficient details to deduce Wellington's peregrinations have
been in the public domain for 160 years, yet not one of the forty-four
accounts consulted for this research has even hinted that Wellington was to be
found wandering around the battlefield, unprotected, at this time. Presumably
Hunter Blair's report was considered to be an aberrant fantasy, or just an
inconvenient truth, best hidden and forgotten.

It cannot be overstressed that the French had not simply been forced to
retreat in good order; they had been thoroughly routed. This was the essential
psychological victory needed to ensure the political collapse of Napoleon's
regime. What is more, this rout had been achieved by and credited to
Wellington.

From the evidence presented there can be little doubt that the 52nd's
achievement was in two parts: the breaking of the final and only plausible
assault by the Garde, followed by the drive at Napoleon and the French
centre. Some may still suspect the evidence is the result of collusion between
the four primary witnesses – the officers of the 52nd. But the surest sign of
collusion is absolute conformity in the smallest detail and there is no sign
of that here: all differed from the others in both major and minor respects.
These disparities have not been reported since they serve only to muddy
further an already complicated story – they are easily found in H.T. Siborne's
Waterloo Letters, which is still in print. What is more, there are clear references
to the 52nd's actions from many disinterested witnesses, including a French
historian. A collusion theory is simply not tenable.

However, there may still be some doubt about the quantity of Garde battalions repulsed by the respective protagonists, 3/1st Guards and the 52nd.
It seems unlikely there will ever be a definitive answer to this question but
the evidence – and lack of evidence – from the British viewpoint strongly

supports the conclusion that there were five, possibly six, in the final thrust, dealt with by the 52nd. Whatever the true numbers may be, the inescapable fact is that the 52nd's subsequent, dramatic charge at Napoleon was of even greater importance.

Before we reach the closing act – the general advance – the next chapter attempts to unravel the contribution to victory by the Light Cavalry brigades of Major General Sir Hussey Vivian and Major General Sir John Vandeleur. It has been claimed by some participants in the light cavalry charge, and by subsequent historians, that credit for the defeat of the French was due to the Allied cavalry. That question and Colonel Halkett's contribution with his Osnabrückers will be discussed next.

THE MOMENT TO
ATTACK WAS ARRIVED

'… The moment to attack was arrived.'

Thus, in a letter to his wife written five days after the battle, did Sir Hussey Vivian describe the moment he led his 6th (Light) Cavalry Brigade into action following the breaking of the final Garde attack by Adam's Light Brigade.[1] Vivian's brigade was composed of three regiments – the 10th, or Prince of Wales's Hussars; the 18th Hussars and the 1st Hussars of the King's German Legion (KGL); the whole totalling some 1,500 men.[2]

The last two regiments had experience in the Peninsula as did Vivian himself, having commanded the 7th Light Dragoons in the retreat to Corunna and then returned for the final campaign in 1813/14. At the start of the battle Vivian's brigade had been posted on the extreme left flank of the Anglo-Allied line. Nothing of note occurred here until after the fall of La Haie Sainte in the evening, when the French artillery began to play upon the Brunswickers and Nassauers at close range. Sensing their incipient collapse Vivian (he claimed on his own initiative) moved across to the west and, by posting his troopers behind them, discouraged the young Germans from decamping completely, although they did give way to shelter behind what little ridge there was in this sector of the line, as described earlier. Vivian's brigade was soon to be involved in the dispersal of Napoleon's army but his was not the only British cavalry to enjoy this role.

Sir John Vandeleur's 4th (Light) Cavalry Brigade was also involved.[3] Under his command, Vandeleur had three regiments of Light Dragoons – the 11th, 12th and 16th, each of three squadrons of about 140 men, say, 1,260 in total at the start of the battle. He had served with the Light Division under Major General 'Black Bob' Craufurd in the Peninsula before transferring in 1813 to command a weak brigade of the 12th and 16th Light Dragoons until the end of the campaign in France. Here at Waterloo, Vandeleur was posted on the left flank until the attack by d'Erlon's corps was repelled by Picton's division together with the massed charge of the Household and Union brigades of

Major General Sir Hussey Richard Vivian, 1775–1842.
He served under Moore in the retreat to Corunna and under Wellington in the last few battles of the Peninsular War. Became inspector general of cavalry in 1825 and ended his career as master general of the ordnance, and Privy councillor in 1835.

heavy cavalry. Vandeleur took his brigade into the valley to cover the retreat of the Union Brigade, and his men suffered severely. Later, Vandeleur tells us, he was ordered to move his brigade:

> … to the rear of the Infantry on the great road behind Hougoumont, where it remained until the Enemy made his last great effort, and was repulsed.[4]

After the 52nd broke the Garde there was one other infantry battalion that moved forward in support of – but operated separately from – the Light Brigade. As already mentioned, Colonel Hugh Halkett had led forward one of his brigade's battalions, the Osnabrück Landwehr, ostensibly to protect the Light Brigade's right flank from cavalry attack. But the Osnabrück militia soon diverged from the Light Brigade's course and became directly involved with one of Vivian's cavalry regiments, and so its actions are described in this chapter (see Map 12, colour section).

Having been told by Colborne why the 52nd was in front of – and at right angles to – the Allied line and parallel to the advancing column of Garde battalions, General Adam returned to the line in order to fetch forward the 71st. At the same time he sought help from other troops in Clinton's division. In his letter to the model-making Siborne he says:

> … request was more than once made for troops from the other part of the Division to… cover the flank of the 3rd Brigade, and at length Lieutenant-Colonel Halkett, with part of his Hanoverian Militia Brigade was sent for this purpose …[5]

Needless to say the commander of the 3rd Hanoverian Brigade has given us a different version. Colonel Hugh Halkett wrote to Siborne:

> The moment General Adam's Brigade advanced I lost no time to follow with the Osnabruck Battalion (2nd Battalion, Duke of York), then on the left of Hougoumont, of which I was in command, one of the Battalions of my Brigade occupying the wood and two others in the ditches in the rear, other troops occupying the enclosures, &c.
>
> During the advance I sent my Brigade Major, Captain v. Saffe, to bring up the two Battalions posted in rear of Hougoumont, but neither he nor the Battalions showed themselves. Next day I found that Captain Saffe was killed before having delivered the message. The Osnabruck Battalion soon got in line and on the right of Adam's Brigade. During the advance we were much annoyed by the Enemy's Artillery. The first Company of the Osnabruck Battalion broke into platoons, and supported by the sharpshooters [Light Company] of the Battalion, made a dash at the Artillery on our right and captured six Guns with their horses.[6]

So the Osnabrück Battalion claimed to have protected the Light Brigade's vulnerable right flank and to have contributed to the disintegration of the French left wing, yet recognition of their contribution is usually limited – if indeed it is mentioned at all – to a debate about two questions; whether or not it was Colonel Halkett who captured the French general, Cambronne, commanding 2/1er Châsseurs; whether the latter actually swore when being captured, rather than uttering the 'bon mot' that is engraved on his tomb? Cambronne was said to have exclaimed, when called upon to surrender, 'Merde' ('s★★t' in the vernacular) but the French claimed he said, 'La Garde meurt, elle ne se rend pas!' ('The Garde dies, it does not surrender.') The theory of 'Inherent Military Probability' strongly suggests it was the former word. Halkett continued his letter:

> During our advance we were in constant contact with the French Guards, and I often called to them to surrender, for some time I had my eye upon, as I supposed, the General Officer in command of the Guards (being in full uniform) trying to animate his men to stand.
>
> After having received our fire with much effect, the Column left their General with two Officers behind, when I ordered the sharpshooters to dash on, and I made a gallop for the General. When about cutting him down he called out he would surrender, upon which he preceded me [to the rear], but he had not gone many paces before my horse got a shot through his body and fell to the ground. In a few seconds I got him on his

legs again, and found my friend, Cambronne, had taken French leave in the direction from where he came. I instantly overtook him, laid hold of him by the aiguillette, [Aiguillette or aglet: a metal-tagged lanyard indicating appointment to Army General Staff.] and brought him in safety and gave him in charge to a serjeant of the Osnabruckers [*sic*] to deliver to the Duke: I could not spare an officer for the purpose, many being wounded.[7] (See Map 13, colour section)

Several accounts of the battle claim that the honour of taking Cambronne should be awarded to other individuals and units, so this seems an appropriate opportunity to clarify the matter. Evidence can be found in John Franklin's excellent *Waterloo. Hanoverian Correspondence*, in which Halkett's capture of Cambronne, at some risk to himself, is confirmed by the three testimonies of Major Dreves and Lieutenant Richers, two of his junior officers and of the (by Halkett, unnamed) serjeant, Conrad Führing, all of the Osnabrück Landwehr.[8] Such credible testimony must surely confirm that the credit for Cambronne's capture can finally be given to Hugh Halkett, despite other claims to the contrary. Cambronne's arrest may be famous only for his use of a scatological swearword but the story of his capture has some real significance to our story. Not only does it show that the morale, even of the Old Garde, had finally collapsed to the extent that a battalion of Napoleon's veterans could no longer stand up to a Hanoverian militia battalion but, most importantly, it determines beyond doubt that the 2/1er Châsseurs was closely involved in the Garde's final assault, albeit its having been the rearmost of the Garde's attacking battalions. Finally, Halkett completes his account with admirable succinctness:

After this [capture of Cambronne] I kept in advance of Adam's Brigade; we soon pushed the two French squares upon the mass of their Cavalry of all descriptions, who at one moment threatened us in a most *vociferous* manner. However, after receiving our fire they went off in all directions. About this time, officers were flying in all directions, seemingly with orders from a superior. Some French Officers, prisoners, said it was Napoleon.

We had the good fortune to take twelve to fourteen more Guns of the Guards, in full play upon us. On our advance the sharpshooters, supported by a Company, were sent among the mass of Guns, and by their fire increased the confusion, made many prisoners, and cut the horses from the leading Guns. Next morning I found marked on these Guns 52nd, 71st, &c., for I had followed the Enemy on the Genappe road, where I met the Prussians, and moved on with them to some houses on the left of the road near Genappe, which houses I occupied during the night, the Battalion being much knocked up, and not seeing any red-coats in the rear.[9]

I remain, yours truly,

Colonel Halkett

There is much valuable evidence to be gleaned from this letter. Halkett says he was both 'in line with' and 'in advance of Adam's Brigade', and this was from a late start with greater distance to cover. This suggests either that Halkett caught up with the 52nd just after the delay caused by the 23rd Light Dragoons, or, more likely, observed he was level with the 52nd, but some distance away to the west. He and his Osnabrückers were heading more directly at the French position, pursuing two Old Garde squares towards La Belle Alliance, and thereby cut the corner, while the Light Brigade took the longer route of the other two sides of a triangle via La Haie Sainte.

As a result Halkett arrived just north of La Belle Alliance before the Light Brigade, still pursuing – he claimed – two Garde battalions. One of these was definitely 2/1er Châsseurs; which was the other? There can be no certainty about this. It might have been the 2/2e Châsseurs, which had been the next ahead in the column of battalions. But, given that Reynell of the 71st claims to have pursued two Garde battalions and that Halkett was slightly

Colonel Hugh Halkett, 1783–1863. Younger brother of Colin Halkett, mistakenly named as William in *Waterloo Letters*; served in the Peninsula with the KGL; commanded the 3rd Hanoverian Brigade at Waterloo and remained in the Hanoverian service, being ennobled by King George V of Hanover.

diverging from the direction taken by the Light Brigade, another possible candidate is 2/3rd Grenadiers, which had been posted several hundred yards to the west of La Belle Alliance, as reported earlier by General Petit. However 2/3e Grenadiers seems unlikely too, when the map is examined. The most likely solution to the question is that the 71st had 2/2e Grenadiers and 2/2e Châsseurs ahead of them initially; that one of these two were then chased by Halkett for a short distance along with 2/1er Châsseurs; that Halkett then concentrated solely on 2/1er Châsseurs and all four Old Garde battalions, including 2/3e Grenadiers came together north of La Belle Alliance.

We have learnt that the morale and fighting spirit of the Old Garde infantry had seriously diminished by this stage of the battle. Indeed, it is hard, if not impossible, to find any unbiased evidence of the legendary death-struggles of the Garde squares, so trumpeted by illustrators and French accounts. It is equally important to recognise from Halkett's evidence that the French cavalry was no real threat, being noisy but easily dispersed.

The Osnabrückers continued to advance alone. That this battalion could move so far ahead of the rest of the Allied infantry as to halt just short of Genappe (if Halkett is to be believed), without being obstructed by the French, shows clearly how completely and quickly the French Army had evacuated its position. Indeed, this was not just a defeat: it was an out-and-out rout. There is, however, one important episode, involving both the Osnabrück Battalion and the British cavalry, that Halkett mentions in another letter and which is spoken of by several cavalrymen. It is claimed the duke himself was very angry with the outcome. This episode will be discussed in detail at the appropriate moment in the cavalry's account. It is time for the cavalry to trot on.

Lieutenant General Lord Greenock, assistant quartermaster general to the cavalry and hence directly responsible to Lord Uxbridge, was part of the headquarters staff as the Garde's attack materialised. He describes his actions:

> On quitting Sir Hussey Vivian, Lord Anglesey joined the Duke of Wellington, and it was about this time that the last attack by the Enemy took place. The Infantry had by then formed into line four deep. We rode towards the left along the rear of the Infantry, crossing the Genappe Road in rear of the Haye Sainte, but immediately returned to the right of the line. It was then that Lord Anglesey sent me to bring up Vivian's Brigade, which I did as he has stated, directing him to make a flank movement to his right in order to clear the flank of the Infantry, and afterwards bring up his right shoulders.[10]

The 'flank movement to his right in order to clear the flank of the Infantry', sounds as if – but may not have specified – that Vivian should come through the line via the gap left by the Light Brigade; that is what actually happened.

While Vivian's brigade was halted in the gap the unfortunate squadron of the 23rd Light Dragoons, having pulled itself together after colliding with the 52nd, now appeared in front of the Allied line and nearly caused yet another problem. It is best described by the officer commanding the squadron, Captain Banner:

> … in consequence of their experiencing a similar annoyance on approaching the British line, [the collision with the 52nd] they were induced to move to its flanks, which movement brought the greater part of this Squadron of the 23rd Dragoons along the front of Sir Hussey Vivian's Brigade. After clearing the Brigade I re-formed the men belonging to the 23rd Dragoons, and proceeded in the direction of Sir Hussey's Brigade, which had just before advanced [to the gap in the line], and on my coming up with the 18th Hussars on the summit of the position, I went to the Honble. Col. Murray … and requested to be allowed to advance with his Regiment, upon which he replied that he had no control over me.[11]

Despite the obvious lack of enthusiasm on Colonel Murray's part, Banner then clung to the 18th Hussars. Apart from the its human interest, this quotation from Banner tells us that Vivian's brigade was still static within the Allied line while the Light Brigade was well on its way to La Haie Sainte. Vivian now moved forward and met Sir Colin Campbell on the slope:

> Then as to what happened when we arrived in the plain at the bottom of the hill. That there was a pause, and I may say a halt in the front [of his brigade] I can positively affirm; the very circumstance of Sir Colin Campbell coming to me from the Duke and desiring me to halt, and the conversation that took place (the affair of a minute, or perhaps moments only, I admit), proves it.[12]

So Campbell has confirmed that Wellington was indubitably 'in the plain at the bottom of the hill' just before Uxbridge was rendered legless. The message that Campbell brought from Wellington was that Vivian should not advance ahead of the infantry. But Vivian decided the infantry would benefit from his assistance and he should ignore Wellington's order (a decision in which Campbell concurred). Besides, where would the glory be in waiting? So, once the squadrons were in line, he ordered the 10th to charge and the 18th to be steady in reserve. Vivian himself gives a racy description of his brigade's initial moves, a description which conjures up the sense of excitement and exhilaration of cavalry combat, given added interest by knowing it was written only three days after the battle; but it is not strictly true:

We were coming up, down went a party of [French] lancers on a party of the 23rd [Light Dragoons] on our right, checked them, then came our right squadron on the lancers, drove them back – then came a body of heavy dragoons on our right squadron – then our centre squadron on them – and away they went – then we soon came on the square which the right squadron charged – and I hear broke it completely – I went with mine to the left of the square … we were among infantry – Imperial Guard, blue [coats] with large fur caps – who were throwing down their arms and themselves roaring *pardon*, on their knees many of them [ex Middle Garde?] – on top of the hill a party of infantry formed, and with cavalry behind them, commenced a sharp fire – we checked … about 35 paces from them – then Lord Robert [Manners] gave a hurrah – and at them we went – they turned directly, horse and foot in most complete flight – infantry throwing themselves down, cavalry off their horses. Soon we came to a deep hollow – on the opposite side a steep knoll – with a square of infantry very well formed – a party of the 18th rushed down the hollow, up the hill and at the square in most gallant style – but as I foresaw were checked and turned by their fire … I decline the honour of charging squares unnecessarily – though one could not but admire the gallantry of the thing.[13]

The prime impression is of rapid move and counter-move, leading to the conclusion that attempting to produce a complete and accurate storyline of a complete cavalry action is impossible. It will not be attempted here. Yet, to tease out specific episodes, especially when they are referred to by separate writers, is not only possible but instructive. For example, Vivian describes the 18th Hussars being checked and turned by the fire of a square. This episode is mentioned in detail by their commanding officer, Lieutenant Colonel Henry Murray (whom we have lately met being icily dismissive to the 23rd Light Dragoons) in his long, exhaustive, informative and sensitive letter to William Siborne. The latter's son, H.T. Siborne, chose to publish only a minimal excerpt from Murray's letter in his *Waterloo Letters* and it is thanks to Gareth Glover that we have the benefit of the whole letter to enlighten us.

Murray explains that 'there was a dip or hollow in the ground between the party of the 18th and the squares, perhaps a fence, but quite close. The squares were inaccessible. Instead, since the signal to retire had been given some time before, he put his men about, to fall back. But tragically they came under fire from artillery (which Murray suspected was Prussian) and lost a lot of men. Murray's long letter included copious footnotes, one of which, referring to the inaccessible squares (note the plural) records 'There is a probability that it was beyond Rossomme …' but it is much more likely to have been south of La Belle Alliance. These squares might well have been the two senior

Grenadier battalions under Petit. There seems little doubt that they would have stood firm, not having suffered the rout and become demoralised, as had the other Old Garde battalions.

Murray indicates that he is conscious of the controversy over the Crisis. He continues:

> Supposing the 52nd to have driven the Ancienne [Old] Garde from near Hougoumont down the space between the two positions, a surmise that is strengthened by my recollection of my fire working (if I might be allowed the expression) in that direction … all which must be conjecture on our part who could not see through the smoke and who could only learn that the 52nd was the regiment so gallantly and memorably employed in achieving so important a feature of the battle. It yet does not appear to me that anywhere on the line, to the front where we went, the 52nd could be ahead of us. But that they might be very near without mutual recognition is easily to be supposed.[14]

It is apparent that knowledge of the 52nd's breaking of the Garde was widespread after the battle and here is another independent recognition of it, but that is not the reason for including this quotation. Rather, it illustrates two important points: first, that the speed of a cavalry action and the effect of smoke render the observation and identification of other units – even those nearby – very difficult if not impossible, and, second, that in his opinion – as in Vivian's too, as we shall shortly learn – the question of the relative importance of the contributions to victory by the infantry and cavalry depended on who was ahead of whom in terms of an imaginary line parallel with the original position. Is this not a little naïve?

The 52nd was indeed ahead of the cavalry in terms of time: that the cavalry was 'out' was solely due to the Light Brigade having broken the Garde's attack. The light infantry had departed from the position minutes before the cavalry but had gone sideways (so to speak) before turning southwards, whereas the cavalry had ridden straight at the French position. For the cavalrymen to assume their contribution was greater because they were further 'ahead' than the infantry is facile. However, in his last-quoted sentence – 'that they might be very near without mutual recognition is easily to be supposed' – Murray turns out to have been very prescient, as will be revealed shortly.

First we must follow the misfortunes of two junior cavalry officers, Robert Arnold and Anthony Bacon, both of the 10th Hussars. Vivian, in response to a query from William Siborne about his brigade's speed of advance, which Major Taylor, commander of the centre squadron of the 10th Hussars, had said was at the gallop but which Vivian was adamant was at the trot, explained the discrepancy as follows:

There is one circumstance to which I have I think to you before adverted, that proves the advance was at a trot and not a hurried one. The leading half-squadron as we were moving off the position, on approaching some of our Guns wheeled to the right instead of to the left, and was consequently moving to the rear. I was on the flank of the Squadron. I immediately (I recollect perfectly well) with a *considerable degree of emphasis, &c., and a good hearty damn*, galloped to the flank of the second half-squadron, and said that it was *towards the Enemy* and *not from the Enemy* they were to wheel. I then took the flank officer's place and I led the Column down the hill in the direction I wished it to move ... Now had our advance been at any very rapid pace the half-squadron which had wheeled from us and been left behind, somewhat perhaps confused and entangled with the Guns, would never have returned to its place in so short a time.[15]

This quotation, which superficially sounds irrelevant, is actually interesting for introducing the two junior officers and for illuminating Vivian's character. The officer in question was Lieutenant Robert Arnold who died in 1841. His 'earliest and dearest' friend, Anthony Bacon, was with Arnold at Waterloo, when they were both wounded.

Here is Vivian damning one of his own officers for a mistake not of his making, an act which might have been understandable immediately after the event but, to do so in 1841 by which time he could have discovered that Arnold was not to blame, was ungentlemanly.

Bacon has given us a mass of evidence, all well and fairly reasoned, yet was completely unpublished by H.T. Siborne, presumably because his evidence contradicted that of Sir Hussey Vivian, who – it should be noted – was not only Siborne's boss but also supported him verbally and financially.[16]

Bacon begins by telling Siborne that he has erred in his description, in the first edition of his *History of the Waterloo Campaign*, of a mistake by the leading half-squadron of the 10th Hussars as they started to advance, by which the half-squadron appeared to be riding away from the enemy. This is the episode Vivian described above. Bacon maintains that the wheeling away was caused by the reckless discharge of a gun or guns between the horses when the squadron was coming through the line. It will come as little surprise to learn that the culprits were the men of the same battery – Rogers' – that had fired whilst the 2/95th was passing through their guns a few minutes earlier. Understandably the horses had taken fright and sheered off in the wrong direction.

It was immediately after this that Bacon describes that 'all at once we burst from the darkness of a London November fog into a bright sunshine'. This observation is sometimes incorrectly attributed to Colonel Murray. As this investigation unfolds it is worth recognising that the smoke from the Allied artillery on the right of the position was a localised bank, obscuring, from the sight of troops in the line, the action taking place in the valley and beyond in the French position, but that adequate visibility beyond the bank was perfectly possible:

> Sir Colin Campbell told me that, when Lord Uxbridge was wounded, he himself again pressed the Duke not to expose, as he was doing, his valuable life, and that he received the same reply which the Duke had immediately before given to Lord Uxbridge that 'he would be satisfied when he saw those fellows go'. He told me several other things about the Duke, most of which I noted down the day after I had the conversation with him. He told me that, when the 52nd advanced, the Duke went off to the right, which would probably be towards the lower part of the inclosures of Hougoumont, and that some little time afterwards they crossed over some rising ground to their left, where they witnessed the unsuccessful charge by Major Howard and a party of 10th Hussars upon a body of French infantry, and that the Duke was very angry when he saw them make the attack without having any support.[17]

That is from William Leeke again. He describes how Wellington moved away from the 52nd, after Lord Uxbridge was wounded and the three Garde squares had retired, to check for French troops in the direction of au Goumont. In the previous chapter we noted how Major Blair, General Adam's brigade major, had been sent on an identical mission and met the duke with a Sardinian officer, Comte de Sales, apparently Wellington's sole companion, who reassured him the ground was clear of French cavalry. It would seem from Leeke's statement that Sir Colin Campbell had been in the vicinity but not immediately with Wellington. The important points that this quotation makes are, first, that Leeke's evidence is reliable and, secondly, that the duke witnessed Major Howard's charge. So what happened to Major Howard and why is it important?

The Honourable Frederick Howard has the dubious honour of probably being the last British officer to die during the fighting at Waterloo. Commanding the right squadron of the 10th Hussars, he was bludgeoned to death by a French grenadier when wounded in a foolhardy charge against one of the Old Garde squares, which held firm amid the chaotic French retreat. The foolhardiness was not his: he was ordered to attack by Vivian. This knowledge puts an interesting slant on Vivian's apparently virtuous statement of 23 June 1815, mentioned earlier:

> ... I decline the honour of charging squares unnecessarily – though one could not but admire the gallantry of the thing.

Although here Vivian was referring to the 18th Hussars, the uncomfortable thought cannot be avoided that he was trying to exculpate himself, or, rather, to deflect inevitable criticism, for having ordered Howard to carry out a suicidal attack on a square. The movements of the three Old Garde battalions after the rout of the final assault are inevitably somewhat obscure: such disasters tend not to be recorded in detail but in this case light has been shed on this particular episode by Anthony Bacon.

Bacon took part in the abortive attack by Howard's squadron and he gives us his eyewitness account of the event, untrammelled by any consideration of protecting his – or anyone else's – reputation. He also helpfully included a sketch plan but honestly points out that a single participant in a cavalry action cannot record events beyond his immediate vicinity. His letters are very detailed and long, so it will be necessary in parts to précis the information rather than quote Bacon in full. They are published complete in Gareth Glover's *Letters from the Battle of Waterloo*. Bacon describes the action as taking place north of La Belle Alliance. He belonged to the right-hand squadron of the 10th Hussars which had crossed the chaussée and was on the east of the axis road (see Map 13, colour section). He says:

> There was a heavy *column* of the Imperial Guards on the opposite side of the road, marching in a diagonal direction towards La Belle Alliance inclining to the right, and on its left flank was a large number of mounted officers, on the high road and close to La Belle Alliance was another *column*, and on our right of the road, and on our right flank which was thrown back about a quarter distance, was a *square* of the Imperial Guard behind which some cavalry was reforming.[18]

Bacon's sketch plan differs from his verbal description.[19] The latter is open to misinterpretation by his use of 'left' and 'right' without it being absolutely clear whether he means his or the French left and right. However, his sketch is carefully annotated, and so that has been taken as the definitive description, and has informed Map 13.

His sketch shows four Garde units. It is possible to make informed guesses as to the identity of each battalion, based on the battalions' positions at the moment of being broken near au Goumont. The most westerly square is probably 2/3e Grenadiers, Of the other two Garde squares placed just north of La Belle Alliance the one astride the road was probably 2/2e Châsseur, and the other was probably 2/2e Grenadiers. This was the square attacked by Howard's squadron with Bacon. The fourth unit, the most easterly of the four, shown in column – not square – can only have been 2/1er Châsseur, pursued by Halkett's single battalion. The 2/1er Châsseurs was still apparently intact (and by inference, this was prior to the capture of Cambronne).

He also records about four squadrons of French cavalry to the west of the three squares and another several hundred yards to his north, roughly midway between La Belle Alliance and La Haie Sainte. The latter may have been the cavalry, described in the previous chapter, that the 52nd's field officers were watching with some concern when the Light Brigade paused to reform just south of La Haie Sainte, before heading southwards.

It is difficult to argue against the supposition that these three Garde squares (excepting 2/1er Châsseurs) were those subsequently attacked, pushed back and eventually dispersed by the Light Brigade. However the Light Brigade was not mentioned by Bacon. Yet he recorded many other bodies of troops – both Allied and French – in considerable detail. That he did not include the Light Brigade strongly suggests it was out of sight due to the convex slope between La Haie Sainte and La Belle Alliance, which is clearly illustrated in the easterly (left-hand) aquatint of the battlefield in the colour plates.

There seems little doubt that Wellington and the Light Brigade were hidden in dead ground to an observer near La Belle Alliance, which would account for the light infantry not being visible to Bacon. The only Allied infantry of which he was aware was Halkett's Osnabrück Battalion beside the road immediately in rear of Howard's squadron (marked 10H, on Map 13). Astonishingly Halkett had come straight across the battlefield from his starting point near the north-east corner of au Goumont, rather than accompanying the Light Brigade on its longer route, and so was well ahead of the latter. By pure chance, he had arrived at this spot simultaneously with Vivian's cavalry. Had the British cavalry not arrived he would have been very dangerously exposed. However, that a single militia battalion could advance with impunity so far into the French position, unopposed, is testimony to the completeness of the French collapse.

Vivian, before riding away to fetch the 18th Hussars, 'desired' Howard to attack the square. Howard, despite recognising the suicidal nature of obeying the order, led his men forward at the trot until about 150 yards from his target when he was persuaded by Lieutenant Arnold to halt and ask Halkett to have his men fire into the square before the Hussars charged. Halkett refused, on the grounds that his force was not sufficient; he maintained his refusal even when Arnold gave the order in General Vivian's name. Vivian claimed to have ridden on the flank of the squadron when it charged but Lieutenant Arnold's having to give an order in Vivian's name suggests otherwise. So, unsupported, Bacon recounts:

> … we immediately charged, they reserved their fire till we were close upon them, and the havoc was dreadful. Howard, Arnold and myself rode close together in front of the squadron, and were all hit about the same moment …

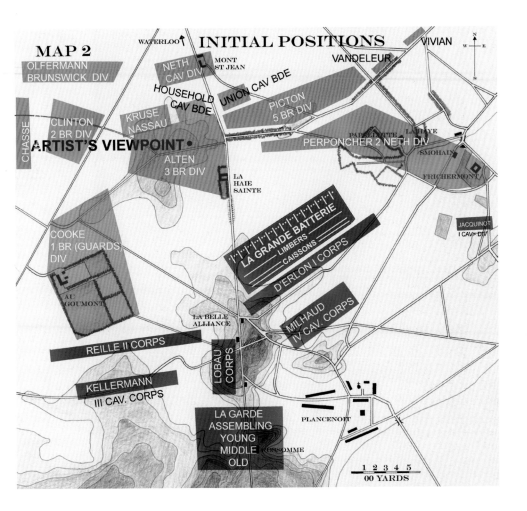

Plate 1

Map 2 illustrates clearly the difference in approach by the two commanders-in-chief to fighting the battle; Napoleon's positions had a certain symmetry to maintain balance while Wellington's distribution of his motley forces paid great attention to the lie of the land. The blocks of colour indicate areas of responsibility rather than the quantity of troops.

The following two coloured engravings were created by Charles Turner from drawings made by Captain George Jones facing South from the point shown left of centre of the Allied line on Map 2 on previous page. They were published by Turner and Booth in 1816.

Plate 2
La Haie Sainte (alternatively La Haye Sainte) and La Belle Alliance

In the left foreground are the buildings and orchard of La Haie Sainte. Just beyond and to the right of the 'hollow road' can be seen the buildings of La Belle Alliance. Note that the valley bottom, where the road appears from behind the orchard, is invisible from La Belle Alliance, because of the shape of the ground. On the horizon, above the right-hand end of the orchard, can be seen the spire of Plancenoit church. On the horizon at the extreme right of the picture stands an observation tower. The same tower is depicted on the extreme left of the other engraving.

Plate 3
Au Goumont

The château, its orchard, garden and woodland dominate the western side of the battlefield. Most importantly, this engraving shows, in its right hand third, the tongue projecting from the ridge of the Allied position, which forced a change of direction by six battalions of the Garde. The tongue no longer exists: in 1821 it was dug away to create the Lion Mound. The observation tower on the left was probably built for the triangulation survey carried out in the 1780s.[1]

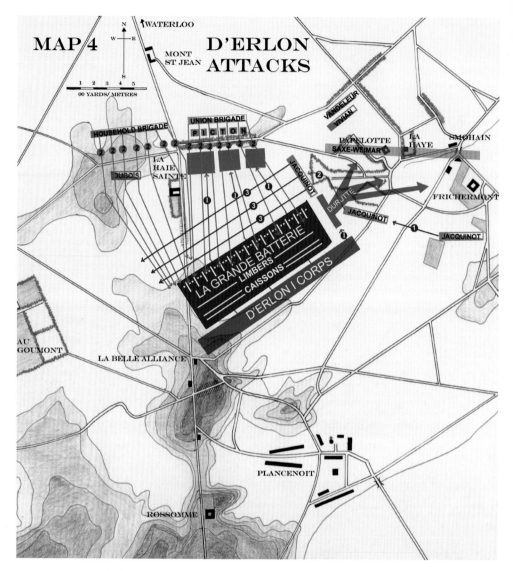

MAP 4 — D'ERLON ATTACKS

WATERLOO
MONT ST JEAN
N
W E
S

1 2 3 4 5
00 YARDS/ METRES

HOUSEHOLD BRIGADE
UNION BRIGADE
PICTON

LA HAIE SAINTE
DUBOIS

VANDELEUR
VIVIAN
PAPELOTTE
SAXE-WEIMAR
LA HAYE
SMOHAIN

FRICHERMONT

JACQUINOT
DUR JTTE
JACQUINOT
JACQUINOT

LA GRANDE BATTERIE
LIMBERS
CAISSONS
D'ERLON I CORPS

AU GOUMONT

LA BELLE ALLIANCE

PLANCENOIT

ROSSOMME

D'Erlon's corps works its way through the Grande Batterie to attack in three massive blocks.
Picton's division stops them and the British Heavy Cavalry disperses them, but the latter is
mauled in turn by a counter-attack by French cavalry. The numbers in circles on directional lines
indicate the sequence of events. (Please note: on this and subsequent maps, for clarity, only units
relevant to the events illustrated are shown. All units are to scale as far as possible.)

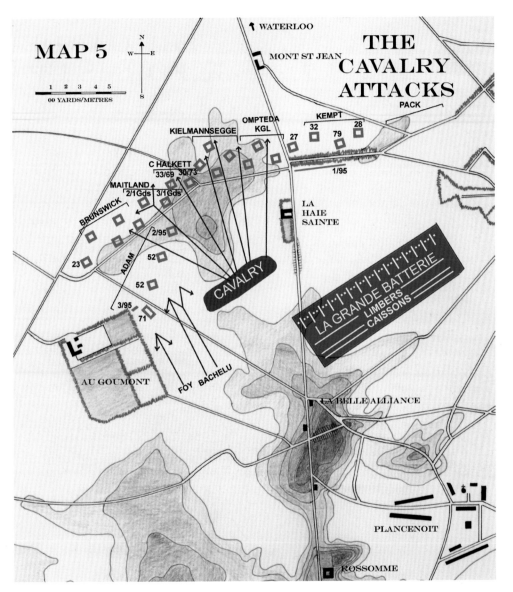

MAP 5

THE CAVALRY ATTACKS

00 YARDS/METRES

WATERLOO

MONT ST JEAN

PACK

OMPTEDA KGL

KEMPT

KIELMANNSEGGE

32   28

27   79

C HALKETT

33/69 30/73

1/95

MAITLAND

2/1Gds 3/1Gds

BRUNSWICK

2/95

LA HAIE SAINTE

23

ADAM

52

CAVALRY

52

3/95

71

LA GRANDE BATTERIE
LIMBERS
CAISSONS

AU GOUMONT

FOY BACHELU

LA BELLE ALLIANCE

PLANCENOIT

ROSSOMME

The experienced troops of Adam's Light Brigade are able not only to act as a groyne to take the energy out of the cavalry charges but also break the belated French attempt at all arms co-operation, the Ligne infantry assault by Foy and Bachelu. The Light Brigade is withdrawn to the Allied line when the cavalry charges are exhausted.

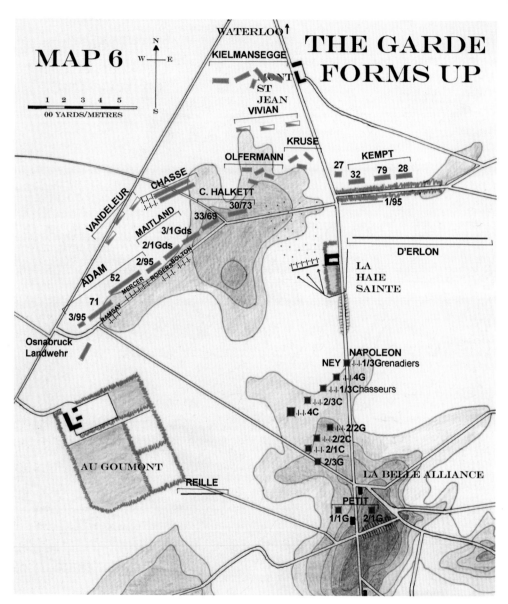

MAP 6

THE GARDE FORMS UP

N
W — E
S

1 2 3 4 5
00 YARDS/METRES

WATERLOO

KIELMANSEGGE

MONT ST JEAN

VIVIAN

KRUSE

OLFERMANN

KEMPT

27   32   79   28

CHASSE

C. HALKETT

30/73

VANDELEUR

33/69

MAITLAND

3/1Gds

2/1Gds

2/95

ADAM

52

71

3/95

MERCER

ROGERS

BOLTON

RAMSAY

1/95

D'ERLON

LA HAIE SAINTE

Osnabruck Landwehr

NAPOLEON

NEY   1/3Grenadiers

4G

1/3Chasseurs

2/3C

4C

2/2G

2/2C

2/1C

2/3G

AU GOUMONT

REILLE

LA BELLE ALLIANCE

PETIT

1/1G   2/1G

La Haie Sainte has fallen and, to its west, there is at least one French battery firing on the Allied line, having been driven from its initial position east of the farmstead by the deadly fire of the 1/95th's rifles. Kielmansegge's brigade has been withdrawn from the line and those of Olfermann and von Kruse are sheltering behind the line, the ridge being less pronounced here than further west. The eight battalions of the Middle and Old Garde are formed in square in echelon. (Please note the unit titles are abbreviated to 'G' for grenadiers and 'C' for châsseurs.)

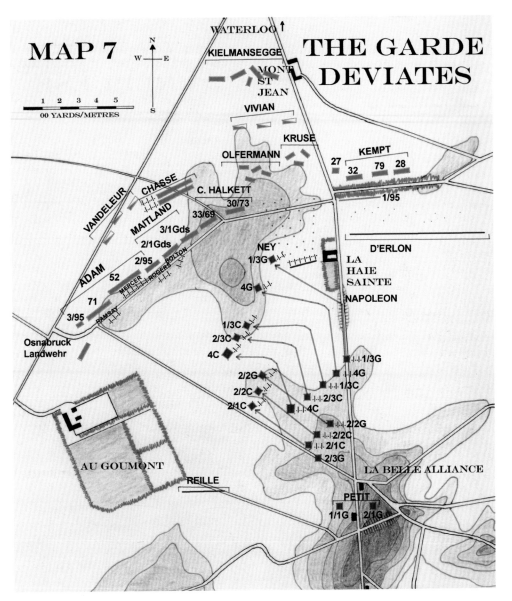

MAP 7

THE GARDE DEVIATES

N
W — E
S

1 2 3 4 5
00 YARDS/METRES

WATERLOO

KIELMANSEGGE

MONT ST JEAN

VIVIAN

KRUSE

OLFERMANN

KEMPT

27   32   79   28

1/95

VANDELEUR

CHASSE

C. HALKETT

30/73

MAITLAND

33/69

3/1Gds

2/1Gds

NEY

D'ERLON

ADAM

2/95

MERCER ROGERS BOLTON

1/3G

LA HAIE SAINTE

52

4G

NAPOLEON

71

3/95   RAMSAY

1/3C

2/3C

4C

Osnabruck
Landwehr

1/3C

2/2G

4G

2/2C

1/3C

2/1C

2/3C

4C

2/2G

2/2C

2/1C

2/3G

AU GOUMONT

LA BELLE ALLIANCE

REILLE

PETIT

1/1G   2/1G

Ney has altered direction to avoid the fire cone of the artillery beside La Haye Sainte and the knock-on effect causes the Middle Garde battalions to separate, the three châsseur battalions choosing to go round the tongue, rather than over its exposed summit. (Note the two-gun sections of horse artillery with each battalion.)

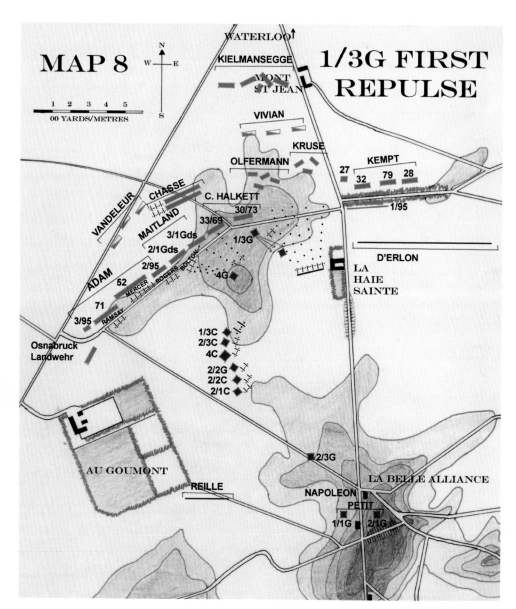

MAP 8

1/3G FIRST REPULSE

1 2 3 4 5
00 YARDS/METRES

WATERLOO
KIELMANSEGGE
MONT ST JEAN
VIVIAN
KRUSE
OLFERMANN
27   KEMPT
32   79   28
1/95
C. HALKETT
CHASSE
VANDELEUR   MAITLAND
30/73
33/69
3/1Gds
1/3G
2/1Gds
2/95
ADAM   52   MERCER   ROGERS   BOLTON
4G
71
3/95   RAMSAY
D'ERLON
LA HAIE SAINTE
Osnabruck Landwehr
1/3C
2/3C
4C
2/2G
2/2C
2/1C
AU GOUMONT
2/3G
REILLE   NAPOLEON   LA BELLE ALLIANCE
PETIT
1/1G   2/1G

1/3e Grenadiers are unexpectedly repulsed for the first time while 4e Grenadiers are exposed to the fire from Bolton's battery. Meanwhile the three châsseur battalions are beginning to coalesce with the three Old Garde battalions in reserve to form a column of battalions.

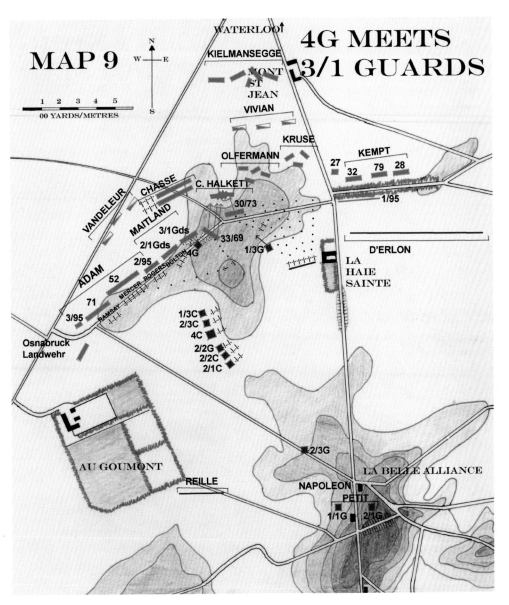

MAP 9

4G MEETS 3/1 GUARDS

WATERLOO

KIELMANSEGGE

MONT ST JEAN

VIVIAN

KRUSE

OLFERMANN

KEMPT

27   32   79   28

1/95

C. HALKETT

30/73

CHASSE

VANDELEUR

MAITLAND

3/1Gds

2/1Gds

33/69

1/3G

D'ERLON

LA HAIE SAINTE

2/95

MERCER ROGERS BOLTON 4G

ADAM

52

71

RAMSAY

3/95

1/3C

2/3C

4C

2/2G

2/2C

2/1C

Osnabruck Landwehr

AU GOUMONT

2/3G

LA BELLE ALLIANCE

REILLE

NAPOLEON

PETIT

1/1G   2/1G

N
W — E
S

1 2 3 4 5
00 YARDS/METRES

1/3e Grenadiers return to the attack. 4e Grenadiers meet 3/1st Guards but the Grenadiers'
cannon, having been firing canister at 3/1st Guards, are now firing at Mercer's troop and at
Halkett's 33rd/69th, the latter having been swung out of line to fire on 4e Grenadiers' flank. 4e
Grenadiers' cannon fire on 30th/73rd. Halkett's two composite battalions retire as a 'mere mob'.

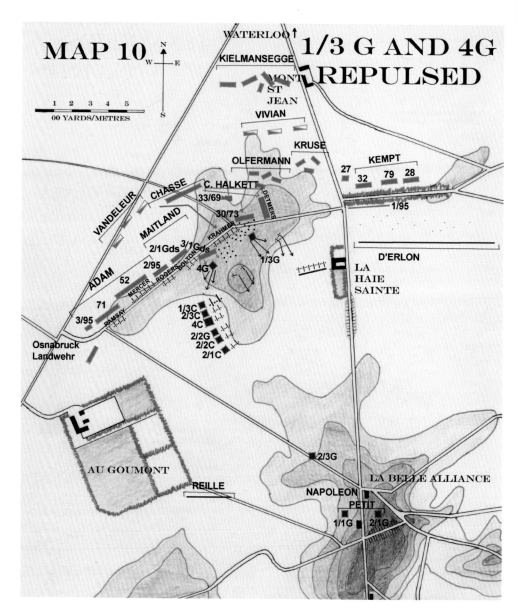

MAP 10

WATERLOO

1/3 G AND 4G REPULSED

1 2 3 4 5
00 YARDS/METRES

KIELMANSEGGE

MONT
ST
JEAN

VIVIAN

KRUSE

OLFERMANN

KEMPT

27   32   79   28

C. HALKETT

33/69

DETMERS

1/95

VANDELEUR CHASSE

MAITLAND

30/73

KRAHMER

2/1Gds 3/1Gds

ADAM   2/95

52   MERCER ROGERS BOLTON

1/3G

D'ERLON

4G

LA
HAIE
SAINTE

71   RAMSAY

1/3C
2/3C
4C

3/95

2/2G
2/2C
2/1C

Osnabruck
Landwehr

AU GOUMONT

2/3G

REILLE

LA BELLE ALLIANCE

NAPOLEON

PETIT

1/1G   2/1G

4e Grenadiers are repulsed and charged by 3/1st Guards; their cannon are seen off by Krahmer's battery, which also repulses 1/3e Grenadiers' second assault, helped by a volley from 30th/73rd, which has returned to the line. Detmers' brigade has moved forward to the front line and threatens 1/3e Grenadiers' cannon section, which decamps.

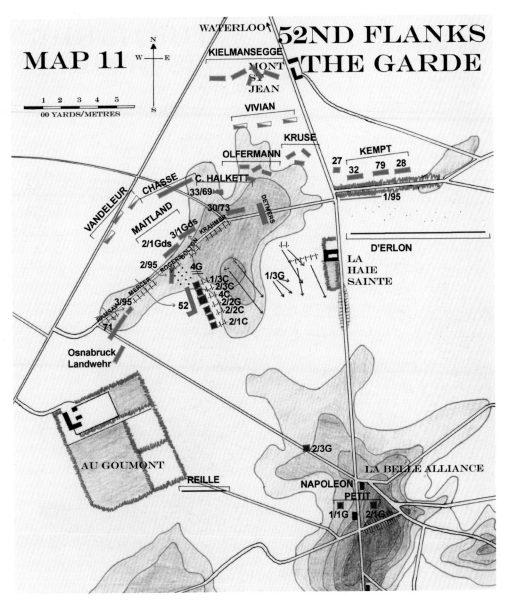

MAP 11

52ND FLANKS THE GARDE

N
W — E
S

1 2 3 4 5
00 YARDS/METRES

WATERLOO
KIELMANSEGGE
MONT
ST
JEAN

VIVIAN

KRUSE

OLFERMANN

KEMPT
27   32   79   28
1/95

CHASSE C. HALKETT
33/69
30/73

VANDELEUR

MAITLAND 3/1Gds
2/1Gds

2/95
ROGERS KRAHMER

MERCER 4G
1/3C
2/3C
4C
2/2G
2/2C
2/1C

3/95
52

1/3G

DETMERS

D'ERLON
LA
HAIE
SAINTE

71

Osnabruck
Landwehr

AU GOUMONT

REILLE

2/3G

LA BELLE ALLIANCE

NAPOLEON
PETIT
1/1G   2/1G

Colborne has brought out the 52nd and the charge against the Garde's six battalions has gone in
before the Light Infantrymen have completed the left-form manoeuvre. The 2/95th leaves the
line, aimed at the remnants of 4e Grenadiers, when the three guns of Rogers' battery are loosed
off blind, to the detriment of the 52nd. The 71st is moving and the two companies of the 3/95th
cross to the 71st's left flank (they may already have done so).

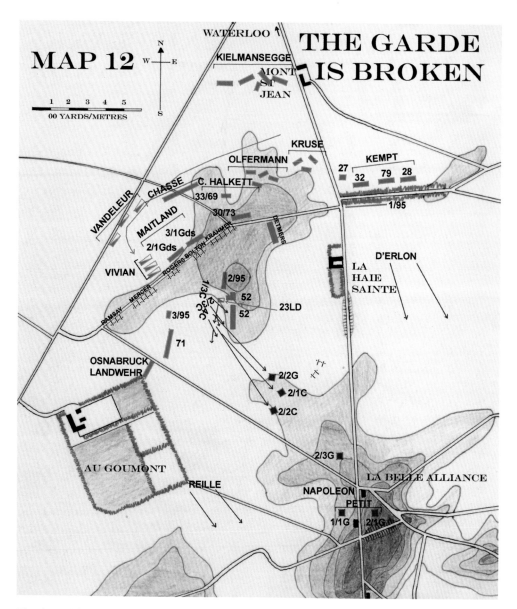

MAP 12

N
W — E
S

1 2 3 4 5
00 YARDS/METRES

WATERLOO

THE GARDE IS BROKEN

KIELMANSEGGE
MONT
ST
JEAN

KRUSE

OLFERMANN

KEMPT
27   32   79   28

1/95

VANDELEUR CHASSE C. HALKETT
33/69
30/73
MAITLAND
3/1Gds
2/1Gds

DETMERS

LA
HAIE
SAINTE

D'ERLON

VIVIAN

ROGERS BOLTON KRAHMER

MERCER

RAMSAY

2/95

1/3CAC

52

52

23LD

3/95

71

OSNABRUCK
LANDWEHR

2/2G

2/1C

2/2C

2/3G

AU GOUMONT

REILLE

LA BELLE ALLIANCE

NAPOLEON
PETIT

1/1G 2/1G

The three châsseur battalions of the Middle Garde are shattered and dispersed; the Old Garde battalions, which were not overlapped by the 52nd, retire towards La Belle Alliance. The 52nd is now charged by the 23rd Light Dragoons (23LD). Vivian's light cavalry comes forward and pauses in the gap in the line. The supporting attacks by Reille and d'Erlon collapse and disperse. The French left wing has been routed. The Osnabrück Landwehr is moving forward.

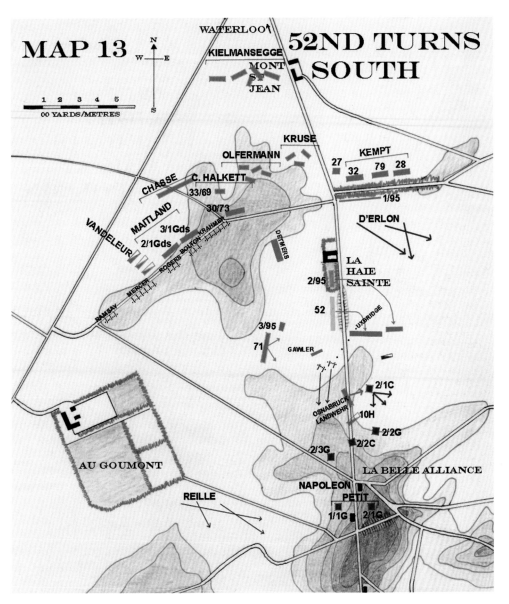

MAP 13

52ND TURNS SOUTH

WATERLOO

KIELMANSEGGE

MONT S. JEAN

N
W — E
S

1 2 3 4 5
00 YARDS/METRES

KRUSE

OLFERMANN

KEMPT

27   32   79   28

1/95

CHASSE   C. HALKETT

33/69

MAITLAND   30/73

VANDELEUR

3/1Gds

2/1Gds

ROGERS   BOLTON   KRAHMER

DETMERS

D'ERLON

MERCER

LA HAIE SAINTE

2/95

RAMSAY

52

3/95

UXBRIDGE

71   GAWLER

2/1C

OSNABRUCK LANDWEHR

10H

2/2G

2/3G   2/2C

AU GOUMONT

LA BELLE ALLIANCE

REILLE

NAPOLEON

PETIT

1/1G   2/1G

The 2/95th has fought through the orchard of La Haie Sainte. The 52nd has halted, crossed the road and reformed. As the regiment sets off up the hill Lord Uxbridge is hit by a shot from artillery, probably some of those that accompanied the Garde's attack. They are about to be seen off by Gawler's detachment. Vivian's brigade's squadrons are racing about the battlefield; only the 10th Hussars is located, fruitlessly charging 2/2e Grenadiers in square, Hugh Halkett having refused to support them. Halkett disperses 2/1er Châsseurs and captures Cambronne.

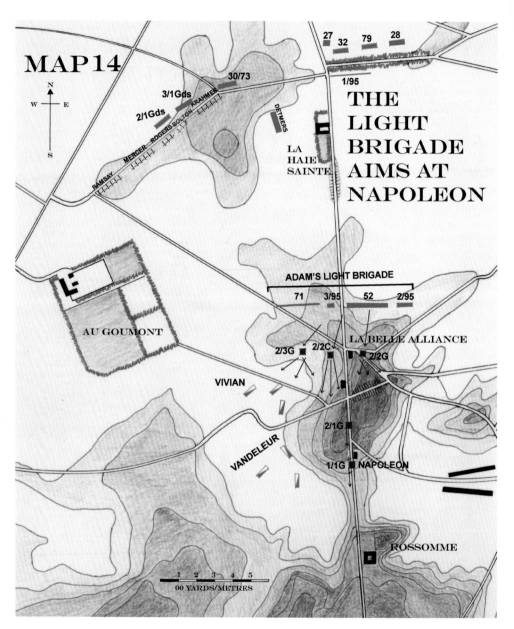

MAP 14

N
W · E
S

27 32 79 28

30/73

3/1Gds

2/1Gds

MERCER · ROGERS · BOLTON · KRAHMER

RAMSAY

1/95

DETMERS

LA
HAIE
SAINTE

THE
LIGHT
BRIGADE
AIMS AT
NAPOLEON

ADAM'S LIGHT BRIGADE

71   3/95   52   2/95

AU GOUMONT

LA BELLE ALLIANCE

2/3G   2/2C   2/2G

VIVIAN

2/1G

VANDELEUR

1/1G   NAPOLEON

ROSSOMME

1 2 3 4 5
00 YARDS/METRES

The Light Brigade has eventually come together and advances south against the three Old Garde squares, which have established a makeshift defensive line in front of Napoleon. He is heading south with Petit's two senior battalions, 1/1er and 2/1er Grenadiers.

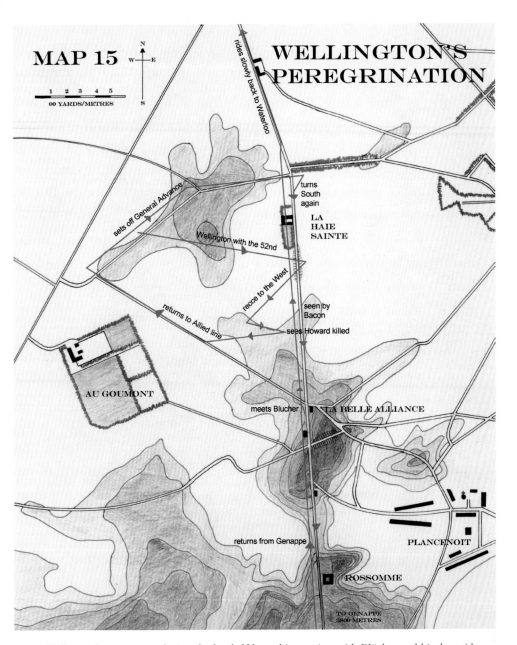

MAP 15   W—E   N / S

1 2 3 4 5
00 YARDS/METRES

WELLINGTON'S PEREGRINATION

rides slowly back to Waterloo

sets off General Advance

Wellington with the 52nd

recce to the West

returns to Allied line

turns
South
again

LA
HAIE
SAINTE

seen by
Bacon

sees Howard killed

AU GOUMONT

meets Blucher ◼ LA BELLE ALLIANCE

returns from Genappe

PLANCENOIT

ROSSOMME

TO GENAPPE
3800 METRES

Wellington's movements during the last half-hour, his meeting with Blücher and his slow ride
back to his quarters in Waterloo are indicated by the thin red line.

    He starts by joining the 52nd's advance across the battlefield. Once assured the Light Brigade
can cope without him, he rides with one staff officer towards au Goumont to check there is no
threat from that direction. Doubling back, he witnesses Major Howard's death and then the three
Old Garde battalions dispersed by the Light Brigade. Then, having initiated the General Advance,
he catches up with the Light Brigade at Rossomme. Having ridden on towards Genappe, he
returns and meets Blücher by chance at La Belle Alliance, before riding morosely back to
Waterloo.

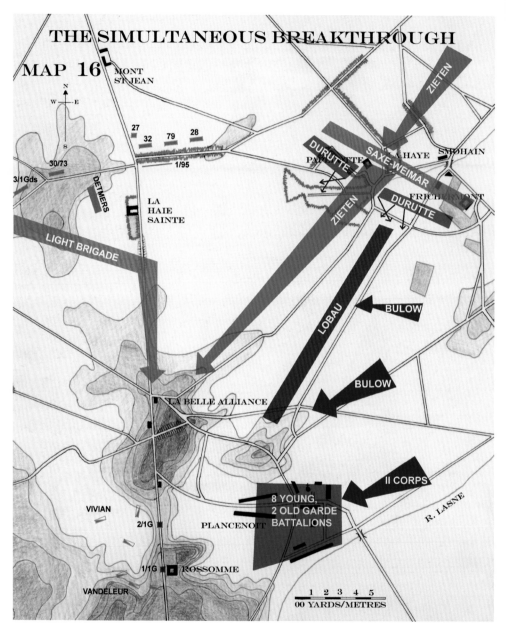

THE SIMULTANEOUS BREAKTHROUGH

MAP 16

MONT ST JEAN

N
W—E
S

27
32   79   28

30/73   1/95

3/1Gds

DETMERS

LA HAIE SAINTE

LIGHT BRIGADE

ZIETEN

DURUTTE

PAPELOTTE

SAXE-WEIMAR

LA HAYE   SMOHAIN

FRICHERMONT

DURUTTE

ZIETEN

LOBAU

BULOW

BULOW

LA BELLE ALLIANCE

II CORPS

R. LASNE

VIVIAN

2/1G

8 YOUNG,
2 OLD GARDE
BATTALIONS

PLANCENOIT

1/1G   ROSSOMME

VANDELEUR

1 2 3 4 5
00 YARDS/METRES

Zieten's advance is initially blunted by fighting the Nassauers but then he breaks through the French, who collapse and run. Lobau and ten battalions of the Garde hold the Prussians in Plancenoit, while Zieten's skirmishers meet the Light Brigade just north of La Belle Alliance.

These Frenchmen were experienced veterans, confirmed by their holding their fire until the most effective moment – and that is confirmed by Howard falling close enough for a grenadier to step out from the square and kill him by a blow to the head with his musket butt. The square was almost certainly of the Garde and it is very difficult to believe the square was dispersed; had it been so, how could a grenadier step forward to smash Howard's skull? For cavalry, unsupported, to break a well formed infantry square – let alone one of the Old Garde – would have been cause for much triumphant trumpeting. There is no evidence of any such. Both Arnold and Bacon were wounded.

Halkett also recorded this incident but – needless to say – to avoid opprobrium he also claimed the square was broken; but he told a different story. In his version he asked the cavalry for assistance, not the other way round. He also suggested the target was no great threat, being just a column of moving infantry:

> Some hundred yards to our right were *some Troops* of Hussars (I believe the 10th). I rode up to them and got them to charge the head of a Column of Infantry, which was drawing to their left in rear of the French Guards. The charge succeeded admirably and the Column dispersed behind some enclosures, after which I saw no more of the Cavalry.[20]

It is difficult to be sure whether his account is true or not, but the most intriguing question is why Halkett was so keen to push on. His prime purpose in advancing in the first place was to protect the flank of the Light Brigade. Clearly he now felt there was no need for that, so maintaining the momentum of the rout was now his best role. To that end he should have attacked any infantry opposed to him and, with cavalry to hand, he had an adequate combination of arms here with which to achieve success.

Had there been horse artillery to hand as well there would have been no excuse, but there was none: all bar one troop had been deployed since the start of the battle in static support of the Allied ridge line. This one troop – Gardiner's – was allocated to Vivian's brigade so he should have been available. But Gardiner had been left to his own devices, because – one suspects – Vivian feared the artillery's manoeuvres would have spoiled the cavalry's magnificent dash. Halkett may have been correct in judging his militia men were not capable of attacking an Old Garde square; but he was sufficiently experienced to know that cavalry alone should not try to attack a formed square either. Instead, he let the 10th Hussars fruitlessly lose good men. His guilty conscience may be evident in his claiming the 10th Hussars attacked a unit in column rather than square, a column being less proof against cavalry.

Halkett's reluctance is even more questionable when his pursuit of 2/1er Châsseurs is considered – these men were genuine veterans of the Old Garde.

Lieutenant Wilhelm Richers, of the Osnabrück Landwehr Battalion, provides a graphic eyewitness description of his battalion's advance, of how the Garde battalion, to which they were opposed, at first stood its ground and his battalion paused.[21] But Halkett's encouraging shout drove the men into a bayonet charge and the Garde first retired and then broke in disorder. Now followed a wild pursuit in which the Hanoverians were able to take many prisoners. A senior officer and two other mounted officers rode back and forth, trying to rally and reform their men until the senior officer's horse was hit by a musket ball and went down, trapping its rider. Halkett galloped forward in amongst the French troops and seized the officer by his gold-braided *aiguillette*. Halkett's own horse then went down to a shot through the body and General Cambronne – as he had revealed himself to be – took French leave in an attempt to rejoin his comrades (who had not stayed to help him) until Halkett got his mount on its feet again and retook the General.

So the question remains – what or who was Halkett pursuing when he declined the invitation to support the 10th Hussars? The only conceivable answer is that he and his Hanoverian troops were still hot on the heels of General Cambronne. None of the published accounts give a clear indication as to precisely where the 2/1er Châsseurs dispersed and finally left Cambronne behind, so the conclusion must be that he was taken near La Belle Alliance, but after Howard's charge. Indeed this seems to be supported by Bacon's evidence, and may in turn clarify his sketch map. There would seem to be very little doubt that the easterly column was in fact 2/1er Châsseurs.

Here we must leave Colonel Halkett to continue his ardent, unopposed pursuit on the way to Genappe, apparently far ahead of any other Anglo-Allied infantry. Instead, we stay with Lieutenant Anthony Bacon, who was seriously wounded in the thigh during the charge. Despite the Hussars' heroism, all three Garde squares were still in position as a screen for Napoleon while Bacon, still mounted, made his way slowly back towards the Allied line.

Given the very considerable numbers of officers killed or wounded during the battle, Bacon's misfortune may seem unimportant but it is far from being so, for he goes on to fix two more moments of great relevance to this investigation, as a direct result of his wound. Recorded by him with no other intention than to prove that his squadron's action had taken place on the east side of the axis road Bacon relates:

> On my way to the rear after being wounded I came upon the Duke attended, it is true, *by one officer only*, but that officer was *Lord George Lennox*, for he rode up to me and directed me the way to La Haye Sainte where I should probably find a surgeon. The Duke was not 200 yards in the rear of our squadron at this time, and about half that distance from the high road;

when I got to the road, I turned to my right, and made [out] Maitland's Brigade of Guards marching along it, I passed on their left flank, at this time I could scarcely sit upon my horse, and I cannot readily forget Colonel Gunthorpe who was with other officers at the head of the column sending a man to lead my horse, I remember passing La Haie Sainte, and soon afterwards being joined by Arnold and several wounded men of the regiment, after which I became senseless, I can remember nothing till I was put into my gig with Colonel Quentin the following morning.[22]

Unintentionally Bacon has given us a fixed point about Wellington's movements (see Map 15, colour section) at this stage of the battle. We know he was with the 52nd from the episode with the 23rd Light Dragoons until the Light Brigade, having turned south in the valley bottom beyond La Haie Sainte, advanced against the three Garde squares north of La Belle Alliance. Howard's charge must have taken place a matter of very few minutes after the Light Brigade resumed its advance when the latter was hidden from Bacon by the spur of higher ground to the north.

Shortly before the three Garde squares were dispersed Wellington must have left the Light Brigade, and 'having gone some distance' to the west to scout for enemy cavalry, was recorded by Major Blair as 'moving at a quick pace', accompanied by only one staff officer, the Sardinian Comte de Sales. This apparently minor incident, recalled in the previous chapter, is vitally important to establishing Wellington's movements at this stage of the pursuit. Wellington next appears, on the slope up to La Belle Alliance where he was chanced upon by Anthony Bacon. Significantly, he had changed staff officers – Lord Gordon Lennox vice the Comte de Sales – thus strongly suggesting that he had returned to the Allied line and was now heading south again. Bacon must have lost track of time because his wound was clearly quite serious, involving major loss of blood. He would eventually spend the night unconscious on the battlefield. In his account he is not explicit about how much time elapsed between his being wounded and his meeting Lord Gordon Lennox with the duke. It seems reasonable to suppose that it was much longer than the young officer realised.

By this time the general advance was under way. We know this because Bacon also tells us that he fell in with Maitland's Guards Brigade on the road just south of La Haie Sainte and we know, thanks to Captain Weyland Powell of the 1st Foot Guards, that the Guards Brigade, when ordered to advance, moved across to the axis road and advanced along it. Powell, despite his many inaccuracies, tells us:

.. we got to the bottom of the valley between the positions. Here our Brigade halted to restore its order by calling out the covering Serjeants and forming Companies. As soon as the Column was formed we proceeded towards the *chaussée* (to Namur), where we found nearly sixty pieces of Artillery jammed together and deserted.[23]

In addition to establishing that the general advance was now in progress he raises three more points of passing interest. Column of companies was not the attacking formation that would have been expected had the general advance been the fighting action Wellington claimed it to have been. Why the Guards moved diagonally across to the Charleroi road instead of heading straight at the French position is not immediately obvious, but may have been in response to a lack of Allied troops to their left able to move, given that neither Colin Halkett's brigade nor the Brunswickers and Nassauers were capable of moving forward, due to exhaustion and casualties. His estimate of the large numbers of artillery pieces may be exaggerated but, nevertheless, his comment may refer to cannon that had been firing from La Haie Sainte and possibly to the remains of the Grande Batterie.

Now it is time to consider the actions of the other light cavalry brigade involved in the pursuit of the French. As we have already heard, the 4th (Light) Cavalry Brigade, consisting of the 11th, 12th and 16th Light Dragoons, was commanded by Major General Sir John Vandeleur. Like Vivian's brigade, it too started the battle on the Allied left wing. Unlike Vivian's men, Vandeleur's had been involved in the aftermath of d'Erlon's corps' initial assault earlier

Major General Sir John Ormsby Vandeleur, 1763–1849. Commissioned into the infantry in 1781. Exchanged to the cavalry in 1792. In 1802 he fought for Wellington in India in the second Anglo-Maratha War. Promoted major general in 1811 in Spain and led the famous Light Division at Cuidad Rodrigo, Salamanca and Vitoria.

in the day, when the British heavy cavalry came under counter-attack by French cavalry. The 12th Dragoons had attacked the French counter-attack, and suffered severe casualties, but they had preserved the lives of some of the heavies. When the Prussian support to the Allied left wing began to materialise, Vandeleur's and Vivian's brigades moved to the Allied centre, with Vandeleur posted in rear of the infantry north of the au Goumont enclosure. Then, along with Vivian's brigade, Vandeleur was ordered forward to support the Light Brigade's meteoric charge, performing as Vandeleur described:

> It then supported Vivian's Brigade, which made several charges on the [French?] left of the retiring Enemy. Vandeleur's Brigade then relieved Vivian's Brigade, pursued, charged, and broke the last Infantry which preserved its order near La Belle Alliance.[24]

Admirably succinct as it was, his account does not tell the whole story. For the sake of balance, we need to explore his brigade's actions in a little more detail, not least because he claims to have broken the 'last infantry that preserved its order' and also because Vivian disputed the relative contributions of his and Vandeleur's brigades. Vivian argued that Vandeleur's brigade came through the same gap in the line, vacated by the Light Brigade, at least twenty – perhaps thirty – minutes after his and achieved very little, compared with his own. He felt so strongly about this that he concluded:

> Truth is history, and history without truth does not deserve the name; and I am anxious for the sake of the gallant men I commanded that one day at least the truth may be known.[25]

Vandeleur, in his previous quotation, claims his brigade 'broke the last Infantry which preserved its order near La Belle Alliance'. Lieutenant J. Luard, 16th Light Dragoons in Vandeleur's brigade, supports this contention. In his letter to William Siborne he mentions this event:

> About a mile and a half from our position, a road runs through the valley on the opposite side of which a Column of French Infantry formed square to oppose us. We instantly wheeled into line, received their fire, and charged, taking or destroying the whole. In this charge Captain Buchanan and Lieutenant Hay were killed, and Captain Weyland wounded. The 10th and 18th Hussars charged a Column of the Enemy at the same moment on our left.[26]

There can be little doubt that the charge was made, because of the casualties sustained, but that the square was broken is highly doubtful. It is possible the charge by the 16th Light Dragoons was inflicted on one of the Garde squares that was pushed on by the Light Brigade and said by the witnesses to have dispersed, but this would have been after Howard's fruitless charge. Anthony Bacon's sketch shows four bodies of Garde infantry all of which can be named with some confidence. If this was the moment that Howard's squadron charged one of them and Halkett pursued and finally dispersed another, and if the 16th Light Dragoons did charge one of the remaining two, they failed to break it: the square was still there, one of the three, when the Light Brigade appeared out of dead ground to push them finally off the battlefield. Besides, the loss of so many officers suggests the 16th Light Dragoons met with determined resistance and the example of Howard's failure to break his square strongly suggests Luard's failed too.

It is even less likely the 16th Light Dragoons would have been successful against the very last two Garde battalions. It is known that the two battalions of the 1er Grenadiers under General Petit moved forward towards La Belle Alliance, to provide protection for Napoleon, but they were unlikely to have come north of the farmstead. No convincing evidence can be found to suggest they did. Besides, given the Grenadiers were the veterans of so many battles it is unlikely they would have succumbed to the 16th Light Dragoons, nor had they been involved in the breaking of the Garde. Petit's evidence tells of both his squares retiring in good order. In a little while Captain Barton will describe a square that eventually surrendered, probably preferring this dishonourable fate to being slaughtered by the Prussians.

So we cannot be sure Luard's square was broken. Neither can we accept at face value his (possibly) linking the action with that by Howard of Vivian's brigade: Luard neither claims to have witnessed Howard's charge nor gives any description that might confirm it. He may – almost certainly would – have heard tell of Howard's charge after the battle and may have linked the two events in his memory. However, if the two charges by the 10th and 16th Hussars did take place simultaneously, then that would give the lie to Vivian's adamant claim that Vandeleur's brigade did not come out of the Allied line until twenty or thirty minutes after his own debouchment. However, the debate is academic since Vivian largely destroys his own case by reporting one of Vandeleur's regiments ahead of him:

Now, without meaning to take away from the merits of my friend Vandeleur, I must claim for my people their due. I assert positively that when I advanced I left Vandeleur's Brigade standing on the position, and they cheered me as I passed. ... And was advancing in pursuit of the broken Enemy, when I found on my right and front the 11th Regiment, part of Vandeleur's Brigade.[27]

But the dispute between Vivian and Vandeleur is not the important issue here – we can conclude that honours would seem to have been even and consider the two light cavalry brigades as a whole. What does need to be determined is the validity of Vivian's claim that the light cavalry deserved the credit for defeating Napoleon's left wing, a claim that recurs with regularity to this day. Is there any truth in it? Captain Taylor, 10th Hussars, one of Vivian's squadron commanders, clearly thought there was and he may have put thoughts into the latter's head. In 1829 he wrote to Vivian as follows:

> It is curious to remember that little notice was ever taken of the charge of this Hussar Brigade in English accounts, whereas there is scarcely a French account in which the Corps of Cavalry that came from the left and completed the rout, [and] which Buonaparte saw cutting into the thick of his troops, is not mentioned as the final blow that decided him to be off.[28]

In a memorandum of the following year, 1830, to William Siborne, providing commentary on public opinions of the battle, Vivian notes 'In one of the Numbers of the *Quarterly Review* the conduct of the British Light Cavalry in the Battle of Waterloo is noticed in the most slighting terms.' In his view, much credit – well deserved – was given to the charge of the heavy cavalry but the contribution by the light cavalry was ignored by British authors, in direct contradiction to French writers who bore testimony to the 'decisive' effect of the light cavalry. To Siborne he wrote:

> I don't know if I sent you a long series of extracts from different French writers speaking of the Battle, in which they all attribute the complete disorder (the *sauve-qui-peut* state) into which the French were thrown at the end of the day to the attack of these six Regiments of fresh Cavalry (Vandeleur's and Vivian's Brigades).[29]

To that claim we should add Captain Taylor's, that the cavalry's assault was '… the final blow that decided him [Napoleon] to be off'. So the question that needs to be answered is: was the disordered state of the French left wing, initially caused by the advance of Adam's Light Brigade, such that Napoleon would have been unable to re-establish sufficient control to mount a counter-attack, or was the advance of the two light cavalry brigades necessary to achieve that disordered state?

One of the earliest French accounts seems to confirm the French view. It comes from *The Battle of Waterloo, also of Ligny, and Quatre Bras, etc.*, which was first published in 1815 and so records French first impressions. In a section headed 'French Official Detail of the Battles with the Prussians and English, with Ney's Observations' the anonymous author wrote:

> At half-after eight o'clock, the four battalions of the middle guard, who had been sent to the ridge on the other side of Mount St. Jean, in order to support the Cuirassiers, being greatly annoyed by the grape-shot, endeavoured to carry the batteries with the bayonet. At the end of the day, a charge directed against their flank, by several English squadrons, put them in disorder ... In an instant, the whole army was nothing but a mass of confusion; all the soldiers, of all arms, were mixed *pêle-mêle*, and it was utterly impossible to rally a single corps. The enemy, who perceived this astonishing confusion immediately attacked with their cavalry, and increased the disorder ...[30]

Thanks to the careful translation of Waterloo as 'Mount St. Jean', it is possible to believe – as is stated in the book – that this was the 'official' French account or, at least, it had a French author and had to be translated into English. The account is, of course, far from accurate. But, leaving aside the inaccuracies – the timing, the quantity of Middle Garde battalions (four was the figure given by Maréchal Ney, four pages later), the omission of the Old Garde Reserve, the misunderstanding about their mission – is the phrase 'a charge directed against their flank, by several English squadrons, put them in disorder' evidence that the light cavalry gained the victory? It is demonstrably confused on two counts. First, replace 'squadrons' with 'battalions' and it clearly describes the 52nd and the Light Brigade; secondly, it follows that the subsequent use of '... immediately attacked with their cavalry' clearly indicates the arrival of the light cavalry in support, brought on *after* the 'disorder' has occurred.

It would be natural to assume cavalry had done the deed – to attribute the defeat to infantry would have seemed degrading; to find infantry performing like cavalry in front of their line and at speed would have been inconceivable. It is impossible to say for certain whether or not this particular account gave rise to Vivian's claim but it is a possibility.

It might be asked, do Maréchal Ney's observations on the end of the battle provide any support for Vivian's claim? Remember, they are primarily an 'apologia':

> I saw four regiments of the middle guard, conducted by the Emperor, arriving. ... he ordered me to lead them on; generals, officers and soldiers all displayed the greatest intrepidity; but this body of troops was too weak to resist, for a long time, the forces opposed to it by the enemy, and it was soon necessary to renounce the hope which this had, for a few moments, inspired.

He then describes how four [*sic*] squares of the Middle Garde were:

> ... forced successively to retire, yielded ground foot by foot, till, over-
> whelmed by numbers, they were almost annihilated. From that moment ...
> the army formed nothing but a confused mass. There was not, however, a
> total rout ...[31]

Apart from wondering how Ney would have described a total rout, it is unfair
to expect the leading general in a disaster to be entirely accurate and honest
about a major defeat but, regrettably, there seems to be hardly a shred of truth
in Ney's account. There is no evidence in the Allied record of the French
squares yielding ground slowly while being ground down – it is just part of
the comforting myth. Indeed, Maréchal de Camp Petit, commanding the two
Old Garde battalions in ultimate reserve south of La Belle Alliance, was quite
sure that, at this stage, only his two battalions were still properly formed:

> The Emperor galloped back and placed himself inside the square of the 1st
> Battalion of the 1st Regiment of Grenadiers. The whole army was in the
> most appalling disorder. Infantry, cavalry, artillery – everybody was fleeing in
> all directions. Soon no unit retained any order except the two squares formed
> by this regiment's two battalions posted to right and left of the main road.[32]

But the myth persists. A modern French expert on the battle, Jacques Logie,
shows, in a map entitled 'The Rout of the French Army', Adam's brigade and
Hugh Halkett advancing towards the three squares north of La Belle Alliance,
while Vivian's and Vandeleur's brigades attack them. This may give an impression of accuracy but it does not give the whole truth: it does not show the
three squares still in position, unbroken, until the Light Brigade came up and
dispersed them. Logie then describes how Vandeleur's and Vivian's brigades
were spreading 'their deadly whirlwind' between La Belle Alliance and au
Goumont. He concluded:

> Several troops of *cuirassiers* tried hard to repel them, but without success, one
> witness reporting that their horses' exhaustion placed them in such a state of
> inferiority that they were unseated like young recruits.[33]

The message is clear – total confusion, panic, no cohesion and the cavalry
already exhausted by the earlier long period of cavalry charges, before the
Allied light cavalry was involved. Captain Barton, of the British 12th Light
Dragoons, reinforces Logie's picture of disorder but emphasises the lack
of resistance:

The only attempt to make anything like a stand against us or interrupt our pursuit, was made by a weak Regiment of Infantry which halted and fired a few shots at us, after which some of the men threw themselves down on their faces in the standing corn, and others effected their escape into the wood on our right. At this time we saw to our left front, a strong Regiment of Cavalry, which we soon ascertained to be the Grenadiers à Cheval of the Imperial Guard; they were formed in a dense column, and appeared to take but little notice of our advance, when opposite their flank they fired a few pistol or carbine shots.

We were some distance in front of our Brigade, and being too weak to make an impression [on them], they literally walked from the field in a most majestic manner.[34]

The overall impression is of a vanquished enemy desperately trying to escape capture or death. The Grenadiers à Cheval were an exception, which impressed many on the Allied side, but their stately departure actually highlights the sad fact that the French Army was absolutely defeated. Captain Barton's statement is representative of many other accounts by officers of Vandeleur's brigade. There are no signs here of aggressive purpose or attempt at counter-attack by the French. On the contrary, the dignified departure without fighting by the Grenadiers à Cheval can only be attributed to their recognition that any attempt at aggressive resistance would be completely useless. Another of Vandeleur's officers, Captain Tomkinson, 16th Light Dragoons, supports Barton's view:

When on the crest of the [Allied] position the whole French Army was [seen to be] in full retreat, their infantry in confusion running at the bottom of the hill.[35]

Captains Barton and Tomkinson were of Vandeleur's brigade: the view presented to the men of Vivian's brigade was little different. Murray, commanding the 18th Hussars, remarked on the apparently calm behaviour of the enemy infantry:

But soon we came into ground entirely covered with French infantry retreating not in a body, but individually, yet with none of that hurry and confusion that might be imagined when thus suddenly ridden upon, and especially some of the Ancienne Garde might be remarked for their coolness and bold countenance (one nearly bayoneted me as I passed).[36]

Perhaps the Garde's coolness was anything but – it has already been suggested they might have been suffering the lethargy that comes from heat exhaustion, which could well account for any sluggishness. Murray's mounts certainly were exhausted after dashing about the field. His party (his men were now disordered and squadrons separated) eventually faced an infantry square but the intervening ground and his inferiority in numbers, together with the signal to retire having been given some time before, persuaded him to withdraw. Unfortunately the light was now so poor that his party was fired on by artillery – probably Prussian, in his opinion – and suffered severely. When he rejoined the 18th Hussars he met Sir Robert Gardiner of the Royal Horse Artillery (RHA).

Sir Robert's troop had initially been brigaded with Vivian's brigade on the left flank and had moved across to the right with Vivian. Neither Vivian nor any of his officers mention Gardiner's troop during their advance: the cavalry was too busy dashing hither and thither in the pursuit of glory to co-operate with them. Had the RHA been able to act in concert with the cavalry, the latter would, almost certainly not have failed against the infantry squares. With cavalry forcing enemy infantry to remain in square, the guns would have annihilated the solid target thus presented. Instead, as Lieutenant W.B. Ingilby, RHA, an officer of Gardiner's troop, tells us:

> Sir H. Vivian's Brigade quickly passed through the intervals [in the Allied front line]. We had now the French in full view before us, completely routed and flying, in the greatest confusion.
>
> Sir Robert Gardiner brought his Guns to fire upon the fugitive crowd instantly, and from that period acted independently from the Brigade of Cavalry, alternately advancing rapidly and halting to fire ...[37]

Once again, the French, from Ingilby's first sight of them, were observed to be in a state of complete chaos. There are many more similar descriptions of the French being, in Ney's words, 'a confused mass'. So, how did Vivian himself recall his first view of the retreating French? In an undated letter written between 1830 and 1841 he claimed:

> The advance of my Brigade ... No doubt threw into confusion all those French troops formed to cover the retreat on their left of the road around La Belle Alliance, whilst Adam's Brigade had before routed the body of reserve covering the attack.[38]

Vivian here gives no hint of the whole French wing being in uncontrollable retreat before he left the Allied position. Claiming his brigade routed 'all those French troops formed to cover the retreat on their left of the road around La Belle Alliance, is clearly untrue since the three squares, of which Howard's was one, were still in position when the Light Brigade came up and pushed them on beyond La Belle Alliance. It is not clear what Vivian meant by 'the body of reserve'. Was he still convinced (or unwilling to admit otherwise, since this was the accepted 'truth' at the time of his writing) that the Guards had achieved the rout of the main Garde attack and that this had caused the rout of the French Army, while Adam's brigade's contribution was to have seen off the rearmost Middle Garde battalion, the 4e Châsseurs – or even the three Old Garde battalions? The latter were at least nominally in reserve. His meaning is uncertain but one fact is not: either the Guards Brigade or the Light Brigade had caused the rout – Vivian had not.

This seems to be the appropriate moment to introduce a note of caution about General Vivian's evidence as a whole. Siborne owed Vivian a favour, having been supported financially by him in the construction of the first model of the battle, his last contribution being £1,000 – a very large sum in those days. So the description of the light cavalry's action in Siborne's history of the battle might be considerably exaggerated. Despite Sir Hussey's avowed passion for the truth, his veracity and claims for success by his brigade are at odds with the contents of the letter he wrote to his wife on 23 June 1815, five days after the battle. In the same letter that introduced this chapter, Vivian had admitted to his wife that he knew perfectly well the French were in rapid retreat even before he left the Allied line:

> No words can give any idea of it (how a man escaped is to me a miracle), we every instant expecting through the smoke to see the Enemy appearing under our noses, for the smoke was literally so thick that we could not see ten yards off. But we at last began to find that the shots did not come so thick, and I discovered the Enemy were, instead of advancing to gain our position, retrograding on theirs. The moment to attack was arrived, and I received orders to advance …
>
> Having cleared the smoke I observed the French retiring up the hill and along the high road covered by their guns – two large bodies of Cavalry, and two Squares of Infantry, whilst our Infantry were gallantly moving on also after them.[39]

Vivian does not express surprise at the sight of the French in disorder but, nevertheless, it must have been abundantly clear to him that the fortunes of battle had finally turned massively in the Allies' favour. However, so keen was Vivian to have the actions of his brigade acclaimed as the final blow to Napoleon's ambitions that he entered wholeheartedly into an acrimonious correspondence in the august pages of the *United Service Journal* with one of the 52nd's officers, Lieutenant George Gawler. Vivian's stance, in essence, was that the 52nd – and by inference the Light Brigade – could not have been responsible for routing the French, because they had not been ahead of the cavalry. Gawler, on the other hand, argued that the 52nd's breaking of the Garde's column of battalions and its rapid advance towards Napoleon had led to the dissolution of Napoleon's left wing (and by inference, his whole army). Until 1833, when the debate took place, the 52nd's action had been completely ignored: Gawler was trying to rectify this. In 1833 Gawler published his *The Crisis and Close of the Action at Waterloo, by an eye-witness*. He made the mistake of stating some facts that he was unable to verify – such as the cavalry's role in relation to the 71st – and thereby weakened his case, allowing critics to dismiss altogether his claim by referring to his errors, as shown by the strongly felt letter from Captain Arthur Shakespear to Vivian:

> … Major Gawler's crisis and your reply, never reached me until Hesse of the 18th [Hussars] came to see me. I have carefully read both. Major Gawler is wrong in many points.
>
> The rapid movement we made off the position, renders it impossible that the 52nd could keep the ground, as stated, we must have been upon them, or they have been in rear of those French troops, who's [*sic*] heads we saw through the smoke, so close to us, but who *never crossed the summit!*
>
> I deny that we came up *'to the support of the 71st'*, we were down the hill, and scoured the plain, to be free of any other troops.
>
> What do the Guards say to this statement, because if true, the 52nd take all the credit from them – as Major Gawler says, they charged across their front!
>
> I think Sir, your reply is excellent but not severe enough – which is bad enough, but his arrogating for the 52nd all the glory of the crisis, deserves severe handling.[40]

Sir John Colborne had hitherto chosen to remain silent on the subject but was now spurred to enter the lists in the *United Service Journal* in support of his erstwhile acting company commander:

> The writer has not been on the ground since; but he is positive, as far as his memory can be relied on, that these facts are correctly stated, and is thus certain that no corps whatever passed between the 52nd and the French from the time the 52nd moved on the flank of the French, for the 52nd were under a heavy fire the whole time and were opposed [up] to the moment they touched the Charleroi road. When they were formed to the left of the Charleroi road no corps was near them. The only corps of cavalry near the 52nd or the French column during the attack was the regiment of cavalry [The 23rd Light Dragoons] that moved in the direction of the left

company of the 52nd. Thus it appears that the movement to which Sir H. Vivian alludes must have been the attack made in retreat, and that all the troops that came in contact with the French must have moved across the track of the 52nd in their movement from the cross-road to the Charleroi road and while the 52nd were charging up to the plateau of La Haye Sainte.[41]

Colborne must have meant the plateau of La Belle Alliance. And what did he mean by 'the attack made in retreat'? Colborne's text is a little opaque but in essence he was saying that he saw no British Cavalry between the 52nd and the French for the last half-hour of the battle.[42] If we cast our minds back to Anthony Bacon's evidence that, at the time of Howard's attack on a Garde square, his detailed description of the troops within his view did not include the Light Brigade, the mystery becomes clear. It is all to do with the shape of the ground.

Vivian's brigade went nearly straight, and rapidly, towards La Belle Alliance, leaving the Allied line at the moment the Light Brigade, which had already reached La Haie Sainte, had just turned south and begun moving up the hill. When Vivian, Howard and Bacon (and possibly Luard) fruitlessly engaged one of the three Garde squares north of La Belle Alliance the Light Brigade was in dead ground, thanks to the convex shape of the slope. By the time Colborne and the Light Infantry pushed the Garde squares away past La Belle Alliance, Vivian had dashed off to the 18th Hussars, Bacon was seriously wounded and Howard was dead. Neither infantry nor cavalry saw the other.

So, leaving discussion of the Prussian contribution to the victory to a later chapter, would Napoleon's left wing have been defeated without the contribution by the two brigades of light cavalry? We have heard from French sources as well as British, from cavalry, infantry and a gunner, and we should bear in mind the repeated testimony from both sides to the French being in a state of complete disorder, apart from a few signs of local, short-lived resistance and controlled retreat by a few units of the Old Garde. But there has been no evidence whatsoever of serious counter-attack. Moreover the British light cavalry declined to attack the only formed body of French cavalry, that of the Garde, which made no attempt at resistance.

We must determine whether or not the three arms of the French left wing, acting either together or individually, would have been able to turn the tables on Adam's Light Brigade (in which, for the sake of completeness, we include the Osnabrück Landwehr) had the light cavalry not been involved. Let us examine, as best we can despite the inevitable confusion, each of the three arms in turn.

Did the French artillery pose a threat? Napoleon's Grande Batterie had been firing as the Garde advanced but would have ceased fire when the Garde neared the Allied Line. Thereafter nothing is heard of it. During its dash across the battlefield the Light Brigade was probably out of its line of sight and in the process of outflanking it. It is probable, too, that the men of the Grande Batterie were mesmerised by the pressure of Prussian troops from their right and rear. On the French left wing there are accounts, such as Gawler's and Leeke's, that mention guns in aggressive action. Halkett is especially strong on cannon but in all these accounts, including those of Colborne and Powell, it is their capture or dispersal, not their fire, which is stressed. Many of these guns would have been those accompanying the Garde's attack but those at La Haie Sainte were also abandoned. Their gunners seem to have been swept away in the panic, leaving their horse teams still in their traces (Colborne had tried to acquire one), so they now posed little threat despite their effectiveness in the early stages of the Garde's advance.

With the exception of the Old Garde battalions, the French infantry showed even less inclination to stand. The sight of the Middle Garde streaming away southwards demoralised the Ligne battalions of Reille's corps around au Goumont. Even the Old Garde retired precipitately. The 2/1er Châsseurs could not resist the persistent pursuit of a single Hanoverian Militia battalion, but eventually broke and dispersed. Three battalions of the Old Garde that attempted to delay the advance north of La Belle Alliance initially repulsed the light cavalry's attempt to move them but were dispersed when faced with superior firepower and the bayonet, delivered with determination by the Light Brigade. Only when dispersed and no longer a formed and disciplined body could they fall prey to the cavalry. There was no sign of any organised and effective resistance by French infantry that might have contained, let alone defeated, the Light Brigade's advance.

Of the three arms, the French cavalry was the most active in retreat. This was to be expected given the cavalry's superior mobility. While it is true the bulk of this arm was exhausted and disordered by the hours of fruitless charges against the Allied squares there were still some cavalry units, in particular some of the Garde, which were fresh and so far unengaged. However, judging by the withdrawal of the Grenadiers à Cheval, the cause was so obviously lost that further resistance was thought to be pointless.

So the impression that the French left wing was defeated by the Light Brigade's advance is inescapable. But the final question is: could Adam's Light Brigade have survived if the scattered remnants of French cavalry had managed to coalesce? The answer is yes, in all probability. *In extremis* the light battalions could have formed square and continued their movement, just as the 52nd did at the Battle of Fuentes de Oñoro; or as happened when charged by the 23rd Light Dragoons, a few minutes before. Here at Waterloo we heard how the battalions of the Light Brigade were formed in four ranks expressly as a deterrent against cavalry, and how the 52nd's officers were carefully maintaining that formation in view of Cuirassiers trying to form to attack but who were prevented from doing so by the speed and determination of the British advance as Colborne describes:

> In going over this ground the Duke was immediately in rear of the 52nd, and when, in consequence of seeing that parties of Cuirassiers, who were retiring before us, were continually trying to form, apparently with the intention of charging us, several of the officers were rather checking the pace of the men for fear of the ranks becoming disordered, he two or three times called out, 'Go on, go on,' and so it was that these Cuirassiers were fairly driven off without ever being able to make any head.[43]

In addition, Halkett's lone battalion was able to traverse the battlefield unaffected by any of the enemy's three teeth arms. Remember his description of 'vociferous cavalry' which went off 'in all directions'. While Vivian and Vandeleur were haring around the battlefield, the Light Brigade advanced inexorably to Rossomme and the Osnabrück Landwehr went further still without hindrance.

The available evidence shows the Light Brigade was able to deter any attack by French cavalry and dominated any momentary show of resistance by infantry. It is impossible to detect from either French or British sources that there was a credible possibility of organised – let alone potentially successful – resistance by the French to the Light Brigade's inexorable advance. The claim that it was the cavalry that persuaded Napoleon himself to leave the field is arguable but is irrelevant, given that, by that stage, not only had he completely lost control of his army (bar the two battalions that gave him temporary shelter) but also had the Light Brigade hot on his heels.

The facts do not support the claim that the Light Cavalry's intervention was critical to the victory: supportive, yes; decisive, no.

In Summary

Despite his repeated claims to the contrary, Vivian's cavalry did not cause the rout that ended the battle. He based his claim on having been ahead of the Light Brigade, but the inference that he was the first out of the line was untruthful, since, immediately after the battle, he told his wife he had seen the infantry advancing through the French position before he left the Allied line. As a result he received a bloody nose – and Major Howard a crushed skull – when he attempted the improbable, to break an Old Garde square by cavalry alone.

Hugh Halkett had been asked to have his Osnabrück militiamen fire on the square, but he was in hot pursuit of Cambronne and refused. He may also have feared the result of a salvo from a Garde square upon his young troops.

A moment's thought will show how bizarre the situation was. Here, with only one battalion of inexperienced militiamen, hundreds of yards ahead of a brigade, which itself was alone in an astonishing advance in front of its army, was a brigade commander (having left his other battalions behind), who was so keen to capture a French general that he refused to support a charge by cavalry, who should not have been there had their commander obeyed his orders, let alone attacking, unsupported, a square of veteran infantry. Halkett must have been in a world of his own, only realising how isolated he was when he and his Hanoverians reached Genappe (if indeed he did so). His contribution to the victory was the dispersal of an Old Garde battalion and the colourful capture of Cambronne. He deserves some credit in the histories, if only for notable enthusiasm.

Vivian's contribution was less definite: his dashing around the battlefield may have dissuaded what little remained of the French cavalry from combining to attack the Light Brigade although it is unlikely that such an attack would have been attempted – let alone successful – without co-ordinated support from artillery or infantry. It was equally evident that the remaining cavalry was not going to risk assaulting such a determined body: the rout had put paid to any possibility of that. Vivian's claim to have persuaded Napoleon to leave the field is refuted by the emperor at this moment having the protection of two stalwart squares of the Old Garde, impervious to cavalry. Had Vivian not erred in failing to co-ordinate his actions with his troop of Royal Horse Artillery matters might have been different. Vandeleur's cavalry performed in much the same fashion, fruitlessly attacking squares and chasing parcels of French horsemen off the field. Both cavalry brigades provided useful support to the Light Brigade but the rout was unstoppable before they arrived.

Lieutenant Anthony Bacon's report – pointedly omitted by H.T. Siborne – is very valuable. His evidence clarifies three separate incidents. He confirms Halkett's single-minded pursuit of 2/1er Châsseurs and how far the latter had reached before its dispersal; he provides a revealing description of the death of Major Howard; he unintentionally confirms that Wellington was later heading south again to catch up with the Light Brigade, having returned to the Allied line to initiate the general advance.

COMPLETE YOUR VICTORY

We reach the final phase of the battle. The emperor's bold bid for victory has been comprehensively beaten and he has left the field in the midst of his fleeing men. Yet his last attack had started well. The Brunswickers and Nassauers had been suppressed by gunfire and forced to retire; then Colin Halkett's brigade had been similarly forced to retire, in confusion, and only one of its composite battalions had immediately returned to the line. But then fortune had deserted Napoleon: his plan of attack had already gone irretrievably awry; the first two individual Garde battalions had been repulsed and his final six battalions had been broken. The forceful follow-through by the Light Brigade caused panic and the collapse of his entire left wing, in which practically every man thought only of saving his own skin. For Wellington the Crisis was over but he still had to initiate the general advance. At some time between joining the 52nd, after it had broken the Garde's six-battalion assault, and speaking to the 52nd's colonel at Rossomme some 2,800 yards to the south, Wellington must have returned to the Allied ridge to launch the general advance. So there will have been a considerable delay between the breaking of the Garde and the order to advance being given: is there any evidence for this?

First a hint: Lieutenant Charles Ellis of 2/1st Guards, who earlier bemoaned the lack of correspondence by officers of his battalion, in the third of his letters to William Siborne confirms the delay between the rout of the Garde and the order to advance:

> My idea has always been the same as yours, that the First Brigade did not advance immediately after the repulse of the second attack of the Imperial Guards.[1]

The acting divisional commander, Sir John Byng does however let slip to William Siborne one very important piece of corroborative evidence:

You are correct also in your remark that the general attack was not commenced until after a short delay, say, ten or twelve minutes.[2]

We must clarify what this does and does not indicate. William Siborne in his
History of the Waterloo Campaign gives no estimate of the delay between the
moment when the Garde's final assault was broken and the general advance,
despite this being what Byng is clearly referring to by his using the phrase
'general attack was not commenced'. What Siborne actually says in his
History of the Waterloo Campaign is: 'between the heads of the two attacking
columns there was a *distance* [Siborne's italics], during their advance, of from
ten to twelve minutes' march'.[3] Siborne is clearly not referring to the general
advance. He has completely misunderstood – or intentionally misinterpreted
– Byng's remark in his efforts to make sense of the myth of the first and
second column. Siborne believed – as do others – that the repulse of the
'second column' by the Guards led immediately to the general advance which
is what was inferred by Wellington's words in the *Waterloo Despatch*. So he
applied the delay of ten to twelve minutes to the pause between the so-called
'first' and the 'second column'. Slight delay there certainly had been, but this
was not the period of time to which Byng was referring.

So what has Byng actually told us? Precisely what he said: that there was
an appreciable time lapse between the moment when the Garde was finally
routed and Wellington's giving the order for the general advance. He has
thus confirmed that there was a ten- to twelve-minute pause during which
Wellington could have followed behind the 52nd across the field in front of
his army; seen the Light Brigade advance against the three Garde battalions;
reconnoitred to check the dead ground towards au Goumont was clear, and
then returned to the Allied line. Needless to say he had taken some minutes
to achieve all this. Had Wellington not been so engaged, why should there
have been any delay between the Garde's retiring 'in great confusion' and his
ordering the general advance?

We know Wellington returned to the right of the line – although not
precisely where – thanks to Captain Johnny Kincaid, adjutant of the 1/95th
positioned at the crossroads in the centre of the Allied line, who described the
moment thus:

Presently a cheer, which we knew to be British, commenced far to the right
[west], and made every one prick up his ears; it was Lord Wellington's long-
wished-for orders to advance; it gradually approached, growing louder as
it grew near – we took it up by instinct, charged through the hedge down
upon the old knoll, sending our adversaries flying at the point of the bayonet. Lord Wellington galloped up to us at the instant, and our men began to

cheer him; but he called 'No cheering, my lads, but forward and complete your victory.'[4]

This moment must have been one of immense relief and Kincaid can be forgiven his hyperbole. Advancing before the order reached them seems unlikely: they would probably have waited for an order from a senior officer, and Wellington would have had some difficulty speaking to them if they were dashing away from him.

As always with mid-battle timings, ten to twelve minutes can only be understood to denote a noticeably lengthy pause, not a precise period of time. However, it is possible to estimate the length of time between the 52nd's breaking the Garde and the Allied army receiving the order to move forward in the general advance. The Light Brigade's advance at the double and Copenhagen's well known 'bottom' ('stamina', in contemporary parlance) makes this perfectly feasible (see Map 15).[5] An average adult's top running speed is 15mph, so about half of that seems a reasonable guess as the Light Brigade's best speed, considering likely energy levels and the state of the ground. Assuming the Light Brigade could move at the same speed as a trotting horse – 8mph, or 235 yards per minute – from the moment of breaking the Garde they would have taken ten minutes to cover 1,550 yards (including two minutes wasted by the 23rd Light Dragoons and a minute's pause as the 52nd reformed south of La Haie Sainte), before the duke left them advancing on the three Garde squares. He now rode westwards presumably at the canter (12mph/350 yards/pm) to satisfy himself there was no threat of an effective French force near au Goumont, turned back towards La Belle Alliance and witnessed Howard's unnecessary death but, reckoning the Light Brigade's inexorable progress would see off the three Garde squares but that extra pressure from his army might be needed, he turned and rode hard (possibly along the track) to the extreme right of his front line. A further five and a half minutes (1,700 yards at the canter) would have elapsed.

It is fairly certain he returned to the extreme right of the Allied line, since the 23rd (Royal Welch) Fusiliers was posted towards the western end of the line and took part in the general advance. This is where Byng was posted. Wellington had been absent for fifteen minutes, or thereabouts, suggesting Byng's estimate of ten to twelve minutes was not far out. Wellington then rode eastwards, to the central crossroads, ordering the advance, and covering another 1,430 yards, taking perhaps seven minutes, including an extra three minutes for slowing to give the order to divisional commanders as he rode along. A total of about twenty-two minutes had elapsed from the moment of the Crisis to the order to advance reaching the 1/95th in the Allied centre.

Such a pause in the action was not unusual: there had been considerable periods of inactivity previously in the battle.

Having told his army to carry out the general advance, Wellington now collected another staff officer and cantered about 900 yards southwards for about three minutes before being seen by the wounded Bacon. To catch up with the Light Brigade at Rossomme, another 2,000 yards, would have taken another six minutes. His full circuit from leaving the Light Brigade north of La Belle Alliance to meeting it again at Rossomme could have been completed in about twenty-two minutes, by which time the 52nd would only just have reached Rossomme, exhausted but exhilarated. Leeke records Wellington coming up to the 52nd and asking Colborne if there was anything he could do for him: Colborne requested a barrel of biscuits since his men had had nothing to eat all day.[6] Leeke admits not having seen or heard this exchange but its pure banality and the fact that Leeke was not using the episode to make a point suggests it is reliable.

The Allied army's situation had now changed dramatically for the better. The Light Brigade had not only defeated the Garde but had caused the French left wing to evacuate the battlefield; the Osnabrück Landwehr Battalion, led by its rather reckless brigade commander, was on its way alone towards Genappe; Vivian and Vandeleur were busy chasing off remnants of the French cavalry. A more dramatic end to a battle would be hard to imagine. Yet this drama is undetectable in Wellington's *Waterloo Despatch* (previously quoted) in which he wrote:

> [The final attack] … which, after a severe contest, was defeated; and having observed that the troops retired from this attack in great confusion, I determined to attack the enemy, and immediately advanced the whole line of infantry, supported by the cavalry and artillery. The attack succeeded in every point; the enemy was forced from his position on the heights, and fled in the utmost confusion …

This 'attack' is what became known as the general advance, often said to have been Wellington's masterstroke, by which the French were finally defeated; but the evidence tells us it was no masterstroke. Having explored Wellington's movements, we know he returned to the Allied line after checking that the ground around au Goumont was clear. His ability to negotiate the battlefield, free from enemy interference, shows there was no enemy threat on that side of the field: the general advance – at least on the Allied right wing – was almost completely unopposed. This was certainly known at the time, hence the opinion of Lieutenant Frederick Pattison, of the 33rd Regiment in Colin Halkett's 5th Brigade, who wrote: 'The advance of the Duke's army was now unimpeded …'[7] Edward Macready of the 30th tells us his battalion did not move forward at all. In his letter to Gawler, he said simply '… the 30th Regiment at the very finish (we did not advance beyond the crest of our own ridge) …'[8] However, his acting brigade commander, Elphinstone, not wishing to be seen to be hanging back when forward movement was expected of him, fantasised:

> The 5th Brigade, which had suffered much during the Action and at Quatre Bras, was not ordered forward. It was afterwards moved a little in advance and remained on the ground during the night.[9]

This statement has the scent of falsehood about it but succeeded in its aim, as did many other untruths in the archive. There is no doubt that all four regiments of Colin Halkett's brigade had had a very hard time during the past three days and there was no shame in not advancing, yet Elphinstone felt he had to pretend the brigade made a token advance. Perhaps bivouacking amongst one's own dead and wounded was best avoided. His ploy worked, despite the testimony of the junior officers to the contrary, H.T. Siborne managed to conclude, in his summary of Halkett's brigade in his *Waterloo Letters*, that 'The Brigade joined in the General Advance …'

Captain Mercer's troop, whose men were exhausted to the point of being too weak to manhandle their guns forward after the recoil of each shot, and having lost a large proportion of their establishment of 200 horses to enfilade fire from the Garde Horse artillery section with 4e Grenadiers, did not move at all:

> Just then an Aide-de-Camp galloped up, shouting to us with all his might, 'Forward, Sir! Forward! It is of the utmost importance that this movement should be supported by Artillery!' We could only point to the miserable remains of our Battery, a glance at which was sufficient, and he rode on.[10]

Maitland's brigade of Guards did advance – as already noted – and bivouacked on the field just south of La Haie Sainte. Unintentional confirmation of this comes from a letter penned a few days after the battle by an anonymous officer of the 1st Guards, who, whilst not being specific about where they slept, makes it clear it was on the battlefield:

> After our bivouac of the 18th after the battle, we marched to Nivelle, over the terrible field; so horrible a scene, scarcely any man ever witnessed; the ground, for the space of a league, was covered with bodies, absolutely lying in ranks, and horses grouped in heaps, with their riders.[11]

Leeke also provides confirmation that the 1st (Guards) Brigade bivouacked on the battlefield. He tells how, after halting at Rossomme, Major William Rowan went back to assist his wounded brother, Charles. He found the Guards north of La Belle Alliance with piled arms. While talking to a Guards officer of his acquaintance, Sir John Byng rode up. On hearing Rowan was of the 52nd, Byng is said to have said, 'Ah, we saw the 52nd advancing gloriously, as they always do.'[12] If this exchange is true – and there seems no reason to suppose it is not – Byng later developed amnesia, as we shall shortly discover.

Gerard Rochell, of Detmers' brigade, whom, after the final retreat of 1/3e Grenadiers, we left standing on the forward slope just north of La Haie Sainte, must have watched the Light Brigade pass across his front. He describes what happened next:

During this [General] advance our battalion became separated; everywhere one could see small groups of men together; I was lucky to keep my loyal company together and they followed me the whole time.

It was in this manner that I saw our battalion commander, Major Boelaard, who called to me: 'where are we to go?' He had no one with him except the Adjutant and 1st Lieutenant van Dijk. But instead of answering him I saw an orchard on the left [La Haie Sainte?], from where a well maintained fire was being delivered by the enemy, and so I hurried to this point with my flankers [light troops]. The enemy was pushed from it, although we did not remain there for long, but advanced while skirmishing the entire time …

It was only with the greatest efforts and the knowledge of the honour we had gained that we steadily advanced; more than once I wanted to throw away my musket, so great was our fatigue, but which I knew would have caused the greatest disgrace thereafter …

While advancing we encountered a mass of Prussian skirmishers approaching because we wore our greatcoats in a manner which led them to believe that [we] were French. We showed them that we were Netherlanders by waving our orange sashes. At this time I witnessed a scene I will never forget as long as I live! They welcomed us with great joy and although we did not know each other we shook hands; everyone shouted: 'the victory is ours!' …

Thus united we continued our victorious advance. Adjutant van Dijk joined me, although he was entirely on his own, and a little later Lieutenant Schouten of our battalion … Both were very tired and asked me to halt. But I did not honour their request, and as they could not go on they remained behind. Afterwards I was glad not to have listened to them, even considering the circumstances, and to have carried on until the end. I am most satisfied to have done so …

We kept on going and pursued the enemy until about ten o'clock in the evening. ... At last the command was heard from behind: 'Netherlanders halt!' We then returned and formed at the head of our brigade, where we found General Constant-Rebècque, our worthy Colonel Detmers ...

It was decided we should stay in this position and bivouac for the night; this was somewhere close to the Maison du Roi [betwween Rossomme and La Caillou]. It was impossible to organise anything more as everyone was mixed together: Prussians, English, Hanoverians and Netherlanders slept on the spot they occupied.[13]

By the end of this scene of confusion and chaos, Rochell had lost only seven men from his company, whereas other companies had completely disintegrated, not from enemy action but a combination of alcohol, of which his company had had none, exhaustion and darkness. But we should remember these men were essentially raw recruits, and Major Boelaard seems to have lost control, and his sense of direction, as soon as his battalion set off on their long march. The faint flicker of resistance from the orchard might be said to be the only attempt to deter the general advance. Besides, the 2/95th had already fought through the farmstead. We do not know for certain when Detmers' brigade resumed its advance, whether he followed close behind the Light Brigade or waited for the general advance to be ordered: the latter seems most likely. Once released for the general advance it seems all control was lost. Rochell paints a picture of almost complete disintegration when his battalion advanced, officers wandering around lost, with few, if any, of their men, the rest having dispersed. His picture provides a sobering antidote to the neat images we have of units moving around the Napoleonic battlefields in immaculate order.

By the time Lambert's Brigade arrived at La Haie Sainte, as part of the general advance proper, all resistance had died, as Lambert himself says:

When the General Advance was ordered, at half-past seven, [it was later] I do not recollect that the Enemy made any stand at the Haye Sainte; all that could get away retired, leaving it full of wounded, and many prisoners were made there.[14]

General Lambert further tells us that the 6th Division, of which his brigade was part, standing to the east of the central crossroads, carried out the required possession of the battlefield and duly halted on the French position around La Belle Alliance.[15] And there are other brief comments in the record, none of which suggest the general advance was anything other than just that — an advance to occupy the battlefield. But no more proof is needed since Wellington himself confirms it.

A *Memorandum upon the Plan of the Battle of Waterloo* by the duke, dated October 1836, was eventually published by the second duke in 1863, eleven years after the first duke's death, in a selection of his father's papers entitled *Supplementary Despatches and Memoranda of Field Marshal Arthur Duke of Wellington.*[16] Wellington was commenting on a plan of the Crisis, presented to him for his approval by William Siborne. For reasons which will become apparent later, the memorandum was never sent. In it the duke first described the advance by the Light Brigade, providing the context to prove he was unquestionably referring to the general advance, when he recorded: 'The infantry was formed into columns, and moved in pursuit in columns of battalions.'

That the battalions were in column, not line, and that brigades were in column of battalions, proves this was no fighting advance, and the use of 'pursuit' confirms it. This statement is the antithesis of his claim, in the *Waterloo Despatch*, that it was his much vaunted general advance that finally defeated the French. Such a loose, uncoordinated movement as the general advance could only have been risked if the enemy had left the field – ergo, they already had, as Wellington clearly stated:

> The enemy did not stand the attack. Some had fled before we halted [referring to the Light Brigade's pause south of La Haie Sainte]. The whole abandoned their position.

It is quite clear that the general advance was, in effect, no more than a symbolic possession-taking of a battlefield that was already clear of all enemy resistance. Except for their dead and wounded the French had gone from this – the western – side of the axis road at any rate. The Allied army halted just after 8p.m., as darkness fell.[17] If further proof were needed that no serious resistance was met during the general advance it is interesting to note that no French regimental eagles were captured by Allied troops at this final stage of the battle.

In Summary

Given the weight of evidence for the dramatic breaking of the Garde by the 52nd and the drive across the battlefield to La Belle Alliance by the Light Brigade it is difficult to deny its truth. If it is true, then we should expect to find evidence of an appreciable delay between the repulse of the French assault and the launch of the general advance. General Byng provides that evidence and confirmation comes from the discovery of Wellington's peregrination during the pause, thanks to Major Blair and Anthony Bacon.

By his reconnaissance towards au Goumont, Wellington knew full well there were no formed bodies of French troops able to oppose his formal possession of the battlefield. He himself admitted that his battalions had moved during the general advance in column, whereas the usual formation for attack – in the British Army at any rate – was line. This is further confirmation that the advance was only a pursuit, not combat against resistance. Wellington even described it, in writing, as a pursuit. In fact very few British units had the energy to advance very far, if at all. By contrast the advance of some of the allied battalions, especially those that had not been under much pressure during the battle, ended in unseemly chaos. History does not record if the men of the 52nd received their biscuits: they certainly received no public recognition of their heroic deed.

THE PRUSSIAN
ASSAULT

The purpose of this book, so far, has been to clarify once and for all what actually happened to cause the complete collapse of the French left wing at Waterloo. In Britain, until only a few years ago, this famous battle was considered to have been an entirely British victory. Thankfully there is now a much wider acceptance of the victory being a joint effort, giving credit, where due, not only to the other nationalities in the Allied army but in particular to the Prussian army. It would be perverse to end the examination of the Waterloo Crisis without clarifying how the actions of the leading elements of both armies related to each other.

It has been said that Napoleon was fighting two battles. That is true insofar as both of his adversaries were armies of roughly similar strength to his own but the proportion of the Prussian army that actually saw action at Waterloo was very much less than its full strength, with the large majority of its men still strung out along the muddy tracks from Wavre. It is closer to the truth to view his dilemma as fighting on two fronts (see Map 16, Colour section).

In chapter 3 we traced the progress of the various Prussian corps as they left their bivouac areas and tried to make headway despite the complicated movement order from Gneisenau, their chief of staff, and hampered by the atrocious state of the roads and tracks after the overnight deluge. The Prussians' twin aims were to deliver Zieten's corps to Wellington's left flank in direct support of the Allied army, and Bülow's corps to attack the strategic crossroads in the village of Plancenoit, to get behind the French and cut their line of retreat.

The struggle for Plancenoit has been fully described in many modern publications and in particularly fine detail by Peter Hofschröer in his *1815, The Waterloo Campaign. The German Victory*, so only an outline of events is given here.

By about 1800hrs Bülow's superior numbers had pushed the French General Lobau's troops out of Plancenoit. Recognising that control of the crossroads gave the Prussians relatively easy access to his rear along the River

'*Alte Vorwärts*'.
Feldmarschall Blücher in
characteristic pose.

Lasne defile, to his right flank and to his command post at La Belle Alliance,
Napoleon despatched all eight battalions of the Young Garde to retake the
village. This was duly effected and the injection of troops allowed Lobau
to extend and strengthen his line to the north of Plancenoit, blocking any
outflanking movement the Prussians might choose to make. Outflanking
movement to the south of Plancenoit was inhibited by the Lasne stream.
However, by committing the Young Garde, Napoleon had lost about a third
of his reserve.

By 1915hrs Prussian numbers had built up again sufficiently to oust the
Young Garde. At this time Napoleon was preparing his masterstroke, the
Garde's attack, against Wellington and no doubt lamenting the lack of the
Young Garde, but instead he was forced to commit yet more of his precious
reserve to the defence of Plancenoit. He sent two battalions of the Old Garde;
1/2e Grenadiers and1/2e Châsseurs. The former pushed the Prussians back to
the churchyard in the middle of the village, the latter, arriving ten to fifteen
minutes later, drove the Prussians by the bayonet out of the village altogether.

Inexorably the numbers of Prussian troops reaching the battlefield increased
again until they were sufficient to mount yet another assault. It was the turn
of the fresh men of von Pirch's II Corps. Sheer force of numbers pushed back

even the Old Garde, but slowly: the village remained in French hands until the final total collapse.

Meanwhile Zieten's corps had been struggling towards junction with Wellington's left wing. The corps had 32km of a single muddy track to negotiate, and progress had been very slow. At one stage the advance guard had to wait for an hour to allow the rear to catch up. And even when they were within striking distance of the Allied left wing they nearly failed to arrive at all. Blücher sent a message in desperation to Zieten – probably when the Old Garde had stormed back through the village – requiring him to change direction and come to his aid in Plancenoit. At the same time a young officer, sent forward by Zieten to assess the situation in the Allied line, mistook the stream of wounded retiring as a sign of retreat. Not wishing to be involved in an Allied collapse, Zieten halted his advance guard and redirected it south-westwards, towards Plancenoit and away from Wellington, who by this stage of the battle was showing signs of concern. It was now about 1930hrs. Fortunately Wellington had given unofficial command of his left wing to the Prussian General Müffling, who, observing this counter-marching, was able to convince Zieten of the error, and to resume his march to join Wellington.

Even then the problems here were not over. Mistaking the Nassauers of the allied Netherlands army for Frenchmen, the Prussians attacked them. Mistaking the Prussians as men of Grouchy's detached corps, although they had appeared from an unexpected direction, the Nassauers fought back. Considerable casualties were incurred on both sides before it was established they were on the same side, and the Prussians turned to attacking the French. The time was now around 2000hrs. Now that the Allied left wing had been reinforced, the light cavalry brigades of Vivian and Vandeleur could be transferred to the Allied right centre, as described earlier.

Eventually, as few as 5,000 men of Zieten's corps came into action against the right angle in the French line formed by d'Erlon's corps facing the Allied army to its north and Lobau's corps facing the Prussian advance to its east. But these were sufficient to tip the balance, aided most probably by a massive fall in morale among the French troops, itself brought on by the realisation that the troops fighting the Nassauers were in fact Prussians, not Grouchy's corps.

We have evidence from the Allied army of the effect on the French of the unexpected appearance of Zieten's men against the traditional weak point in any army's formation, the junction between two separate corps. Here, on the Allied left, we meet a new witness, Lieutenant Kevan Leslie, who was in the Light Company of the 79th (Cameron) Highlanders. Leslie was proud (and possibly quite relieved) to be one of only three officers of the 79th to march with his regiment out of the action at the end of the day. As described earlier, the Imperial Garde's attack in the west was part of a French general attack, along the whole Allied line. At the left end of the Allied line General Durutte's 4th Infantry Division of d'Erlon's corps had been pressing hard on the Nassauers under Prince Bernard of Saxe-Weimar – not to be confused with the Nassau contingent under von Kruse beside the axis road – who were giving way:

> This attack was late in the day, and we had not long regained our position when, at the period to which you allude, [the French general advance] the Enemy in front of us seemed moving forward a fresh Column for a simultaneous attack to that on the right of our Line [the Garde's attack]. This [the attack on the 79th] was checked by the appearance of the Prussians breaking from the wood on the left of our position. ....[1]

The row of dots deprived Leslie's letter, as published in H.T. Siborne's *Waterloo Letters*, of its final sentence; the letter actually ended:

> This eruption caused all the French to our front and as far as the eye could see to recoil and depart as fast as they could.[2]

Presumably this historically essential sentence was omitted by H.T. Siborne because it contradicted the description of the end of the battle in his father's *History of the Waterloo Campaign*. Such censorship is understandable but regrettable. One wonders what other uncomfortable but important facts were hidden by the Sibornes.

So, remarkably, it transpires that both wings of the French Army were broken near-simultaneously by the sudden and unexpected appearance of enemy troops; the French right wing collapsed under the unexpected onrush of Zieten's men, while the unconventional counter-attack against the Garde by the Light Brigade routed Napoleon's left wing.

The next report in the sequence of conjunctions between French and Allied troops may provide a clearer idea of the low state of French morale. Ensign Leeke told us earlier how the 52nd surprised a party of about 100 infantry and horse artillery in a 'hollow road', after the Light Brigade's dispersal of the three Garde squares south of La Belle Alliance.[3] Just beyond the hollow road the Light Brigade met the leading Prussians. Captain John Cross may have been referring first to Leeke's party in the hollow road before registering the appearance of Prussians:

> ... the 52nd and moved on in line keeping their right on the road, passed La Belle Alliance, and were joined by the skirmishers at the head of Bülow's corps, that shortly after that came obliquely from the left.[4]

That Cross assumed the skirmishers were from Bülow's corps is natural but not necessarily correct. At the time of writing he was probably unaware of Zieten's rout of the French right wing since it had not been mentioned in the *Waterloo Despatch*, whereas the Prussian breakthrough was said to have occurred at Plancenoit. The memorandum from which the above passage is taken was undated but clearly followed the first letter from Cross, dated 1835, in response to William Siborne's round-robin. H. T. Siborne included none of Cross's communications in his *Waterloo Letters*. Colonel Colborne may have similarly been unaware of Zieten's success and also attributes the Prussians to Bülow's corps:

> At the junction of the Genappe road and the road leading, I believe, from Wavre to Nivelles, the skirmishers of the 52nd and the advance of the Prussians under General Bulow [*sic*] mixed. … We halted a few hundred yards from it, and the whole of General Bulow's Corps passed our right on the road leading to Genappe.
>
> The Duke of Wellington, on returning from La Belle Alliance [on his way back to the Light Brigade after ordering the general advance], passed the left of our Column and inquired for me, and left a message that we were to halt for the night.[5]

That both officers should attribute to Bülow's corps the Prussians they met at La Belle Alliance is understandable: they might have been the tip of Bülow's thrust to the north of Plancenoit, remembering that Pirch's corps was now tasked with capturing the village itself. However, one word from Cross hints at the possibility the Prussian troops were from Zieten's corps. 'Obliquely' can literally be taken two ways: to mean at an angle from behind, or an angle from in front. A glance at Map 16 reveals that the distance that the 52nd had travelled to reach La Belle Alliance is almost precisely the same as that from Zieten's point of breakthrough. Assuming the French right wing collapsed as completely as the left, the two groups could have arrived at La Belle Alliance simultaneously and – in the Prussians' case – 'obliquely'.

Some French authors speak of the collapse of their right wing being caused by the breaking of the Garde on the left wing, to shouts of 'La Garde recule!' The opposite is sometimes suggested – that the Prussian breakthrough in Plancenoit caused the collapse of the Garde's attack. It is certainly difficult to believe the latter, that the Garde could actually have been aware of a collapse of the French right although they could have been aware of the importance of the titanic struggle in Plancenoit. However, our detailed examination of primary sources shows quite clearly that each and every element of the Garde's attack was defeated by Allied action. It is most unlikely that the Garde

Generalleutnant Count
August Graf von Gneisenau,
1760–1831.
Joined the Prussian service
as a staff captain in 1786
and saw action in Poland
and then against Napoleon.
Between 1807 and 1813
he helped to reform and
modernise the Prussian army
including the establishment
of the highly trained General
Staff.

climbed the ridge to the west of La Haie Sainte into the maelstrom of Allied fire whilst simultaneously keeping a weather eye on the progress of the battle far to their right. Besides, would Ney not have been the first to blame his attack's defeat on the collapse of the French right, had that been the case? He did not.

Although the question of whether either breakthrough caused the other can probably never be fully resolved, the question of whether the breakthrough by Zieten preceded or followed the final capture of Plancenoit can be. The Prussian chief of staff, Gneisenau, tells us clearly, in *Marshal Blucher's Official Report of the Operations of the Prussian Army of the Lower Rhine* (undated) in Booth's compendium, that Zieten's success came first. Gneisenau was writing shortly after the battle on behalf of Marshal Blücher:

> It was half an hour past seven, and the issue of the battle was still uncertain. The whole of the 4th corps, and a part of the 2d, [*sic*] under General Pirch, had successively come up. The French troops fought with desperate fury: however, some uncertainty was perceived in their movements, and it was observed that some pieces of cannon were retreating [could these be the ones the 52nd 'captured'?] At this moment, the first column of the corps of General Ziethen arrived on the points of attack, near the village of

Smonhen [*sic:* Smohain], on the enemy's right flank, and instantly charged. This moment decided the defeat of the enemy. His right wing was broken in three places; he abandoned his positions. Our troops rushed forward at the pas de charge, and attacked him on all sides, while, at the same time, the whole line advanced.

And eight irrelevant lines later:

The enemy, however, still preserved means to retreat, till the village of Planchenoit [*sic*], which he had on his rear, and which was defended by the guard, was, after several bloody attacks, carried by storm. From that time the retreat became a rout ...[6]

As one might expect, Zieten being in the lead of the Prussian army at this time, his corps alone took over the pursuit of the French.[7] Peter Hofschröer reckons Plancenoit was finally in Prussian hands by 2030hrs:

The 2/1er Châsseurs under Pelet formed the rearguard. The remnants of the Guard left in a great rush. By 8.30 [2030hrs] the Prussians were masters of [Plancenoit] the key to the French rear and broke through towards the Brussels road all along the front.[8]

So it seems reasonable to assume the sequence of events was as follows (relevant maps are 3 and 16):

By about 1800hrs	Bülow's superior numbers had pushed Lobau's troops out of Plancenoit. The entire Young Garde ousts Bülow's men.
By 1915hrs	Prussian numbers had built up again sufficiently to oust the Young Garde.
By 1930hrs	Napoleon regained the village when he sent in two battalions of the Old Garde, first 1/2e Châsseurs and then 1/2e Grenadiers.
Also at 1930hrs	Zieten finally headed for his junction with Wellington's line and attacked the Nassauers.
At around 2000hrs	discovering the Nassauers were allies, the Prussians turned to attacking the French forward right wing. At the same time Napoleon lead the final Garde assault towards La Haie Sainte.
At about 2015hrs	both wings of the French were broken, simultaneously but independently of each other.

At 2030hrs   the Light Brigade and men (probably) of Zieten's corps met south of La Belle Alliance.

At 2045hrs   the Light Brigade halted at Rossomme and Zieten's corps passed them in pursuit of the French. Then Plancenoit finally fell.

There seems little doubt that the complete rout of Napoleon's army was brought about by near-simultaneous successes by Zieten on the east flank and by Adam's Light Brigade, lead by the 52nd, on the west. The coincidence of routs to left and right is borne out by the leading troops of both victorious armies meeting between La Belle Alliance and Rossomme.

If we accept that both routs occurred together without one causing the other, is it possible to say one contributed more to the ultimate victory than the other? Arguably, the breaking of the 'all-victorious' Garde was the more important of the two events since the Garde's attack, supported all along the line, was intended to be the masterstroke that would win for Napoleon. Indeed, given the large gap created in the Allied line, the Garde's attack came within a whisker of succeeding. But there are, of course, other arguments for awarding the honours to the Prussians. Amongst these are two that merit consideration here. The first is the rather sweeping claim that the battle would not have been won if the Prussians had not entered the fray. The response is that Wellington would not have fought at Waterloo at all without Blücher's assurance that the Prussians would support him. Even when assured of Blücher's intention to support him, had he known how late the Prussians' arrival was going to be he would probably have retired in haste. Wellington might even reasonably complain of Prussian dilatoriness, especially in view of Gneisenau's convoluted movement plan.

The other argument for awarding laurels to the Prussians is that the battle for Plancenoit bled Napoleon of his reserve. It is true that Napoleon's first reserve – Lobau's corps – and then the Young Garde and two battalions of the Old Garde were siphoned off. If Lobau's corps had been deployed further beyond Plancenoit there is a possibility that Bülow's Prussians could have been held, in which case both the Young Garde and the two battalions of the Old Garde might still have been available for the Garde's final blow. Had the Garde been complete, the question arises of whether or not the 52nd – or even the complete Light Brigade – could have seen it off. The immediate and obvious response is that numbers would have given the French the edge.

However, there are two points worth considering. The first is that the Young Garde was of little worth when compared, for example, to its quality when advancing into Russia in 1812. For the Waterloo campaign the Young Garde had been made up of drafts from the Ligne regiments and put up a poor showing even against the inexperienced Prussian militiamen in Plancenoit. Secondly, the final Garde attack was defeated more by the element of surprise than by numbers or firepower.

In the event the 52nd was outnumbered by about three to one and yet even the Old Garde battalions retreated – albeit in some degree of order – despite their not all having been directly opposed by the 52nd. Had the 71st had time to come forward to be alongside the 52nd and the same surprise achieved – there is no reason to suppose another two Old Garde battalions would have presented a problem. But, if the eight battalions of the Young Garde had spearheaded the Garde attack, the result might have been different. There is little doubt that the Light Brigade would have ousted the Young Garde but what might have happened then? Would the Middle and Old Garde have panicked and run?

It seems likely the veterans would have advanced through the gap left by the Light Brigade's departure. Under the circumstances, Sir John Colborne would surely have recognised the danger and kept the 52nd in line. But if these questions are to be debated, if the relative values of the individual allies' contributions are to be considered seriously, the other similar what-ifs should be considered too. For instance, Grouchy's 30,000 men might have disrupted the Prussian advance to Waterloo, or they might have advanced to the sound of gunfire and joined Napoleon at the battlefield. There are so many imponderable possibilities that arguing them all through to a conclusion may be entertaining but is otherwise pointless.

And yet there is another possibility that is worth thinking about. What would have happened if Zieten had been expected to arrive in time at Wellington's left flank, but had failed and, consequently, had not caused the French right wing to break? This nearly occurred when Zieten was ordered by Blücher to change direction to help him in Plancenoit. At this time the French definitely had the upper hand. The east end of Wellington's line was weakly defended and Durutte's men were even making progress. Lobau's corps were holding the line against the Prussians north of Plancenoit and the two battalions of the Old Garde still had a grip on the village. Without Zieten's unexpected thrust the French right might have held on for some time until Prussian numbers had built up yet again. If, before that moment had been reached, Durutte had broken through the Allied line, what effect might that have had on the battle in the two possible outcomes; if the Garde's attack succeeded, and if it failed?

The proper answer is that we cannot tell for sure, but there can be little doubt that Wellington would have been in considerable difficulty if the Garde had broken through, although the outcome would not necessarily have been a foregone conclusion. Outnumbered the Garde would certainly have been but the British battalions in the front line were exhausted and – in most cases – seriously depleted, while the morale of the allied infantry in reserve was fragile. The Garde was in square with only light cavalry to oppose them and little Allied artillery support was available for cavalry attacks to be successful even if – unlike Vivian – the cavalry showed some inclination to co-ordinate with gunners.

On the other hand, had the Garde been beaten and had simply retreated, Wellington would have been in a stronger position to cope with the breakthrough in his left flank, especially if Zieten had eventually arrived. But if the Garde had been broken and consequently the entire French left wing had been routed, as did occur, there would have been a strong possibility, even likelihood, that the French right would have followed suit. This follows because of an exceptional element to the Light Brigade's thrust: its drive down the axis road, straight at Napoleon and his headquarters, which, together with the light cavalry's support, deprived the French of their command and control. This surely highlights the overriding importance of the 52nd's momentous move.

In Summary

It is tempting to interpret Gneisenau's complicated plan for the movement of the various Prussian corps from Wavre as a reflection of his disgruntlement with Wellington for having failed to honour his promise of support at Ligny. On the other hand it seems implausible that he should have risked losing the campaign simply out of pique. Nevertheless the two Prussian thrusts arrived so late in the day as to more than justify Wellington's description of the battle as 'a close-run thing'.

The long-drawn-out struggle for Plancenoit and its capture was not the cause of the French right wing's collapse, but it had another significant effect on the battle: the reduction of Napoleon's final reserve, the Garde. That the Garde's strength might have been greater is often quoted as one of the reasons why the Prussian contribution to the battle's victorious outcome is pre-eminent. However, given that the charge by the 52nd succeeded largely through its element of surprise and the threat of the bayonet rather than overwhelming musketry, there is no certainty that a larger force of Garde battalions would not have suffered the same instantaneous collapse as did the last six battalions.

It is clear that Zieten's breakthrough preceded the Prussian breakthrough at Plancenoit, which did not occur until after the collapse of both wings. It is also clear that Zieten's breakthrough and the 52nd's breaking of the Garde were near-simultaneous. Both forces headed for Napoleon at La Belle

Alliance and arrived together; the only difference is that the Light Brigade was a formed body, impervious to cavalry, while the Prussian troops were skirmishers, although no doubt the main body was not far behind.

Whether the French would have lost in the event of the Garde breaking through the Allied line or if Zieten had not broken through on the French right are questions that are eminently debateable but are purely academic: honours must surely go equally to both the Prussian and the Anglo–Allied armies.

And so ends the examination of the Crisis in slow time, step by step. Now we can break into quick time.

13

THE CRISIS IN QUICK TIME

Hitherto the pace of the action has, of necessity, been very measured, in order to draw out convincing evidence of the facts, many of which will have directly contradicted the long-established myths of the Crisis. Reading through the evidence will have taken longer than the action itself. Now is the moment to break into quick time, to race through the action, to obtain a sense of the rapid pace of events.

Napoleon's assault group of eight Garde battalions was formed up in battalion squares – in anticipation of enemy cavalry – in echelon with the right-hand square leading, each square both behind and to the left of the one on its right, allowing each square to volley from any face without firing into a neighbouring square. Each battalion had a section of two cannons of Garde Horse Artillery on its right, in support.

Napoleon led the way along the road to Brussels with the 1/3e Grenadiers à Pieds and the other four Middle Garde battalions – 4e Grenadiers, 1/3e Châsseurs, 2/3e Châsseurs and 4e Châsseurs – conformed, still in echelon angled diagonally to the left rear, each with supporting artillery. A reserve of three battalions of the Old Garde – 2/2e Grenadiers, 2/2e Châsseurs and 2/1er Châsseurs – followed in their rear. The 2/3e Grenadiers was posted separately, between La Belle Alliance and au Goumont. The Imperial Garde was not alone, this was to be a general advance. Both d'Erlon on the right and Reille at au Goumont on the left, were ordered by Napoleon to advance in support of the Garde's attack. On the east side of the Brussels road that divided the battlefield, troops of d'Erlon's corps engaged in a fire fight with the riflemen of 1/95th and the exhausted troops on the Allied left. Reille's attack had not materialised before the Garde was defeated.

While the Garde was forming up, from north of the newly captured enclosure of La Haie Sainte on the western side of the Brussels road, a French battery (or batteries), once it had moved from east of the enclosure to the west to escape the close-range sniping fire from the rifles of 1/95th, had brought its cannon fire to bear upon the Brunswickers and Nassauers at a range of little more than 200m, with devastating effect, driving them back behind the ridge. No other French infantry were involved here, on the west of the Brussels road.

As helpful as this may have seemed, the artillery bombardment from La Haie Sainte had a real disadvantage. Its arc of fire over the Garde's planned approach route – unexpected due to the battery's move from east to west of La Haie Sainte – forced Ney (to whom command had been handed by Napoleon when he reached La Haie Sainte) to veer at least 30° to the left to avoid it. When 1/3e Grenadiers made the sharp and sudden change of direction to its left, the 4e Grenadiers were forced to change direction too in order to maintain their relative position. The other Middle Garde battalions also veered left in succession in order to maintain the echelon formation. The second battalion over-corrected and had separated from the first by some 300m when it arrived at the Allied line.

The knock-on effect of this sideways shift was to change the châsseur battalions' formation fundamentally. The pronounced tongue of land projecting from the Allied ridge was almost certainly a contributory factor. Due to the leftwards shift the châsseurs were now faced either with climbing its forward slope and then crossing an exposed plateau, or moving further left, round the tip of the tongue, and approaching the ridge via the re-entrant on the tongue's western side. They chose the latter route and the three châsseur battalions moved into a line-ahead formation, a genuine column of battalions. Evidence suggests the three Old Garde battalion commanders concluded their duty as the reserve was to give added punch to the châsseurs' assault so they moved at the 'pas de charge' to close up behind them. Napoleon's attempt to correct Ney's direction of advance was too late.

As a result of the change of direction, the 1/3e Grenadiers met the four ranks of Colin Halkett's left-hand battalion, the combined 30th/73rd of Foot. One volley was enough to stop them and – to the surprise of the British – the 1/3e Grenadiers retired into the smoke. The Garde's artillery section, however, did not retire but maintained a devastating, close-quarter cannonade on the 30th/73rd. At much the same time as 1/3e Grenadiers retired, the men of 4e Grenadiers, the next Garde square in the echelon, having climbed the tongue, marched stolidly across its 300m plateau under shrapnel fire from Bolton's battery of Foot Artillery, and eventually appeared in front of the 3/1st Foot Guards. Halkett swung out the 33rd/69th to engage the Grenadiers' right flank but were fired on by one gun of the 4e Grenadiers' artillery section, while the other gun played on 3/1st Guards with serious effect until obstructed by the arrival of 4e Grenadiers, whereupon it switched its fire to Mercer's battery. Meanwhile 3/1st Foot Guards, prompted by Wellington's high-pitched orders, rose from the ground, volleyed and charged. The 4e Grenadiers tumbled back down the slope, pursued by the Guards. Unfortunately, the charge did not sweep up the Garde's supporting artillery, which continued to fire on the 33rd/69th and Mercer's battery. Halkett was wounded and his battalions, both now under severe artillery pressure, were ordered by Colonel Elphinstone to retire; in doing so, they collided, and momentarily became a 'mere mob'. Fortunately there were no French troops to take advantage of the large gap that had opened in the Allied line, effectively some 700 yards from the crossroads to the left of the Guards brigade.

The 30th/73rd recovered and was back in line in time to receive the renewed attack by 1/3e Grenadiers. Many historians have assumed this second attack on 30th/73rd was actually the 4e Grenadiers' and hence that the unit repulsed by the 1st Foot Guards was a châsseur battalion, but the evidence strongly indicates otherwise. This second attack by 1/3e Grenadiers was repulsed with timely assistance from Krahmer's battery and a pursuit of sorts by Detmers' brigade, which halted on the forward slope of the ridge, shortly after passing through the front line. These Belgian gunners had been sent forward from the second line by General Chassé, one of Napoleon's erstwhile commanders. Detmers' brigade came forward at Wellington's instigation, although Chassé claimed to have sent them. He had however increased the quantity of battalions, causing a traffic jam.

Meanwhile, 3/1st Guards pursued the survivors of 4e Grenadiers down the forward slope for some 100–150 yards. But then the Guards' relative inexperience let them down. Misunderstanding of an order led to confusion and a somewhat untidy and precipitate withdrawal to their original position behind the crest of the ridge, where order was restored.

However, there were still six Garde battalions advancing, so the repulse of 4e Grenadiers was definitely not the decisive blow that broke the French. Three Middle Garde battalions of châsseurs with three of the Old Garde in support, with a combined strength of at least 3,000, now remained of the original attacking force. This was still a formidable body of veteran troops, who had snatched victory for Napoleon in the past. Moreover the Anglo-Allied forces were tired and short of ammunition. The battle hung in the balance.

The remaining six Garde battalions, in column of battalions, had come round the base of the tongue, one behind the other with the only visible gap of about twenty paces between the Middle and Old Garde contingents. They were heading, like a battering ram, at the part of the Allied line where the British Guards had retired behind the ridge. Sir John Colborne, mounted and on the crest of the ridge forward of the 52nd, recognised that this was a very serious threat. Deciding that immediate, urgent and decisive action was needed, on his own initiative he ordered his left-flank company, No 10, forward to skirmish, to distract and possibly halt the enemy, while he led his remaining 900 men down the forward slope in four ranks. The leading battalions of the Imperial Garde shuddered to a halt when fired on by the

skirmishing company. When the 52nd's left flank was level with the head of
the column of battalions Colborne ordered the now left-flank company –
No 9 – to wheel left and halt to act as a marker opposite the head of the
oncoming column of battalions. He then gave the command 'right-shoul-
ders-forward' (today's 'left-form') to his regiment to bring the 52nd into a
position roughly parallel with the French column of battalions.

Ensign William Leeke, carrying the regimental colour of the 52nd, marched
about 150 yards down the forward slope and saw French troops attempting to
reform some distance in front of the leading square. He surmised they were
skirmishers but what he saw were, in fact, the survivors of the 4e Grenadiers.

The 52nd advanced until it was about 50 yards from the now-stationary
French column of battalions and its left flank was level with the head of the
leading square. Even in four ranks (as defence against cavalry, rather than the
normal two of 'in line') the 52nd had a frontage of about 200 yards but still it
did not overlap the rear of the French column of battalions. Now the troops
on the flanks of the Garde squares turned outwards and fired a ragged volley.
Despite the speed of the 52nd's attack the regiment suffered upwards of 150
casualties in a few seconds; most were probably caused by blind British gunfire.

To maximise the surprise effect of his manoeuvre, even before the right
flank companies had completed the movement Colborne ordered a volley
on the move by the two left-hand companies, followed immediately by the
full battalion charge. Caught by surprise, the three Middle Garde battalions
crumpled and then broke in the face of this unprecedented attack. Never
before had anyone dared to treat the Garde in this manner! Morale collapsed
completely and, each man now thinking only of his own safety, they streamed
back towards La Belle Alliance. Only the three battalions of the Old Garde in
the rear, which had not been fully overlapped by the 52nd, were able to retire
in some sort of order. The 1st Foot Guards took no part in the breaking of this
final attack by the Garde: not only were they behind the crest, out of sight,
but were also out of ammunition and so did not fire on the oncoming French
column of battalions at all. Both the brigade commander, Sir Peregrine
Maitland, and the commanding officer of 3/1st Foot Guards, Lord Saltoun,
attested to this in letters to William Siborne, the model maker and historian.

Next, British cavalry disrupted the 52nd's manoeuvre. Out of the smoke
galloped a squadron of the 23rd Light Dragoons, chased by French cavalry,
heading for the 52nd's left wing. According to Leeke, the 23rd Light Dragoons
had specially chosen blue for their uniform, making identification difficult.
But in fact blue was widely worn in the Allied cavalry.. The 52nd's left-hand
companies duly formed square and fired on the oncoming horsemen before
they could identify them as 'friends'. Wellington, who had now ridden out to
join Colborne, simply said 'Never mind: go on, go on.'

The 52nd had shown the way but soon its colleagues in Adam's brigade caught up with it. On its left the six companies of the 2/95th Rifles were ordered forward by Wellington and were soon alongside, since they were on the hub of the wheel and had less far to go. They swept away the remnant of 4e Grenadiers. The 71st with two companies of 3/95th came forward on the right, but, with a late start and greater distance to cover, were some way behind. Colonel Hugh Halkett led one of the four battalions in his brigade – the Osnabrück Landwehr Battalion – straight forward in support from north of au Goumont and found himself pursuing two Garde battalions, one of them 2/1er Châsseurs.

Colborne now advanced the 52nd not straight at the French lines but diagonally across the battlefield, towards La Haie Sainte. The combined effect of the sight of the Garde dissolving in panic and the threat to their flank by the 52nd and the 2/95th may have encouraged the 1/3e Grenadiers to break off their second attack against Colin Halkett's brigade. And now the sight of the Light Brigade sweeping majestically, at the double, across the battlefield in full view of the French Army (for the smoke was localised at the Allied front line), combined with the shouts of 'La Garde recule!', panicked the bulk of Napoleon's men on the west of the Brussels road into headlong retreat.

When the 52nd reached the Brussels road, Colborne halted his men to straighten his line, to change direction and to allow the 71st to catch up. Wellington had ridden forward with the 52nd, and, seeing three squares of the Old Garde, with their guns, still formed near La Belle Alliance, cried 'Well done Colborne, well done. Go on, don't let them rally'.

The 52nd and its comrades advanced to drive the Old Garde squares, with supporting French cavalry, off the battlefield. This advance directly threatened Napoleon and his staff. One of the guns with these squares fired canister at what was now the complete Light Brigade, and it was probably by this shot that Lord Uxbridge lost his leg. Uxbridge, in command of the cavalry, and next senior after Wellington, had come forward and was with the duke behind the 52nd, just south of La Haie Sainte.

The Light Brigade was astride the axis road south of La Haie Sainte, and climbing the slope when Vivian's Light Cavalry Brigade came through the Allied line and, after a brief pause in the valley bottom, clashed with several parcels of cavalry before meeting the three Garde squares north of La Belle Alliance. The Light Brigade was out of sight from the French at this time, in dead ground to the north, but Hugh Halkett with the Osnabrück Landwehr appeared at this moment, still pursuing the 2/1er Châsseurs. Halkett was asked to fire on one of the static squares before Major Howard of the 10th Hussars charged it with his squadron but Halkett declined, possibly because he was obsessed with capturing General Cambronne who was with 2/1er Châsseurs.

Howard charged nevertheless, was killed, and the square was not broken. All three squares stayed put until the 52nd, with six companies of the 2/95th on its left and the 71st of Foot with two companies of the 3/95th on its right, came over the rise and drove the squares before them, directly threatening Napoleon and his staff, while the bulk of the French Army's left wing streamed away towards Genappe. After passing the farmstead of La Belle Alliance, where Napoleon had had his headquarters in the later stages of the battle, the Old Garde squares disintegrated and dispersed.

Wellington, now satisfied the French were on the run, had ridden to the west, towards au Goumont, with one staff officer to check there was no sign of resistance from that quarter. He rode back towards La Belle Alliance to confirm the three squares had dispersed and witnessed Howard's abortive charge upon 2/2e Grenadiers. Immediately the Light Brigade came over the brow and the squares duly broke up. Wellington now returned at speed to the western end of the line of his exhausted army. Riding at speed along the line he gave the order for a general advance, to take possession of the battlefield as a token of superiority. But the response was mixed: some battalions did move forward but only to the bottom of the valley; others managed 50 yards or so, while others moved not at all. However, this hardly mattered. The French were gone from the battlefield and were retiring at speed and in a state of complete chaos.

Meanwhile, on the Allied right centre, Zieten's Prussian I Corps had at long last connected with Wellington's left flank. Once the mistake of firing on the Nassauers, their allies, had been resolved, Zieten's advanced units attacked the junction between d'Erlon's corps (whose men had themselves been attacking the Allied left, as part of Napoleon's final attack) and Lobau's corps. Under the impact of Zieten's sudden, unexpected assault, the right-hand, eastern half of Napoleon's army also broke and ran, just as his left flank crumbled in the face of the Light Brigade's dramatic thrust. South of La Belle Alliance the 52nd met Zieten's leading elements. Soon afterwards, with the mass of the French Army retiring precipitately, the ding-dong struggle for possession of Plancenoit, the village on Napoleon's right flank, was finally resolved in the Prussians' favour. Zieten's corps pursued the hapless French until late into the night.

Colonel Halkett, who, with his Osnabrückers, had eventually captured General Cambronne, continued towards Genappe together with the disorganised and somewhat inebriated men of Chassé's division.

At the farm of Rossomme, well in rear of the original French position, the light infantry and riflemen of Adam's brigade halted and bivouacked for the night with the comfort of the straw and discarded blankets of the Imperial Garde, and – possibly – a barrel of biscuits sent by Wellington.

14

MYTH MAKING

It is easy to imagine the adrenalin rush that must have lifted Wellington's spirits while the French Army swirled in routed chaos around its emperor, who was escaping as best he could, protected by the loyal veterans of the two senior Old Garde battalions under the command of Maréchal de Camp Petit.

Wellington, having returned to his army to give the orders for the general advance, rode southwards again. Near Rossomme he met several senior officers including Major General de Constant-Rebècque, chief of staff of the Netherlands army, who had come forward with the Netherlands troops of whom Gerard Rochell and his company were rare, sober examples. Constant-Rebècque described Wellington as being 'with the happiness of the victory which was shining within him' and recorded their conversation as they approached Rossomme:

> Wellington asked: 'Well, what do you think of it?'
> Rebècque replied: 'I think, Sir, it is the most beautiful thing you have ever achieved.'
> Wellington: 'By God, I saved the battle four times myself!'
> Rebècque: 'I suppose the battle will take the name of Mont-Saint-Jean.'
> Wellington: 'No, Waterloo.'[1]

Having caught up with the Light Brigade, Wellington ordered the light troops to halt, while he rode on a little further towards Genappe to make sure there were no signs of French recovery. There is no evidence to suggest he discovered Hugh Halkett and his Osnabrück Landwehr ahead of him. Then he made his way back and chanced to meet Blücher at La Belle Alliance. Here Blücher suggested the battle be named after La Belle Alliance, but Wellington had already made up his mind and rejected this reasonable suggestion. La Belle Alliance was in the centre of the battlefield, more so than the farm of Mont-Saint-Jean, after which the battle is known in France. In Germany the battle is still called 'La Belle Alliance', a title which would have recorded for posterity the fraught, short but fortuitous co-operation between the two nations.

The meeting of the two commanders was recorded by General Gneisenau, in his official report on the campaign:

> In the middle of the position occupied by the French Army, and exactly upon the height, is a farm, called La Belle Alliance. The march of all the Prussian columns was directed towards this farm … There, too, it was, that, by a happy chance, Field Marshal Blücher and Lord Wellington met in the dark, and mutually saluted each other as victors.
>
> In commemoration of the alliance which now subsists between the English and Prussian nations, of the union of the two armies, and their reciprocal confidence, the Field Marshal desired, that this battle should bear the name of La Belle Alliance.[2]

Strangely, for many years after the battle, Wellington denied having met Blücher at La Belle Alliance, declaring Genappe in its stead, in defiance of all the eyewitness accounts of the meeting. This denial is puzzling. What did it gain? Was he trying to prove he had been further ahead than the Prussians, or was he trying to show he was ahead of – not behind – Adam's brigade, which he had halted at Rossomme? In later years he forgot himself and stated La Belle Alliance to have been the site of the famous meeting. Lord Stanhope

It was at La Belle Alliance that Marshals Blucher and Wellington Accidentally Met.
The British public evidently believed the two marshals met here rather than in Genappe, as Wellington claimed initially.

recorded this lapse of memory – in 1840, at a dinner party, Wellington had forgotten his earlier insistence that the meeting took place at Genappe:

> Blücher and I met near La Belle Alliance, we were both on horseback, but he embraced and kissed me, exclaiming Mein lieber Kamerad, and then Quelle affaire! Which was pretty much all he knew of French.[3]

Why did Wellington choose to name the battle after a village some considerable distance away from the battleground? Several possible but seemingly petty reasons have been proposed, all of which can be almost instantly dismissed. For example, it has been suggested that he did not want his victory to sound French, and chose 'Waterloo' because it sounded more English or because it would be easier for the English to pronounce. In fact it was standard practice at this period to name battles after the victor's headquarters. Almost certainly he objected to 'La Belle Alliance' because it emphasised the equally successful contribution by the Prussians, and Wellington could not accept that. Did that thought lead to another? Could the meeting of the two commanders have been the shocking moment when he realised he could not actually claim the victory against the French left wing for himself, let alone the battle as a whole?

The truth was that he had essentially been a spectator to the 52nd's dramatic eruption from the line and its meteoric crossing of the battlefield. Did he believe that if this truth were to become the accepted version of events he might, at best, be denied the plaudits and honours he longed for, or, at worst, become the laughing stock of Europe? This could explain why he was described as being in a mood of black depression as he rode back in total silence to Waterloo. Lieutenant Colonel Basil Jackson, one of the staff officers with Wellington, records how his chief looked 'evidently sombre and dejected' and said not a word to his staff as he took over thirty minutes to ride slowly back to his headquarters in Waterloo from his meeting with Blücher.[4]

Historians attribute his black mood to the trauma of the daylong battle, or to his losing so many of his staff. But would even these emotions have been so strong as to obliterate 'the shining happiness of victory'? The only matter that could extinguish the sensation of personal triumph would be something that directly affected that sensation, something that lessened his personal glory, or destroyed it altogether. Blücher's bid for an equal share in the victory was bad enough, but even worse would have been the realisation that he could not rightly claim the victory as his, even against the French left wing, because Colonel Colborne had struck the winning blow.

In the bright light of hindsight this may seem to be a farfetched conclusion. After all, there is little doubt in the modern mind, and even less in contemporary opinion (with the possible exception of Prussian), that Napoleon would have dined in Brussels that very night had the Allied army not been led by Wellington – his sheer presence had ensured the victory, a point he himself repeatedly stressed. The Allied army had, arguably, borne the brunt of the day's fighting and he was its commander-in-chief, therefore, to the British public at any rate, it was his victory. But in his mind, just after the battle, the situation may have seemed very different. He was exhausted and the adrenalin had ceased to flow; he had been on tenterhooks for hours, especially in his wait for the promised Prussian pressure to materialise; he had been on horseback the entire day; many of his 'family' of staff were dead; as usual he had had to take all the decisions (or thought he had) and even taken command at battalion level. The strain must have been almost unbearable. He can be forgiven for having heightened emotions and a loss of coherent thought. But, as he rode slowly back to his quarters in Waterloo village, was he furiously turning over in his mind whether he could risk creating a version of the battle's endgame that would give him the credit for the victory, like Salamanca?

Of course, this version of Wellington's thought process is pure surmise, but it is the most likely precursor to his composing the long letter to Lord Bathurst, which is now known as the *Waterloo Despatch*, in which it is impossible to find any mention of the Light Brigade's independent action. Any slight possibility of its inclusion in his description of the battle's ending is ruled out by the phrase 'the whole line of infantry, supported by the cavalry and artillery', which can only refer to the general advance:

> These [cavalry] attacks were repeated till about seven in the evening, when the enemy made a desperate effort with the cavalry and infantry, supported by the fire of artillery, to force our left centre, near the farm of La Haie Sainte, which, after a severe contest, was defeated; and having observed that the troops retired from this attack in great confusion, … I determined to attack the enemy, and immediately advanced the whole line of infantry, supported by the cavalry and artillery. The attack succeeded in every point; the enemy was forced from his position on the heights, and fled in the utmost confusion, leaving behind him, as far as I could judge, one hundred and fifty pieces of cannon.[5]

Judging by the first-hand evidence so far adduced, there can be little or no doubt that the 52nd's dramatic *coup de main* was the crucial blow that brought success for Wellington, yet he omitted it from his despatch, effectively hiding the battle's last half-hour from history. Ensign Leeke was convinced Wellington ungenerously and mysteriously forgot the 52nd's action, but that seems singularly unlikely, given Wellington's active involvement in the movement, coupled with his famous memory for detail. Moreover, in later years he had ample opportunity to correct his omission, had he wanted so to do. The inescapable conclusion is that the omission was intentional.

Intentional deceit is a serious accusation to make against one of Britain's iconic figures. The hypothesis must be very carefully tested. To do so effectively we should expect certain aspects of evidence to be apparent. First, Wellington must establish a persistent version without committing himself to any detail that, in the event of the truth being revealed, can prove him to be a liar. Secondly he must do his utmost to ensure that the truth is not revealed by others by controlling all that is printed about the battle and dissuading others from enquiring or writing about it.

A hypothesis of intentional deceit presupposes that absolute proof will be difficult to find because efforts to eliminate or hide incriminating evidence will have been made. We must accept that Wellington is unlikely ever to admit to the deed, so a lack of incriminating evidence does not necessarily imply innocence. Occasionally we can expect the absence of evidence to be as telling as its existence, when, for example, documents that should exist are missing. We should also be aware of the possibility that many statements by him, or his associates in the deceit, if there be any, will be worded in such a way as to allow their meaning to be understood two ways, in order to provide an escape, should the deceit be uncovered. Put another way, what he says may seem to have an innocent meaning but, in light of the hypothesis of his deceit, it may also mean something entirely different.

That others – either willing or unwilling – may be implicated in the deceit is very likely, but it is impossible to find anyone else but Wellington himself who could have the authority, desire and the motive to carry out such a manipulation of the historical record. That being so, the inevitable question arises: could a man with such a reputation for moral rectitude in later life actually be capable of such dishonesty?

Freud has taught us to look first at childhood for the secrets behind adult behaviour. Arthur Wellesley was the fifth son of the 1st Earl of Mornington, an Anglo-Irish peer and professor of music at Trinity College, Dublin, who had failed in his attempt to marry into the British aristocracy and settled instead for Anne Hill-Trevor, the eldest daughter of the banker, the 1st Viscount Dungannon. Arthur was a shy and sensitive boy who enjoyed poetry but had no aspirations to academic or sporting success. We know that he attended Eton from 1781 until 1784 when he was removed, possibly for academic reasons, but more probably they were financial: his father had been careless with money and died early. His mother took him to Brussels, where the cost of living was known to be cheaper, but it could equally have been because of his academic record.

He had failed to distinguish himself at Eton in any way. Even the result of a fight, with a boy named Robert Smith, is in doubt. His removal and the whiff of poverty could well have given him a heightened sense of inadequacy, which he tried to conceal by overcompensating. He gave the impression of a strong belief in his own capabilities, yet he achieved little of note during the next decade. He attended the Royal Academy of Equitation in Angers, more finishing school than military academy, where he learnt fluent French and rubbed shoulders with the aristocracy, probably acquiring a lifelong preference for aristocratic rule. At Angers he did apply himself assiduously to learning to play the violin, which – according to a fellow lodger – he played very well, his only apparent talent at the time.[6] His mother believed he would never amount to anything.[7] Until this moment his upbringing by status-anxious parents would seem to have been designed specifically to engender in the young man a marked sense of insecurity, inadequacy and snobbery.

In 1787 he was bought a lieutenancy in the 73rd Regiment, but soon moved to the 76th, then to the 41st, thus avoiding disease-threatening service in the West Indies. He then served in two cavalry regiments before settling in the 33rd Regiment of Foot, having bought himself a majority.

In 1793 the spark of ambition brought him alive at last. He sold (some say burned) the symbol of his misspent youth – his violin – and set about becoming a professional soldier. At the cost of about £500,000 at today's value he had purchased commissions to reach lieutenant colonel of the 33rd by 1794 when he came under fire for the first time in the Low Countries.[8] The 33rd was subject to the overall command of the hill-climbing Duke of York, and did not distinguish itself.

Was it wounded pride and the intense desire never to be proved wrong or bested by someone else – a characteristic that was to be so pronounced in later life – that now fired his ambition? This characteristic can certainly be found in his approach to marriage. After the Low Countries, he spent ten years obtaining distinction in India, whence he returned as a rich major general. Years before, he had proposed to Kitty Pakenham, Lord Longford's daughter, but was rejected by her father on the grounds that he was undistinguished. On returning from India he promptly proposed to – and married (sight unseen) – the said Kitty, despite remarking, on their wedding day, on her having grown ugly in the interim. Having thus eliminated the ten-year-old snub of rejection by her aristocratic family, he then proceeded systematically to humiliate his wife by his numerous dalliances with other women, both single and married.

Holding a grudge for ten years and then resolving it by concluding an unhappy marriage is surely an indicator of character. Such tenacity of purpose might be interpreted as the unfortunate outcome of loyalty but a more cynical view suggests he was driven by a determination not to be worsted by anybody. He was determined to be seen to succeed under all circumstances, whatever the consequences might be.

Another less-than-attractive trait of Wellington's, linked to this desire for superiority, was his refusal to give credit to others, possibly due to believing that praise of others would detract from the credit due to himself. He was infamous for this habit from his early days – even the Duke of York was strongly prejudiced against Wellington on this account:

> He [York] does not deny his military talents, but he thinks that he is false and ungrateful, that he never gave sufficient credit to his officers, and that he was unwilling to put forward men of talent who might be in a situation to claim some share of credit, the whole of which he was desirous of engrossing himself. He [York] says that at Waterloo he [Wellington] got into a scrape and allowed himself to be surprised, and he [York] attributes in great measure the success of that day to Lord Anglesea [sic], who, he says, was hardly mentioned, and that in the coldest terms; in the Duke's despatch.[9]

The corollary of the desire to gain sole credit for success is a similar wish to avoid, or alleviate, the blame for failure. Wellington's handling of Lord Uxbridge before Waterloo is possibly a case in point. Uxbridge had fought in the Corunna campaign with Sir John Moore, who had written 'it was impossible to say too much in praise of the cavalry',[10] but had to give up the command of the cavalry on Wellington's arrival. So Wellington had no personal experience of Uxbridge as a cavalry commander and was suspicious of his reputation as a dashing hussar. As is well known, Wellington was not impressed by the cavalry under his command in the Peninsula, accusing it of 'galloping at everything'.

Nevertheless, for the 1815 campaign, Wellington had to accept Uxbridge as commander of the cavalry, since his preferred nominee was unavailable. In effect, but not in name, Uxbridge was second-in-command of the Allied army. During the evening before Waterloo, Wellington did an extraordinary thing. In Spain he had been a micromanager of his armies, overseeing all details of both administration and operations, frequently bypassing his generals to give orders to mere battalion or squadron commanders. Yet Wellington now delegated full control of all his cavalry – some 13,350 horsemen, about 22 per cent of his forces – to a man whom he did not trust as a leader of cavalry and may have disliked. Lord Uxbridge had sought out the duke to find out the plan of battle in case he had to take over command. Wellington had replied:

'Who will attack first tomorrow, I or Bonaparte?'

'Bonaparte', replied Uxbridge.

'Well, Bonaparte has not given me any idea of his projects: and as my plans will depend on his, how can you expect me to tell you what mine are?' But then the Duke, conscious of having been unhelpful almost to the point of rudeness, rose and added, 'There is one thing certain, Uxbridge, that is, that whatever happens, you and I will do our duty.'[11]

Even had he been uncertain of both Bonaparte's and Blücher's intentions; even if he genuinely believed he had the Almighty's protection; however much he might have disliked or distrusted Uxbridge for eloping with his brother's wife (as is often quoted as an excuse for his rudeness, although his own philandering might cast doubt on this), there was much that should have been shared with the man who might have to assume command. Could Wellington's patronising and uninformative attitude be another indication of his ambition to be able to claim sole credit for what he could – at this stage – only pray would be a victory over Napoleon? After all, if Uxbridge had been aware of Wellington's plans he might have laid claim to some credit in the victory. Alternatively, was Wellington expecting the cavalry to 'gallop at everything' – as indeed it largely did, including the 52nd – and was inoculating himself from involvement in the subsequent criticism?

In accordance with his delegated command of the cavalry, when d'Erlon's corps – nearly 20,000 strong (and so reasonably visible, one might imagine) – attacked the Allied left wing, Uxbridge had to make the decision and give the orders for the heavy cavalry to attack the massed French force. Lord Uxbridge said in his letter to William Siborne: 'I received no order from the Duke of Wellington to make the first charge or any other during the day.'[12] Then, after the French cavalry's counter-attack had resulted in the near extinction of the two brigades of heavy cavalry, Wellington is reputed to have said to Lord Uxbridge: 'Well, Paget, I hope you are satisfied with your cavalry now.' However much it may have been deserved, this disparaging remark was clearly not intended to boost the recipient's confidence at a moment when a little encouragement would have been more appropriate.

Uxbridge had ridden with the first line of cavalry, and admitted later that he should have been with the second, reserve line, to exercise control. Despite the near destruction of the heavy cavalry, it had to its credit the defeat of Napoleon's first, and expectedly decisive, thrust, as well as an invisible contribution to the breaking of the Garde's final attack, when, by the heavy cavalry's potent and invisible – but practically non-existent – threat, Napoleon (or Ney) was persuaded to deliver the Garde's attack in battalion squares in echelon formation, which in the event was probably a mistake. When the Crisis finally came, Uxbridge was with

Wellington and the 52nd during its chase across the battlefield. When the 52nd halted to dress its line just south of La Haie Sainte, a parting shot from a French cannon smashed Uxbridge's knee. Wellington mentioned Uxbridge's leg in his despatch, but he gave the rest of him not a word of praise.

Failure to give credit is entirely consonant with believing one is the only person of any ability and, so too, is never admitting error. All these traits can be indicators of a strong personality, a characteristic eminently desirable in a commander of a tiny volunteer army, but they can also be viewed as evidence of an insecure personality, desperate to achieve and to create and hold a reputation as strong and decisive.

Arguably, there is another trait that a weak personality has, which a strong one does not – the habit of claiming other peoples' success as his own. Wellington was certainly guilty of this. One example can suffice. During the Peninsular War, Major George Scovell had succeeded in deciphering the French security codes, giving Wellington many strategic advantages. The codes had been of varying complexity with *le grand chiffre* the hardest of all to crack, but Scovell had done so and, for example, made a major contribution to Wellington's victory at Salamanca. The later editions of Wellington's *Despatches* contained the deciphered versions of many of the French marshals' letters, but none of those in *le grand chiffre* for the obvious reason that revealing Wellington's knowledge of the enemy's plans lessened the importance of the duke's apparent powers of deduction and divination.

John Gurwood may have been the titular editor of the *Despatches* but Wellington had retained the power of veto. In 1836 Wellington was dining at a Mr Rodgers' town house. When drawn on the subject of French ciphers he replied that the lesser codes had been broken easily. When asked if his Grace had had anybody on his staff for the especial purpose of making out ciphers, the duke, recognising his audience's potential approval of the intellectual power implied in this, replied 'No. I tried, everyone at headquarters tried, and between us we made it out.'[13] Stealing somebody else's thunder came naturally to him, so falsely claiming to have ordered the winning blow at Waterloo seems entirely in character.

Wellington can also be accused of triumphalism to emphasise his personal superiority over Napoleon. Two of Napoleon's mistresses were amongst his sexual conquests. One of these was Marguerite Weimar, an actress with the stage name of 'Mademoiselle George', who was heard to remark that, of the two senior soldiers, 'Le Duc était de beaucoup le plus fort.' Indeed so strong was he that he added the other erstwhile imperial mistress, Guiseppina Grassini, to his list.

And Wellington acquired other Napoleana. The emperor's sword was a gift from Blücher; and as a gift from Louis XVIII came sixty-six flags with

Napoleonic bees and 'N' motifs in laurel wreaths, flags which had been presented by Napoleon to his new battalions at the Champ de Mai two weeks before the campaign; amongst other acquisitions were numerous portraits and Canova's nude statue of the emperor, now standing immensely at the bottom of the staircase of Apsley House. The two mistresses and his cook seem to be the most telling items in this respect, being the most personal. But to find triumphalism of such proportions in this so-called epitome of rectitude suggests a deeper seated psychological trait than mere immodesty.

He professed to have little or no interest in decorations but, nevertheless, accepted the highest honours from all the crowned heads of Europe. By Louis XVIII of France he was admitted to the ancient Order of the Holy Ghost; Prussia awarded him the Order of the Black Eagle; he became one of only thirty Knights of the Danish Order of the Elephant; Russia produced the Order of St Andrew; and the Prince Regent honoured him with the Royal Hanoverian Guelphic Order. He much enjoyed dressing up with the all the insignia – although over time he forgot which Order came from which country – and did not mind his new nickname of 'the Beau'.[14]

There were lesser rewards for others, too. Wellington's suggestion that every man who fought in the campaign should receive a medal was, apparently, a magnanimous gesture. This was to be the first medal to be awarded generally, rather than just to generals, and might be construed as a generous sign of his gratitude. But this is questionable. A cynic might suggest the issue of a medal with his name upon it was engineered by Wellington to cement in the public mind the concept of his sole responsibility for the victory. By contrast, his reaction to the much later suggestion that a campaign medal would be appropriate for all those who had fought in the Peninsular War was completely negative. Inevitably the Peninsular veterans queried why they should not receive something similar to the Waterloo medal, but Wellington refused to support their case on the grounds that it was the army at Waterloo that had beaten Napoleon and had achieved the coup de grâce that brought peace to Europe. He accepted that the campaigns in the Iberian Peninsula had been useful but said that Waterloo was 'an occasion of major importance'. In his view, to put the Peninsular War on a par with Waterloo would have diminished the latter's super-importance.

So the Peninsular veterans did not receive a medal. Time passed but the sense of grievance did not diminish until a precedent was set by the award of a medal for the First Afghan War, 1841–1842, in which an entire British Army was so gloriously lost by the same Elphinstone who had dithered at Waterloo. This time the Peninsula veterans' case was taken up by the 5th duke of Richmond, who, as the Earl of March, had served in the 52nd during the Peninsular War, and also at Waterloo, where he was attached to Wellington's staff. Richmond presented a petition to the House of Lords. Wellington objected. He insisted that Waterloo was a special case; he claimed the award of 1,300 medals to senior officers and the thanks of Parliament was sufficient reward and that a campaign medal could not be awarded to the soldiers if those of other successful British armies were not similarly rewarded, along with the sailors involved too.

The Royal Navy had indeed played a major role in the campaigns in Spain and richly deserved recognition. Richmond countered with two arguments; that the senior recipients of medals would not have received them without the effort and bloodshed of the junior officers and men, and that the sixteen votes of thanks by Parliament were worthless unless those thanked had something by which they could be distinguished. He won the day and the Military General Service Medal (GSM) 1793–1814 was authorised. The first impression of Wellington's behaviour over the GSM tends to label him as an old stick-in-the-mud. But a more critical mind might interpret his attitude in another way. There is more than enough evidence to show that he was absolutely determined to receive the full and sole credit for the victory at Waterloo. In much the same way that awarding the title 'Grenadier' to the 1st Foot Guards highlighted his role in the Crisis, so the issue of the Waterloo Medal, which uniquely carried his name, would reinforce both the importance of the victory and his role in it. By the same token the issue of a General Service Medal might have detracted from the value of his bid for all the glory implied by the issue of the Waterloo Medal, hence his continued opposition to a proposal that common sense suggests he should have whole-heartedly supported.

Self-pride was one of Wellington's strongest characteristics. John Croker, a Tory Member of Parliament, recorded a conversation at Walmer Castle, during which Wellington claimed credit for world peace:

> Salamanca changed all the prospects of the war, and was even felt in Russia. Vitoria freed the Peninsula altogether, broke off the armistice at Dresden, and this led to Leipzig, and the deliverance of Europe; and Waterloo did more than any battle I know of, towards the true object of all battles, the peace of the world.[15]

And to Thomas Creevey, Wellington had said 'By God I don't think it would have been done if I had not been there.'[16] He had used much the same words to General Baron Constant-Rebècque near Rossomme when catching up with the Light Brigade. It is perfectly true that his presence was all important but such frequency of repetition suggests either immoderate self-pride or considerable insecurity – or both. Wellington was also acutely aware of the personal nature of the conflict between him and Napoleon. Two or three times Wellington is on record as having exclaimed: 'Thank God I have met him!'

Many people still see Wellington as a national treasure, and with good reason: his military genius made a major contribution to the overthrow of the 'Corsican ogre'. After Waterloo he was worshipped, as an anonymous Guards officer made abundantly clear in a letter written four days after the battle:

> I constantly saw the noble Duke of Wellington riding backwards and for-wards, like the Genius of the storm, who, borne upon its wings, directed its thunder where to burst. He was every where to be found, encouraging, directing, animating. He was in a blue short cloak, and a plain cocked hat, his telescope in his hand; there was nothing that escaped him, nothing that he did not take advantage of, and his lynx's eyes seemed to penetrate the smoke, and forestall the movements of the foe. How he escaped, that merci-ful Power alone can tell, who vouchsafed to the allied arms the issue of this pre-eminent contest ... [17]

Idolatry leaves no room for fault, yet this overview of Wellington's charac-ter surely warns us not to dismiss sound evidence that contradicts sentiment or sycophancy.

In Blücher's suggestion of La Belle Alliance as the battle's name inferring a joint Prussian-Allied victory Wellington recognised a threat to his pride and reputation, and so he rode slowly back to Waterloo, morose and deep in thought. Once back at his quarters he called for dinner. Christopher Hibbert records (and there seems no reason to doubt him) that a few of his remaining staff, including General Müffling and General Miguel d'Álava were present at the post-battle meal. [18]

Born in 1770, d'Álava, a Spaniard, had risen to captain a Spanish frigate and was present at the Battle of Trafalgar in 1805, but he then contrived to be transferred into the army at equivalent rank – hence his claim to be the only person present at both battles. When the British established an army in the Spanish Peninsula, d'Álava was appointed by the Spanish ruling Cortes to the headquarters of the then General Arthur Wellesley, as liaison officer. He soon found favour with the future Duke of Wellington and became a trusted aide-de-camp. The two men were clearly good friends, as is illustrated by an incident at the Battle of Orthez in 1814, when d'Álava sustained a blow to his backside and Wellington was having a laugh at his expense when he too was struck by a spent musket ball on the thigh. He fell, exclaiming, 'By God, I am ofendida [wounded] this time.' Fortunately the force of the shot was taken by his sword but he limped for days afterwards. [19] Later, on 12 April 1814 when official notification of Napoleon's abdication, six days previously, arrived as

Lieutenant General
Miguel-Ricardo d'Álava,
1770–1843.
Believed to have been the
only man present at both
Trafalgar in a Spanish
frigate, and at Waterloo
as an aide to Wellington.
He acted as the Spanish
liaison officer to Wellington
throughout the Peninsular
War. Latterly much
involved in the fluctuating
politics of Spain, from
which he took refuge at
Wellington's expense at
Stratfield Saye, Wellington's
gift from a grateful nation.

Wellington was dining at the Toulouse Préfecture, he called immediately for champagne and proposed a toast to the French king. It was not one of his own officers but d'Álava, who straightaway proposed a toast to 'El Liberador de España.' The cheering lasted ten minutes.[20]

Once the Peninsular War had ended, General d'Álava returned to Spain but, when Napoleon again threatened the peace of Europe, he was appointed minister plenipotentiary to the king of the Netherlands. He nevertheless managed unofficially to join Wellington's staff at Waterloo. Before he dined after the battle Wellington may have already decided what was needed for public consumption was a direct link between him and the winning blow. It would have been clear to him that, in order to avoid criticism, the link had to be established by proxy: he could neither promote the link himself nor be seen to be connected to its promotion. He seems to have decided the link could be provided by his friend, d'Álava, and had concluded that the fortuitous moment when he gave orders to the 3/1st Guards could be spun into an iconic episode. He needed an account that would describe him achieving the masterstroke, but worded in such a way that would not contradict the true version in the event of the truth becoming public. So it seems more than likely he gave d'Álava a colourful description of how he had judged the right moment, given a few orders to the Guards and 'guided them on with his hat'.

This is certainly the story that can be found in a letter d'Álava wrote, dated 20 June 1815, and published in full in Booth's *The Battle of Waterloo, also of Ligny, and Quatre Bras, etc.* The letter was addressed to Don Pedro Cevallos, Principal Secretary of State to Ferdinand VII of Spain. This account was published in the *Madrid Gazette* of Thursday 13 July 1815 and the relevant passage was printed by *The Times* of London on 3 August 1815. This was the first widely read description of the battle since the publication of the 'Waterloo Despatch' in *The London Gazette*. In contrast to the *Waterloo Despatch*'s reticence about the conclusion of the Allied army's struggle with Napoleon, d'Álava's put more flesh on the bones, especially so far as Wellington's heroic part in it was concerned. The extract reads as follows:

> At last, about 7 in the evening, Buonaparte made a last effort, and putting himself at the head of his guards, attacked the above point of the English position with such vigour, that he drove back the Brunswickers who occupied part of it, and for a moment the victory was undecided, and even more than doubtful ...
>
> Fortunately at this moment we perceived the fire of Marshal Blucher [*sic*], attacking the enemy's right with his usual impetuosity; and the moment of decisive attack being come, the Duke put himself at the head of the English foot-guards, spoke a few words to them, which were replied to by a general *hurrah*, and his Grace himself guiding them on with his hat, they marched at the point of the bayonet, to come to close action with the Imperial Guard. But the latter began a retreat, which was soon converted into flight and the most complete rout ever exhibited by soldiers. The famous rout of Vittoria [*sic*] was not even comparable to it.

The gallant Spaniard then added 'several reflections' including:

> Of those who were by the side of the Duke of Wellington, only he and myself remained, untouched in our persons and horses. The rest were either killed, wounded, or lost one or more horses. The Duke was unable to refrain from tears on witnessing the deaths of so many brave and honourable men, and the loss of so many friends and faithful companions, and which can alone be compensated by the importance of the victory.[21]

It is not impossible that this 'reflection' was not d'Álava's own but that he was prompted by Wellington to include it in order to provide a plausible reason to account for his post-battle 'black depression', to head off any awkward questions. Should this idea be thought far-fetched we should remember Wellington's known skills in deceiving the enemy. It is reasonable to recognise that he would cover his tracks with as much care as he could muster, for clearly his reputation would be severely at risk were his deceit to be discovered. Whatever the case, the Spaniard had certainly now lodged in the British psyche the legend of Wellington giving the commands that won Waterloo. It is impossible to be sure whether or not d'Álava knew at this stage if he was being used to start a myth, nor if he was asked to ensure his account was published in England. Taking a chance that *The Times* would pick it up from the *Madrid Gazette* would seem a rather uncertain means of transmission to the British public, leaving open the possibility that d'Álava sent the cutting or a copy of his letter to *The Times* himself.

One thing is certain: Wellington was so exceptionally pleased to have d'Álava's account in the public domain that he recommended it as a source of 'facts' about the battle in addition to his own despatch. For example, to a budding historian he wrote, with the let-out clause which the hypothesis suggests we should expect:

> General Alava's report is the nearest to the truth of the other *official* reports published, but that report contains some statements not exactly correct.[22]

D'Álava's involvement with Wellington did not end there. After the battle and once more back in Spain, he became involved in the highly convoluted political situation around the restored Francophile King Ferdinand. This resulted in self- imposed exile, first in Gibraltar and then in England, when he rejoins this story, at which moment the question of whether or not he was complicit in the deception is probably answered.

The day after the battle, the 'shining happiness of victory', reported by Constant-Rebècque, was still eluding Wellington. Contrary to most accounts, he did not write his *Waterloo Despatch* in Waterloo but in Brussels. There are several witnesses to this – one is General Pozzo di Borgo who wrote the Russian Account in Booth's *The Battle of Waterloo*: 'He [Wellington] is gone to Brussels to make up his despatches (pour faire son expedition).'[23] Di Borgo's account is undated but his phrase '… is gone to Brussels…' suggests di Borgo wrote on the 19 June. Another witness is Constant-Rebècque, who neatly establishes that Wellington had already decided during his gloomy ride back to Waterloo to return to Brussels. In his day-by-day report to the Prince of Orange, Constant-Rebècque recorded on 18 June:

> … towards 11 o'clock [p.m.] we arrived at Waterloo … I went to the Duke to ask for orders and found him with Count Lobau who had been taken prisoner … I asked him for permission to visit the Prince of Orange at Bruxelles and he informed me that he would see me there in the morning.

And on the 19 June he recorded:

> I took leave of the Prince [at Bruxelles] and after having received orders
> from the Duke of Wellington, who arrived at that very moment, remounted
> my horse and rode to the headquarters at Nivelles. It was 10 o'clock.[24]

Yet another witness to his writing in Brussels rather than at Waterloo – to convince any remaining doubters – is Lady Salisbury. According to Christopher
Hibbert, Lady Salisbury asked Wellington to tell her what he was thinking
when he rode back early on Monday morning from Waterloo to Brussels to
write his despatch.[25] Wellington did not repudiate the suggestion that he had
written his despatch in Brussels, although he was not very communicative.
But, when pressed by the question 'Did it never occur to you that you had
placed yourself on such a pinnacle of glory?' he replied, 'No, I was entirely
occupied with what was necessary to be done. I have no recollection of any
sensation of delight.'

No sensation of delight? He must have been acutely troubled by some
matter of serious concern for this to be true. At this period in his life his pinnacle of ambition surely would have been to defeat the military genius of
Europe. He had effectively said as much – now he had succeeded. Moreover,
he was riding away from his army, showing he had absolute faith in his victory and that his troops could – for the time being at least – be left to their
own devices. So he had no need to consider what had to be done on a day-
to-day basis. Yet he claimed to have been 'entirely occupied with what was
necessary to be done'. Did he mean he had been pondering deeply whether
he could successfully obscure the unpleasant fact that the final blow that saw
off Napoleon's last attack was dealt by a subordinate, not by himself, and if so,
'what was necessary to be done' to hide the fact?

It seems reasonable to ask what reasons would justify his retiring many
miles behind his army in order to write his despatch. After all, his usual style
was to be available with his army to take the multitude of decisions needed
to be dealt with by the commander-in-chief. Even if he had 'delegated' to
Blücher the task of pursuing the French, on the day after a major engagement
there would have been many questions requiring his attention, especially
of one who insisted on taking all important decisions himself. He had no
second-in-command to take decisions for him, his quartermaster general,
Colonel de Lancey, had been seriously injured and was soon to die, and Lord
Uxbridge had lost his leg. Besides, it is only with hindsight that we know the
French were practically out of the war. Although Blücher had accepted the
task of pursuing them there could have been no certainty on the morning
of 19 June that the Anglo-Allied forces would not be needed to fight again,

and yet here was their commander retiring to a place of quiet to compose his report on the previous day's proceedings.

The most likely reason for separating himself as far as possible from his troops would have been a desire to escape to find the peace and quiet he needed for composing an especially important despatch. But he had composed many other important despatches without such seclusion: why was this one different? The answer may be that this one had to be more – and less – than a statement of fact. If he had indeed decided to hide the truth of how the battle ended (including the Prussian intervention on his left flank) he had, first, to consider if it was really feasible, in both the short and the long term, to maintain the falsehood. In addition he needed to work out what actions would have to be taken to establish the myth and what would have to be avoided. For this he needed peace and quiet, to concentrate on judging the risk and creating a plan.

At this point it is worth asking what factors persuaded the duke that he could succeed in creating a myth about the battle's end that would redound to his credit and, at the same time, not result in discredit if the truth were to come into the open. The decision as to whether or not he could succeed in hiding the facts of the battle's conclusion may have been quite easy to make; he would have recognised several factors in his favour. His standard policy of placing his troops on the reverse slope would help: the 52nd's action took place some way down the forward slope and would have been out of sight of most of his troops, with the curtain of smoke, described as 'a London November fog', helping to hide it from observers on the ridge top. If the smokescreen was that thick, even mounted field officers on the ridge top and the gunners on the forward slope may not have witnessed the 52nd passing below them. If they had, it would still be his word against theirs, and everyone would believe the commander-in-chief in preference to any other. Anyway, who would dare to risk their career and their social status by contradicting him in public?

His taking command of the Guards at their critical moment was a perfect story to promote as the cause of the French rout, and the silence of the 1st Guards' officers could be ensured by special awards, whilst the other ranks would be convinced the success was theirs. The Light Brigade's officers would be unlikely to make a fuss, in order to avoid ostracism or career stagnation; besides, who would believe their word against his? The several generals who had witnessed the Light Brigade's action could be bought off by honours and awards. The French might know the truth, but who would listen to the enemy? Surely not even the French marshals would be believed, even if they could be induced to talk about their humiliation – if their story included the 52nd's decisive blow it would probably have been treated as an implausible excuse.

And there were other matters to address. He would have recognised the urgent need to establish his version firmly in the minds of both the establishment and the general public; he would have to suppress any dissent from those few who would know he was dissembling; he would have to discourage all attempts to discover the truth. All this would have to be achieved without his exposing himself to charges of falsehood in anything he said or wrote. He would also have to avoid tacitly approving anything that contradicted his version.

One particularly taxing question was how to ensure due credit was given to Blücher without losing Wellington's own desired reputation as the man who beat Napoleon. Given the importance of the battle to the affairs of Europe and the consequent interest in its dramatic conclusion, his task, when he sat down to compose his despatch, was to turn out to be much harder to accomplish than he may have imagined it would be. But his lie has survived for 200 years.

Once in Brussels, almost immediately he allowed himself to be distracted by another witness to his having been there. Thomas Creevey MP tells how he was beckoned by Wellington up to his room.[26] If, as it is suggested, Wellington had come back to Brussels to write his despatch away from the hassle of the battle's aftermath, why would he then distract himself by summoning to his upstairs room, in order to offer him his innermost thoughts, a civilian of only slight acquaintance who had been highly critical of him in the past? Perhaps Wellington identified Creevey, in his role of Member of Parliament, as a useful, albeit unwitting, ally in the cause of creating the myth?

Creevey recorded Wellington's 'greatest gravity all the time, and without the slightest show of anything like triumph or joy' and his repeating '... so nearly run a thing'. 'Then he said "By God! I don't think it would have been done if I had not been there."'

Wellington even took the rare step (for him) of praising the courage of all his troops, mentioning especially the Guards who had defended au Goumont, a theme he reinforced when he came to writing the despatch. Creevey interpreted Wellington's somewhat agitated demeanour as a soldier unburdening himself to a civilian as he began to realise that it was his personal presence on the battlefield that was the key to his success, rather than his skill as a general. By contrast, a cynic might be forgiven for seeing his outpouring to Creevey, unplanned as it was, as an opportunistic attempt to sow the seeds of the myth by emphasising three points – it was a near-run battle, won by his presence and by the Guards; and what of his agitated demeanour?

When completed, the *Waterloo Despatch* was an extraordinarily low-key report with no sense of triumph about it; indeed some readers thought it was a clever way of describing a defeat. It is, however, worth examining for other clues. It is often said that Wellington was always economical with words –

especially of praise – in his battle reports. It has been claimed that his failure to give praise to individual units was his standard practice and explains why he did not see fit to mention the Light Brigade, let alone the 52nd. But one needs only to read his description of the earlier battle at Quatre-Bras to find the disproof of this theory: 'I must particularly mention the 28th, 42nd, 79th, 92nd regiments, and the battalion of Hanoverians.' However he was certainly less generous with his praise when it came to Waterloo; no infantry unit, other than the Guards division, is mentioned, and yet the Guards are praised twice, once for defending au Goumont, which was doubtless well deserved but many other units had held their ground equally well, and again later he reiterated his approval of them:

> It gives me the greatest satisfaction to assure your Lordship, that the army never, upon any occasion, conducted itself better. The division of Guards, under Lieutenant-General Cooke, who is severely wounded, Major-General Maitland and Major-General Byng, set an example which was followed by all.

To praise the Guards twice, but no other infantry, might not be questioned were it not for our knowing what other praiseworthy deeds were performed, even apart from the Light Brigade's dramatic intervention. Such singling out of the Guards smacks inevitably of a none-too-subtle way of giving them the credit for the victory, supporting d'Álava's account of Wellington's 'waving them on with his hat'. The *Despatch* continues with apparently sincere gratitude to the Prussians:

> … and having observed that the troops retired from this attack in great confusion, and that the march of General Bulow's [*sic*] corps by Frichermont upon Planchenoit [*sic*] and La Belle Alliance, had begun to take effect; and as I could perceive the fire of his cannon, and as Marshal Prince Blucher [*sic*] had joined in person, with a corps of his army to the left of our line by Ohain, I determined to attack the enemy, and immediately advanced the whole line of infantry, supported by the cavalry and artillery.
> I should not do justice to my feelings, or to Marshal Blucher and the Prussian army, if I did not attribute the successful result of this arduous day to the cordial and timely assistance received from them.
> The operation of General Bulow upon the enemy's flank, was a most decisive one; and, even if I had not found myself in a situation to make the attack, which produced the final result, it would have forced the enemy to retire, if his attacks should have failed, and would have prevented him from taking advantage of them, if they unfortunately should have succeeded.[27]

We have already identified how Wellington intentionally omitted any reference to the breaking of the French right wing by Zieten's corps. Here we find him damning the Prussians by faint praise and, in the process, ensuring their contribution to victory would not be recognised in Britain, by inserting 'even if I had not found myself in a situation to make the attack, which produced the final result'.

Indeed, so successful was he that the Prussians' contribution was sidelined, except in Prussia, and has been almost ever since. So it is pertinent to ask if there is any further evidence of his actively trying to denigrate the Prussian achievements?

To this end let us look again at this part of the *Waterloo Dispatch*. We have learned from Lieutenant Leslie's evidence that there is little doubt that it was Zieten's corps' unexpected debouchment in support of the Allied left wing that caused the rout of Napoleon's troops on the east side of the battlefield, and that the breakthrough at Plancenoit came later, as we learnt from Gneisenau. We heard that Prussian skirmishers reached La Belle Alliance at the same time as did the Light Brigade, but it is not certain from whose corps they came. The 52nd's officers stated them to have been from Bülow's corps, probably because, at the time of their writing, the then-current version of history had Plancenoit falling before Zieten's corps' breakthrough, a belief almost certainly intentionally fostered by the *Waterloo Dispatch*. However as Plancenoit had not yet fallen when the two nationalities met, Zieten's corps is the most likely source of the skirmishers while Bülow's is less so.

When he wrote his dispatch, was Wellington aware of Zieten's breakout? It is quite difficult to believe he was not. Even if Wellington had missed all the visible clues, he must have heard of it at the post-battle dinner from General Müffling, who surely would have told him of Zieten's near diversion to Plancenoit and his eventual routing of Durutte's men.[28] This was news that – one suspects – Wellington did not want to hear, let alone to repeat in his dispatch.

Therefore, to deny any Prussian claim to share the honours equally, Wellington needed to deflect attention from Zieten's actions and emphasise Bülow's. In the dispatch there is no mention at all of Zieten. Instead we find Bülow named twice and Blücher three times. The only hint of Zieten's approach is Blücher's supposed presence at 'Ohain [did he mean Smohain?] with a corps of his army to the left of our line'. In fact, Blücher was at neither place: he was at Plancenoit and had ordered Zieten to change direction to join him there, an order which fortunately Zieten was persuaded by Müffling to ignore. Wellington's phrase 'the operation of General Bulow [*sic*] upon the enemy's flank, was a most decisive one; ...' is as clear a denial of Zieten's involvement as we are likely to find.

We know that Blücher and Wellington had met at La Belle Alliance in the middle of the erstwhile French position when Wellington was returning from his reconnaissance forward to Genappe. Why did Wellington choose not to publicise his having been a long way further forward than Blücher as a means of claiming sole responsibility for beating the French? His having been near Genappe (whether or not he actually went that far) while the Prussian commander was still on the battlefield would have been the perfect story to support the claim. One possibility is that he recognised he had no means of proving he had been as far as Genappe and hoped that pretending to have met Blücher there would validate his claim. However, the most rational answer to the mystery as to why Wellington insisted he and Blücher met at Genappe, rather than at La Belle Alliance, is linked to his smokescreen to hide Zieten's breakthrough? His original and puzzling claim to have met Blücher at Genappe may be explained by his attempting to add conviction to the statement that the Prussians had first broken through at Plancenoit, and hence that the Prussian success came after the 52nd's breaking of the French left wing.

It is hard to avoid the conclusion that the famous *Waterloo Dispatch* is full of guile. However, once finished, it was dispatched to England in the hands of Major the Honourable Henry Percy. Still dressed for the Duchess of Richmond's ball but carrying the two captured, gilt French eagles, Percy had a difficult journey, especially when his boat became becalmed when crossing the Channel, necessitating his having to row to shore with the sloop's Captain White and four sailors. Eventually he delivered the eagles to the Prince Regent and the *Dispatch* to Earl Bathurst. Bathurst duly announced the victory in the House of Commons on 23 June. His words were recorded in *Hansard*:

> Towards the close of the day Bonaparte himself, at the head of his Guards, made a desperate charge on the British Guards, and the British Guards immediately overthrew the French.[29]

At first it seems odd that Bathurst knew that it was the British Guards who had overthrown the Garde, since there was no mention of this in the *Dispatch*, other than obliquely by the Guards being the only unit praised by name. But the source of his information may have been a letter from his elder son – Lord Apsley – telling him that both he (a civilian on the staff) and his younger son Seymour (ensign in the 1st Guards) were both safe. Seymour had written, 'He [Napoleon] led the Imperial Guard in person. He was met by our Guards, which threw them quite over. Seymour was in this affair …'[30] Seymour, and indeed the bulk of the 3/1st Guards, may genuinely have believed that their repulse of 4th Grenadiers had led to the overthrow of the French. The Guards having retired behind the ridge, the Light Brigade's actions were almost certainly out of their sight as well as being obscured by smoke. But Percy must have been aware that Seymour's statement was only partially true yet he seems to have made no effort to put Bathurst straight on this matter. Perhaps Percy had no opportunity; perhaps Bathurst ignored his description, preferring his son's; perhaps Percy had been carefully briefed by Wellington to avoid any mention of the 52nd. We shall probably never know but, whether or not Wellington had any direct influence on this crediting of the victory to the Guards, Bathurst's announcement was definitely a bonus, helping to fix the Guards' role in Parliament's mind, if not immediately in the public's.

It is safe to assume that more than a statement in the House of Commons would be needed to ensure the myth's acceptance by the nation as a whole. Arguably the most influential factor in its creation was the Royal Acclamation issued by the War Office dated 29 July 1815, which read:

> The Prince Regent, as a mark of his Royal approbation of the distinguished gallantry of the Brigade of Foot Guards in the victory of Waterloo, has been pleased, in the name and on behalf of his Majesty, to approve of all the Ensigns of the three Regiments of Foot Guards having the rank of Lieutenants, and that such rank shall be attached to all the future appointments to Ensigncies in the Foot Guards, in the same manner as the Lieutenants of those regiments obtain the rank of Captain.
>
> His Royal Highness has been pleased to approve of the 1st Regiment of Foot Guards being made a Regiment of Grenadiers, and styled 'The 1st, or Grenadier Regiment of Foot Guards,' in commemoration of their having defeated the Grenadiers of the French Imperial Guards upon this memorable occasion.[31]

This was a unique honour: never before or since has a British regiment been awarded the title of the enemy it defeated. As such, the award must have impressed on the public that the recipients had achieved something very important indeed, namely striking the blow that won the battle, as has been the belief ever since.

It is unlikely this impression was simply fortuitous, it surely must have been intentional. Certainly, it was never contradicted. Moreover, the term 'grenadier' carried overtones of considerable superiority. Even before the award of the title 'Grenadiers', the Guards regiments, like other British infantry regiments, had ten companies of which one was designated light and another grenadier, the latter being the senior. In the seventeenth century grenadiers had literally been armed with grenades in addition to a musket and sword. The grenades of the time were cast-iron spheres filled with black powder and assorted bits of metal, with a wooden tube, containing slow-burning powder as a fuse. The overloaded grenadier also had to carry and manipulate the slow match, with which to ignite his infernal devices. He then had to stand still within throwing range of the enemy and judge how soon to throw his grenade to avoid self destruction in the event of his waiting too long, or having it thrown back if he threw too soon.

Needless to say, the Grenadier company contained the strongest, tallest and bravest (but perhaps not the most imaginative) men. Their headgear – the mitre shape – was tall and slim both to increase the impression of power, and to avoid it being knocked off by the overarm action of grenade throwing, as the then-currently-worn tricorne hat would have been. By 1768 the mitre had been replaced by the bearskin cap (so it was not awarded for Waterloo) but this was for full-dress occasions. In the Napoleonic wars the shako was worn in the field, the men of grenadier companies being distinguished by a white plume on the left side. The use of grenades had long since been discontinued but the title 'grenadier' still implied superiority. So, when the Prince Regent decreed, six weeks after Waterloo, that the 1st Guards were to be titled the 'First or Grenadier Regiment of Foot Guards' every man was entitled to wear the insignia of a grenadier, signifying the superiority of the 'Grenadiers' over all other infantry regiments. The new Grenadiers still had separate grenadier and light companies.

The Royal Acclamation followed Bathurst's announcement and preceded the publication of d'Álava's account so all three together would authoritatively have verified the 'fact' that this award had been made to acknowledge the defeat of the whole Garde attack, which, in turn, had caused the rout of Napoleon's army. However, if the whole Garde attack had been routed, the title should logically have been 'Imperial' or 'Garde' or some title both grander and less unit-specific than 'Grenadier'. Therefore 'Grenadier' fits the hypothesis – it was chosen not only to imply superiority but also to evade accusations of deceit if the truth should ever be revealed.

So the acclamation was true, as far as it went. The 3/1st Guards had indeed defeated one battalion of the French grenadiers. It was d'Álava's account that established the 3/1st Guards as battle-winners. According to the hypothesis we should expect there to be a complete lack of documentary evidence of Wellington having been involved in suggesting the award. None has been found. Some may claim that, since there is no evidence of Wellington having initiated the idea, it could equally well have come independently from the Duke of York. Indeed, that is perfectly true, but there is no known evidence of that either. Besides, even a letter from York, suggesting the award, would not be proof that Wellington had not originated the proposal by word of mouth, either directly or by proxy.

Given his known ability in the field of deception and the evidence of his being careful not to commit himself to the deception in print, it is singularly unlikely he would put a proposal for the award in writing. Only a letter from Wellington, stating he disapproved of the award, would actually guarantee the proposal was not his own. York had nothing to gain from the award: Wellington had much. The suggestion may not even have come either from the Duke of York or via him. Given the evidence that York did not much care for Wellington, he may have been disinclined to support his proposal. Is there not a distinct possibility that Wellington made the suggestion direct to the Prince Regent, whose style favoured the grand gesture, such as this was? There is at least one example of Wellington communicating directly with the Prince Regent. On 2 July 1815 he wrote in terms designed to please him and which might well have earned a favour:

> Your Royal Highness will see ... the strong grounds we have for hoping we shall bring affairs here to the conclusion most wished for by your Royal Highness, without a further effusion of blood; and, if that should be the case, your Royal Highness will again have saved the world.[32]

By contrast, there is written evidence of Wellington suggesting the award of the Waterloo medal. Only ten days after the battle Wellington wrote to the Duke of York ' ... the expediency of giving to the non-commissioned officers and soldiers engaged in the Battle of Waterloo a Medal ...'[33] Hitherto medals had only been awarded to senior officers. York replied on 4 July:

> I have the pleasure to acquaint you that your idea of granting a medal to *all* concerned in the Battle of Waterloo had already been in contemplation, and I am in hopes that it will be immediately acted upon.[34]

It is not clear if the proposal for the issue of the medal to officers too came from Wellington or from someone else. Given York's poor opinion of Wellington it is possible York was not going to give Wellington the opportunity to claim credit for this break with tradition. Nevertheless Wellington's name appeared on the medal. Needless to say, this was another good way to link indelibly the victor's name with his victory.

There were other events that emphasised the pre-eminence of the Guards in the victory. In January 1816 the only two French eagles captured by the British were lodged in Whitehall Chapel.[35] Neither had been captured by a Guards battalion, yet the leading part in the parade was taken by 2/1st Guards, now titled Grenadier Guards – 3/1st Guards were still in France. Whilst the sovereign would have been perfectly entitled to have his Guards carry out this

The Waterloo Medal. The reverse of the medal, with 'WELLINGTON' above the figure of winged victory, who has a victor's sprig of laurel in one hand and an olive branch for peace in the other, the ribbon crimson with dark-blue edging. Cast in silver, given to all who took part in the campaign and to relatives of those killed, with the recipients name and his regiment engraved around the edge.

ceremonial, one might, with hindsight in our age of equal opportunities, be permitted to wonder why the regiments that actually took the eagles were not given at least a share in the glory. Instead, the impression given to the public at large must have been that the 1st Guards had been responsible for their capture. Intentional or not, this public preference will have helped to set in stone the Grenadier Guards' Waterloo-winning reputation.

Finally, if he was trying to create a myth, what a perfect gift to Wellington was the phrase 'Up Guards and at 'em', the five iconic words that are known to any one with a passing interest in history, let alone of the purely military sort. They sum up all that any Briton thinks he needs to know about the Battle of Waterloo, namely that Wellington gave the order and the Guards beat the French. We now know they were not Wellington's words and that the Guards did not beat the French. Nevertheless this well-known phrase must have been welcomed by Wellington for its power to establish in the public's mind his supposed battle-winning act. He could have denied having used the expression, or that it did not achieve the success attributed to it; but there is no evidence that he ever did.

In conclusion we must ask if the evidence is sufficient to prove beyond reasonable doubt that Wellington intentionally attempted to create a myth. The *Waterloo Dispatch* extolled the bravery of the Guards but made no mention of other infantry units. The opinion that such omission was normal is contradicted by his having highlighted the performance at Quatre-Bras of several individual battalions. The emphasis, in the *Dispatch*, on the Guards was repeated by his statements to individuals such as Creevey. The Prince Regent's grant of the unique title of 'Grenadiers' was an impressive signal that the 1st Guards deserved the highest accolade. That Wellington originated this idea is not certain but neither is it disproved. There is no doubt that the award has been a major factor in establishing and maintaining the deceit. His description in the *Waterloo Dispatch* of the battle's end was exceptionally vague. However the detail – especially of Wellington's commanding the Guards battalion which repulsed 'the Garde' – was provided by a close acquaintance, with whom he is said to have dined after the battle, and whose account Wellington subsequently promoted as an official history. The most telling and indisputable point in support of the hypothesis is that Wellington, despite being fully aware of what actually happened, did not report the true account of the battle's last half-hour.

Taken together, there is no denying a myth was created, from which Wellington stood to benefit.

Avoiding the Issue

Wellington, having created a myth of how he personally achieved the victory at Waterloo, was now committed to a lifetime of maintaining the lie. Unfortunately he had failed to anticipate that this battle would be the first to receive the detailed attention of what would today be described as military historians. Unexpectedly (we may assume), by providing so little detail about the Crisis he had inadvertently stirred up a hornet's nest of curiosity about what actually happened when – in the few bland words of his dispatch – Napoleon's final attack, ' … after a severe contest, was defeated'. Before a year had elapsed he found himself besieged by budding authors seeking either information about the battle, or his imprimatur on their guesses.

Our hypothesis suggests we should now find him trying to nip their efforts in the manuscript. We do – Mr Mudford provides an example. In May 1816, Mr W. Mudford put Wellington on the spot by asking him to accept the dedication of his history. This might have seemed a compliment but Wellington knew it was really a device to increase sales, and had no compunction over refusing the dedication. Perhaps he hoped to discourage publication completely when he wrote:

> More accounts have been published of that transaction than of any other that for many years has attracted the public attention; and those who have written them have thought they possessed all the necessary information for the purpose when they have conversed with a peasant of the country, or with an officer or soldier engaged in the battle. Such accounts can not be true; and I advert to them only to warn you against considering them as any guide to the work which you are about to publish.[1]

Poor Mr Mudford then had the temerity to write back, asking where the truth might be found. Wellington duly pointed him at his own dispatch and to d'Álava's report:

You now desire that I should point out to you where you could receive information on this event, on the truth of which you could rely. In answer to this desire, I can refer you only to my own dispatches published in the 'London Gazette.' General Alava's report is the nearest to the truth of the other *official* reports published, but that report contains some statements not exactly correct. The others that I have seen can not be relied upon. To some of these may be attributed the source of the falsehoods since circulated through the medium of the unofficial publications with which the press has abounded, of these a remarkable instance is to be found in the report of a meeting between Marshal Blücher and me at La Belle Alliance; and some have gone so far as to have seen the chair on which I sat down in that farm-house. *It happens that the meeting took place after ten at night, at the village of Genappe* [original emphasis]; and any body who attempts to describe with truth the operations of the different armies will see it *could not be otherwise.*[2]

This apparently innocuous letter contains not only evidence of his trying to discourage investigation of the Crisis but also his false claim of having met Blücher at Genappe. However, the most telling sentence is:

General Alava's report is the nearest to the truth of the other *official* reports published, but that report contains some statements not exactly correct.

This is as good as admitting that he had generated and sanctioned d'Álava's account. What is more he follows one of the principles of his deceit by using words designed, in the event of truth breaking out, to escape censure by including the caveat 'some statements not exactly correct'.

Mr Mudford refused to be discouraged. In 1817 he published *An Historical Account of the Campaign in the Netherlands in 1815 &c.* As the hypothesis suggests, we should expect Wellington's public stance on published articles and histories to be to feign complete indifference, despite there being an appreciable number that were critical. There is no sign in *Wellington's Dispatches* of any written comment upon them, with one exception – that of the Prussian general, and author of the famous *Vom Kriege,* Karl von Clausewitz, who had fought as a major at Ligny and Plancenoit. Clausewitz had criticised Wellington's handling of the 1815 campaign, prompting a unique, detailed and lengthy response. In addition to answering Clausewitz's argument the duke concluded:

Surely the details of the battle could have been left [as] in the original official reports. Historians and commentators were not necessary. The battle, possibly the most important event in modern times, was attended by advantages sufficient for the glory of many such armies as the two great Allied armies engaged. The enemy never rallied; Buonaparte lost his empire for ever; not a shot was fired afterwards [not true]; and the peace of Europe and of the world was settled on the basis of which it rests at the moment.[3]

Clearly it was von Clausewitz's professional criticism that stung Wellington into print. He was annoyed that anyone should see fit to carp over the detail of his performance, given its successful outcome. The memorandum runs to sixteen pages and his case is carefully argued. Since he put so much thought into a subject clearly of import to him, one might expect to find it published in the 'official' *Dispatches*, which were edited under the watchful eye of the duke himself. But for reasons unknown he decided not to publish it in his lifetime and it fell to the 2nd duke's lot to bring it to the light of day. It covers much ground in considerable detail and one would be forgiven for hoping it might have thrown light on the Crisis, but it does not; the description of the battle's end is quoted verbatim from the *Waterloo Dispatch*.

In 1830 another unanticipated difficulty arose. Plans were made to construct a United Service Museum, with a 'Waterloo Room' in which the chief

Captain William Siborne, 1771–1849.
Ensign of 9th Regiment of Foot in 1813, he was not at Waterloo but joined the Army of Occupation in France in 1815. He published two books on topographical surveying and, in 1826, was appointed assistant military secretary to the commander-in-chief, Ireland. In 1830 he was commissioned by Sir Rowland Hill, then commander-in-chief Britain, to produce a model of the battle of Waterloo. This large model is now at The National Army Museum. He later created a smaller model, now at The Royal Armouries, Leeds.

exhibit would be a model of the battle, as a tribute to the Duke of Wellington. The tale of the construction of this model of the battle is admirably told in two books: Peter Hofschröer's *Wellington's Smallest Victory* and Malcolm Balen's *A Model Victory*. The story has been touched upon in previous chapters of this book. It is a sad story which displays the dark side of Wellington's character. The story, however, is even darker than the two authors realised.

Captain William Siborne was in the army at the time but was not present at Waterloo. Commissioned into the 9th Regiment of Foot in 1813, he joined the army of occupation in France just after the battle. By 1830 Siborne had already created a miniature Borodino.[4] That same year, he was tasked by the commander-in-chief of the army, Sir Rowland Hill, to construct a model of Waterloo, to be paid for out of public funds. He was a precise young man who took a delight in surveying. Indeed, so obsessive was he over detail that he spent eight whole months surveying the battlefield, living the while at La Haie Sainte.

Whilst a survey would be needed for constructing the model, the need for mapping may also have been in response to an early attempt at the development of the battlefield for housing. Unfortunately, development of a sort had already dramatically altered the topography of a key feature of the battlefield. Between 1823 and 1825 the Lion Mound had been constructed by the Belgians as a memorial to the Prince of Orange, who had sustained a shoulder wound at the spot. The soil for the mound came not only from the banks of the sunken road north of La Haie Sainte but mostly from the spur of land that projected southwards from the Allied ridge, the very same tongue that caused the divergence of the châsseur battalions of the Middle Garde and the following battalions of the Old Garde.[5]

The loss of this feature is much to be regretted, not least because its absence has obscured its importance. Fortunately Siborne heard of its existence from his hosts at La Haie Sainte and consequently it features on his model, extending from the ridge as far out as the farmhouse. The tongue is clearly shown on a map, of which the relevant section has already been illustrated (see p.105). Its form is shown clearly in the right-hand aquatint by Charles Turner. Both map and aquatint are dated 1816.

He placed in the *United Service Journal* a request for information about the Crisis and was surprised by the public debate this inspired. Most bitter was the dispute about who dealt the final blow to the French, which erupted between his superior officer in Ireland, Sir Hussey Vivian, and Lieutenant Colonel George Gawler, late of the 52nd. Clearly a model would generate many more such disagreements. This led Siborne to decide to send a circular letter to nearly all the surviving British officers. His questionnaire was aimed specifically to resolve what happened at the Crisis. His first question was:

What was the particular formation and position of the -----------Division, Brigade, Regiment or Battery, at the moment (about 7pm) when the French Imperial Guards, advancing to attack the right of the British forces, reached the crest of our position?

And the second:

What was the formation of the Enemy's forces immediately in front of the ---- Division, etc.?[6]

Of course a model can freeze only one moment and Siborne chose what he called 'the eventful crisis of the battle upon the issue of which hung the destiny of Europe', namely the breaking of the Garde, primarily, one suspects, because this was the instant when possible defeat was turned into overwhelming victory, and therefore the crucial moment by which Wellington should be honoured.

Siborne probably shared everyone's fascination, not only about what actually happened, but also about the inter-unit rivalry that the debate about it generated. Being a serving officer, Siborne was duty-bound to obtain permission to distribute his circular.

Instead of this being the mere formality he expected, his application initially produced resistance from Wellington's military secretary at Horse Guards, Fitzroy Somerset. Somerset was no slouch.[7] He was commissioned into the 4th Light Dragoons in 1804, transferred to the 43rd Light Infantry in 1808, joined Wellington as ADC at Copenhagen, was wounded at Buçaco, volunteered with the 52nd's stormers at Cuidad Rodrigo, was first into the breach at Badajos, and took the surrender of the city. He lost his right arm at Waterloo, and served as military secretary to Wellington, until the latter's death in 1852. He objected to Siborne's request on the grounds that it would produce such a mass of contradictory facts as to make the task of determining the truth impossible.

Not for the first time was it suggested that the correct way to elucidate the sequence of events was to follow the *Waterloo Dispatch*. From this suggestion alone it is fairly clear that Somerset was following Wellington's instructions. But we know how useless this guidance was, because Wellington had carefully omitted from his dispatch the salient facts about the Crisis. Somerset's response also included the objection that Siborne's gathering information in this way 'must in a great measure tend to weaken the high authority of the Duke of Wellington's Despatch'.

Siborne failed to detect the implied threat, namely that Wellington did not intend to allow his version to be queried, let alone contradicted, and piously assured Somerset:

… it [the model] will contain nothing at variance with one syllable of that document, and, moreover I do not intend to fasten a single figure upon my Model, until I shall have submitted for his Grace's approval and correction, a plan of the action, showing the manner in which I propose to distribute the Troops at the moment in question.[8]

Perhaps reassured by Siborne's intention of submitting a plan, Somerset reluctantly agreed Siborne could send out his survey but, on the bottom of Siborne's letter, wrote 'Then let him have his circular and the Lord give him a safe deliverance.'[9] This ominous comment was then inadvertently transmitted by an insensitive clerk to Siborne, who still failed to detect the menace in the two responses from Somerset. He should have been suspicious of how vehemently members of Wellington's staff were responding to his apparently innocent request for permission to issue a circular to enquire about an event which was intended to glorify Wellington's reputation. The inference is inescapable, that Wellington had something to hide – and his staff knew it.

After the replies to his circular had been digested, Siborne's plan was duly sent to Wellington. It was last heard of with Somerset, but has, unsurprisingly, disappeared. This is of no import (other than to raise the question why it was lost when such a massive archive otherwise survived) because we have the model itself to tell us (presumably) what the plan showed. We know Wellington did not like it – on the grounds that it showed some 48,000

Lieutenant Colonel Lord Fitzroy Somerset, 1788–1855. Commissioned into the 10th Hussars in 1804, he first served Arthur Wellesley in the Copenhagen campaign, then as aide-de-camp and military secretary throughout the Peninsular War, taking time off to fight with the 52nd at the assaults on Cuidad Rodrigo and Badajos. He was created 1st Baron Raglan and commanded the British forces in the Crimean War in 1855.

Prussian troops in Plancenoit, implying explicitly that it was the Prussian presence that had beaten Napoleon.

The model can now be viewed at the National Army Museum in Chelsea. It depicts the 52nd's independent flanking action that routed the Garde, as well as 3/1st Guards firing on the head of the Garde column. Wellington knew the 52nd's action was correct but he wanted to hide it; he knew the 3/1st Guards firing on the final Garde assault was incorrect but he wanted that to be believed. Having the two actions shown together was awkward, to say the least.

Wellington's response to Siborne's plan was to dictate a memorandum, dated October 1836, accepting Siborne's map of the ground but with no comment on Siborne's version of events but, instead, describing his own version.[10] This is probably the only documented description of the Crisis by Wellington and is therefore of especial importance. Recorded here in full, it reads as follows:

> I have looked over the plan of the ground of the Battle of Waterloo, which appears to me to be accurately drawn.
>
>   It is very difficult for me to judge of the particular position of each body of the troops under my command, much less of the Prussian army, at any particular hour.

Bearing in mind that his original complaint was about the supposed excess of Prussians, it is contradictory that he now denies any detailed knowledge of their dispositions and, by inference, their numbers, suggesting – perhaps confirming – that the Prussian question was not the real reason for his objecting to Siborne's enquiries. He continues:

> I was informed that the smoke of the fire was seen occasionally from our line, behind Hougoumont, at a distance, in front of our left, about an hour before the British Army advanced to the attack of the enemy's line.
>
>   That attack was ordered possibly at half-past seven, when I saw the confusion in their position upon the result of the last attack of their infantry, and when I rallied and brought up again into the first line the Brunswick infantry.

In the *Waterloo Despatch* the words 'confusion' and 'last attack of their infantry' stated that it was this that gave rise to the general advance – but not so here. In the final sentence of his memorandum he distinctly describes the general advance as a later episode.

We should also note, in passing, that his rallying of the Brunswick infantry occurred before the Garde's advance first struck Halkett's brigade and so is either irrelevant or, perhaps, is an attempt to place the rout of the Garde (and hence the winning blow) earlier than it actually occurred, in order to establish that this action preceded the defeat by the Prussians of the French right wing. Stating the time to have been 'half-past seven' may be in similar vein.

Next he recounts ordering the light cavalry of Vivian and Vandeleur to the centre:

> The whole of the British and Allied cavalry of our army was then in rear of our infantry. I desired that it might be collected in rear of our centre; that is between Hougoumont and La Haye Sainte.

This is followed by a sentence that unarguably establishes his deceit beyond doubt, by almost telling the truth:

> The infantry was advanced in line. I halted them for a moment in the bottom, that they might be in order to attack some battalions of the enemy still on the heights.

This last sentence is an exact, albeit succinct, description of the Light Brigade's pause at La Haie Sainte when turning south, reforming and then advancing uphill and dispersing the three battalions of the Old Garde just north of La Belle Alliance, as described in chapter 9.

This sentence from his own pen is Wellington's admission that he accompanied the advancing Light Brigade and therefore confirms his being knowingly guilty of dishonesty, of attempting to erase from history an action in which he took part as an observer and which he knew to have been the winning manoeuvre. To add insult to injury, Wellington was as keen as ever to claim all the credit. According to William Leeke the 52nd was halted by Sir John Colborne – not by the duke – and the latter is innocently reported by Leeke to have cried 'Go on, go on, don't let them rally!' Surely Wellington would not have used those words if he – Wellington – had ordered the halt. The memorandum's next three sentences are a precise and correct description of the 52nd's advance:

> The whole moved forward again in a very few moments. The enemy did not stand the attack. Some had fled before we halted. The whole abandoned their position.

That was not the general advance, however.

Next, Wellington describes the advance by the cavalry of Vivian's and Vandeleur's brigades, and finally the infantry in columns, which can only be the general advance, recalling Anthony Bacon's memory of 3/1st Guards being in column formation when he met them near La Haie Sainte. It also shows that the two terms – column and column of battalions – were clearly differentiated. The use of the word 'pursuit' should also be noted:

> The cavalry was then ordered to charge and moved round the flanks of the battalions of infantry.
> The infantry was formed into columns, and moved in pursuit in columns of battalions.

It is significant that he omitted any mention of the 52nd's flanking manoeuvre and breaking of the Garde, hoping – one assumes – that Siborne would accept the carefully established myth of his well-timed deployment of the 1st Guards creating the French 'confusion'. What he does describe is the all-important drive by the Light Brigade at Napoleon, thereby admitting his involvement in the hidden last half-hour of the battle.

Having written the memorandum, he must have realised he was in danger of committing himself in print to an account that was in direct contradiction to the version he had been promoting for twenty years. His solution was not to reply at all, and the memorandum seems never to have been sent to its intended recipient. Nevertheless he kept it, despite its incriminating content. That it was one of those documents Wellington did not wish to be published is suggested, since it could – and logically should – have appeared in Gurwood's *The Duke of Wellington's Despatches*, the last volume of which was published in 1839. But it did not appear. Instead, it was unwittingly brought into the public domain in 1863 (eleven years after the First Duke's death), by the 2nd duke in the selection of his father's papers entitled *Supplementary Despatches*.

The dispute between Wellington and Siborne over the scale and timing of the Prussian intervention grew rapidly. Having decided not to send his memorandum, Wellington instructed Somerset to write to Siborne, request- ing him to attend a secret meeting with the duke. Siborne, whose job was assistant military secretary in Ireland, declined on the grounds of ill-health and lack of money to travel, both possibly brought on by the struggle to make progress with the model.

Siborne was certain of his facts, having been in contact with the Prussian general staff. When this became known to the duke, his resultant displeas- ure ended any hope of a satisfactory result for Siborne. Derogatory rumours now began to circulate that Siborne had been duped by the Prussians; even (although untrue) that Siborne was of German descent. Poor Siborne, stung by these innuendoes – one can not help guessing who had started the rumours – wrote again to Somerset. Somerset, in response, spelled out the problem: if the Prussians were to be placed on his model as he had shown on his plan then 'those who see the work will deduce from it that the result of the Battle was not so much owing to British valour, and Wellington's great generalship as to Prussian force'.

Despite all the attempts to deflect him from his purpose, Siborne duly finished his project. However, Wellington refused to visit the model when it opened to view by the public in 1838. This was the only sure way he had of avoiding giving tacit approval not only to the 'Prussian question' but also to the presence on the model of the 52nd Light Infantry, with its colleagues in Adam's brigade, attacking the flank of the final and main column of battalions of the Imperial Garde at the moment of the Crisis. For years to come Wellington persisted in denigrating the model, claiming it was thoroughly inaccurate whilst knowing it was anything but – except in showing the British Guards firing on the Garde's final attack and too few Prussians in Plancenoit.

Meanwhile, Siborne, by now financially embarrassed by his project, had finally capitulated on the question of the Prussians and had offered to reduce their number and withdraw them if that would encourage the duke to relent and agree to the government purchasing the model. Had his only concern been the dominance of the Prussians, this could have been Wellington's moment to relent. If, however, his disgruntlement over the Prussians was actually a convenient smokescreen for trying to hide the 52nd's brilliant manoeuvre, he could be expected to refuse.

Needless to say, the duke refused. And no one – not even Hill who had initiated the project – had the courage to act contrary to his wishes. Nevertheless, Siborne admitted his 'error' in public and removed from his model some 40,000 Prussian troops (or rather the number of tiny figures representing them), already made at no little expense, thereby vandalising the superb accuracy for which he had aimed from the start.

The model was mortgaged and went on display. Siborne, encouraged by its popularity but cheated of its income, set about creating another model, illustrating the Allied cavalry's rout of d'Erlon's attack at the start of the battle. This time he ensured he had sufficient funds by enlisting the financial support of Sir Hussey Vivian. This model is currently displayed in the Leeds Armoury. Meanwhile Wellington continued his denigration of Siborne's work and, as commander-in-chief, obstructed the acquisition by the government of both models.

The interest generated by the models showed clearly that there was a demand for an authoritative history of the battle. From his enquiries to the participating officers, Siborne was able to compose his *History of the War in France and Belgium in 1815*, which later assumed the title *History of the Waterloo Campaign*. This work was first published in 1844 and is still in print 150 years later, despite criticism of its balance and accuracy. It represented Siborne's hopes of making a profit to reduce the debts accrued from the first model, the profits of which had been creamed off by an unscrupulous business associate. However his financial hopes for his *History* were ruined by the Reverend George Gleig, whose *Story of the Battle of Waterloo* was published in a cheap edition – six shillings against Siborne's two guineas – before Siborne could get his second edition into print.[11] Moreover, to add insult to injury, Gleig's version was a direct plagiarism of Siborne's first edition, which had sold out between March and August 1844. This theft of intellectual property is proved not only by the way the two texts march in parallel, but also by Gleig's including in his version several errors in Siborne's first edition that Siborne corrected in his second edition. The suspicious element of this is that Gleig had become a close associate of Wellington in 1826, and his book was written with the duke's permission.[12]

Siborne's hopes of staving off bankruptcy with sales of his second edition were destroyed by Gleig's success. It is difficult to ignore the suspicion that Gleig's book was a deliberate ploy, prompted by Wellington, to disparage, if not destroy, Siborne. In particular Gleig, in his preface, airs criticism of Siborne's work that could have come directly from Wellington's mouth, since it echoes the duke's frequent complaint that the accounts of the battle were simply collections of anecdotes which ignored the 'truth', which – Wellington continually claimed – was to be found in the official accounts, such as the *Waterloo Despatch* and d'Álava's account. Compare Wellington's words (previously quoted) to Mr Mudford:

> The people of England may be entitled to a detailed and accurate account of the Battle of Waterloo, and I have no objection to their having it; but I do object to their being misinformed and misled by those novels called 'Relations', 'Impartial accounts,' &c. &c., of that transaction, containing the stories which curious travellers have picked up from peasants, private soldiers, individual officers, &c. &c., and have published to the world as the truth.[13]

With Gleig's words:

> His [Siborne's] History will always stand on its own merits; I am glad to acknowledge my own obligations to it; and his plans I have found, while studying my subject, to be invaluable. But I confess that my recollections of war lead me somewhat to undervalue – perhaps in a measure to distrust – the stories told in perfect good faith by parties who happen to be the heroes of them. Modern battles are not won by feats of individual heroism; indeed, many gallant deeds [that are] achieved embarrass more than they facilitate

the accomplishment of the General's plans. I have, therefore endeavoured as much as possible to avoid entering into minute narrations of these things, except where simple facts were to be stated; and I hope that this course will prove satisfactory to my readers.[14]

He then proceeds to reproduce practically every 'minute narration' from Siborne's work, but slightly rewritten. It was blatant plagiarism – no wonder the book was subtitled 'From Authentic Sources' – and Gleig was a man of the cloth! It comes as no surprise to learn that he was appointed Chaplain General to the Forces in the year of publication, 1844, the-no-doubt remunerative post he held until 1875. In 1846 he was also appointed Inspector General of Military Schools. Wellington must have been very pleased indeed with his *Story of the Battle of Waterloo* – or very desirous of keeping Gleig from whistle blowing.

It will also come as no surprise to learn that the stress of battling against the titan of the age probably caused Siborne's premature death. However the models and his *History* remain as testaments to his determination to establish the truth. But he never quite resolved the answer to the question of what actually happened at the Crisis. He remained faithful to Wellington's myth, having 3/1st Guards firing on the final Garde attack, but he also describes in some detail in his book the Light Brigade's action thereafter, without fully grasping its importance.

It is time to return to General Miguel d'Álava. After Waterloo, Wellington was a rich man. He very reasonably returned to the Treasury £40,000 of his £60,000 share of the prize money distributed after Waterloo. To mark its appreciation the nation had purchased for him the Stratfield Saye estate. When d'Álava was exiled from Spain, the duke provided him with a house on the estate and said to Coutt's, his bankers, 'This is my friend; and as long as I have any money at your house, let him have it to any amount that he thinks proper to draw for.'[15]

Wellington is known to have lent money to friends and relations. He suspected his wife of wasting his money, but found she had been supporting not only her relations but also his – he forgave her, after her death. He spent almost uncontrollably on alterations to Stratfield Saye House, although he tried to curb the expenditure. So he was quite content to spend but less happy about giving. Yet he clearly felt himself indebted to d'Álava beyond the simple bond of friendship. A lump sum would have paid the debt; an annual pension might have been more satisfying for the recipient. But is it not highly questionable to give, to another, even a close relative, free access to one's own bank account, however much indebted one is for services rendered unless, that is, the service is such that one would prefer it not to be revealed?

In other words, does not the possibility of blackmail of Wellington by d'Álava raise its ugly head? And does such blackmail not tend to support the theory that Wellington had a secret, a 'Pandora's Box', to which d'Álava held the key?

There seems little doubt that the truth about the rout of the Garde by the 52nd was general knowledge within military circles and wider. So we can be all but certain that d'Álava knew, sooner or later, that he had connived with the duke to establish a falsehood. Public revelation of this unsavoury fact would have lost d'Álava his 'unlimited pension' and a friendship. But the damage to Wellington's reputation would have been immense, perhaps catastrophic. And d'Álava seems to have had difficulty keeping secrets, as Lady Salisbury noted in the *Hatfield House Papers*, of June 1835. According to Lady Salisbury, d'Álava became less welcome at Stratfield Saye than before, because of 'many reasons but among others from his habit of gossiping which, of all propensities the Duke most detests'.[16] It would have been a somewhat undesirable trait in someone who may have been blackmailing his host.

When King Ferdinand died, d'Álava was able to return to Spain, but promptly returned to Britain as ambassador. He eventually died in France in 1843, to the immense relief – one suspects – of the Duke of Wellington, if he had indeed been the victim of blackmail. It must be stressed that the supposition is based purely on circumstantial evidence.

There is no doubt that Wellington did his best to discourage 'histories' of the battle but he was unable to achieve anything like complete control. His control of his officers was more effective. For example we have the case of Lord Uxbridge's leg, which has already been recorded by Uxbridge himself as having been struck by canister shot when he was '… in the low ground beyond La Haye Sainte …', in other words not in the Allied line on the ridge but just behind the 52nd during its dash across the battlefield. Uxbridge waited thirty-seven years before he released this information.[17] The loss of his leg had been the subject of massive public interest since the day after the battle but the myth placed its loss within the Allied line just prior to the general advance. To have revealed the true location earlier would have destroyed Wellington's version of events. Perhaps Uxbridge had been sworn to secrecy but, after the lapse of a third of a century, he felt it was safe to let the cat out of the bag.

Easiest of all 'histories' to control were, of course, the volumes of his own despatches, especially number 8, which contains the Waterloo archive. Wellington retained overall control over the contents of these publications, as we hear a little later. In this volume – at least for the period of the campaign itself – there is not a single incoming document with the exception of the mass of encomiums from all the legitimately crowned heads of Europe, extolling Wellington's virtues. The most obviously missing documents are the customary post-battle reports by senior officers, which would have been of great interest to contemporaries and posterity alike. But their absence from the *Despatches* is entirely in accord with our hypothesis.

Fortunately the 2nd duke saw fit to publish several of these reports in volume 10 of the *Supplementary Despatches,* affording an opportunity to discover whether the 52nd's action left any trace in the record. Needless to say it does.

At 8am on 20 June, Lord Rowland Hill, in whose II Corps Adam's Light Brigade was part of Sir Henry Clinton's 2nd Division, wrote:

My Lord Duke,

Although your Grace witnessed the conduct of that part of the troops under my command which had the good fortune to be employed in the action of the 18th instant, still I think it my duty to transmit the accompanying report from Lieutenant General Sir H. Clinton, commanding 2nd Division, and beg leave to express my entire concurrence with the Lieutenant General's sentiments respecting the gallant conduct of the troops on this occasion.

I have also to mention the steady conduct of the 3rd Division of the troops of the Netherlands, under the command of Major General Chassé, which was moved up in support of Major General Adam's brigade, to repulse the attack of the Imperial Guard.[18]

Major General Frederick Adam, 1781–1853.
Of Scottish descent, Adam joined the British Army in 1796 and trained for the artillery. Between 1812 and 1813 he fought in Spain but on the eastern side, not under Wellington's command. After Waterloo he continued in the army becoming governor – or its equivalent – of the Ionian Islands, Corfu and Madras.

Hill, aware that Wellington knew all about the Light Brigade's exploit, saw no need to describe it, but Clinton's letter clearly establishes the truth of it. Hill enclosed Clinton's report which refers first to the Light Brigade's period in echelon of squares forward of the Allied line during the French cavalry attacks. Clinton's report reads thus:

> I have the honour to report to your Lordship that the conduct of the 2nd Division during the action of yesterday was such as to entitle it to the appro-bation of your Lordship and to that of the Commander of the Forces ...
>
> It then fell to Major General Adam's brigade to take its share of the same honourable service: the manner in which the several regiments – the 52nd, under Colonel Sir J. Colborne; the 71st under Colonel Rennell [*sic*]; and the 2nd and 9th [typographical error: 2nd and 3rd/95th], under Lieutenant Colonels Norcott and Ross – discharged their duty, was witnessed and admired by the whole army ...

Clinton then reports the 52nd's action against the Garde, which he describes in outline, but assumes Hill knows the detail and so omits a detailed descrip-tion, knowing that Adam's letter contains a full account:

> When the handsome repulse of the enemy's last attack afforded the opportu-nity to become ourselves the attacking body, so judiciously taken advantage of by Major General Adam's brigade, under your Lordships immediate direction, [Sycophancy? There is no evidence of Hill's direct involvement] I directed Colonel Halkett to reinforce the attacking line with the Osnabrück Battalion, under Lieutenant Colonel Count Münster ... I beg too that your Lordship, in making your report to the Commander of the Forces, will have the enclosed letter from Major General Adam laid before his Grace.[19]

Not unexpectedly, Adam's letter was not reproduced in the *Supplementary Despatches* and must be presumed lost. This would appear to be the prime case of a lack of evidence being evidence. The letter's disappearance is too predictable to be coincidental: there can really be little doubt that Wellington destroyed it. But the loss is not irretrievable because we have Adam's response to Siborne's letter of enquiry. Sure enough, his description of the action is a little opaque and some of his statements do not agree with the sequence of events determined by other witnesses. Nevertheless he describes the action adequately:

> ... a very sharp tussle with its [the Garde's] Tirailleurs, but this did not extend to our right further than the right of the 52nd ... When their

Tirailleurs were disposed of, the 52nd were right shouldered forward ...
The 3rd Brigade advanced, the Imperial Guard was driven back, and the
Brigade, continuing to advance, crossed the Genappe *chaussée*, which was at
some little distance to the right [left?].

While advancing, the Duke of Wellington being with the Brigade, some
Battalions of the Enemy were re-formed, and appeared inclined to stand.
... After a few moments [halt] the Duke said, 'They won't stand, better
attack them,' and the 3rd Brigade was accordingly again put in motion, and
the Battalions of the Enemy withdrew, and fell into the mass of confusion
which existed in our front.

There is no reason to suppose Adam's letter to Clinton would have contained
much more detail than this, given that Adam knew perfectly well that Wellington
had been alongside him for much of the movement, although words of praise
would, no doubt, have been in evidence. It makes it quite clear that there was
more to the battle's end than Wellington claimed so it is fully understandable
why Wellington did not wish to keep Adam's letter for the record.

The most serious case of evidence control is the case of John Gurwood,
who carried out the immense task of editing *Wellington's Dispatches*. In 1808,
at the age of 18, John Gurwood obtained an ensigncy in the 52nd Regiment
of Foot, lately converted to Light Infantry by Sir John Moore. He served with
the famous Light Division in Spain. As a subaltern he had commanded the
Light Division's Forlorn Hope at the storming of Cuidad Rodrigo. 'Forlorn
Hope' was an apt name for the group of volunteers whose role was to be
the first to attack a breach in the wall of a city under siege. 'Forlorn' is probably derived from the German or Dutch 'verloren' meaning lost. The French
called these men 'Les enfants perdus'. Any 'children' who were not 'lost' were
usually commissioned and awarded the Legion d'Honneur, which obliged
their comrades to salute them.

The British were far less generous, giving no rewards, with one exception
– the 52nd recognised the extraordinary bravery by awarding a badge, worn
on the right arm, of a laurel wreath and the letters 'VS', for 'Valiant Stormer'.
Leading the assault Gurwood received a severe wound to his head but still took
prisoner the governor, General Barrie, and received the latter's sword from
Wellington in recognition of the deed. He transferred to the 10th Hussars in
1814 and was wounded for a third time at Waterloo where he was supposed to
be an ADC to General Clinton but had fallen out with him and fought instead
with the 10th Hussars. Such transfer between units by officers was common and
a change of arm, from infantry to cavalry by no means unusual.

His years of service with the 52nd in Spain must have been a source of
great pride to him and his affection for his 'home' regiment very strong.

Captain T. W. Taylor, his squadron commander in the 10th Hussars, told Siborne how Gurwood was struck in the knee and his horse killed as Vivian's Light Cavalry Brigade was moving west to the right centre of the Allied position shortly before the Crisis.[20] So Gurwood was not a witness to the events that concluded the battle and the pursuit that followed, but, nevertheless, he must have been very proud to hear of his ex-regiment's exploits.

By 1828 he was employed by Wellington to compile and edit the *Despatches* and, like so many others of his generation (one suspects) was keen to learn what exactly had transpired at the Crisis. William Leeke records quoting from a letter from a Colonel Bentham of November 1853:

> I [Bentham] met Gurwood in London, about 1828; he was then staying at Apsley House, and I asked him why he never drew the Duke out about the catastrophe [of the Garde's defeat] at Waterloo. He said that he had repeatedly made the attempt, but that it was a subject which always excited great impatience. On the last attempt the Duke said, 'Oh, I know nothing of the services of particular regiments; there was glory enough for us all.'[21]

In 1835 in *Letters from the Battle of Waterloo*, Gurwood tells Siborne, in reply to the latter's circular letter seeking information on which to base his model:

> I wish you every success in your enquiries that your labours may be satisfactory in this very national undertaking, and I congratulate you on having completed the most essential part of it. The position of the troops at the hour you mention is of little importance in comparison with the ground, and cannot display the merit of particular corps.[22]

Here Gurwood seems to be acting the dutiful secretary by quoting Wellington's own position in the matter. Yet, to deny the importance of the positions of individual units sounds particularly odd from a man who had served so bravely in the 52nd in the Peninsula and had made repeated attempts before 1828 to discuss with the duke what exactly happened at the Crisis. To have to deny repeatedly the fact of his 'home' regiment's moment of glory and to have to lie or obscure that and other facts about the battle must have been extremely frustrating and contrary to his conscience. Nevertheless he soldiered on with his task of editing the thirteen volumes (including the index) of *The Duke of Wellington's Despatches 1799–1815*, a task he had completed by 1839. In 1845, on 27 December at Brighton, he slit his own throat.

An accusation of having driven Gurwood to take his own life was made against Wellington by the Rev. G. R. Gleig in his *Personal Reminiscences of the First Duke of Wellington,* written in 1885 but not published until 1904.[23] This is the man who had gained notoriety by having totally plagiarised William Siborne's *History of the Waterloo Campaign,* possibly at Wellington's instigation. As already noted, he had also been appointed chaplain general to the army but now – after some years of friendship – he had fallen out with Wellington. His accusation was based on the belief that Wellington had forced Gurwood to burn the record of his conversations with the duke.

However his accusation is apparently refuted by Wellington's actions just prior to Gurwood's suicide. Not only had he assigned to Gurwood the proceeds from the sale of the *Despatches* in 1845 but, during the month of his death, had offered to help him obtain sick leave and invited him to stay at Stratfield Saye. Gurwood had written of severe insomnia brought on by the stress of revising one of the volumes of the *Despatches.* He spoke of having wasted three years of his life on producing the index, and that the exertions of the fifteen years working on the *Despatches* might prove fatal to him.[24] From the correspondence between Wellington and Gurwood's widow, Fanny, and his daughter, Adele, it is clear that Wellington had not realised, until after Gurwood's death, that he might have compromising material. That he had burned much of it was bad enough: what was worse, there was more. With great urgency – but taking care not to alert the grieving family to his great anxiety – he had the papers retrieved. Then – and only then – he gave the newly bereaved women a tongue lashing. For example:

> The Duke does not believe there is an instance in history of a similar act. It is anti-social; it puts an end to all the charms of society, to all familiar and private communication of thought between man and man; and, in fact, it places every individual in the situation in which he puts himself in a publick assembly, with a gentleman of the press to report what he says ...[25]

Wellington's severity has been excused on the grounds of old age. It is true, the apparent breaking of trust must have hurt, and the duke had shown much favour towards Gurwood. But, since Mrs Gurwood had been obliging in the first instance and had shown no inclination to be difficult about returning the material, why did Wellington burst into such intemperate language? Why was Wellington so agitated? Did he have something to hide?

A man of his stature might well have many secrets he would prefer to keep. However, there is one strong possibility, which – if true – implicates the duke in Gurwood's death. It is possible – indeed very likely – that Gurwood's papers contained evidence relating to the 52nd's contribution to the battle and of Wellington's decision to keep it out of the public domain. Gurwood's papers may have comprised some or all of three separate elements – first, his letters from Wellington; second, his notes of conversations with the duke; third, all the paperwork concerned with his editing of Wellington's dispatches.

The latter two elements may well have contained evidence of Wellington's duplicity over the 52nd's action. This could – for example – have included copies of the proofs of *Wellington's Despatches* in which all mentions of the 52nd's (and the Light Brigade's) action at Waterloo had been deleted by Wellington. It is significant that Wellington is said to have retained editorial control of all twelve volumes of the *Despatches*. Indeed Gurwood had written: 'Your Grace may draw your pen through what may be deemed unnecessary to print' – and Wellington had destroyed the amended proofs.[26] But it would seem unlikely Wellington would then have dealt with the printers himself, surely Gurwood would have done that. It follows that he must have seen the deletions and may have kept a record of Wellington's alterations to the proofs, or at the very least, copies of his own original drafts, which, when compared with the published version could show Wellington's deletions.

Gurwood would have had a particular interest in doing so, not only for the sake of historical accuracy but also for personal reasons, having served with the 52nd throughout the Peninsular War. Having to edit out from the eighth volume of the *Despatches* all mention of the 52nd's part in the Crisis, or – worse still – including them, only to have Wellington edit them out, must have been very frustrating. Indeed, having the fruits of his careful labours censored at all must have been stressful in the extreme. To be made party to deliberate falsification of history must have been galling. For someone with a desire not only to present accurate history but also to preserve the reputation of his esteemed employer, finding him in fact to be dishonest would have been psychologically unsettling.

This puts Wellington's generosity to Gurwood in a potentially very different light. It is difficult to avoid the suspicion that, by 1845, Wellington was seriously concerned that Gurwood was about to break down and, perhaps, to reveal all. Awarding him the income from the sales – said by one source to have been about £10,000 – of the *Despatches*, in the same month that Gurwood took his own life, might be interpreted not so much as an encouragement or token of thanks as an attempt to buy his silence.[27]

During the correspondence, Mrs Gurwood also expressed regret that her husband had burned all the duke's letters to him, 'all expressive of Your Grace's esteem and confidence', to which his widow attached a high value, hoping they would be an heirloom for his children.[28] Destruction of letters of praise indicates a complete reversal of erstwhile feelings of loyalty and affection. Does this not emphasise that Gurwood had finally lost all faith in, and attachment to, his employer? We can only surmise what Gurwood's motives were in destroying part of the incriminating evidence.

That he genuinely wished not to cause embarrassment to Wellington seems unlikely in the light of the flames consuming the duke's letters of approbation. Did he wish to protect his own reputation by destroying the evidence of his having kept secret records (a matter he must have known Wellington abhorred) or did he want to protect his wife and family from the opprobrium he suspected would be heaped on them after his death, were his criticism of Wellington – even if unspoken – to enter the public domain? Answers to these questions are unlikely ever to be found but one thing is clear: whatever Gurwood had been hiding was of the greatest importance to Wellington.

Wellington's clearest attempt at suppressing evidence is the disappearance of General Adam's letter. That the letter once existed is unquestionable. In addition, there is a broad range of examples of Wellington doing his best to prevent knowledge of his deceit being discovered and published, from his discouragement of straightforward histories of the battle, via an argument over a model, the possibility of blackmail, and an excited response to the discovery that Gurwood had been hoarding incriminating documents. However persuasive these are in favour of the hypothesis of Wellington's guilt when taken together, individually none of them unarguably proves the hypothesis – all are

Lieutenant-Colonel John Gurwood, 1790–1845.
He joined the army in 1808 as an ensign in the 52nd, and fought through the Peninsular campaign until the assault on Cuidad Rodrigo, in which he lead the Forlorn Hope. He was severely wounded but, nevertheless, captured the French commanding general. He then transferred to the cavalry and was wounded in a preliminary skirmish early in the battle of Waterloo. After the war he became Wellington's military secretary and editor of the *Dispatches*.

open to other interpretation. All, that is, bar one. In the memorandum written in answer to Siborne's proposed plan for the model, Wellington unambiguously shows his involvement in the 52nd's dramatic advance. Since Siborne's model clearly shows the 52nd 'flanking' the Garde, we can be sure the plan also included this. Thus he now knew the 52nd's action was about to become public knowledge and must have assumed that the Light Brigade's charge at Napoleon was too.

Epilogue

The hypothesis we have been examining posed three questions to resolve the 200-year-old argument about the battle's end – what actually happened; why and by whom was the true version omitted; and was its omission an accident or intentional?

The facts of what actually occurred at the battle are now clear, beyond all reasonable doubt. It has to be admitted – however regrettable it may be – that Wellington is the only possible candidate to blame for obscuring the truth and intentionally hiding the last half-hour. One very important question remains: why did Wellington decide to obscure this glorious manoeuvre from history, and, by so doing, not only inflict a blatant injustice upon an officer and a regiment that had served him so brilliantly and faithfully in the Peninsular War, but also to put at risk his own desired reputation as an honest and responsible English gentleman?

There was no doubt whatsoever that it was his Allied army that had routed the French or, more precisely, their left wing. As commander-in-chief he was unarguably the victor or, again more precisely, the joint victor with Blücher. He could so easily have claimed that Colborne, one of his 'Spanish' protégés who, knowing his commander's mind, had anticipated his order, thus giving glory to them both. Indeed Waterloo was not the first battle in which the 52nd had turned the tide for Wellington: the regiment's exploits in the Light Division in Spain and France are well documented elsewhere. The Battle of Orthez is a prime example.

In 1813, the British, having chased Marshal Soult into France, had caught up with his army in a strong position on the heights above the Gave de Pau, near Orthez. Wellington attempted to turn both of Soult's flanks while advancing against his centre, hoping, after defeating him, to cut off his retreat. To oversee the battle, he placed himself on a commanding knoll, an old Roman camp. Beresford with the 4th and 7th Divisions attacked the French right, under Reille. Picton, with the 3rd and 6th Divisions, attacked the centre under d'Erlon. Hill, with the 2nd Division, was tasked with turning the French left commanded by Clausel, while von Alten, with the Light Division, stood by as a reserve. But all did not go well. After three hours fighting both Beresford and Picton had been forced back. Historian and general, C.W. Robinson described what happened next:

> At this juncture Wellington's quick grasp of the battlefield and handling of his troops saved the day. A sudden counterstroke upon Reille secured victory (as at Talavera and Salamanca) at a critical moment.
>
> Observing from the Roman camp that Reille, in pressing back Beresford on the right, had become separated from D'Erlon, he directed the 52nd Regiment, wading through a marshy ravine which took them to their knees, to mount the ridge on Reille's flank and rear, while he himself, with the 3rd and 6th Divisions, closed upon D'Erlon; and Beresford, with the 7th and 4th, again attacked.
>
> In a short time the tide of battle had changed. Colonel Colborne, so often distinguished before, was soon upon the ridge, between Reille and the French centre, with the 52nd; Beresford, turning, faced Reille again; ... Wellington had thus won the battle ...
> In its conception and its rapidity this counterstroke, for such it was, was as brilliant as that of Salamanca...[1]

A cogent case has been made by Huw J. Davies that proposes that Wellington was very conscious of the Prussian drive for hegemony of the German speaking states and was loath to give to their claim the boost that Prussian victory over Napoleon would inevitably bring.[2] It follows that the playing down of the Prussian contribution in the *Waterloo Despatch*, already identified, may have had a political aim. But had his priority been the need to prove the Anglo-Allied superiority over the Prussian claim, would not the dramatic and very effective dash across the battlefield and through the French position by the Light Brigade have been infinitely more impressive and persuasive than the near non-event he described in the *Waterloo Despatch*? Moreover, the Light Brigade's dash occurred before the Prussian breakthrough at Plancenoit, which – largely thanks to his *Despatch* – is still generally accepted as the moment of Prussian breakthrough.

Zieten's breaking of the French right wing could have been ignored, as it largely has been until now. Some or all of these factors may have affected his decision to exclude Colborne and the 52nd from his honours list. However, a strong contender for the prime reason was that Wellington, well aware that in truth he shared the victor's laurels equally with the Prussians, decided the most effective way of achieving precedence over Blücher, was to establish himself as the man who personally gave the order that broke the French. Bearing in mind his decision was made in the heat of the moment just after the battle, as well as his personality, this would have been an aim surely much closer to his heart than diminishing the influence of Prussia in post-war Europe.

Perhaps Wellington was motivated by other emotions. Was it simply pique, that not he but a mere colonel had dealt the death blow to Napoleon's hopes, a deed which he – the duke – had dreamed of for many years? Naturally he would have wanted to beat Napoleon by a stroke of his own invention rather than be 'saved' by one of his own officers, let alone by the Prussians.

Was it because of his obsession with having to be in sole control of the army's movements that he could not tolerate someone acting on their own initiative, especially one – it could be argued – who had put the army at risk by his action? Colborne's manoeuvre could have been misjudged – if there had been French cavalry to take advantage of the 52nd's movement out of line by charging through the considerable gap vacated by Adam's brigade's departure, disaster could have ensued.

Was he jealous of Colborne's achievement, especially of his stroke of genius in driving for the Imperial jugular? Did Wellington believe he had been outclassed – or at least that his peers might think he had been? Did he, perhaps, believe that his performance at Waterloo had not been up to the mark, and imagined he would be criticised for it? Despite any failings, personally dealing the winning blow would have deflected all criticism. On the other hand he may simply have been concerned at the potential loss of face, that his reputation might be damaged, that the adulation, which had put him in charge of negotiations with the heads of the other victorious nations about the fate of France after Napoleon's 1814 abdication, might be diminished.

Had he acquired an inflated view of his own importance when appointed British plenipotentiary to the Congress of Vienna, and then as commander-in-chief to the Allied army when Napoleon broke out of Elba? Did he feel he had to live up to the omnipotent image others had of him? It is fair to suggest that, had his reputation been tarnished at this juncture, his influence over the future of Europe might have been massively reduced. But surely he would have considered the potentially greater damage to his reputation of being exposed as a liar, had his deception been discovered. This should have been a major factor against the decision to hide the last half-hour.

Wellington did not, as far as we know, record his thoughts on the reason why he chose to manipulate history. Some or all of these possible reasons may have influenced his decision but the weight of evidence suggests that he desired, above all else, and despite the very serious risk to his reputation, to go down in history as the man who gave the order that beat Napoleon. In other words, his prime purpose in writing the 52nd's independent action out of history was to ensure that he could claim to have won the Battle of Waterloo by his own judgement of the critical moment and his own delivery of the commands, just as he had beaten Marmont at Salamanca.

In support of this theory, we have a record of the moment when he revealed his inner ambition. On hearing the news of Napoleon's death, he remarked to his friend, Harriet Arbuthnot: 'Now I may say I am the most successful general alive.'[3] It must be admitted that his success brought him magnificent rewards. However, for all ranks of the Light Brigade, to have achieved such a meritorious result but then to have it completely ignored, brought no reward except disappointment and frustration. Sir John Colborne's feelings are recorded by his son:

> However much he [Sir John Colborne, Lord Seaton] disliked interfering personally in this ... controversy, ... it always caused him a certain amount of surprise and annoyance to find the long movement and march of the 52nd denied, a movement which was the talk, indeed, of the whole army on the march to Paris and during the time it was there stationed, and on account of which movement he had been daily receiving congratulations from numerous officers of the English army, including Sir John Byng, of the Guards, himself. The conversion of this extended and dangerous movement of the 52nd into a mere wheel of the regiment on the flank of the Guards [Garde] annoyed him as much almost as seeing the movement altogether ignored [as it was] in the meagre despatch of the Duke of Wellington.[4]

Like Colborne, the officers of the 52nd had to keep silent about the issue, in order to avoid almost universal opprobrium for contradicting the great national hero, until Gawler and Vivian had their public spat in the *United Service* Journal, which was touched on earlier. But did the other ranks' feelings enter the record? In a strange and round about way it transpires they did. When the Metropolitan Police Force was established, Colonel Charles Rowan, late of the 52nd Light Infantry, had been appointed the first joint commissioner, along with a Richard Mayne, possibly on Wellington's recommendation to Sir Robert Peel.

When drawing up the 'New Police' rules and regulations they decided that superintendants in charge of companies/divisions would not be ex-officers of the military, in order to avoid politicisation. Instead, senior retired non-commissioned officers would be appointed, predominantly from the Guards regiments. The Metropolitan Police orders for 8 July 1833 reveal that Serjeant William Randall, of the 6th Company of 'F' Division, was to be dismissed 'for making use of improper language respecting the Grenadier Guards, calling them Sandbags'.[5] Presumably, the officer who dismissed Randall felt the nickname to be offensive although 'Sandbags' does not sound overly rude.

However, calling somebody a 'sandbag' is not exactly complimentary either, referring, as it may, to an item that is inert and only good for defensive purposes. The present-day Grenadiers accept the nickname, but in honour – according to the regimental website – of their defence, against overwhelming odds, of the Sandbag Battery in thick fog during the Battle of Inkerman in the Crimean War. Perhaps this was, as described, 'one of the epics of Military History', but it can not be the origin of the nickname since Inkerman was fought in November 1854, whereas Randall was sacked in 1833. Given that we now know the 1st Guards stood inert and defensive while Adam's brigade broke the main body of the Garde at Waterloo, it seems very possible the nickname 'Sandbags' arose from that event.

This supposition is supported by the roll of recipients of the Waterloo Medal, which reveals four men by the name of William Randall (or Randle, spelling being a more fluid matter then than now). A corporal in the 71st is a likely candidate for the unfortunate Serjeant Randall. The 71st – as we know – was part of Adam's Light Brigade, positioned on the 52nd's right. It is entirely plausible that a soldier of the 71st Light Infantry might have strong feelings about a perceived lack of support at a critical moment. Indeed, there is a possible link with Waterloo. The police officer who took offence and sacked Serjeant Randall was Joseph Thomas. At Waterloo there was a Lieutenant Colonel Charles Thomas, who was killed.[6] If the two were related it would explain the sensitivity over the offending nickname – Colonel Thomas was of the 1st Foot Guards.

It is reassuring to learn that the Grenadier Guards will not be overly concerned about losing the reputation of winning Waterloo. *The British Grenadiers,* the latest printed version of the history of the Grenadier Guards, published in 2006, stated:

> Thus it would have been the two fresh battalions of the 3rd Châsseurs, closely followed by the 4th Châsseurs, that assaulted the two battalions of the First Guards.[7]

These three battalions are said to have been Napoleon's last throw and *The British Grenadiers* generously gives credit to the 52nd for helping to repulse the last one; the three Old Garde battalions in reserve are said to have been occupied solely with covering the eventual retreat and escorting the defeated emperor off the field. However, as our analysis has shown, the assumption that three battalions attacked 3/1st Guards is an exaggeration: our analysis shows there is no evidence that more than one battalion attacked the Guards' brigade. A check in 2013, of the British Army website of the Grenadier Guards now reveals the following text:

Napoleon directed his final assault with fresh troops – the Imperial Guard, which had hitherto been maintained in reserve. That assault was utterly defeated and in honour of their defeat of the Grenadiers of the French Imperial Garde, the 1st Guards were made a Regiment of Grenadiers and given the title of 'First or Grenadier Regiment of Foot Guards'.

Near truth has prevailed and it is now recognised that their opponents were indeed grenadiers, not châsseurs, as explained earlier. But it is also now clear their enemy was only a single battalion since the only other grenadier battalion had already been repulsed by Colin Halkett's brigade. It is unfortunate that the inference still lingers that this success lead to the 'utter defeat' of the Garde, whereas the three châsseur battalions and certainly two, possibly three, Old Garde battalions were still to come, to be broken by the 52nd. However regrettable it might seem, it must be realised that another regiment deserved the Prince Regent's accolade; of 'Imperial' perhaps?

But it might be observed that this realisation may have come to at least one very senior Guards officer over 170 years ago. Major General Byng wrote to HRH the Duke of York on the day after the battle:

> I had also to witness the gallantry with which the last attack made by Grenadiers of the Imperial Guard ordered on by Bonaparte himself; the destructive fire they [the Guards] poured in, and the subsequent Charge, which together completely routed the Enemy, a second attempt met with a similar reception and the loss they caused to the French of the finest Troops I ever saw, was immense.[8]

His statement bears notable similarity to the website text, quoted above. Naturally he omitted to reveal who had routed the 'second attempt' but, at least, he acknowledged there had been one. However, in a letter dated April 1835 in reply to William Siborne's request for information about the Crisis, Byng had a remarkable change of mind, caused, apparently, by the sudden onset of amnesia:

> I think the inference you have drawn from information received is generally correct … but I fear giving too decided an opinion, as I was at the moment suffering much from the contusion I received.[9]

Byng quite clearly did not wish to be party to the lie of the myth, but nor did he dare contradict his commander-in-chief.

One aspect of the 52nd's astonishing success in routing the French left wing is that the 52nd not only charged the Imperial Garde at the run but also then doubled across the battlefield until they reached the axis road, at which point Colonel Colborne ordered a halt to recover both their dressing in line and – presumably – their breath. This dramatic movement must not only have been a wonderful sight for those few on the Allied side able to witness it but a mind-numbing sight to the French.

Intriguingly, there is a precedent from classical Greek times. The Battle of Marathon is vaguely known to everyone for the modern race of some 26 miles, invented for the Olympic Games in 1895. In 490 BC some 10,000 men of a combined Athenian and Plataean force faced the invading Persian army of some 25,000 men. According to Herodotus, the Greek forces, for the first recorded time in battle, attacked the Persian centre at the double, creating such a startling impression that the Persians broke and ran, and Greece was saved. A memorial and burial mound still survive to remind us of their deed.

It is too much to hope that a similar memorial to the 52nd and its comrades of the Light Brigade might mark the site of their triumph. But there is one method of commemoration which could be established and for which there are precedents. The key role played by the 52nd at Waterloo could be formally recognised, in retrospect, by the award of a 'Waterloo Distinction', a piece of the Waterloo Medal Ribbon, to be worn on the sleeve of the appropriate uniform by all ranks of the 52nd's successor battalion in the Rifles. Similar distinctions were awarded in the cases of the Devonshire Regiment (French Croix de Guerre, 1914–18 War) and the Gloucestershire Regiment (US Presidential Unit Citation, Korean War). Thus the 52nd's brilliant achievement at Waterloo would be perpetuated, albeit some 200 years late.

The essential memorial for the 52nd's action at Waterloo is for its achievement to be recognised and so firmly established in everyone's mind that both its breaking of the Garde and its drive across the battlefield at Napoleon become part of the nation's historical narrative.

The chief impediment to fixing in the public mind the true version of events that concluded the Napoleonic wars is the syndrome noted by Napoleon himself: 'History is a lie that nobody contests.' So firmly embedded in the nation's mythology is Wellington's lie that it will take a major counter-offensive by all who believe in the desirability of truth and particularly by those who dispense history in its many forms to the nation – indeed to the world – to rout it.

But it must be done – at the double.

The 52nd's post-Waterloo cap badge, and a bugle horn stringed.

APPENDIX

Essential Facts

An understanding of the terminology and fighting techniques of the Napoleonic era will have considerable importance as this story unfolds. It is a fascinating but wide subject. Only the facts that are absolutely relevant to an understanding of the events of the hidden last half-hour of the battle are detailed here.

Rank-and-File, and Line.
'Rank-and-file' is still the term used for the men in a body of troops to distinguish them from the supernumeraries – the officers, warrant officers and serjeants. Rank can be a grade, such as captain, but that is not what is implied in the term 'rank-and-file'. Here the term 'rank' implies a single line of men, shoulder to shoulder. But beware, the word 'line' has to appear here but complicates matters.

'Line' is a specific formation which, when taken up by a unit, implies, in the French Army three ranks, but in the British Army only two ranks. To complicate matters further, 'line' can refer both to the formation of the basic tactical unit, a battalion of infantry, or to the entire front of an army, when, for example, used as 'the Allied line', which is formed primarily of infantry but can include cavalry and artillery. Yet another use of the word is in 'the skirmishing line', when men are expressly not shoulder to shoulder but are fighting as files (see below) in a loose formation. Skirmishing was the particular skill of light infantry and rifle regiments, both of which were also capable of fighting in the line, as they did at Waterloo.

Like 'line', 'file' in English is a multi-meaning word, but militarily at least is easier than 'line' to explain. A file is the man in the front rank and the man (or men) directly behind him. In the Light Infantry the two men of a file remained together as 'buddies' so long as both were unwounded.

Line Infantry

During the eighteenth and early nineteenth century a line infantryman was essentially an automaton, drilled endlessly on the parade ground to perform without thinking, to the command of the drum, the drill manual's prescribed movements in the hope that he would instinctively carry out the same manoeuvres amidst the thunder and carnage of battle. His incentive to succeed was often the fear of the punishment he would receive if he failed.

Light Infantry

Before 1803 each line battalion had a light company, the men of which were expected to act as skirmishers when the need arose. That year General Sir John Moore put a proposal to the British government for light infantry regiments to be created, to replace the light company system. Sir John suggested the men should be 'not men of stature, but intelligent, quick, hardy and young'. 'Stature' implied height – military thought of the time considered the taller the soldier the more impressive he was, and that is why so much of the headgear – the almost universal shako in the British Army for example – had been designed to increase the impression of height. Light infantry were to be capable of fighting in both the skirmishing and the line infantry roles.

The first two regiments to be converted to light infantry were the 52nd of Foot followed by the 43rd of Foot. Moore was offered the option of a green uniform for the light infantry, but preferred to retain the traditional scarlet jacket, to avoid any sense of elitism when light infantry were employed alongside the line regiments.

When Wellington (Arthur Wellesley as he then was) assumed command in Spain, he brigaded the two light infantry regiments together with riflemen of the 95th in the 'Light Brigade', an appellation which will occur frequently in this tale. The reader is asked not to confuse the use of this title with the glorious cavalry disaster in the Crimean War, the charge of the so-called Light Brigade.

The term 'light brigade' was first coined in Wellington's Peninsular army half a century before the Crimean War. So successful was the Light Brigade that it was soon expanded to the Light Division of two brigades centred on the 43rd and 52nd Regiments and including riflemen of the 95th and Portuguese rifle battalions, together with the Chestnut Troop of the Royal Horse Artillery (RHA).

Apart from the obvious differences in uniform, the Rifle and Light Infantry regiments differed in other ways, most particularly in their weapons. The advantages of the rifle were its accuracy and its longer range, compared to that of the muzzle-loading musket, even in well-trained hands. The light infantry musket was a shorter version of the old 'Brown Bess', which had hardly altered since Marlborough's day, 200 years before. The shorter barrel of the New Land Pattern Light Infantry Musket was intended to make reloading easier when lying behind cover and it now had a rear sight where Brown Bess had none. The rifle's disadvantage was its slower rate of fire – one shot per minute against two or three by musket – resulting from having to hammer home the ball that was enclosed in a leather patch to give it a grip on the rifling and ensuring a good gas seal. Slow loading could be a disadvantage when pressed by cavalry. Napoleon had rejected rifles on logistical grounds, not favouring a variety of ammunition.

Here at last was the modern infantryman, trained to think and act for himself, independent of the mutual support provided by being part of a solid phalanx. Moore's soldierly dictum for the Rifles and Light Infantry was 'Do everything that is necessary, and nothing that is unnecessary.'

Infantry Formations and Movements

Column, Echelon and Square

For ease of control, battalion movement both off and on the battlefield was in column. A British battalion moving across the battlefield would have been on a one company frontage, one company behind another, each company in two ranks, for ease of directional control. A variable aspect of the column was its length, depending on the distance between companies, the latter dictated by the likelihood of having to change formation into square or line.

For the moment of attack the British retained the supposedly old-fashioned, but still highly effective, line formation, which, in attack as well as in defence, gave the important advantage of maximum firepower. However, its success in attack – the ability to maintain the line under enemy fire – depended on the absolute steadiness of the well-trained, regular soldier. Line was also very susceptible to being broken by cavalry.

The Revolutionary and Napoleonic armies of France and its allies were largely composed of conscripts, for which there was a running debate about the respective advantages of attacking in column or line, a debate that was not even resolved by the revision of the *Règlement* – the French drill manual – of 1808.

The French used a two-company frontage for their '*colonne d'attaque*' – each company in three ranks – because their technique, necessitated by having a conscript army (whose less than unshakeable morale benefited from move-

THE GARDE
IN

COLUMN

SQUARE

& ECHELON

SUPPORT MUTUAL
SUPPORT MUTUAL
ECHELON
SUPPORT MUTUAL
SUPPORT MUTUAL

REFUSED

DIRECTION
OF
ADVANCE

ment *en masse*), was to advance in column-of-attack until close to the enemy when the men would deploy into line. Against similarly conscripted armies the threat of a blow from a massed body of men usually resulted in the enemy's breaking and running before the column needed to shake out into line. Deploying into line – *ordre mince* to the French – was always a dangerous moment; too soon and there was a risk of being cut down by cavalry and too late risked the loss of momentum at the critical moment. The British Army was not conscripted (although its sources of recruits were often less than ideal) and its iron discipline in defence in line almost always saw off the French in column, mostly by the mathematics of fire power. A British battalion of 600 in line (two ranks deep) could bring 600 muskets to bear on a Ligne battalion of equal strength, which, formed in six companies each of 100 men in three ranks, in column of two-company frontage, could volley with only 132 muskets (assuming the third rank did not fire, to avoid murdering their own front rank).

As in the Peninsula, so at Waterloo, the French columns were wrong-footed by Wellington's technique of hiding his battalions out of sight behind a crest, rendering almost impossible the judging of the correct moment to go into *ordre mince*. But mathematics was not the sole reason for the effectiveness of the British line in defence: psychology had a role to play.

Stemming from its revolutionary days the French infantry customarily advanced with a noisy clamour, which both sustained the conscripts' morale and intimidated the enemy. Under Napoleon the rhythmic cries of '*Vive l'Empereur*' became famous. The British response was to stand motionless and silent until the leading French battalion halted to shake out into line, when one devastating close-range volley would be delivered, followed by a cheer and an immediate charge with lowered bayonets.

Finally in our consideration of 'column' there is the need to distinguish between one battalion and a number of battalions in 'line ahead' (to borrow a nautical term that would be very well known to Wellington and his contemporaries). In army parlance, line ahead was properly a 'column of battalions', as Wellington himself clarified for us when he wrote: 'The infantry was formed into columns, and moved in pursuit in columns of battalions.'[1]

However, it has to be remembered that few people were as precise as the duke. In many accounts, the imprecise use of the word column may imply either one battalion or a column of battalions. Much misunderstanding has arisen over the years thanks to this imprecision in the use of the term 'column'.

Echelon

When advancing to the attack, an 'echelon' formation was sometimes employed, in which each successive battalion was positioned behind and to one side of its predecessor. This was a technique much favoured by Frederick the Great of Prussia. Its chief proponent in France during the Napoleonic wars was Maréchal Ney. The concept was that the heaviest and most destructive blow (usually the senior regiment) should fall on a weak point in the enemy's line and that the following series of hammer blows in succession would be overwhelming. No two battalions would be directly behind one another, with one exception: if a flank was 'refused', the last battalion would be tucked in directly behind the one in front, to strengthen the flank defence against cavalry. A further advantage of echelon was that volleys fired at attacking cavalry by one battalion would not hit another. If attack by cavalry was expected, the battalions would have moved in 'square'.

Square

British regiments, including Light Infantry and Rifles, had ten companies. Each side of the square was four ranks deep, the two front ranks kneeling and the rear two standing. All four ranks would have been interleaved, each man with a clear view outwards. The two kneeling ranks had bayonets fixed and musket butts firmly planted in the soil. They would not have fired except in extremis. There is some debate as to whether the rear two, standing, ranks had fixed bayonets or not. Early photographs of the Grenadier Guards in square show them fixed but it is argued that reloading would have been easier if bayonets were not in the way. However, the counter-argument to this is that the only dangerous part of the bayonet was the point and this was largely kept out of harm's way by its length. The square's prickly effect would have been much enhanced if all ranks had fixed bayonets. The Prussians certainly saw no difficulty in loading with bayonets fixed since theirs were fixed the entire time: scabbards were not even issued.

So long as the troops were not caught in the act of forming square and kept their nerve, the square was a complete defence against cavalry. No horse, however hard-driven, would run itself onto the bayonets, unless it had already been shot dead, when momentum might slide it and its rider through the side of the square, creating a gap for other riders to penetrate. As often as not these brave souls would then have been despatched anyway.

Fire control was very important. No side of a square would feel safe if they had 'thrown away' all their fire, leaving them offenseless until reloaded. Reloading took the British about fifteen seconds, and the KGL even less. No other army could compare with this rate of fire. It was achieved through practising with live ammunition. The need to adjust or replace flints would have reduced the rate of fire. There are recorded instances of a stand-off between cavalry and an infantry square, the cavalry tempting the infantry to 'throw away their fire' and the infantry unwilling to fire until the cavalry were committed and presented an unmissable target. The key to such an impasse was to introduce the third teeth arm: the artillery. If horse artillery worked with the cavalry, the square – if not similarly supported – was lost. If it stood, the men died on the spot from gun fire; if it broke the men would be cut down by the cavalry's sabres or lances.

Wheel and Form.

Manoeuvring formed bodies of troops on the battlefield by battalion or company or half-company (division), to change from line, to square, to column, and to change direction required familiarity with many drill movements. Some are still demonstrated to perfection by the Foot Guards on Horse Guards Parade at the annual trooping the colour. Two of these movements, for changing direction in line through 90°, have particular relevance to this story – the 'wheel' and the 'form'. The wheel is easy to imagine – one end

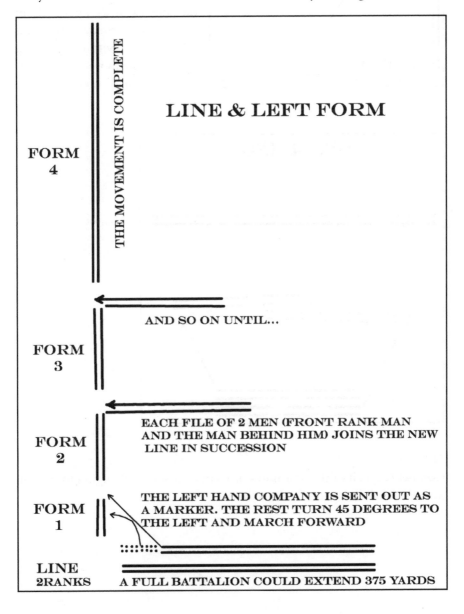

THE MOVEMENT IS COMPLETE

LINE & LEFT FORM

FORM
4

FORM
3

AND SO ON UNTIL...

FORM
2

EACH FILE OF 2 MEN (FRONT RANK MAN
AND THE MAN BEHIND HIM) JOINS THE NEW
LINE IN SUCCESSION

FORM
1

THE LEFT HAND COMPANY IS SENT OUT AS
A MARKER. THE REST TURN 45 DEGREES TO
THE LEFT AND MARCH FORWARD

LINE
2 RANKS

A FULL BATTALION COULD EXTEND 375 YARDS

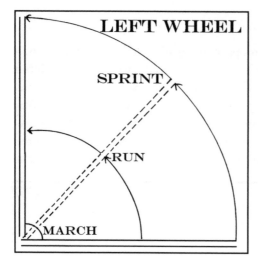

of the line is the hub while the line moves round it like a spoke. The longer the line, the faster the men at the outer end must move. The alternative is the left or right form. In this movement the right or left file turns 90° and halts while the remainder of the unit turns 45°. Each file in turn marches forward and halts when in line with the growing new line. The movement is completed when all files are in line again.

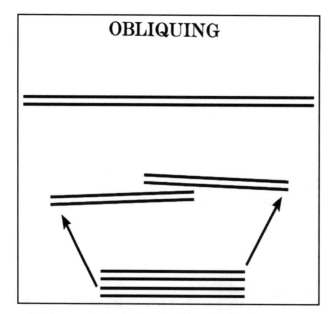

Obliquing
Colonel Reynell of the 71st uses this term to describe changing formation from double line, i.e. four ranks, to line.

Artillery

Ammunition

The most frequently fired ammunition was 'round shot' (also known as 'solid shot' or 'ball') of cast iron, whose weight defined the size of the cannon, such as a 6-pounder, for example. Round shot was best used at long range because of its carrying power and, ideally, it ricocheted once so that it travelled at chest height for a considerable distance to achieve its maximum effect. Even when spent and rolling along the ground it could take off a foot. When the mass of an infantry square was the target, round shot could be devastating but against a two- or three- deep line it was far less telling, except perhaps for its effect on the morale of inexperienced troops, for they could see it coming. If the ground was saturated – as it was at Waterloo – round shot was almost useless as it tended to bury itself in soft ground.

Next there was 'common shell'. This was the equivalent of the modern high explosive (HE) shell. It was spherical like solid shot, but the hollow cast-iron shell was filled with gunpowder and it had a fuse, ignited by the flash from the propellant charge. Its effect came from the shards of metal casing as well as the force of the explosion. It often burst after striking the ground so it was somewhat ineffectual at Waterloo because of the soft, rain-sodden earth.

Similar in appearance to common shell, but invented and used only by the British, was 'case shot' (sometimes confusingly called 'common case' or 'spherical case'). This was an air-burst weapon with an adjustable time fuse. The iron case contained not only gunpowder but also musket balls, and thus provided a means of firing at the enemy infantry over the heads of one's own troops. The fuse was a little unreliable, sometimes resulting in 'friendly fire', as at least one of the infantry battalions at Waterloo was to discover. Spherical case, known officially only from 1852 as 'Shrapnel' (after the inventor) is referred to in this book by its inventor's name. The French tried to replicate it but were unable to design a satisfactory fuse.

All three types – round shot, common shell and case (shrapnel) – were mounted on a sabot of wood (sabot is the French for a clog or a hoof), and held in place by tin strapping. Having the ball strapped to the sabot also ensured that the fuse's slight projection on the opposite side from the sabot did not snag on the barrel and that the blast from the charge did not strike the fuse directly but came round the sphere before igniting it. The sabot provided a flat surface against which to maximise the force of the explosion of the propellant.

Finally there is the close range ammunition known as 'canister' or 'grape'. Canister (again confusingly occasionally called 'case' or 'common case') comprised a cylindrical metal container of musket balls on a sabot attached to a canvas propellant bag. Grape obtained its name from the appearance of the naval gun round which was so strapped in canvas as to resemble (to the imaginative mind) a bunch of grapes. The military version consisted of nine larger balls in three layers of three separated by discs on a central spigot. In accounts of the time, both are often referred to as 'grape shot'. Both the French and British used the two different sizes of ball, the heavier being fired initially at a longer range – because a heavier ball travelled further – and then the lighter but more numerous musket ball was most effective at short range. It may be the heavier version carried the vernacular name of grape while the lighter was known as canister.

Cannon

So much for the projectiles, what of the projectors? In all three armies involved at Waterloo there were two basic types of cannon – the gun and the howitzer. In essence the gun was long-barrelled and aimed directly at its target, while the howitzer had a stubby barrel and lobbed its projectile, thus being able to reach behind ridges and other obstacles such as woods. It followed that some projectiles could be fired by both types of ordnance, some by only one. Round shot was fired by all calibres of gun, but not by howitzers; common shell was fired only by howitzers; spherical case (shrapnel) could be fired from both guns and howitzers; canister, the ammunition of last resort, was common to all ordnance.

Organisation

Artillery on all sides was either horsed or on foot. For the British, the Royal Horse Artillery (RHA) was organised in 'troops' and the Royal Foot Artillery (RFA) organised in 'brigades'. Both units were often called 'batteries', by non-gunners, and, to avoid potential confusion in this publication, both will usually be so called. The French called their batteries *compagnies*.

At Waterloo, Wellington gave two explicit instructions to his artillery. The first was not to engage in counter-battery fire. Conservation of ammunition was the prime purpose behind the duke's edict. At long range, at least, such fire was largely ineffective given the poor accuracy of smooth-bore cannon. Near the end of the battle, when the Garde artillery approached the Allied line, this instruction was ignored by at least one troop commander. To hide this supposed misdemeanour from Wellington, Captain Mercer invented a story about a German officer (i.e. one who could have been either of the KGL or Prussian) who rode up and demanded Mercer should stop firing on a pair of guns that were firing with effect at Mercer's battery.

In fact, Mercer was right to be firing because the two guns were French horse artillery, firing in support of the Garde's attack. The second instruction was that the gunners should desert their cannon, and shelter in the nearest infantry square when enemy cavalry approached, leaving the guns unspiked for reuse when the cavalry had retired. One unfortunate British serjeant spiked his piece at Waterloo in the face of the first French cavalry charge and had to go to the rear to have the vent hole drilled out. He did not return to action.

The Theory of Inherent Military Probability

On occasions when it is necessary to resolve doubts on the veracity of unreferenced points or, as is sometimes the case, to deduce a fact where no evidence can be found, the theory of 'Inherent Military Probability' has been employed.[2] Propounded by Colonel A.H. Burne in the 1920s, the theory states that the solution of an obscurity can be achieved by an estimate of what a trained soldier would have done in the circumstances. This theory has also been found useful for dismissing improbable suggestions. It can, of course, be employed only by trained soldiers, of which the author was one, albeit of a much later era.

NOTES & REFERENCES

Colour Plates

1 The story of its linking with the British triangulation survey is admirably told in Rachel Hewitt's *Map of a Nation* (London: Granta, 2010), in which a drawing of a similar construction can be found on p.85.

Chapter 1: The Reason Why

1 Weller, *Wellington at Waterloo*, p.xiv.

2 Gurwood (ed.) *The Despatches of Field Marshal the Duke of Wellington*, Vol. 8, p.149.

Chapter 2: The Campaign so Far

1 Adkin, *The Waterloo Companion*, p.23.

2 Ibid. p.24.

3 Harvey, *The War of Wars*, p.473.

4 It has always seemed to me to be overly patronising to convert to English from French such words as 'Ligne' and 'Garde'. Indeed retaining the French spelling aids clarity in a subject where the French Garde assaults the British Guards, while the French Ligne Regiments attack the Allied line. This rule will be observed except where words have been anglicised in a quotation. As a courtesy to our French and German friends I also intend to show accents, as far as an Englishman is able, except on Napoléon, who has no need of accentuation.

5 The words 'regiment' and 'battalion' can cause confusion. In British and French armies (for the Prussians I have not detailed units below corps level) the regiment is the family; battalions are individual members of that family. Thus 1/1er Grenadiers would indicate the first battalion of the First (premier) Grenadiers; the second battalion would be 2/1er. 1/2e would be the first battalion of the second (deuxième) Grenadiers. The same rule applied in the British Army, but in both armies – particularly the British – there was often no more than one battalion of most regiments in any campaign. The 52nd of Foot, for example, had a second battalion but it was in England, so there is no need to specify 1/52nd. The 95th, on the other hand, had elements of three battalions present at Waterloo so we find 1/95th, 2/95th and 3/95th.

6 Adkin, p.197.

7 Nations represented in the Allied army included Germans from Hanover, Nassau and Brunswick, as well as Dutch and Belgian together with the British element, which included the King's German Legion – partly commanded by British officers. This well respected force was comprised of refugee Hanoverians from George III's

possession in Germany. Hanover had been subjugated and occupied by Napoleon. It is subsequently usually referred to as the KGL.

8 Adkin, p.37.

9 Weller, *Wellington at Waterloo*, p.64.

10 Logie, *Waterloo, the 1815 Campaign*, p.58.

11 Weller, p.65.

12 Pattison, *Personal Recollections of the Waterloo Campaign*, p.41.

13 Full histories of the battle for Quatre-Bras are available. Mike Robinson's *The Battle of Quatre Bras 1815* gives the latest and fullest description of the battle.

14 Logie, p.72.

Chapter 3: Hard pounding this, gentlemen.

1 Leeke, *The History of Lord Seaton's Regiment, (The 52nd Light Infantry) at the Battle of Waterloo*, p.15.

2 La Haie Sainte translates as the 'Sacred Hedge'; no one seems to know why.

3 Logie, *Waterloo, the 1815 Campaign*, p.89. Given that the purpose of this book is to establish truth it seems logical to try to correct an error of nomenclature. I intend to refer to au Goumont when Hougoumont would be more readily recognised by a British audience, except where it is used in a quotation. The esteemed French historian, the late Jacques Logie, who held a doctorate from the Sorbonne and was president of the Committee for Historical Study of the Battle of Waterloo, explains that Hougoumont was known at the time of the battle as 'Gomont' or 'Goumont', first recorded as such in 1358. On a map of the battlefield, published by J. Booth, *The Battle of Waterloo, etc.*, dated 1816, the chateau [*sic*] and farm of Goumont is clearly so named. 'Hougoumont' probably arose from 'au Goumont', and so the latter version will be used here. Strangely, Booth's book contains a second, smaller map of the battle on which the château is named as Hougoumont. This map is annotated 'Drawn and engraved from a Plan Delivered from the Horse Guards from a Sketch by Capt. Thornton.' Perhaps we now know whom to blame for the error – and how he pronounced his 'haitches'.

4 Hugh Halkett – not to be confused with Colin Halkett, his elder brother – has mysteriously acquired the alternative name of William. A letter dated 1837 to a Captain Benne, eventually found its way to William Siborne and was mistakenly signed 'William' in H.T. Siborne's *Waterloo Letters*. A misreading of a handwritten 'Colonel' perhaps?

5 Weller, *Wellington at Waterloo*, p.127.

6 Between 1687 and 1871 officers of the Guards regiments carried – confusingly to modern ears – two different ranks, one linked to their regimental position and the other their status in the army. Majors in a battalion were ranked as full colonel; captains as lieutenant colonel; lieutenants ranked as major. Finally in 1815 ensigns were given the army rank of lieutenant as a reward for the conduct of the 1st Foot Guards at Waterloo.

7 Adkin, *The Waterloo Companion*, p.24.

8 Ibid. p.298.

9 It seems only fair to point out that no British cavalryman thought to do the same when the Household and Union brigades got amongst the guns of the Grande Batterie.

10 Leeke, p.30.

11 Use of square brackets indicate comments by the present author whereas parentheses within quotations indicate the comment is the original author's.

12 Logie records this episode as described by Foy's ADC, J.B. Lemonier-Delafosse, p.115.

13 Siborne, H.T. (ed.), *Waterloo Letters*, Letter No 120 from General Adam, p.276.

14 Shaw-Kennedy, *Notes on the Battle of Waterloo*, p.123. Shaw was commissioned in the 43rd Light Infantry, who shared with the 52nd the honour of fighting in Wellington's Light Division in the Peninsula. He later took the name Kennedy to accept a bequest.

15 Wintle, 'Memoirs of Caulaincourt 1935', quoted in the *Dictionary of War Quotations*, London: Hodder & Stoughton, 1989.

Chapter 4: Formez le Carré!

1 Levasseur, *Souvenirs Militaires d'Octave Levasseur etc.*, p.304.

2 Houssaye, *1815. Waterloo*, p.221.

3 Smith, *The life of John Colborne, Field-Marshal Lord Seaton*, copied from a memorandum by Petit in the Morrison Collection, London.

4 Ibid, p.424.

Chapter 5: En Avant la Garde!

1 Siborne, H.T. (ed.), *Waterloo Letters*, Letter No 160 from Captain J. Leach, p.365.

2 Pontécoulant, *Napoleon à Waterloo*, pp.245–246.

3 Siborne, H.T. (ed.), Letter No 160 from Captain J. Leach, p.365.

4 Pontécoulant, p.246.

5 Houssaye, *1815. Waterloo*, p.225.

6 Crabbé, *Jean-Louis de Crabbé: Colonel d'Empire*, p.16, quoted in Andrew Field's *Waterloo: The French Perspective*, Pen and Sword 2012

7 Siborne, H.T. (ed.), Letter No 139 from Ensign E. Macready, p.330.

8 Kruse, *Report, dated 21st June 1815, concerning the events of the 15th, 16th and 17th June, and the battle of the 18th at Mont St. Jean*, online by 1815 Limited.

9 Franklin, (ed.) *Waterloo. Netherlands Correspondence*. Account by Major General de Constant -Rebècque, p.19.

10 Hessisches Staatsarchiv Darmstadt: abt.011, E60. Letter dated 26 July 1815 from Fähnrich (Ensign) Heinrich von Gagern, published online by 1815 Limited.

11 Niedersächsisches Staatsarchiv, Wolfenbüttel: 24 Neu 11. Report, dated 9 o'clock in the morning 19 June 1815, by Oberst Johann Elias Olfermann, commanding the Brunswick Contingent, to the secret council at Braunschweig, published online by 1815 Limited.

12 Franklin, (ed.) *Waterloo. Hanoverian Correspondence*, report dated 9 December 1824 by Major Otto Heinrich Müller, Bremen Light Infantry, p.106.

13 Smith, *The life of John Colborne, Field-Marshal Lord Seaton, etc.* p.400.

14 Pontécoulant, p.252.

15 Mercer's *Journal of the Waterloo Campaign*, London, 1870.

Chapter 6: Slap came their Grape

1 Siborne, H.T. (ed.), *Waterloo Letters*, Letter No 135, from Major General Sir Colin Halkett, p.320.

2 Barbero, *The Battle: A History of the Battle of Waterloo*, quoting Edward Macready in the *United Service Magazine*, p.316.

3 Houssaye, *1815. Waterloo*. p.225. Houssaye errs on two counts: eyewitnesses confirm the gun sections were on the right of each square and his use of the term echelon is confused. (See the appendix.)

4 Adkin, *The Waterloo Companion*, p.55.

5 Chandler, David. *The Campaigns of Napoleon*, 1995.

6 Lying down behind a ridge to shelter from incoming gunfire was perfectly acceptable behaviour, frequently ordered by Wellington himself. However, when standing, even to duck when solid shot could be seen to be heading straight at you was very bad form, and sternly discouraged.

7 Glover, G. (ed.), *Letters from the Battle of Waterloo.* Letter No 139 from Captain Robert Howard, p.215.

8 Adkin, quoting Edward Macready in the *United Service Magazine.* p.393.

9 Siborne, H.T. (ed.), Letter No 139 from Ensign E. Macready, p.330.

10 Holmes (ed.), *Battlefield*, p.231.

11 Adkin, quoting Edward Macready in the *United Service Magazine*, p.393.

12 Siborne, H.T. (ed.), Letter from Captain J.A. Wilson, p.241.

13 Ibid. Map facing p.186.

14 de Chair, (ed.), *Napoleon's Memoirs*, p.535.

15 Napier, *History of the War in the Peninsula and in the South of France*, book XXIV, p.106.

16 Petit, *Petit's report on the Garde at Waterloo.*

17 Siborne, H.T. (ed.), Letter No 135 from Major General Sir Colin Halkett, p.320.

18 Adkin, p.205.

19 Pattison, *Personal Recollections of the Waterloo Campaign*, p.41.

20 Siborne, H.T. (ed.), Letter No 139 from Ensign E. Macready, p.330.

21 Adkin, quoting Edward Macready in the *United Service Magazine*, p.398.

22 Ibid. Letter No 145 from Major Dawson Kelly, p.340.

23 Ibid. Letter No 145 from Major Dawson Kelly, p.340.

24 Ibid. Letter No 146 from Major Dawson Kelly, p.341.

25 Adkin, p.393.

26 Franklin, (ed.) *Waterloo. Netherlands Correspondence*, quoting from a report, dated 4 July 1815, from Lieutenant General Baron David Hendrik Chassé, to HRH the Prince of Orange. p.119.

27 Ibid. from an undated account by Captain Antoine von Omphal, ADC to Lieutenant General Baron David Hendrik Chassé, p.132.

28 Siborne, H.T. (ed.), Letter No 89 from Captain A.C. Mercer, p.220.

29 Franklin, (ed.) a report, dated 4 July 1815, from Lieutenant General Baron David Hendrik Chassé to HRH the Prince of Orange, p.119.

30 Ibid. quoting a report to Baron Jean-Victor de Constant-Rebècque, dated 11 November 1815 by Lieutenant Colonel Baron Leonhard Albrecht Carl van Delen, p.125.

31 Ibid. quoting from an undated account by Captain Gerard Rochell, p.148.

32 Adkin, quoting Edward Macready in the *United Service Magazine*, p.397.

33 Franklin, (ed.) *Waterloo. Netherlands Correspondence*, a letter from General Lord Hill to Lieutenant General Baron Chassé, p.121.

34 Wellington, 2nd Duke of, (ed.) *Supplementary Despatches and Memoranda of Field Marshal Arthur Duke of Wellington*, vol. 1. Hill had mentioned Chassé's action to Wellington in a letter dated 8am, 20 June 1815, p.544.

35 Franklin, (ed.), *Waterloo. Netherlands Correspondence*, quoting from an account by Captain Gerard Rochell, p.148.

36 Leeke, *The History of Lord Seaton's Regiment*, p.52.

Chapter 7: Up Guards and at 'em

1 Siborne, H.T. (ed.), *Waterloo Letters*, Letter No 106 from Captain and Lieutenant Colonel Lord Saltoun, p.248.

2 Booth, (ed.), *The Battle of Waterloo, etc.*, p.63.

3 Siborne, H.T. (ed.), Letter No 105 from Major General Peregrine Maitland, p.243.

4 Hanning, *The British Grenadiers*, p.64.

5 Adkin, *The Waterloo Companion*, p.205.

6 Siborne, H.T. (ed.), Letter No 96 from Captain Pringle, p.227.

7 Glover, G. (ed.), *Letters from the Battle of Waterloo*, Letter No 105 from Ensign Thomas Swinburne, p.167.

8 Siborne, H.T. (ed.), Letter No 109, from Lieutenant and Captain H.W. Powell, p.255.

9 Glover, G. (ed.), Letter No 100 from Lieutenant Charles Ellis, p.162.

10 Siborne, H.T. (ed.), Memorandum with Letter No 105 from Major General Peregrine Maitland, p.244.

11 Leeke, *Supplement to The History of Lord Seaton's Regiment, etc.*, in his letter to the editor of the *Army and Navy Gazette* dated 30 May 1867, p.6.

12 Harrington Collection. Letter dated 21 June 1815, from Ensign Robert Batty.

13 Siborne, H.T. (ed.), Memorandum with Letter No 105 from Major General Peregrine Maitland, p.244.

14 Siborne, H.T. (ed.), Letter No 106 from Captain and Lieutenant Colonel Lord Saltoun 1st Foot Guards, p.248.

15 Ibid. Memorandum with Letter No 123 from Colonel Sir John Colborne, p.287.

16 Leeke, p.80.

17 Glover, G. (ed.), Letter No 95, from Lieutenant Colonel Henry Rooke, p.158.

18 Regimental Headquarters Scots Guards, letter dated 19 June 1815 from Major General Sir John Byng to HRH, the Duke of York. Published online by 1815 Ltd.

19 Leeke, p.85.

20 Ibid. p.124.

21 Glover, G. (ed.), Letter No 101, from Lieutenant Charles FR Lascelles, p.163.

22 Ibid. Letter No 99 from Lieutenant Charles Parker Ellis, p. 162.

23 University of Nottingham, Drury Lowe Collection – Dr.C.30/6, letter dated 19 June 1815 to his father Thomas Nixon, from Captain James Lock Nixon, published online by 1815 Ltd.

24 Siborne, W., *History of the Waterloo Campaign*, p.342.

25 Ibid. p.341.

Chapter 8: Make that Column Feel our Fire

1 Siborne, H.T. (ed.), *Waterloo Letters*, memorandum with letter No 105 from Major General P. Maitland, p.244.

2 Petit, General Jean-Martin. *Petit's report on the Garde at Waterloo*, translated by George Jeffrey, edited by John Koontz.

3 The Garde was organised in regiments, each commanded by a maréchal de camp (barring casualties), each regiment being of two battalions commanded by majors. But the battalions were deployed individually. Hence Petit has Christiani (grenadiers) and Pelet (châsseurs) in command of 2nd battalions because their 1st battalions had already been detached to retake Plancenoit. However, Mark Adkin says Pelet had actually gone to Plancenoit: 2/2 Châsseurs was commanded by Major Mompez.

4 Smith, *The life of John Colborne, Field-Marshal Lord Seaton*, p.424.

5 Siborne, H.T. (ed.), Letter No 124 from Lieutenant G. Gawler, p.292.

6 Ibid. memo with Letter No 123 from Colonel Sir John Colborne, p.284.

7 Smith, G.C. Moore, remarks in Appendix II, p.400.

8 Ibid., a memorandum by James, son of Sir John Colborne, p.421.

9 Ibid. p.411.

10 Ibid. p.411.

11 Glover, G. (ed.), *Letters from the Battle of Waterloo*, Letter 118 from Captain William Rowan, p.182.

12 Ibid. Letter No 121 from Captain John Cross, p.184.

13 Siborne, H.T. (ed.), *Waterloo Letters*, memorandum with Letter No 123 from Colonel Sir John Colborne, p.284.

14 Smith, p.411.

15 Siborne, H.T. (ed.), memorandum with Letter No 123 from Colonel Sir John Colborne, p.284.

16 Glover, G, (ed.), Letter No 121 from Captain John Cross, p.184.

17 Siborne, H.T. (ed.), memorandum with Letter No 123 from Colonel Sir John Colborne, p.284.

18 Smith, a memorandum by James, son of Sir John Colborne, p.421.

19 Siborne, H.T. (ed.), Letter No 124 from Lieutenant G. Gawler, p.292.

20 Smith, a memorandum by James, son of Sir John Colborne, p. 421.

21 Siborne, H.T. (ed.), Letter No 103 from Lieutenant G.S. Maule, p.239.

22 Ibid. Letter No 128, a statement by Corporal William Aldridge, of 2nd Battalion 95th Rifles, forwarded by Colonel G. Gawler, p.302.

23 Leeke, *The History of Lord Seaton's Regiment, etc.*, p.43.

24 Leeke, supplement to *The History of Lord Seaton's Regiment, etc.*, his letters to the editor of the *Army and Navy Gazette*, p.4.

25 Siborne, H.T. (ed.), facing p.186.

26 Ibid. Letter No 90 from Lieutenant P. Sandilands p.223.

27 Leeke, p.43.

28 Ibid. p.43.

29 Siborne, H.T. (ed.), Letter No 109, from Lieutenant and Captain H.W. Powell, p.255.

30 Adkin, *The Waterloo Companion*, p.205.

31 Petit, *Petit's report on the Garde at Waterloo*, translated by George Jeffrey, edited by John Koontz.

32 Siborne, H.T. (ed.), Letter No 124 from Lieutenant G. Gawler, p.292.

33 Adkin, p.204.

34 Booth, (ed.) p.274.

35 Leeke, p.45.

36 Ibid. p.47.

37 Glover, G. (ed.), Letter No 118 from Captain William Rowan, p.182.

38 Leeke, p.47.

39 Ibid. p.51.

40 Glover, G. (ed.), Letter No 122 from Captain John Cross, p.187.

41 Ibid. Letter No 130 from Lieutenant Thomas Smith, p.197.

42 Smith, p.415.

43 Glover, G. (ed.), Letter No 130 from Lieutenant Thomas Smith, p.197.

44 Siborne, H.T. (ed.), Letter No 127 from Captain T.R. Budgen, p.300.

45 Ibid. Letter No 125 from Lieutenant Colonel Thomas Reynell, p.297.

46 Ibid. Letter No 129, from Captain W. Eeles, p.306.

47 Ibid. Letter No 126 from Major S. Reed, p.298.

48 Glover, G. (ed.), Letter No 115 from Captain W.G. Moore, p.179.

49 Ibid, Letter No 114 from Captain Lord Charles Fitzroy, p.178.

50 Quinet, *Histoire de la Compagne de 1815*, Paris: 1862.

51 Petit, *Petit's report on the Garde at Waterloo*.

Chapter 9: Don't let them Rally

1 Glover, G. (ed.), *Letters from the Battle of Waterloo*, Letter No 134 from Captain Albertus Cordemann, p.207.

2 Siborne, H.T. (ed.), *Waterloo Letters*, Letter No 160 from Captain J. Leach, p.366.

3 Ibid. Letter No 128, statement by Corporal Aldridge, p.302.

4 Ibid. Memorandum to Letter No 123 from Colonel Sir John Colborne, p.285.

5 Glover, G. (ed.), *Letters from the Battle of Waterloo*, Letter No 122 from Captain John Cross, p.187.

6 Leeke, *The History of Lord Seaton's Regiment, etc.*, p.48.

7 Smith. *The life of John Colborne, Field-Marshal Lord Seaton*, a memorandum by James, son of Sir John Colborne. p.421,

8 Siborne, H.T. (ed.), Letter No 48 from Lieutenant John Banner, p.98.

9 Ibid. Letter No 49 from Major P.A. Latour, p.100.

10 Holmes, *Wellington: The Iron Duke*, p.140.

11 Siborne, H.T. (ed.), Letter No 4, from Lieutenant General the Earl of Uxbridge, p.6.

12 Ibid. Memorandum to Letter No 123, from Colonel Sir John Colborne, p.285.

13 Glover, G. (ed.), Letter No 116 from Captain Patrick Campbell, p.180.

14 Siborne, H.T. (ed.), Memorandum to Letter No 123, from Colonel Sir John Colborne, p.286.

15 Ibid. p.286.

16 Leeke, p.51.

17 Glover, G. (ed.), Letter No 120 from Captain John Cross, p.183.

18 Ibid. Letter No 121 from Captain John Cross, p.184.

19 Siborne, H.T. (ed.), Letter No 128 from Corporal Aldridge, p.303.

20 Adkin, p.399.

21 Colonel Sir Colin Campbell was of the 2nd (Coldstream) Foot Guards and Commandant of Headquarters.

22 Leeke, p.55.

23 Ibid. p.56.

24 Anglesey, Marquess of, *One Leg*, p.148.

25 Adkin, p.399.

26 Leeke, supplement to *The History of Lord Seaton's Regiment*, p.56.

27 Foulkes, N., *Dancing into Battle*, p.79.

28 Anglesey, p.148.

29 Booth, (ed.) *The Battle of Waterloo, also of Ligny, and Quatre Bras, etc.*, p.185.

30 Smith, p.411.

31 *Oxfordshire and Buckinghamshire Light Infantry Chronicle*, Vol XXIII, p.134.

32 Petit, *Petit's report on the Garde at Waterloo*.

33 Siborne, H.T. (ed.), Letter No 124 from Lieutenant G. Gawler, p.295.

34 Ibid. Letter No 125 from Colonel T. Reynell, p.297.

35 Ibid. Letter No 126 from Captain S. Reed, p.298.

36 Leeke, supplement, p.63.

37 Leeke, p.61.

38 Siborne, H.T. (ed.), Letter No 126 from Captain S. Reed, p.298.

39 Ibid. Letter No 129, from Captain W. Eeles, p.306.

40 Leeke, p.67.

41 Siborne, H.T. (ed.), Letter No 120 from Major General Frederick Adam, p.275.

42 Ibid. Letter No 121 from Major T. Hunter Blair, p.279.

43 Glover, G. (ed.), Letter from Major the Comte de Sales, p.27.

Chapter 10: *The Moment to Attack was Arrived*

1 Siborne, H.T. (ed.), Letter No 70, from Major General Sir John Vandeleur, p.149.

2 Adkin, *The Waterloo Companion*, p.108.

3 Beware: on page 107 in *The Waterloo Companion*, Adkin attributes the 6th Cavalry Brigade to both Vivian and Vandeleur.

4 Siborne, H.T. (ed.), Letter No 51 from Major General Sir John Vandeleur, p.106.

5 Ibid. Letter No 120 from Major General Frederick Adam, p.277.

6 Ibid. Letter No 130 from Lieutenant Colonel Hugh Halkett, p.308.

7 Ibid. Letter No 130 from Lieutenant Colonel Hugh Halkett, p.309.

8 Franklin (ed.), *Waterloo. Hanoverian Correspondence*, pp.51, 55, 61.

9 Siborne, H.T. (ed.), Letter No 130 from Lieutenant Colonel Hugh Halkett, p.309.

10 Ibid. Letter No 7 from Lieutenant General Lord Greenock, p.15.

11 Ibid. Letter No 48 from Lieutenant John Banner, p.98.

12 Ibid. Letter No 74 from Major General Sir Hussey Vivian, p.163.

13 Black, *The Battle of Waterloo, a New History*, p.146.

14 Glover, G. (ed.), *Letters from the Battle of Waterloo*, Letter No 63 from Lieutenant Colonel the Honourable Henry Murray, p.115.

15 Siborne, H.T. (ed.), Letter No 74 from Major General Sir Hussey Vivian, p.163.

16 Glover, G. (ed.), Letter No 61 from Lieutenant Anthony Bacon, p.98.

17 Leeke, *The History of Lord Seaton's Regiment*, p.57.

18 Glover, G. (ed.), Letter No 62 from Lieutenant Anthony Bacon, p.105.

19 Ibid. Letter No 61 from Lieutenant Anthony Bacon, p.101.

20 Siborne, H.T. (ed.), Letter No. 130, from Lieutenant Colonel Hugh Halkett to Captain Benne, p.308.

21 Franklin, (ed.), *Waterloo. Hanoverian Correspondence*, p.55.

22 Glover, G. (ed.), Letter No 62 from Lieutenant Anthony Bacon, p.106.

23 Siborne, H.T. (ed.), Letter No 109 from Captain H.W. Powell, p.255.

24 Ibid. Letter No 51 from Major General Sir John Vandeleur, p.106.

25 Ibid. Letter No 72 from Major General Sir Hussey Vivian, p.160.

26 Ibid. Letter No 61 from Lieutenant J. Luard, p.122.

27 Ibid. Letter No 71 from Major General Sir Hussey Vivian, p.157.

28 Ibid. Letter No 75 from Captain T.W. Taylor, p.177.

29 Ibid. Letter No 71 from Major General Sir Hussey Vivian, p.157.

30 Booth, (ed.) *The Battle of Waterloo, also of Ligny, and Quatre Bras, etc.*, p.259.

31 Ibid. p.263.

32 Adkin, p.399.

33 Logie, *Waterloo, the 1815 Campaign*, p.125.

34 Siborne, H.T. (ed.), Letter No 58 from Captain A. Barton, p.116.

35 Ibid. Letter No 59 from Captain W. Tomkinson, p.118.

36 Glover, G. (ed.), Letter No 63, p.112.

37 Siborne, H.T. (ed.), Letter No 82 from Lieutenant W.B. Ingilby, p.201.

38 Ibid. Letter No 73 from Major General Sir Hussey Vivian, p.162.

39 Ibid. Letter No 70 from Major General Sir Hussey Vivian to Lady Vivian, p.149.

40 Glover, G. (ed.), Letter No 58, from Captain Arthur Shakespear to Sir Hussey Vivian, p.93.

41 Smith, *The life of John Colborne, Field-Marshal Lord Seaton*, p.403.

42 Ibid. p.411.

Chapter 11: *Complete your Victory*

1 Glover, G. (ed.), *Letters from the Battle of Waterloo*, Letter No 100, from Lieutenant Charles P. Ellis, p.163.

2 Siborne, H.T. (ed.), *Waterloo Letters*, Letter No 113 from Major General Sir John Byng, p.261.

3 Siborne, W., *History of the Waterloo Campaign*, p.344.

4 Kincaid, *Adventures in the Rifle Brigade, in the Peninsula, France and the Netherlands, from 1809 to 1815*, p.170.

5 Wellington's horse was named 'Copenhagen' because, when unborn, he was carried by his dam, unknown to her owner, during the Copenhagen campaign in 1807, in which Arthur Wellesley (as Wellington then was) was a divisional commander. The campaign's aim was to divest the Danes of their navy, to prevent it aiding Napoleon in his attempt to blockade Britain's trade with Europe.

6 Leeke, *The History of Lord Seaton's Regiment, etc.*, p.65.

7 Pattison, *Personal Recollections of the Waterloo Campaign*, p.51.

8 Siborne, H.T. (ed.), Letter No 139 from Captain E. Macready, p.332.

9 Ibid. Letter No 141 from Lieutenant Colonel W.K. Elphinstone, p.332.

10 Ibid. Letter No 89 from Captain A.C. Mercer, p.221.

11 Booth, (ed.), *The Battle of Waterloo, also of Ligny, and Quatre Bras, etc.*, p.69.

12 Leeke, p.71.

13 Franklin (ed.), *Waterloo. Netherlands Correspondence. An account of military service and the Waterloo campaign*, by G.J. Rochell, p.148.

14 Siborne, H.T. (ed), Letter No171 from Major General Sir John Lambert, p.393.

15 Ibid. Letter No 170, from Major General Sir John Lambert, p.392.

16 Wellington, second Duke of, *Supplementary Despatches*, p.513.

17 It is remarkable that dusk was as early as 8pm three days before the longest day of the year. Was the early dusk the result of the cataclysmic eruption of Tambora in Indonesia, which threw 4,600ft (1,400m) off the top of the mountain killing 88,000 people? The ejected gas and ash blanketed the globe, leading to failed harvests throughout the world in 1816. On the day of the battle a blood-red sunset was recorded. Was the eruption also the cause of the torrential rainstorm the evening and night before the battle?

Chapter 12: *The Prussian Assault*

1 Siborne, H.T., *Waterloo Letters*, Letter No 155 from Lieutenant K.J. Leslie, p.356.

2 Hamilton-Williams, *Waterloo, New Perspectives*, quoting BL MS 34704, note 35, p.396.

3 Leeke, *Supplement to the History of Lord Seaton's Regiment*, p.61.

4 Glover, G. (ed.), *Letters from the Battle of Waterloo*, No 122 from Captain John Cross, p.188.

5 Siborne H.T., memorandum with Letter No 123 from Colonel Sir John Colborne, p.286.

6 Booth, (ed.), *The Battle of Waterloo, also of Ligny, and Quatre Bras, etc.*, pp.205–6.

7 Hofschröer, P., *1815. The Waterloo Campaign. The German Victory*, p.144.

8 Ibid. p.145.

Chapter 13: *The Crisis in Quick Time*
None

Chapter 14: *Myth Making*

1 Franklin, *Waterloo. Netherlands Correspondence*, account by Major General Baron Jean-Victor de Constant-Rebècque, p.21.

2 Booth (ed.), *The Battle of Waterloo, also of Ligny, and Quatre Bras, etc.*, 'Marshal Blücher's Official Report of the Operations of the Prussian Army of the Lower Rhine' by General Gneisenau, p.207.

3 Stanhope, *Notes of Conversations with the Duke of Wellington*, p.245.

4 Seaton (ed.), *Lt-Col Basil Jackson's Notes and Reminiscences of a Staff Officer, etc.*, p.60.

5 Gurwood, (ed.) *The Despatches of Field Marshal the Duke of Wellington*, Vol. 8, p.149.

6 Hibbert, *Wellington, a Personal History*, p.6.

7 Foulkes, *Dancing into Battle*, p.63.

8 Ibid. p.67.

9 Strachey and Fulford (eds), *The Greville Memoirs 1814–1860*, vol. 1, p.120.

10 Hibbert, p.170.

11 Anglesey, *One Leg*, pp.132–133.

12 Siborne, H.T. (ed.), *Waterloo Letters*, Letter No 3 from Lieutenant General the Earl of Uxbridge, p.3.

13 Urban, *The Man who broke Napoleon's Codes*, p.285.

14 Hibbert, p.152.

15 Jennings (ed.), *The Croker Papers*, vol. II, p.235.

16 Creevey, *The Creevey Papers. A selection from the correspondence and diaries of the late Thomas Creevey MP*, pp.236–7.

17 Leeke, *The History of Lord Seaton's Regiment, etc.*, p.63.

18 Hibbert, p.181.

19 Harvey, *The War of Wars*, p.757.

20 Larpent (ed.), *The Private Journals of Lord Judge-Advocate Larpent*, p.487.

21 Booth (ed.), p.215.

22 Wellington, 2nd Duke of, *Supplementary Despatches*, vol. 10, Letter to Mr W. Mudford, p.508.

23 Booth, p.210.

24 Franklin (ed.), *Waterloo. Netherlands Correspondence*, p.22.

25 Hibbert, p.185.

26 Creevey, pp.141–142.

27 Gurwood, p.149.

28 Hibbert, p.181.

29 *Hansard*, vol. 31, 23 June 1815, col. 973.

30 HMC Bathurst, pp.356–57.

31 Booth, p.285.

32 Gurwood, p.188.

33 Ibid. p.178.

34 Wellington, 2nd Duke of, vol. 8, p.656.

35 Hanning, Henry, *The British Grenadiers*, p.73.

Chapter 15: Avoiding the Issue

1 Wellington, 2nd Duke of, *Supplementary Despatches*, vol. 10, Letter to Mr W. Mudford, p.508.

2 Ibid. p.508.

3 Wellington, 2nd Duke of, *Supplementary Despatches*, vol. 14, p.530.

4 Balen, Malcolm, *A Model Victory*, p.20.

5 Adkin, *The Waterloo Companion*, p.148.

6 Siborne H.T. (ed.), *Waterloo Letters*, p.xvii.

7 Hofschröer, *Wellington's Smallest Victory*, p.100 et seq.

8 Glover (ed.), *Letters from the Battle of Waterloo*, Letter No 7, p.329.

9 Ibid. Letter No 9, p.331.

10 Wellington, 2nd Duke of (ed.), vol. 10, p.513.

11 Siborne, W., *History of the Waterloo Campaign*, p.xiv.

12 Wellington Papers, 1/865/11, at Southampton University.

13 Wellington, 2nd Duke of, vol. 10, Letter from Wellington to Sir John Sinclair, p.507.

14 Siborne, W., p.x.

15 Stanhope, Philip Henry, 5th Earl. *Notes of Conversations with the Duke of Wellington, 1831–1851.*

16 Hibbert, *Wellington, a Personal History*, footnote, p.343.

17 Anglesey, *One Leg*, 1961.

18 Wellington, 2nd Duke of, vol. 10, p.544.

19 Ibid. p.544.

20 Siborne, H.T., Letter No 75 from Captain T.W. Taylor, p.172.

21 Leeke, p.97.

22 Glover, G. (ed.), Letter No 54 from Captain John Gurwood, p.90.

23 Gleig, *Personal Reminiscences of the First Duke of Wellington*, edited by his daughter, Mary.

24 Hussey, *Journal of the Society for Army Historical Research*, 80 (2002), pp.104–8.

25 Ward, *A Romance of the Nineteenth Century*, pp.176–181.

26 Balen, p.27.

27 Hofschröer, p.227.

28 Ward, pp.175–6.

Epilogue

1 Robinson, *Wellington's Campaigns 1808–15*, part III, Nivelle to Waterloo, 1907.

2 Davies, *Wellington's War: The Making of a Military Genius*.

3 Bamford and Wellesley (eds), *The Journals of Mrs Arbuthnot 1820–1832*, Macmillan, 1950.

4 Smith, *The life of John Colborne, Field-Marshal Lord Seaton, etc.*, p.420.

5 *Metropolitan Police Orders*, 1833, 8 July, MEPO 7, p.384.

6 Booth (ed.), *The Battle of Waterloo, also of Ligny, and Quatre Bras, etc.*, pp.273 and 311.

7 Hanning, Henry, *The British Grenadiers*, p.64 et seq.

8 Byng, Major General Sir John, Letter dated 19 June 1815 to HRH, The Duke of York, published online by 1815 Ltd.

9 Siborne, H.T. (ed.), *Waterloo Letters*, Letter No 113, from Major General Sir John Byng, p.261.

Appendix

1 Wellington, 2nd Duke of (ed.), *Supplementary Despatches and Memoranda of Field Marshal Arthur, Duke of Wellington*, vol. 10, p.513.

2 Keegan, *The Face of Battle*, p.34.

BIBLIOGRAPHY

Adkin, Mark, *The Sharpe Companion*, HarperCollins, London, 1998.

Adkin, Mark, *The Waterloo Companion*, Aurum Press Ltd, London, 2001.

Anglesey, Marquess of, *One Leg*, Jonathan Cape, London, 1961.

Balen, Malcolm, *A Model Victory*, Harper Perennial, London, 2006.

Bamford, Francis and Gerald Wellesley, 7th Duke of Wellington (eds), *The Journals of Mrs Arbuthnot 1820–1832*, Macmillan, 1950.

Barbero, Alessandro, *The Battle: A History of the Battle of Waterloo*, Atlantic Books, London, 2006.

Black, Jeremy, *The Battle of Waterloo, A New History*, Icon Books Ltd, London, 2010.

Booth, J., publisher of *The Battle of Waterloo, also of Ligny, and Quatre Bras, etc.*, 1815, tenth edition 1817.

Boulger, Demetrius C., *The Belgians at Waterloo*, London, 1901.

Byng, Major General Sir John, *Letter dated 19 June 1815 to HRH the Duke of York*, Regimental Headquarters Scots Guards, published online by 1815 Ltd.

de Chair, Somerset, *Napoleon's Memoirs*, Faber and Faber, London, 1948.

Chandler, David. *The Campaigns of Napoleon*, Weidenfeld and Nicolson, 13th Edition, London, 1995.

Chappell, Mike, *Wellington's Peninsula [sic] Regiments (2) The Light Infantry*, Osprey Publishing Ltd, 2004.

Crabbé, J., *Jean-Louis de Crabbé, Colonel d'Empire*, Nantes, Editions du Canonnier, 2006

Creevey, Thomas, *The Creevey Papers. A selection from the correspondence and diaries of the late Thomas Creevey MP*, John Murray, London, 1906.

Davies, Huw J., *Wellington's War: The Making of a Military Genius*, Yale University Press, 2012.

Esdaile, Charles, *The Peninsular War*, Penguin Books, London, 2003.

Field, Andrew W., *Waterloo. The French Perspective*, Pen & Sword, 2012.

Fletcher, Ian, *A Desperate Business: Wellington, the British Army and the Waterloo Campaign*, Spellmount, Staplehurst, 2001.

Foulkes, Nick, *Dancing into Battle*, Weidenfeld and Nicolson, 2006.

Franklin, John (ed.), *Waterloo. Netherlands Correspondence*, 1815 Limited, Ulverston, 2010.

Franklin, John (ed.), *Waterloo. Hanoverian Correspondence*, 1815 Limited, Ulverston, 2010.

Gleig, Rev. G.R., *The Story of the Battle of Waterloo*, John Murray, 1847.

Glover, Gareth (ed.) *Letters from the Battle of Waterloo*, Greenhill Books, London, and Stackpole Books, Pennsylvania, 2004.

Glover, Gareth, 'Somerset's Account of the Battle of Waterloo', *The Waterloo Journal*, vol. 29, spring 2007.

Glover, Michael (ed.), *A Gentleman Volunteer: The Letters of George Hennell from the Peninsular War, 1812–13*, William Heinemann Ltd, London, 1979.

Griffith, Paddy, *French Napoleonic Infantry Tactics 1792–1815*, Osprey Publishing, Oxford, 2007.

Gurwood, John (ed.), *The Despatches of Field Marshal the Duke of Wellington*, vol. 8, London, in a facsimile edition by Cambridge University Press.

Hamilton-Williams, David, *Waterloo, New Perspectives*, Brockhampton Press, 1993.

Hanning, Henry, *The British Grenadiers*, Pen and Sword Ltd, Barnsley, 2006.

Harrington Collection, The, a letter dated 21 June 1815 from Ensign Robert Batty, 3/1st Foot Guards, to his father, Dr Robert Batty, published online by John Franklin, 1815 Ltd.

Harvey, Robert, *The War of Wars*, Constable and Robinson, London, 2007.

Hathaway, Eileen (ed.), *A True Soldier Gentleman. The Memoirs of Lt John Cooke 1791–1813*, Shinglepicker Publications, Swanage, 2000.

Haythornthwaite, Philip, *Napoleon's Guard*, Osprey Publishing, 1997.

Hibbert, Christopher, *Waterloo*, Wordsworth Military Library, Ware, 1997

Hibbert, Christopher, *Wellington, A Personal History*. HarperCollins, London 1997, pb. 1998.

Hill, General Lord, Letter dated 11 July 1815 to Lieutenant General Baron Chassé. Stadsarchief, Zütphen: collectie familie van Löben Sels; Nr.II, nr.8.2, annex C, published online by 1815 Ltd. Hofschröer, P., *1815 The Waterloo Campaign. The German Victory*, Greenhill Books, London, 1998.

Hofschröer, P., *Wellington's Smallest Victory*, Faber and Faber, London, 2005

Holmes, Prof. Richard (ed.), *Battlefield*, Oxford University Press, 2006.

Holmes, Prof. Richard, *Oxford Companion to Military History*, Oxford University Press, 2001.

Holmes, Prof. Richard, *Wellington: the Iron Duke*, HarperCollins, London, pb. 2003.

Houssaye, Henri, *1815. Waterloo*, 31st edition translated by Evans, A.C., Black, London, 1900.

Humphrys, Julian, 'A Tale of Two Medals', *BBC History Magazine*, vol. 10, no 1.

Hussey, John, *Journal of the Society for Army Historical Research*, 80 (2002).

Jennings, L.J. (ed.), *The Croker Papers. The Correspondence and Diaries of John Wilson Croker, Secretary to the Admiralty from 1809 to 1830*, John Murray, 1884.

Journal of the Society for Army Historical Research, vol. XXX, No 122.

Kennedy, General James Shaw, *Notes on the Battle of Waterloo*, London, 1865.

Kincaid, J., *Adventures in the Rifle Brigade, in the Peninsula, France and the Netherlands, from 1809 to 1815*, facsimile of 1909 edition, Richard Drew Publishing Ltd, Glasgow, 1981.

Kruse, General Major Baron August von, report dated 21 June 1815, concerning the events of the 15, 16 and 17 June, and the battle of the 18 June at Mont-Saint-Jean. Hessisches Hauptstaatsarchiv, Wiesbaden: Abt.130 II, Nr.5716, translated from the German and published online by 1815 Limited.

Leeke, Rev. W., *The History of Lord Seaton's Regiment, (The 52nd Light Infantry) at the Battle of Waterloo*, Hatchard and Co, London, 1866.

Leeke, Rev W., *Supplement to The History of Lord Seaton's Regiment, (The 52nd Light Infantry) at the Battle of Waterloo*, Hatchard and Co, London, 1871.

Logie, Jacques, *Waterloo, The 1815 Campaign*, English version, Spellmount, 2006.

Longford, Elizabeth, *Wellington – Pillar of State*. Weidenfeld and Nicolson, 1972, and in paperback by Panther Books, 1975.

Longford, Elizabeth, *Wellington – the Years of the Sword*, The Literary Guild, London, 2nd imprint, 1970.

McNab, Chris, *Armies of the Napoleonic Wars*, Osprey Publishing, Oxford, 2009.

Metropolitan Police Orders 1833, 8 July, MEPO 7, p.384.

Miller, David, *Commanding Officers*, John Murray, 2001.

Mockler-Ferryman, A.F., *The Oxfordshire and Buckinghamshire Light Infantry Chronicle*, vol XXIII, January–July 1914, Eyre and Spottiswoode, London, 1914.

Mudford, W., *An Historical Account of the Campaign in the Netherlands in 1815 etc.*

Napier, Major General Sir William, *History of the War in the Peninsula and in the South of France*, book XXIV, Murray, London, 1830.

Nixon, Captain James Lock, 2nd Battalion, 1st Regiment of Foot Guards, letter dated 19 June 1815 to his father Thomas Nixon, University of Nottingham, Drury Lowe Collection: Dr. C. 30/6, published online by 1815 Ltd.

Oxfordshire and Buckinghamshire Light Infantry Chronicle, January–July 1914, vol. XXIII, London.

Pattison, Lieutenant Frederick Hope, *Personal Recollections of the Waterloo Campaign*, Blackie, Glasgow, 1870; new edition by the Association of Friends of the Waterloo Committee, 1997.

Petit, General Jean-Martin, 'His report on the Garde at Waterloo', translated by George Jeffrey, edited by John Koontz.

Pontécoulant, *Napoleon à Waterloo*, reprinted by À la Librairie des Deux Empire, Paris, 2004.

Quinet, Edgar, *Histoire de la Compaigne de 1815*, Paris, 1862.

Roberts, Andrew, *Napoleon & Wellington*, Weidenfeld & Nicholson, 2001, and in paperback, Phoenix Press, 2003.

Robinson, Major General C.W., *Wellington's Campaigns 1808–15*, Part III Nivelle to Waterloo, 1907.

Robinson, Mike, *The Battle of Quatre Bras 1815*, The History Press, 2009.

Scott, Michael, 'The Battle of Marathon', *BBC History Magazine*, vol. 11, no 5, May 2010.

Seaton, R. (ed.), *Lt Col Basil Jackson's Notes and Reminiscences of a Staff Officer, chiefly relating to the Waterloo Campaign and to St Helena matters during the captivity of Napoleon*, John Murray, London, 1903.

Siborne, Major General H.T., *Waterloo Letters, A Selection from Original and Hitherto Unpublished Letters Bearing on the Operations of the 16th, 17th, and 18th June, 1815, By Officers who served in the Campaign*, first published by Cassell in 1891, and reproduced in facsimile by Greenhill Books in 1993.

Siborne, Captain W., *History of the Waterloo Campaign*, Greenhill Books, London, and Presidio Press, California, 1990. Facsimile of the Third Edition.

Smith, G.C. Moore, *The Life of John Colborne, Field-Marshal Lord Seaton, compiled from his letters, records of his conversations and other sources*, John Murray, London, 1903. Verbatim records of letters in Appendix II.

Stanhope, 5th Earl, *Notes of Conversations with the Duke of Wellington*, John Murray, London, 1889.

Strachey and Fulford (eds), *The Greville Memoirs 1814–1860*, Macmillan, 1938.

Urban, Mark, *Generals*, Faber and Faber, London, 2006.

Urban, Mark, *The Man who broke Napoleon's Codes*, Faber and Faber, London, 2001.

Ward, Dudley, *A Romance of the Nineteenth Century*, John Murray, London, 1923.

Weller, Jac, *Wellington at Waterloo*, Greenhill Books, London and Stacpole Books, Pennsylvania, 1992.

Wellington, 2nd Duke of, *Supplementary Despatches and Memoranda of Field Marshal Arthur Duke of Wellington*, vol. 10, Murray, 1863.

INDEX